SLAPPED TOGETHER

THE DILBERT BUSINESS ANTHOLOGY

SLAPPED TOGETHER

THE DILBERT BUSINESS ANTHOLOGY

SCOTT ADAMS

The Dilbert Principle

The Dilbert Future

The Joy of Work

HarperBusiness
An Imprint of HarperCollins *Publishers*

THE
DILBERT™
PRINCIPLE

A Cubicle's-Eye
View of Bosses, Meetings,
Management Fads &
Other Workplace Afflictions

SCOTT ADAMS

HarperBusiness
A Division of HarperCollins*Publishers*

A hardcover edition of this book was published in 1996 by HarperBusiness, a division of HarperCollins Publishers.

THE DILBERT PRINCIPLE. Copyright © 1996 by United Feature Syndicate, Inc. All rights reserved. Printed in the United States of America. No part of this book may be used or reproduced in any manner whatsoever without written permission except in the case of brief quotations embodied in critical articles and reviews. For information address HarperCollins Publishers, Inc., 10 East 53rd Street, New York, NY 10022.

HarperCollins books may be purchased for educational, business, or sales promotional use. For information please write: Special Markets Department, HarperCollins Publishers, Inc., 10 East 53rd Street, New York, NY 10022.

First paperback edition published 1997.

Designed by Caitlin Daniels

The Library of Congress has catalogued the hardcover edition as follows:

Adams, Scott, 1957–
    The Dilbert principle : a cubicle's-eye view of bosses, meetings, management fads & other workplace afflictions / Scott Adams.
        p.   cm.
    ISBN 0-88730-787-6
    1. Management.   2. Office politics.   3. Personnel management.   I. Title.
HD31.A294   1996
650.1'3—dc20   96-388

ISBN 0-88730-858-9 (pbk.)

08 09 10 ❖/RRD 10 9 8 7 6 5 4 3 2

For Pam

CONTENTS

Foreword: Big Opening   ix

Introduction: Why Is Business So Absurd?   1

1   The Dilbert Principle   11

2   Humiliation   18

3   Business Communication   35

4   Great Lies of Management   51

5   Machiavellian Methods   62

6   Employee Strategies   91

7   Performance Reviews   101

8   Pretending to Work   112

9   Swearing: The Key to Success for Women   121

10   How to Get Your Way   124

11   Marketing and Communications   131

12   Management Consultants   151

13   Business Plans   162

14   Engineers, Scientists, Programmers, and Other Odd People   170

15   Change   196

16   Budgeting   201

17   Sales   212

18   Meetings   220

19   Projects   227

20   ISO 9000   240

21 Downsizing   244

22 How to Tell If Your Company Is Doomed   264

23 Reengineering   274

24 Team-Building Exercises   280

25 Leaders   287

26 New Company Model: OA5   315

BIG OPENING

These days it seems like any idiot with a laptop computer can churn out a business book and make a few bucks. That's certainly what I'm hoping. It would be a real letdown if the trend changed before this masterpiece goes to print.

As some of you may know, my main profession is cartooning. It's a challenge for a cartoonist to write a whole book. Cartoonists are trained to be brief. Everything I've learned in my entire life can be boiled down to a dozen bullet points, several of which I've already forgotten.

You'd feel kinda perturbed if you bought a big thick book and all it had in it was a dozen bullet points, particularly if several of them seemed to be "filler." So my "plan for excellence" is to repeat myself often to take up some page space. In marketing terms, this is called "adding value." And for your reading pleasure I will include many colorful but unnecessary metaphors. In fact, the metaphors in this book are more useless than a weasel in a cardboard shirt.*

---

*I can't promise that the rest will be that good.

THE
DILBERT™
PRINCIPLE

INTRODUCTION

WHY IS BUSINESS SO ABSURD?

Most of the themes in my comic strip "Dilbert" involve workplace situations. I routinely include bizarre and unworldly elements such as sadistic talking animals, troll-like accountants, and employees turning into dishrags after the life-force has been drained from their bodies. And yet the comment I hear most often is:

> "That's just like my company."

No matter how absurd I try to make the comic strip I can't stay ahead of what people are experiencing in their own workplaces. Some examples for the so-called real world include:

- A major technology company simultaneously rolled out two new programs: (1) a random drug testing program, and (2) an "Individual Dignity Enhancement" program.

- A company purchased laptop computers for employees to use while traveling. Fearing they might be stolen, the managers came up with a clever solution: permanently attach the laptop computers to the employees' desks.

- A freight company reorganized to define roles and clarify goals. Management decided to communicate the changes by ordering each department to build floats for a "Quality Parade."

- A manager at a telecommunications company wanted to reinforce the "team" concept in his department. He held a meeting to tell the assembled "team" that henceforth he will carry a baseball bat with him at all times and each team member will carry a baseball while at work. Some team members found a way to hang the baseball around their necks so they don't have to carry it. Others fantasized about wrestling the bat away from the manager and using it.

- A company decided that instead of raises it will give bonuses if five of seven company goals are met. At the end of the year the employees are informed that they have met only four of seven goals, so no bonuses. One of the goals they missed was "employee morale."

Thousands of people have told me workplace stories (mostly through e-mail) that are even more absurd than the examples above. When I first started hearing these stories I was puzzled, but after careful analysis I have developed a sophisticated theory to explain the existence of this bizarre workplace behavior: People are idiots.

Including me. Everyone is an idiot, not just the people with low SAT scores. The only differences among us is that we're idiots about different things at different times. No matter how smart you are, you spend much of your day being an idiot. That's the central premise of this scholarly work.

MANDATORY SELF-DEPRECATION

I proudly include myself in the idiot category. Idiocy in the modern age isn't an all-encompassing, twenty-four-hour situation for most people. It's a condition that everybody slips into many times a day. Life is just too complicated to be smart all the time.

The other day I brought my pager to the repair center because it wouldn't work after I changed the battery. The repairman took the pager out of my hand, flipped open the battery door, turned the battery around, and handed the now functional pager back to me in one well-practiced motion. This took much of the joy out of my righteous indignation over the quality of their product. But the repairman seemed quite amused. And so did every other customer in the lobby.

On that day, in that situation, I was a complete idiot. Yet somehow I managed to operate a motor vehicle to the repair shop and back. It is a wondrous human characteristic to be able to slip into and out of idiocy many times a day without noticing the change or accidentally killing innocent bystanders in the process.

MY QUALIFICATIONS

Now that I've admitted that I can't replace the battery in my pager, you might wonder what makes me think I'm qualified to write this important book. I think you'll be impressed at my depth of experience and accomplishment:

1. I convinced a company to publish this book. That might not seem like much, but it's more than you did today. And it wasn't easy. I had to have lunch with people I didn't even know.

2. I worked in a cubicle for seventeen years. Most business books are written by consultants and professors who haven't spent much time in a cubicle. That's like writing a firsthand account of the experience of the Donner party based on the fact that you've eaten beef jerky. Me, I've gnawed an ankle or two.

3. I'm a trained hypnotist. Years ago I took a class to learn how to hypnotize people. As a byproduct of this training I learned that people are mindless, irrational, easily manipulated dolts. (I think I paid $500 to learn that.) And it's not just the so-called good subjects—it's everybody. It's how our brains are wired. You make up your mind first and then you rationalize it second. But because of the odd mapping of your perceptions you're convinced beyond a doubt that your decisions are based on reason. They aren't.

Important scientists have done studies° proving that the area of the brain responsible for rational thought doesn't even activate

---

°They were important scientists, but not so important that I would remember their names and not so important that you'd care. But I'm sure it's true because I read it in a magazine.

until *after* you do something. You can confirm that fact using hypnosis, by giving a person an irrational post-hypnotic suggestion and asking later why the subject did what he did. He will insist it made sense at the time, employing a logic more tortured than Pavarotti at a Tiny Tim concert.

A hypnotist quickly develops a complete distrust for the connection between a person's reasons and his actions. The class fundamentally changed the way I look at the world.

4. Nobody believes statistics anyway. This is a huge time-saver for me as an author. It removes any guilt I might have about fabricating statistics. If you're a "normal" person, you tend to believe any studies that support your current views and ignore everything else. Therefore, any reference I might make to legitimate research is wasted. If we can agree on the futility of trying to sway you with legitimate research it will save us both a lot of trouble.

That doesn't mean I will ignore statistics. Far from it. Throughout this book I will make references to scientific studies. Of course, they'll all be total fabrications. But my versions will make better reading than legitimate research, and ultimately the impact is the same.

If you think about it, most of the studies you see in the media are either completely misleading or intentionally biased. This book is no different, except that I don't underestimate your intelligence. I mean, how could I?

THE ROLE OF INTELLIGENCE IN BUSINESS

I don't know why the economy works, but I'm sure it isn't because brilliant people are managing it. My guess is that if you sum up all the absurd activities of management, the idiocies somehow cancel out, thus producing cool things that you want to buy, such as Nerf balls and Snapple. Add the law of supply and demand to the mix and you've pretty much described the whole theory of economics.

Ninety percent of all new business ventures fail. Apparently, ten percent of the time you get lucky, and that's enough to support a modern economy. I'm betting that's what separates us from the animals; animals are lucky only nine percent of the time. I suspect this is true because I play strip poker with my cats and they rarely win. In fact, it's gotten to the point where they run like cowards at the sound of my electric shaver.

The world has become so complicated that we're all bluffing our way through the business day, hoping we're not unmasked for the boobs that we really are. I see the world as a massively absurd endeavor, populated by people who struggle every minute to rationalize the silly things they do.

It's not the business world that brings out our idiocy, but it might be the place where we notice it the most. In our personal lives we tolerate bizarre behavior. It even seems normal. (If you don't believe me, take a look at your family members.) But at work we think everyone should be guided by logic and rational thinking. Any absurdity in a business setting stands out like a dead nun in a snowbank.° I'm convinced that the workplace doesn't contain more absurdity than everyday life, but the absurdity is definitely more noticeable.

I find great humor in the fact that we ever take ourselves seriously. We rarely recognize our own idiocies, yet we can clearly identify the idiocies of others. That's the central tension of business:

> We expect others to act rationally even though we are irrational.

It's useless to expect rational behavior from the people you work with, or anybody else for that matter. If you can come to peace with the fact that you're surrounded by idiots, you'll realize that resistance is futile, your tension will dissipate, and you can sit back and have a good laugh at the expense of others. This can be a very healthy book.

THE EVOLUTION OF IDIOTS

Scientists believe that humans are the grand result of billions of years of evolution. I can't explain the entire theory of evolution here, but it can be summarized this way.

Theory of Evolution (Summary)

First, there were some amoebas. Deviant amoebas adapted better to the environment, thus becoming monkeys. Then came Total Quality Management.

I'm leaving out some details, but the theory itself also has a few holes that are best left unquestioned.

° If it bothers you to think of a dead nun, imagine that she's only badly wounded and she'll recover.

Anyway, it took us many years to get to this lofty level of evolution. That leisurely pace of change was okay because there wasn't much to do except sit around and hope you didn't get eaten by wild pigs. Then somebody fell on a sharp stick and the spear was invented. That's when the trouble started.

I wasn't there, but I'm willing to bet that some people said the spear would never replace fingernails as the fighting tool of choice. The naysayers probably hurled bad names at the spear-users—names like "moog" and "blinth." (This was before the merchant marines had been created, so swearing wasn't very good yet.)

But "diversity" was not celebrated back then, and I expect the "Say No to Spear" people finally got the "point" if you catch my drift.

The good thing about a spear is that almost everybody could understand it. It had basically one feature: the pointy end. Our brains were fully equipped for this level of complexity. And not just the brains of the intelligentsia either—the common man could find his way around a spear too. Life was good, save for the occasional plague and the fact that the average life expectancy was seven . . . and the fact that you'd be praying for death after the age of four. But almost nobody complained about how confusing the spears were.

Suddenly (in evolutionary terms) some deviant went and built the printing press. It was a slippery slope after that. Two blinks later and we're switching batteries in our laptop computers while streaking through the sky in shiny metal objects in which soft drinks and peanuts are served.

I blame sex and paper for most of our current problems. Here's my logic: Only one person in a million is smart enough to invent a printing press. So when society consisted of only a few hundred apelike people living in caves, the odds of one of them being a genius were fairly low. But people kept having sex, and with every moron added to the population, the odds of a deviant smarty-pants slipping through the genetic net got higher and higher. When you've got several million people running around having sex all willy-nilly,°

° If you haven't tried having sex "all willy-nilly" you really should.

the odds are fairly good that some pregnant ape-mom is going to squat in a field someday and pinch out a printing-press-making deviant.

Once we had printing presses, we were pretty much doomed. Because then, every time a new smart deviant came up with a good idea, it would get written down and shared. Every good idea could be built upon. Civilization exploded. Technology was born. The complexity of life increased geometrically. Everything got bigger and better.

Except our brains.

All the technology that surrounds us, all the management theories, the economic models that predict and guide our behavior, the science that helps us live to eighty—it's all created by a tiny percentage of deviant smart people. The rest of us are treading water as fast as we can. The world is too complex for us. Evolution didn't keep up. Thanks to the printing press, the deviant smart people managed to capture their genius and communicate it without having to pass it on genetically. Evolution was short-circuited. We got knowledge and technology before we got intelligence.

We're a planet of nearly six billion ninnies living in a civilization that was designed by a few thousand amazingly smart deviants.

True Example

Kodak introduced a single-use camera called the Weekender. Customers have called the support line to ask if it's okay to use it during the week.

The rest of this book builds on my theory that we're all idiots. I'm sure there are other plausible explanations for why business seems so absurd but I can't think of any. If I do, I'll write another book for you. I promise I won't stop searching for an answer until you run out of money.

THE DILBERT PRINCIPLE*

I use a lot of "bad boss" themes in my syndicated cartoon strip "Dilbert." I'll never run out of material. I get at least two hundred e-mail messages a day, mostly from people who are complaining about their own clueless managers. Here are some of my favorite stories, all allegedly true:

- A vice president insists that the company's new battery-powered product be equipped with a light that comes on to tell you when the power is off.

*This article originally appeared in the *Wall Street Journal* on May 22, 1995. It got a huge response and led to the creation of this book.

- An employee suggests setting priorities so the company will know how to apply its limited resources. The manager's response: "Why can't we concentrate our resources across the board?"

- A manager wants to find and fix software bugs more quickly. He offers an incentive plan: $20 for each bug the Quality Assurance people find and $20 for each bug the programmers fix. (These are the same programmers who create the bugs.) Result: An underground economy in "bugs" springs up instantly. The plan is rethought after one employee nets $1,700 the first week.

Stories like these prompted me to do the first annual Dilbert Survey to find out what management practices were most annoying to employees. The choices included the usual suspects: Quality, Empowerment, Reengineering, and the like. But the number-one vote-getter in this highly unscientific survey was "Idiots Promoted to Management."

This seemed like a subtle change from the old concept by which capable workers were promoted until they reached their level of incompetence—best described as the "Peter Principle." Now, apparently, the incompetent workers are promoted directly to management without ever passing through the temporary competence stage.

When I entered the workforce in 1979, the Peter Principle described management pretty well. Now I think we'd all like to return to those Golden Years when you had a boss who was once good at something.

I get all nostalgic when I think about it. Back then, we all had hopes of being promoted beyond our levels of competence. Every worker had a shot at someday personally navigating the company into the tar pits while reaping large bonuses and stock options. It was a time when inflation meant everybody got an annual raise; a time when we freely admitted that the customers didn't matter. It was a time of joy.

We didn't appreciate it then, but the much underrated Peter Principle always provided us with a boss who understood what we did for a living. Granted, he made consistently bad decisions—after all, he had no management skills. But at least they were the informed decisions of a seasoned veteran from the trenches.

Example

Boss: "When I had your job I could drive a three-inch rod through a metal casing with one motion. If you're late again I'll do the same thing to your head."

Nitpickers found lots of problems with the Peter Principle, but on the whole it worked. Lately, however, the Peter Principle has given way to the "Dilbert Principle." The basic concept of the Dilbert Principle is that the most ineffective workers are systematically moved to the place where they can do the least damage: management.

This has not proved to be the winning strategy that you might think.

Maybe we should learn something from nature. In the wild, the weakest moose is hunted down and killed by dingo dogs, thus ensuring survival of the fittest. This is a harsh system—especially for the dingo dogs who have to fly all the way from Australia. But nature's process is a good one; everybody agrees, except perhaps for the dingo dogs and the moose in question . . . and the flight attendants. But the point is that we'd all be better off if the least competent managers were being eaten by dingo dogs instead of writing Mission Statements.

It seems as if we've turned nature's rules upside down. We systematically identify and promote the people who have the least skills. The usual business rationalization for promoting idiots (the Dilbert Principle in a nutshell) is something along the lines of "Well, he can't write code, he can't design a network, and he doesn't have any sales skill. But he has *very* good hair . . . "

If nature started organizing itself like a modern business, you'd see, for example, a band of mountain gorillas led by an "alpha" squirrel. And it wouldn't be the most skilled squirrel; it would be the squirrel nobody wanted to hang around with.

I can see the other squirrels gathered around an old stump saying stuff like "If I hear him say, 'I like nuts' one more time, I'm going to kill him." The gorillas, overhearing this conversation, lumber down from the mist and promote the unpopular squirrel. The remaining squirrels are assigned to Quality Teams as punishment.

You may be wondering if you fit the description of a Dilbert Principle manager. Here's a little test:

1. Do you believe that anything you don't understand must be easy to do?

2. Do you feel the need to explain in great detail why "profit" is the difference between income and expense?

3. Do you think employees should schedule funerals only during holidays?

4. Are the following words a form of communication or gibberish:

The Business Services Leadership Team will enhance the organization in order to continue on the journey toward a Market Facing Organization (MFO) model. To that end, we are consolidating the Object Management for Business Services into a cross strata team.

5. When people stare at you in disbelief do you repeat what you just said, only louder and more slowly?

Now give yourself one point for each question you answered with the letter "B." If your score is greater than zero, congratulations—there are stock options in your future.

(The language in question four is from an actual company memo.)

THE DILBERT PRINCIPLE ILLUSTRATED

HUMILIATION

Employee morale is a risky thing. Happy employees will work harder without asking for extra pay. But if they get too happy, endorphins kick in, egos expand, and everybody starts whining about the fact that with their current pay they'll have to live in a dumpster after retirement.

The best balance of morale for employee productivity can be described this way: happy, but with low self-esteem.

You can test your own level of employee happiness with this test. If you laugh out loud at any of the "office witticisms" shown here, then you are happy in exactly the right amount to be productive:

HAPPINESS PRODUCTIVITY TEST

Below are several witticisms encountered in your office every day. How many do you find irresistibly funny?

1. "Are you working hard or hardly working?"

2. "Are you holding up the wall?"

3. "You look different today!" (said to someone at a borrowed desk)

4. "It's not my day to watch Bob."

5. "Not bad for a Wednesday!"

If you laughed at any of the five witticisms, you have the proper Dopey-from-the-Seven-Dwarfs kind of happy that spells productivity. But if during this test you suddenly got a mental image of a co-worker you'd like to bludgeon with a speakerphone, then you might have too much self-esteem to be productive.

THE SOLUTION: HUMILIATION

Over the years, businesses have developed a broad range of techniques that bring employees' self-esteem back into the "productive zone" without sacrificing happiness. This chapter discusses the most important humiliation techniques.

- Cubicles

- Hoteling

- Furniture

- Dress clothes

- Employee Recognition Programs

- Undervaluing employee contributions

- Making them wait

CUBICLES

Cubicles—sometimes called "work spaces" or "pods"—serve as a constant reminder of the employee's marginal value to the company. I've never seen a brochure from a cubicle manufacturer, but I think it would look something like this:

The Cubicle 6000™ Series

Think of The Cubicle 6000™ as a lifestyle, not just a big box to keep your crap in one place!!

We used nature as our guide when we designed The Cubicle 6000™. Every unit has the unmistakable motivational feel of the four most inspiring locations on earth:

VEAL-FATTENING PEN:

Imagine the security that those lucky young cows feel, snug in their individual living units, without a care in the world. The reaffirming message is "Live for today!"

CARDBOARD BOX:

It's the same architecture that has transported the possessions of successful people for hundreds of years!

BABY'S PLAYPEN:

A reminder of the exuberance of youth and the thrill of being held captive by strange people who speak gibberish and punish you for reasons you don't understand!

PRISON CELL:

We've "captured" the carefree feeling of a convict serving twenty to life. Experience the security that was previously available only in the penal system!

And look at these features!!

- Open top so you'll never miss a surrounding noise.
- Small size so you can enjoy the odors of your co-workers.
- No annoying windows.
- Available in battleship gray or feces brown.
- Movable— discover the thrill of frequent office shuffling.
- Coat hanger (only available on the Admiral Series).

HOTELING

The only drawback to the cubicle-oriented office is that some employees develop a sense of "home" in their little patch of real estate. Soon, pride of ownership sets in, then self-esteem, and *poof*—good-bye productivity.

But thanks to the new concept of "hoteling," this risk can be eliminated. Hoteling is a system by which cubicles are assigned to the employees as they show up each day. Nobody gets a permanent work space, and therefore no unproductive homey feelings develop.

Another advantage: Hoteling eliminates all physical evidence of the employee's association with the company. This takes the fuss out of downsizing; the employee doesn't even have to clean out a desk. With hoteling, every employee has "one foot out the door" at all times.

Hoteling sends an important message to the employee: "Your employment is temporary. Keep your photos of your ugly family in the trunk of your car so we don't have to look at them."

FURNITURE

You're only as important as your furniture. And that's at peak levels of dignity. Often you're less important than your furniture. If you think about it, you can get fired but your furniture stays behind, gainfully employed at the company that didn't need *you* anymore.

It's no surprise that people invest a great deal of ego in their office furniture. Depending on your status in the company, your furniture sends one of these two messages:

"Ignore the worthless object sitting on this chair."

Or . . .

"Worship me!! Kneel before the mahogany shrine!"

Given a choice, you want furniture that sends that second message. Unfortunately, impressive furniture is available only at higher levels of management. Statistically speaking, the reader of this paragraph is not likely to be a member of senior management. So I'll skip that discussion.

Assuming you're not in senior management, you might be lucky to have a big ol' board that stretches the length of your cubicle and keeps the telephone from falling in your lap. Let's call it a "desk" for the sake of argument. This desklike arrangement is the perfect complement to the tiny chair that will be your home for seventy hours a week.

If you're a secretary, your chair probably has no armrests. That's okay; you weren't hired to rest your arms. You should be busy finding ways to prevent the professional staff from meeting with your boss. *That's* what you're getting paid to do, dammit.

But if you're not a secretary, you might be enjoying the luxury of armrests. Those armrests are essential for balance if you plan to nap in your cubicle. During my career at Pacific Bell I spent many blissful hours sound asleep in my cubicle, thanks to armrests. I always located my computer so my back faced the aisle when I looked at the screen. That way I could pull up a document, balance my arms on the armrests, close my eyes, and drift into Sugarland, all while looking like a dedicated employee. Sometimes the phone would ring, but I learned to screen it out. (The brain is an amazing thing!)

Despite being well-rested, sometimes even "Dopey Happy," I never achieved enough self-esteem at Pacific Bell to become cocky. My furniture did its job, providing just the right level of humility to maintain my fever-pitch of productivity.

E-mail From the Cubicle Trenches

As you can see from these examples, money is no object compared to the importance of keeping the employees in their proper place.

> From: (name withheld)
> To: scottadams@aol.com
>
> Scott,
>
> Now that we've reengineered, we have fewer managers than we have windows! Big problem, but we have a solution. We've erected five-foot-high partition walls in front of the windows, so that non-managers can sit there without offending the pecking order.

> From: (name withheld)
> To: scottadams@aol.com
>
> Scott,
>
> I thought you'd enjoy this:
> Someone I know works at a government agency—they recently reorganized people in the Engineering Department and a lowly non-management type was put into the corner space of the work areas. Since the space had walls put up a year ago to accommodate a manager, they are actually hiring contractors to come in and have the walls taken out for the lowly nonmanager!

From: (name withheld)
To: scottadams@aol.com

Scott,

Recently, our office moved down the street. Around the same time, I was fortunate to be promoted to a new job.

As with all large companies, the allotment of cubicle and office space is associated with grade level (for example, if you are grade X, you get a sixty-four-square-foot cubicle; if you are grade Y, you get a one-hundred-square-foot office). Finally, after a few diligent years of corporate service, my grade level afforded me an office.

This is all well and good; however, my grade level did not specify nice, wooden office furniture. I still have many levels yet to go. Therefore, in an effort to reuse cubicles from the previous facility, the real estate arm of my company installed a cubicle within my office. Imagine for the moment how ridiculous this looks.

Now, the funny part is that the office I occupy has a window; however, it is completely blocked by the cubicle wall.

DRESS CLOTHES

Nothing is more adorable than one of those little organ-grinder monkeys with a tiny vest and a hat. That would be the official uniform at your company too if not for the fact it would be considered a "uniform" and there's no budget for that sort of thing.

Companies have discovered a low-cost method for making people dress in the same humiliating fashion as the monkey but without the expense of buying uniforms. The secret is to specify a style of acceptable dress that has the same symbolism as the monkey's outfit but allows some variety:

CLOTHING	SYMBOLISM
Necktie	Leash
Pantyhose	Leg irons; prisoner
Suit jacket	Penguin; incapable of flight
High heels	Masochism

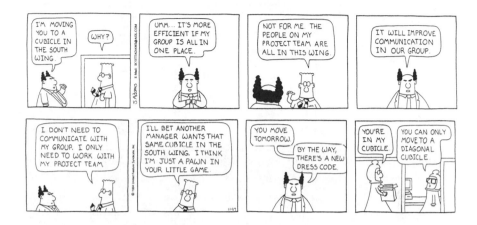

EMPLOYEE RECOGNITION PROGRAMS

Recognition programs send an important message to all the employees in the group, not just the "winners." Specifically, the message is this: "Here's another person who won't be downsized until after we nail *you*."

But that's not the only benefit. Recognition programs help identify which social caste the employees belong to.

RECOGNITION PROGRAM	CASTE
Employee of the Month Program	"Paper Hat" Caste
Certificate of Appreciation	"No Overtime Pay" Caste
Token Cash Award	"Mushroom in the Cubicle" Caste
None	"Executive" Caste

There are no recognition programs at the highest levels of the organization. This is a motivating factor for lower-level employees. They know that if they work hard they have a chance of reaching a level of management where "recognition" programs don't exist.

I once won a "Recognition Award" at Pacific Bell. As I approached the front of the room to accept my award it became apparent that the executive running the program didn't know what I did for a living. Thinking quickly, he invented an entirely fictitious project for the benefit of the audience and thanked me for my valuable contribution to its success.

I felt "happier" after that, but my self-esteem didn't increase enough for me to think it was a good time to ask for a raise. Morale-wise, this was a home run for the company. I was so motivated that I gave serious thought to working right through my siesta that afternoon.

From E-mail: The All-Time Most Humiliating Recognition Program Ever

From: (name withheld)
To: scottadams@aol.com

Scott,

In the wake of a recent senior staff retreat, it was announced that as a reward for outstanding work, one employee would be selected each month to receive the "Fuzzy Bunny" award. Another employee, dressed in a rabbit suit (I swear I am not making this up) would visit the chosen employee's cubicle bearing balloons, a coffee mug, and a certificate of merit. This would presumably encourage us to work harder. The plan was killed (thank God) because nobody would agree to be the bunny.

UNDERVALUING EMPLOYEE CONTRIBUTIONS

Employees like to feel that their contributions are being valued. That's why managers try to avoid that sort of thing. With value comes self-esteem, and with self-esteem comes unreasonable requests for money.

There are many ways to tell employees that their work is not valued. Here are some of the crueler methods, which incidentally work the best:

- Leaf through a magazine while the employee voices an opinion.

- Ask for information "urgently" and then let it sit on your desk untouched for weeks.

- Have your secretary return calls for you.

- Use an employee's document for something other than its intended purpose, as in this example:

MAKING THEM WAIT

One of the most effective methods of humiliation used by managers is the practice of ignoring an underling who is in or near the manager's office while the manager pursues seemingly unimportant tasks. This sends a message that the employee has no human presence. It is similar to changing clothes in front of the family pet; the animal is watching but it couldn't possibly matter.

This tool of humiliation can be fine-tuned to any level simply by adjusting what activities are performed while the employee waits.

ACTIVITY	LEVEL OF HUMILIATION
Taking phone calls	Not so bad
Reading other things	Bad
Flossing	Very bad
Learning a foreign language	Very very bad

3

BUSINESS COMMUNICATION

Any business school professor will tell you that the objective of business communication is the clear transfer of information. That's why professors rarely succeed in business.

The real objective of business communication is to advance your career. That objective is generally at odds with the notion of "clear transfer of information."

The successful manager knows that the best kind of communication is one that conveys the message "I am worthy of promotion" without accidentally transferring any other information. Clear communication can only get you in trouble. Remember, you can't be wrong unless you take a position. Don't fall into that trap.

MISSION STATEMENT

If your employees are producing low-quality products that no sane person would buy, you can often fix that problem by holding meetings to discuss your Mission Statement.

A Mission Statement is defined as "a long awkward sentence that demonstrates management's inability to think clearly." All good companies have one.

Companies that don't have Mission Statements will often be under the mistaken impression that the objective of the company is to bicker among departments, produce low-quality products, and slowly go out of business. That misperception can be easily cured by writing a Mission Statement such as this:

Mission

"We will produce the highest quality products, using empowered team dynamics in a new Total Quality paradigm until we become the industry leader."

But you're not home free yet. The company Mission Statement will be meaningless until all the individual departments write their own Mission Statements to support the company's overall mission. That can be a bit harder because most departments have a variety of distinct functions and you wouldn't want to leave any of them out. So you might end up with individual Mission Statements that look like this:

Mission

"Perform world-class product development, financial analysis, and fleet services using empowered team dynamics in a Total Quality paradigm until we become the industry leader."

Individually, the Mission Statement of the company and the Mission Statement of the department might mean nothing. But taken together you can see how they would inspire employees to greater heights.

VISION

If for some reason the company's Mission Statements do not cause a turnaround in profitability, you might need a Vision Statement. In stark contrast to the detailed road map provided by a Mission Statement, a Vision Statement is more of a "high-level" guide for the company. The higher the better, because you want a vision that will last the ages.

The first step in developing a Vision Statement is to lock the managers in a room and have them debate what is meant by a "Vision Statement" and how exactly it differs from a "Mission Statement" or a "Business Plan" or "Objectives." These are important questions, because one wrong move and the employees will start doing "vision things" when they should be doing "mission things" and before long it will be impossible to sort it all out.

The debate over the definition of "vision" will end as soon as the participants become too tired and cranky to enjoy belittling each other's intelligence. At that point somebody will start suggesting various visions just to get the meeting over with. All good Vision Statements are created by groups of people with bloated bladders who would rather be doing anything else.

You know you've got a rockin' Vision Statement when it inspires the employees to think of themselves as being involved in something much more important than their pathetic little underpaid jobs, when they feel part of a much larger plan—something that can shape the society they live in. Here are examples of successful Vision Statements:

Example #1

"We will have all the wealth in the world while everybody else dies in the gutter wishing they were us."

Example #2

"We will evolve into pure energy and exist on a new temporal plane, BUWHAHAHAHAHA!!!!"

Example #3

"A computer on every desktop."*

NAMING YOUR GROUP

One of the toughest challenges in corporate communications is to develop a name for your department that makes you sound vital to the company

*This is Microsoft's actual Vision Statement.

without attracting too much work. You can do this by using empty but important-sounding words like "excellence" and "technology" and "district" in your name.

Your name should be vague enough to legitimately claim responsibility for anything that looks like it might be a success. If the CEO suddenly develops a hot interest in multimedia, you can swoop in and say, "That sounds like a job for the 'Excellence in Technology District'—because it requires technology and excellence." It's a hard argument to refute.

Then after six months, when the winds change, or you get a new CEO, and you've steered the project onto a sandbar, you can say, "Our work is done. I think this project needs to be championed by Marketing." Then transfer the responsibility, but not the budget. (Colloquially, "Throw that dead cat into somebody else's backyard.")

It may be necessary to rename your group every several months, just to avoid getting a bad reputation. Luckily there is no shortage of empty but important-sounding words to choose from. Depending on your area of expertise, you can generate new names for your group by randomly combining words from this handy list:

Technology Jobs

Information
Technology
Development
Implementation

User
Advanced
Multimedia
Data
Services
Systems
Computing
Telecommunications
Network
Research
Support

Marketing Jobs

Market
Product
Channel
Development
Communications
Evangelist
Promotions

Sales Jobs

Customer
Client
Representative
Service
Center

TALKING LIKE A MANAGER

If you want to advance in management you have to convince other people that you're smart. This is accomplished by substituting incomprehensible jargon for common words.

For example, a manager would never say, "I used my fork to eat a potato." A manager would say, "I utilized a multitined tool to process a starch resource." The two sentences mean almost the same thing, but the second one is obviously from a smarter person.

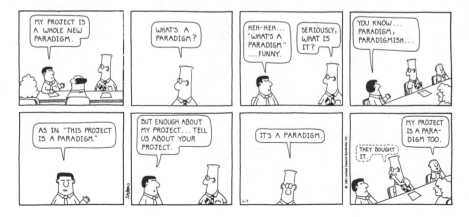

ANNOUNCEMENTS

The purpose of a company announcement is to convey the message that something is happening—something that you aren't important enough to be informed about in any meaningful detail. But if you're clever, you can sometimes read between the lines and understand the true meaning, as in this example:

MOTIVATIONAL TALKS

You may have a bunch of undertrained employees who are using inadequate tools, mired in bureaucratic processes, all of which makes your company uncompetitive. The solution is motivational talks. Gather your team together and put the "fire in their bellies" with your own brand of inspirational oratory.

It's not important that your words carry any specific useful information. As I've already explained, information can never lead to anything good. The goal is to elevate the employees to a competitive frenzy, and for that you need not transfer any information. Here are some phrases that have been known to inspire troops through the ages:

Inspirational Messages

- "It's going to be a very tough year."
- "Frankly, I don't think our project will get funded."
- "Don't expect much in terms of raises. Work should be its own reward."

- "If we don't have more profits next year we'll have more layoffs. Actually, we'll probably have more layoffs anyway."
- "There are no reorganizations planned. It's business as usual."

PRESENTATIONS

Throughout your career you will be asked to make many presentations. The purpose of a presentation is to transfer resources away from accomplishing objectives and concentrate them on explaining how well you're doing.

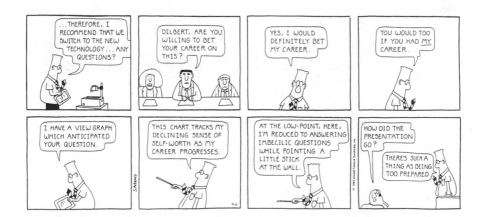

GROUP WRITING

Stephen King writes very scary books. Shakespeare wrote several excellent plays. Unfortunately, they worked alone.* If only they had worked together there's no telling how much better the results would have been. That's the theory behind "group writing," and it's hard to find fault with the logic.

You've heard the saying that if you put a thousand monkeys in a room with a thousand typewriters and waited long enough, eventually you would have a room full of dead monkeys. (Tip: It's a good idea to feed monkeys.) Group writing is a lot like a room full of dead monkeys, except not as "fun."

*Some scholars contend that Shakespeare had other people write his plays and all he did was grab the credit while making crude jokes about his codpiece. Either way, you have to admire his spunk.

The main goal of group writing is to ensure that every sentence satisfies all the objectives of every person in the room. This can be problematic if all the participants have different objectives. You can minimize the impact of different objectives by focusing on the goals that all parties can agree on:

1. Don't convey any information whatsoever.

2. See number one.

The best of all worlds is to be asked to comment on the writing of a co-worker. You get to savor the experience of shredding another person's ego while taking no personal risk. It can be very satisfying.

For fun, suggest changes that would completely reverse the message intended by the author. This puts the author in the awkward position of having to reroute the document for further unhelpful comments or choosing to ignore your "upgrades." If your comments are ignored you have the God-given right to ridicule the end product and claim you had no input. Your activity will look just like "work" even though it's easy and it requires no personal risk. And on the off chance that the document you ridiculed becomes successful you can claim it as part of your accomplishments.

EXAMPLES OF CLEAR BUSINESS COMMUNICATION

From: (name withheld)
To: scottadams@aol.com

Scott,

Some years ago, I was in the habit of sending my staff a yearly recap memo, what we did, what we were looking forward to, etc. We were going to be installing an automated system and I said that even though we had accomplished a lot the past year we couldn't stand pat during the coming year.

A day after the memo was handed out, a woman asked to see me and then, after breaking down into tears, asked what did I have against a co-worker of hers, a woman whose first name was Patricia. It seems Patricia was herself very upset and crying in the ladies' room because the both of them couldn't understand for the life of them why I couldn't "stand pat."

Oh well . . .

From: (name withheld)
To: scottadams@aol.com

Scott,

My boss had these in my performance planning for 1995. (Really!)
I just got them today.
"Utilize issue clarification processes."
"Make sure appropriate people are involved in the process."
"Visibly act or function as a team player."
"Act in the best interests of achieving the team."
These are the ones I came up with. I think mine are better.
"Streamline processes for maximizing propensities."
"Enable full contrivances of empowerment."
"Eliminate occurrences of proliferate randomness."
"Managerially balance data compilation with process ownership."

From: (name withheld)
To: scottadams@aol.com

Scott,

Please help me interpret the instructions from my team leader, as
the drop-dead date is approaching.
No joke, this is real . . .
———

(1) Validate the supporting activities and remaining gaps,

(2) Identify any new gaps, and

(3) Determine the year-end stage assessment.

When determining the attainment stage, please use following cri-
teria:

(1) The attainment stage defines seven [an acronym].
Clarifications listed in the attachment called [a filename] apply.

(2) The solutions to the gaps will be developed and implemented as indicated in attachment marked [a filename].

(3) The Attainment Definition with the lowest attainment stage governs the Management Practice Attainment Stage (i.e., if a management practice has four attainment definitions with no gaps and one attainment definition with a gap, the attainment stage for the management practice is that of the attainment definition with the gap).

HELP!!!!

From: (name withheld)
To: scottadams@aol.com

Scott,

The following is an excerpt from an announcement memo from one of our general managers concerning a personnel change.

"This change will allow us to better leverage our talent base in an area where developmental roles are under way and strategically focuses us toward the upcoming Business System transition where Systems literacy and accuracy will be essential to maintain and to further improve service levels to our customer base going forward."

Several of us sat down and tried to understand what was supposed to be communicated and came up with the following by just crossing out most of the double-talk:

"This change will improve service to our customers."

From: (name withheld)
To: scottadams@aol.com

Scott,

The dean here in the college of business (call him upper management) wanted the faculty to develop a "Mission Statement" that we would all be willing to "own." But he knew he couldn't get 110 people to work together on anything, let alone a Mission Statement. So he formed a committee.

Guess what the committee did. Right—it split into groups and drafted all 110 faculty to be part of those various groups. We formed "teams" which were supposed to "determine our core competency" and find a way to "satisfy our customers" in the context of "continuous improvement" (preferably on half of the current budget).

The result was predictable. Some of us resented the waste of our time, some of us used witty, yet biting sarcasm, and some actually thought it was a great opportunity to "get to know each other better." These guys were the ones who asked us all to hold hands at commencement because "You are special. This is a very special moment."

The final product was a document no one would support. We all got a note from the dean that essentially said, "You didn't read my mind and got the wrong answer!"

4

GREAT LIES OF MANAGEMENT

For your convenience I have compiled and numbered the most popular management lies of all time. I do this as a service to the business community. Now when you're telling a story about the treachery of your managers you can simply refer to each lie by its number, for example, "She told us number six and we all went back to our cubicles and laughed." This will save you a lot of energy that can then be channeled into whining about your co-workers.

Great Lies of Management

1. "Employees are our most valuable asset."

2. "I have an open-door policy."

3. "You could earn more money under the new plan."

4. "We're reorganizing to better serve our customers."

5. "The future is bright."

6. "We reward risk-takers."

7. "Performance will be rewarded."

8. "We don't shoot the messenger."

9. "Training is a high priority."

10. "I haven't heard any rumors."

11. "We'll review your performance in six months."

12. "Our people are the best."

13. "Your input is important to us."

It's not always easy to tell the difference between a scurrilous management lie and ordinary nitwittism. When confronted with an ambiguous situation you can usually sniff out the truth by using a handy method that I call the "What Is More Likely" test. Here's how it works:

State each of the plausible interpretations of reality (using humorous metaphors when possible), then ask yourself this question:

"What is more likely?"

You will discover that this technique will greatly clarify the communications of your managers. Allow me to demonstrate its usefulness on the Great Lies of Management.

"EMPLOYEES ARE OUR MOST VALUABLE ASSET"

On the surface this statement seems to be at odds with the fact that companies are treating their "most valuable assets" the same way a leaf blower treats leaves. How can this apparent contradiction be explained?

An example will be useful. Let's say your boss has a broken desk chair and there's no money left in the budget to replace it. Is it more likely that your boss would:

A. Sit on the floor until the next budget cycle.

B. Use a nonmanagement chair despite the lower status it confers on the sitter.

C. Postpone filling a job opening in the group, distribute the extra work to the "most valuable assets," and use the savings to buy a proper chair.

As employees we like to think we're more valuable than the office furniture. But the "What Is More Likely" test indicates that it's not the case. Realistically we're someplace toward the lower end of the office supply hierarchy.

I used to take great pride in opening a new box of staples and informing them that they worked for me and I was their undisputed ruler. But eventually I had to stop naming them individually because it was such an emotional roller coaster when one went crooked. This may be off the point but if anybody sees Walter, tell him I miss him.

"I HAVE AN OPEN-DOOR POLICY"

What is more likely?

A. Your boss genuinely wants a never-ending trail of Bozos to walk into her office and complain about things that can't be fixed. Her long-term goal is to be distracted from her real responsibilities, fail in her job, and eventually become homeless.

Or . . .

B. She knows she can intimidate people into avoiding her office by scowling and assigning work to the first ten people who try it. That way she gets the benefit of sounding "open" without any of the costs.

"YOU COULD EARN MORE MONEY UNDER THE NEW PLAN"

Is it likely that your company changed the entire compensation plan to give all of you more money? Are raises so rare these days that your company actually forgot about that option?

Or is it more likely that the new compensation system is a complicated maneuver to disguise the fact that from now on your health benefits will be administered by the Christian Scientists?

"WE'RE REORGANIZING TO BETTER SERVE OUR CUSTOMERS"

Is it likely that the current reorganization—in stark contrast to all the ones that preceded it—will be the one that turns your company into a revenue-generating dynamo? And is it likely that the main reason your customers hate you is that your organization chart is suboptimal?

Or is it more likely that your management has no clue how to fix your fundamental problems and they think that rearranging the existing supply of nitwits will look like progress?

CHANGE FOR THE SAKE OF PROMOTION

22 BUILD A BETTER LIFE BY STEALING OFFICE SUPPLIES Dogbert's Big Book of Business

"THE FUTURE IS BRIGHT"

Is it likely that your boss is a visionary who can predict the future even though he can't operate the computer on his desk? And if he can see the future, is it likely that he prefers to waste this ability in his current job versus using his powers to cure cancer and make a few bucks in the process?

Or is it more likely that the future isn't much brighter than your boss?

"WE REWARD RISK-TAKERS"

By definition, risk-takers often fail. So do morons. In practice it's difficult to sort them out.

Is it likely that your manager will begin rewarding people who have failed, knowing that a good portion of them are morons and every one of them has caused the boss to receive at least one executive-induced wedgie?

Or is it more likely that people who fail will be assigned to Quality Teams while the people who succeed will leave the company faster than a cheetah leaves a salad bar?

Bonus Question

If the successful people leave, will they make more money or less money at another company?

"PERFORMANCE WILL BE REWARDED"

Is it likely that this is the year the officers of your company will say, "To hell with the stock prices and our bonuses. What were we thinking? Let's distribute more money to the employees!"?

Or is it more likely you'll be put through a tortuous Performance Review process that would result in approximately the same tiny raise whether you were Mother Teresa or the Unabomber?

"WE DON'T SHOOT THE MESSENGER"

Is it likely that all the managers of your company have simultaneously found Buddha dancing in their desk drawers and decided to give peace a chance?

Or is it more likely that these Satan-spawned, coffee-torqued managers will continue to extract revenge on any target that is dumb enough to stand still?

(Note: It helps to add a little "attitude" to some of these questions to increase the contrast.)

"TRAINING IS A HIGH PRIORITY"

Let's say, hypothetically, that the budget for your department gets tight. Is it more likely your manager will leave your high-priority training budget intact and save money by delaying the launch of your product instead, thus reducing his own raise and bonus?

Or is it more likely that the training budget will disappear faster than the hors d'oeuvres at a Richard Simmons *Sweatin' to the Oldies* reunion.

From E-mail . . .

From: (name withheld)
To: scottadams@aol.com

Scott,

. . . an experience I had with [company] a few years ago. A survey determined that employees required more training. At the same time, training budgets were slashed drastically. I was literally forced to attend a bunch of little $39 Holiday Inn training sessions on time management, etc.

"I HAVEN'T HEARD ANY RUMORS"

Is it likely that the perpetual flow of rumors has suddenly stopped just at the time when the odds are highest that something might actually happen?

Or is it more likely that your manager knows the news is so bad that the slightest whiff of the truth will make the employees less productive than a truckload of Chihuahuas?*

*Maybe this analogy is a stretch. But just maybe I've done exhaustive studies of Chihuahua work habits and discovered that a truckload of Chihuahuas is the least productive organizational size.

"WE'LL REVIEW YOUR PERFORMANCE IN SIX MONTHS"

The best thing about the future is that it isn't here yet. When your manager promises to review your performance in six months for a possible raise, what is more likely?

A. Your manager believes that you could become smarter and more productive in 180 days, thus earning such a large increase in salary that you'll be glad you waited.

Or . . .

B. Your manager expects he will be in a new job within six months and your chances of getting a raise are deader than a Fishstick at a cat festival.

"OUR PEOPLE ARE THE BEST"

This lie is appreciated by the employees. Unfortunately only one company in each industry can have the best employees. And you might be suspicious about the fact that your company pays the lowest salaries.

Is it likely that the "best" employees would be drawn to your company despite the lower-than-average pay? Is it possible that there's a strange mental condition that makes some people brilliant at their jobs, yet unable to compare two salary numbers and determine which one is higher? Let's call these people "Occupational Savants." If they exist, what are the odds that they all decided to work at your company?

And is it likely that the people you work with all day appear to be denser than titanium, yet in reality are the most skilled professionals in their field?

Or is it more likely that the Nobel Prize–winning economists of the world are right—the market system works—and your company has exactly the doltish quality of employees that it's willing to pay for?

"YOUR INPUT IS IMPORTANT TO US"

To the manager, the following equation holds true:

$$\text{Employee Input} = \text{More Work} = \text{Bad}$$

As an abused and powerless employee you know it's fun to give your manager impractical suggestions such as this:

"If you care about the health of the employees you should ask the CEO to fund research on the effects of fluorescent lights on fertility."

This suggestion is thoroughly impractical, but the beauty of it is that your manager can't discard it offhand without appearing uncaring. Nor can the work be delegated, since no manager wants a subordinate to talk to his superior and maybe say embarrassing things.

Most employee suggestions are either clueless or sadistic. Once in a great while a good idea slips through, but a good idea is indistinguishable from a bad one unless you're the person who thought of it. It's never entirely clear in advance when employee input will be a good thing. So managers have to treat all input as bad.

Here's the test to see if managers really want employee input:

Is it likely that your boss enjoys the extra work involved in pursuing the well-meaning, sagelike suggestions of your gifted colleagues?

Or is it more likely your boss will pretend to listen to your thoroughly impractical suggestions, thank you for the input, do exactly what he planned all along, and then ask you to chair the United Way campaign as punishment?

See how easy this is?

5

MACHIAVELLIAN METHODS

(WRITTEN BY DOGBERT)

This chapter contains many surefire tips for gaining wealth and personal power at the expense of people who are studying how to be team players. Naturally I have withheld my most effective tips so that I can crush you later if it's absolutely necessary, or if it just looks like fun. But what you find here should still be enough to brush aside the kindhearted dolts that litter your path to success.

Use these techniques sparingly, at least until you've gained total power over the simpletons around you. If you use all these techniques at once you'll probably scare the neighboring cubicle dwellers into thinking you're a witch. They might form an unruly mob, storm your office, and kill your secretary. This would be a tragedy, especially if you need some copies made.

PROVIDE BAD ADVICE

During the course of your career many people will come to you for advice. This is your chance to steer them off the corporate speedway and—if you're skillful—help them plow into a crowd of innocent spectators.

It's not always easy to give advice. For one thing, your tail might wag uncontrollably, thus signaling your impending treachery. Moreover, your advice has to sound plausible, no matter how destructive and self-serving it really is. The best way to give bad advice that still sounds well-meaning is to "take the high road."

For example, let's say your manager has engaged in unethical conduct and your co-worker discovers this activity and comes to you for advice. You should "take the high road." Tell your co-worker to confront the boss and also blow the whistle to the authorities. This will simultaneously open your boss's job for you while most likely eliminating your co-worker from competition, all in the name of what is "right."

You don't need to take the high road in all cases. Your co-workers might be sufficiently moronic to accept plain old bad advice without questioning it, as in these examples:

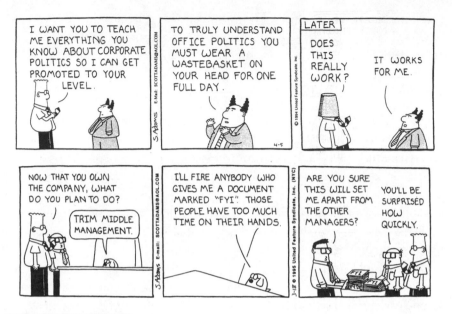

SHADE THE TRUTH

The great thing about the truth is that there are so many ways to avoid it without being a "liar." You can avoid the stigma of being a liar while still enjoying all the benefits of misleading people by simply omitting important qualifiers to your statements.

TRUE STATEMENT	OMITTED QUALIFIER
"I'm a team player"	. . . for the other team.
"You're next on my list"	. . . of things to ignore.
"I'll call you when I know"	. . . that you won't be there.
"I love what you've done with your hair"	. . . Medusa.

WHOM YOU ASSOCIATE WITH

People will judge you by the company you keep, especially during lunch.
Never eat lunch with a person of lower salary.

Exceptions

- Your secretary during National Secretaries Week (obligatory).
- Your boss's secretary (indirect sucking up).

- A person widely known to be terminally ill (makes you look compassionate).

If you get tricked into dining with a person of lower salary you can salvage the situation by spreading a rumor that the person is terminally ill. This is not technically lying, since we're all going to die eventually. If anybody spots you together, hold your napkin over your mouth like a surgical mask whenever the low-ranking person speaks to you.

Ideally, you want to dupe higher salaried people into being seen at a meal with you. They will try every trick to avoid you, so you must be nimble and devious. For example, you could schedule a department lunch and not bother to invite the other people in the department. Or, if you possess vital information that is needed by the higher-paid person, take the knowledge hostage and demand lunch as your ransom.

WITHHOLD INFORMATION

A good way for ineffective people to cling to power in an organization is by creating a monopoly on information. This information should seem important, but not critically important. In other words, your co-workers should want the information you're withholding, but not so badly that they'll choke you to death when you prevent them from getting it.

Form a multilayered protective defense for your strategically withheld information. With the right mixture of attitude and complete psychopathic behavior you can withhold just about anything. Here's how.

Layer One

Insist that you don't have the information and act like the requesters are insane for expecting that you do. Repeat their request aloud as if to underscore the fact that what they're asking for makes no sense. Grill them mercilessly as to why on God's green earth they would ever think you had this information. If they present a convincing case that they know you have the information, smile and act like the problem was in the way they asked the question. Go to layer two.

Layer Two

Say you're too busy to explain all the information to the requesters. Remind them that it took you years to understand it all. Ask them to leave you an easily ignored voice mail to schedule a time when you can sort through it together. That's because you "want to help." If the requesters persist, proceed to layer three.

Layer Three

Insist that the information is not ready yet—either because you're waiting for somebody else's input or because you need to "massage" the numbers to remove all the misleading data. If the requesters insist on settling for last month's information—or even misleading information—proceed to layer four.

Layer Four

Exhibit an exceptionally bad personality. Be rude, negative, and condescending. This layer is not a defense in itself, but it makes the requesters more vulnerable to the next layers of defense.

Layer Five

Give the requesters incomplete or irrelevant information and hope they go away thinking they got what they needed. By the time they get back to their offices and discover they've been duped they might be discouraged. If you did a convincing job with the layer four bad-personality step, there's a good chance the requesters will give up on you altogether and leave you safe and happy.

Damage Control

If the requesters leave your cubicle with any sort of information whatsoever, complain to anybody who will listen that the information is faulty because the requesters either didn't understand the information or misinterpreted it.

TWO WRONGS MAKE A RIGHT, ALMOST

Your simpleminded relatives were technically correct when they told you "Two wrongs don't make a right." What they failed to mention is that two wrongs can sometimes cancel each other out, and although it's not as good as a "right" it's much better than one wrong. If you're clever, you can neutralize any blunder through a series of offsetting destructive acts, as in this example:

RETRIBUTION

Retribution is your best friend, especially when it's combined with its natural companion: hypocrisy. For some reason, retribution has become a dirty little word in business. But only the word itself is a problem; the practice of retribution is as popular as ever. Use it whenever you get the chance.

While an actual act of retribution can be fun and deeply fulfilling, it's the *threat* of retribution that has the most potential to help your career. For the threat to be taken seriously you must have actual or potential power to carry out your retribution. If you're at a low level in the organization you must create the impression that you're likely to be promoted or you're likely to be having an affair with somebody in power. If you're ugly and unlikely to be "bopping up" then your best bet is to create an aura of imminent promotion by simply looking managerial:

- Dress more expensively than your peers.

- Conceal any traces of technical competence.

- Use the word "paradigm" several times a day.

- Tell everybody that you're preparing for a meeting with the president.

- Refer to articles from the *Wall Street Journal*.°

These things are not enough to guarantee a promotion—although they come close—but they're enough to make your peers hedge their bets and do some preemptive butt kissing.

All your threats of retribution will seem hollow unless you can demonstrate your ability to detect those transgressions that merit retribution even when they occur beyond your presence. One way to appear all-knowing is to build a reliable network of spies in the organization.

°Don't waste your time actually reading the *Wall Street Journal*. Many people subscribe to it, but nobody actually reads it. It's easier just to say, "Hey, did you see that article in the *Journal* yesterday?" and see what happens. If the other person says yes, he's bluffing too, so you can both give a hearty laugh about the insights of the article and leave it at that. If the other person indicates he did not read the article, give a condescending look and mutter, "It figures" before changing the subject.

The best way to encourage spies to give *you* information is by being willing to give *them* information in exchange—preferably false information. Don't be afraid to invent plausible-sounding rumors that you know won't pan out. Inaccurate rumors are often an indication that you have direct contacts in the inner circles of the organization where lots of ideas are floated that don't materialize. Always couch your rumors in weasel terms like "They're considering..." or "One of the plans is..." so you can't be proven wrong no matter what happens.

The final and most important part of making retribution work for you is to broadcast your intention to use it, as in this example:

VIRUS MANEUVER

If you're in charge of a project that's a sure loser, or if the people who work for you are losers, you must distance yourself from them as soon as possible. The direct method is to simply switch jobs or fire your bad employees. But that's settling for too little. Instead, think of your bad assets as potential viruses that can be used to infect your enemies within the corporation. All you need to do is artificially inflate their value and wait for some unsuspecting manager to try to take them off your hands.

Never make the mistake of giving bad Performance Reviews to bad employees. That will limit their ability to switch jobs within the company and shackle them to you forever until their corrosive effect destroys you. It's better to focus on the positive aspects of every employee's performance, even if you have to assault the truth a bit.

If you can't transfer bad employees to other departments, move them into positions in which they are the key support for projects that are closely identified with other managers. If that opportunity doesn't exist, as a last resort, put the poor performers in charge of the United Way campaign and let everybody suffer with you.

DEMAGOGUERY

You can achieve notoriety by speaking out against things that are already unpopular. The focus of your attacks could be a project, technology, or strategy, or even an incompetent manager. There will be no shortage of worthy targets to choose from. But pick carefully. Make sure your target is already doomed and despised. When the inevitable happens, you'll look like a genius for accurately forecasting collapse.

Here are some good examples of projects for which you can confidently predict failure:

- Any morale building effort.

- Any large-scale reengineering effort.

- Any project that takes more than two years.

- Any market-driven technology product.

- Anything that hasn't been done before.

By sheer chance, some of the projects that you attack will succeed. But no project is so thoroughly successful that you can't pick out a few weak areas and highlight them as examples of "just what you were afraid would happen."

Once you've built a track record for consistently forecasting the failure of other people's work, higher-level managers will begin to think you're a brilliant visionary. Promotion is inevitable, at which point you'll be in a much better position to take advantage of other people for personal gain.

DISPARAGE CO-WORKERS

All success is relative. You can improve your relative success by disparaging the skills and accomplishments of those who surround you. This will be fairly easy since the people who surround you are idiots. Focus like a laser on every misstep they make and take every opportunity to broadcast the mistakes to your boss in clever ways that don't make you look like a backstabber.

You can avoid the backstabber appearance by badmouthing your peers to your boss's secretary. This guarantees that the information will reach your boss without your direct involvement, and as a bonus the facts usually become exaggerated in the process. Best of all, once the boss's secretary believes your co-workers are losers, they won't be able to schedule time on the boss's calendar to prove otherwise.

Don't make the mistake of criticizing your co-workers to their faces. That will tip your hand and invite retaliation. The only constructive criticism is the kind you do behind people's backs.

FORM OVER SUBSTANCE

The earth is populated by shallow and ignorant people. That's why form will always be more important than substance. You can waste your time complaining about how that should not be the case in a perfect world, or you can snap out of it and follow my advice.

Documents

If a document is over two pages long, few people will ever read it. And those who do read it won't remember it in twenty-four hours. That's why all your documents should be over two pages long. You don't want your readers to be influenced by a bunch of facts. You want them to look at your creative use of fonts, your brilliant application of white space, and your inspired graphics. Good formatting leaves the reader with the clear impression that you are a genius and therefore whatever you're writing about must be a good idea.

Clothing

Contrary to popular belief, it's often your clothing that gets promoted, not you. You reap some benefit by being the person inside the clothes. Always dress better than your peers so your clothes will be the ones selected for promotion. And make sure you're in your clothes when it happens. One man made the mistake of bringing his dry cleaning to work and ended up as a direct report to his own sports jacket.

Looking Busy

Never walk down the hall without a document in your hands. People with documents in their hands look like hardworking employees heading for important meetings. People with nothing in their hands look like they're heading for the cafeteria. People with the newspaper in their hands look like they're heading for the bathroom.

Above all, make sure you carry loads of stuff home with you at night, thus generating the false impression that you work longer hours than you do.

APPEAL TO GREED

You can short-circuit the two or three neurons that people use for common sense by appealing to their greed. Nothing defines humans better than their willingness to do irrational things in the pursuit of phenomenally unlikely payoffs. This is the principle behind lotteries, dating, and religion. You can use this quirk of human nature to your advantage and it won't cost you a dime.

The psychological explanation for this phenomenon is that life sucks and we'd all rather fantasize about being someplace else. Your job as a Machiavellian manipulator is to give people a microscopic chance of gaining riches by doing your bidding.

GET OTHERS TO DO YOUR WORK

Take every opportunity to delegate the unglamorous and hopeless portions of your workload downward, sideways, and upward.

Delegating to subordinates is easy. The hard part is delegating to co-workers and your boss. Always appeal to the principle of "efficiency" when you try to fob off your work sideways or upward. Support your argument by creating a record of being incompetent and unreliable for any tasks that are boring or thankless.

For example, if you are put in charge of bringing the donuts to the staff meeting, bring the kind that nobody likes. If you are asked to type up notes from the meeting, intentionally write bad grammar into people's quotes. If you are asked to chair the company's United Way campaign, start each meeting by stating your opinion that these people should "get a job and stop freeloading." Eventually, you'll be in a much stronger position to convincingly say things like "Well, I could make those photocopies, but in the interest of efficiency, Ted would do a much better job."

But the real "low-hanging fruit" of work avoidance involves any task that has more importance to somebody else than it has to you. If you ignore this type of task long enough, eventually the person who really needs it done will offer to do it, even if it's clearly your job.

EXAGGERATE YOUR TALENTS

Everybody exaggerates his or her talents. There's no trick to that. You need to take it to the next level: complete fantasy. It's not enough to say you performed well at your assigned tasks; you must take credit for any positive development that ever happened in the company or on earth.

What You Did

Attended some meetings, ate donuts, nodded head to bluff comprehension.

Worked on a project that got canceled after management figured out what you were doing.

What You Can Claim

Created a strategy to bring the company into the next century. Increased revenues by $25 million.

Reengineered the company's core processes and increased market share by ninety percent.

Got stuck organizing the company's U.S. Savings Bond drive.

Stabilized the monetary system of the wealthiest nation on earth.

INTIMIDATION BY LOUDNESS

Speak loudly and act irrationally. Co-workers and even bosses will bend to your will if you use this method consistently. Consistency is the key. Send a clear signal that you cannot be swayed by reason and that you'll never stop being loud and obnoxious until you get your way. This method is effective because the law prevents people from killing you and there's no other practical way to make you stop.

At first, your victim might try to wait you out, hoping you'll get tired and go away. That's where most Machiavellian wannabes fail with the loudness method—they give up too early. You must be persistent, bordering on loony. Never let up.

After you get your way, turn instantly into the sweetest person your victim has ever seen. Buy candy. Call the victim's boss and leave kudos. Sing the victim's praise while others are nearby. This widens the gap between the experience people have when they satisfy you and the experience they have when they don't.

This method is most effective when used on people who were raised in dysfunctional families. Fortunately, that's nearly everybody. These people will start to believe you're their best personal friend. At that point you can abuse them even more.

MANAGE SEXY PROJECTS

The worth of any project is based on how it will sound on your résumé. Don't get caught up in the propaganda about how important something is for the stockholders. The stockholders are people you'll never meet. And since most projects fail or turn into something you never intended, the only lasting impact of your work is the impact on your résumé. Keep your priorities straight.

Nobody can read a résumé and get any real sense of what the author actually did on a job. All judgments are necessarily based on the collective quality of the individual words. That's why you have to work on projects that have good words in the names.

Avoid any project that has one of the following words in its description:

- Accounting

- Operations

- Reduction

- Budget

- Quality

- Analysis

Seek out any project that has one of the following résumé-ready words in its description:

- Multimedia

- Worldwide

- Advanced

- Strategic

- Revenue

- Market

- Technology

- Rapid

- Competitive

GET INPUT (BUY-IN)

Many dolts will try to impede your brilliant plans. You can minimize their collective resistance through a process called "getting buy-in." This involves collecting the opinions of people who care about a decision, acting interested, then pretending that your plan is a direct reflection of what the majority of people want.

This might sound silly, but if you compare it to the alternatives it's the only practical solution. You can't accommodate a hundred different opinions, and you can't ignore them. All you can do is provide people with the illusion that they participated in the decision. For some reason, that's enough to make people happy.° This is the basis for all democracies.

SELF-SERVING STRATEGIES

There are documented cases of employees who experienced low-level food poisoning in the company cafeteria and later, when this was combined with the hypnotic trance state induced by the boredom of the job, reacted to the inspirational message on a company bulletin board and accidentally acted in the best interest of the company.

It could happen to you. Just be careful what you eat. That's the best advice I can give.

MANIPULATE THE MEDIA

Reporters are faced with the daily choice of painstakingly researching stories or writing whatever people tell them. Both approaches pay the same.

Contrary to what you might believe, the quotes that you see in news stories are rarely what was actually said and rarely in the original context. Most quotes are engineered by the writers to support whatever notion they had before starting the story. Avoid any mention of a name or topic that you wouldn't want to see yourself misquoted about.

°The reason would be that people are idiots.

For example, see how an innocuous corporate statement can be edited slightly to alter the original meaning while still being a legitimate quote:

You say: "Our company is skilled in many other things that are never reported by the biased media."

Media reports: "Our company _____killed _____m_____other t_____er_____e____s_____a."

All news stories focus on one of two things: something that is very bad or something that is very good. Help the writer determine what is very good about your situation; otherwise the default story is generally about something that is very bad.

THE HONESTY TRAP

You might be tempted to give your honest opinions to upper-level managers. Resist this temptation at all costs.

Don't be lulled into a sense of false security by management's oft-stated interest in getting feedback. There are only two safe things to say to a manager:

- "Your decisions are brilliant!"

- "I have an idea on how to save some paper!"

Any other feedback is a direct challenge to the manager's intelligence and authority. If your impulse for honesty grows too strong, try this simple exercise to tame your masochistic tendencies:

1. Find a large kitchen spatula.

2. Beat yourself on the head with it.

3. Repeat.

TAKE CREDIT FOR THE WORK OF OTHERS

Millions of employees do millions of things every day. By sheer chance, some of them will accidentally do something valuable. Identify these rare situations and make every effort to attach your name to them.

If you're the boss, make sure your name is prominently written on any piece of good work produced by your people. Your people will hate that, but if you've studied the section on retribution it won't be a problem.

If you're part of a team effort, make sure you're the one who presents the conclusions and distributes the documents to upper management. Staple your business card to documents when you distribute them. That makes you look like the primary contributor even if all you did during the meetings was eat donuts and fantasize about making love to an attractive co-worker in the utility closet.

OFFER FALSE SACRIFICES

An essential part of being a team player is the willingness to make false sacrifices that other people perceive as genuine. Offer to give up things that you know won't be accepted or won't be missed. Here are some good things to offer up as sacrifices:

- Offer to reduce the rate of increase in future budgets and refer to it frequently as a budget reduction.

- Transfer your worst employees to another department to "help."

- Reduce your budget by shutting down a project that was doomed to fail because of your management.

- Offer to fire employees in your department who were supporting other groups in the company. The managers of the other groups will have to do the fighting to rebuild your empire while you look like a team player for offering the sacrifice.

- Offer to cut support to the most critical function in the company. This offer will never be accepted and it makes the things you didn't offer seem like they must be comparatively more important.

WORK ON PROJECTS WITH NO VERIFIABLE RESULTS

The best jobs are those that have results that cannot be measured. Stay away from jobs in which your value can be measured in quantity and timeliness. You can exaggerate your impact on quality much more easily than you can exaggerate your impact on quantity.

Bad Jobs

Sales
Programming
Operations

Customer service
Shipping

Great Jobs

Strategy
Anything with "Media" in the name
Marketing (for mature products)
Long-term reengineering projects
Advertising
Procurement

SEND PEOPLE TO THE LEGAL DEPARTMENT

From time to time it will be necessary for you to kill a project without being identified as the assassin. That's why large companies have legal departments. No project is so risk-free that your company lawyer can't kill it.

MANAGE THE BUDGET GROUP

It can be unglamorous work to manage the budget function for your group. Most managers wouldn't want that duty, so it will be easy for you to move the budget tasks under your control. Once you have it, you effectively control the strategy and careers of every person in the department.

There is a widespread misconception that the budget is set by senior management and the budget analysts are merely tools of their policies. In reality of course, it's the other way around. Senior managers are so bored by the budget process, and so overwhelmed by its complexity, that they jump at the chance to accept a budget analyst's recommendation for budget changes.

EMPLOYEE STRATEGIES

You're working more hours than ever. And if you're one of the so-called exempt employees you aren't getting paid for overtime. It might seem that your average hourly pay is shrinking like a cheap cotton shirt.

Not true!

Nature has a way of balancing these things out. You have to consider the total compensation picture, which I call "Virtual Hourly Compensation."

Definition

Virtual Hourly Compensation is the total amount of compensation you receive per hour, including:

- Salary
- Bonuses
- Health plan
- Inflated travel reimbursement claims
- Stolen office supplies
- Airline frequent flyer awards
- Coffee
- Donuts
- Newspapers and magazines
- Personal phone calls
- Office sex
- Telecommuting
- Illegitimate sick days
- Internet surfing
- Personal e-mail
- Use of laser printer for your résumé
- Free photocopies
- Training for your next job
- Cubicle used as a retail outlet

ADAMS'S LAW OF COMPENSATION EQUILIBRIUM

Adams's Law of Compensation Equilibrium states that an employee's Virtual Hourly Compensation stays constant over time. Whenever an employer finds a way to increase your workload, nature will adjust either your compensation or your perceived work hours to create equilibrium.

For example, when companies went hog-wild on downsizing in the early nineties, the surviving employees began working longer hours to avoid identification as low performers. Salaries didn't increase much because the supply of employees was greater than the demand. On the surface, it looked as if average hourly wages were permanently lowered.

Predictably, nature responded to the temporary imbalance by creating new activities that looked like work but weren't; for example, Internet access and telecommuting.

This is the same process of deception and disguise that nature provides to other parts of the animal kingdom. For example, the Elbonian Puffer Bird can expand to twice its normal size when threatened.° Similarly, employees puff up their *perceived* hours of work without increasing their *real* work. Equilibrium is maintained.

TOTAL WORK EQUATION

Real Work + Appearance of Work = Total Work

You can be a participant in nature's grand plan by actively pursuing the activities that create equilibrium. Try to keep your *Total Work* at a constant level without increasing your *Real Work*. Do that by beefing up your *Appearance of Work* using any of the following activities:

°Yes, I did make that up. But we both know that somewhere there must be a bird that puffs up when it's threatened. If I'm not mistaken, my parakeet Goldie did that just before the tragic basketball incident that I later blamed on my brother.

- Internet surfing

- Personal e-mail

- Attending meetings

- Talking to your boss

- Conventions

- Upgrading your computer

- Testing new software

- Waiting for answers from co-workers

- Project consulting

- Hiding behind voice mail

TELECOMMUTING

Telecommuting is nature's gift to our generation. Just when it seemed that the combination of long commutes, pollution, congested highways, and long meetings would kill us, nature gave us telecommuting.

Now you can spend time at home, sitting around in your pajamas, listening to your stereo, and playing with your hand puppet. If you feel generous and slam out two hours of productivity, it's more than you would have done in the office, so you can feel good about it.

The office is designed for "work," not productivity. Work can be defined as "anything you'd rather not be doing." Productivity is a different matter. Telecommuting substitutes two hours of productivity for ten hours of work.

To cover your joy of telecommuting (and avoid having the program canceled because of excess joy) take every opportunity to lie about how much more "work" you do at home. Leave lots of inane and unnecessary voice mail messages to your boss and co-workers while you're home. This creates the illusion that you are as unhappy and unproductive as they are, thus justifying a continuation of telecommuting.

RUNNING A SIDE BUSINESS FROM YOUR CUBICLE

A cubicle is an excellent retail space, suitable for selling stuffed dolls, earrings, cosmetics, semiprecious gems, plant arrangements, household cleaning products, real estate, and vacation packages. Don't miss your opportunity to "moonlight," or as I like to call it, "fluorescentlight."

All you need is a tacky handmade sign on the outside of your cubicle that tells people you're open for business. A brochure or product sample can help lure people in.

You don't need high-quality merchandise. Let's be honest—if your co-workers were bright enough to know the difference between diamonds and monkey crap they wouldn't be working at your company. So don't waste a bunch of time on "quality." It's shelf space that matters, and you've got 180 cubic feet to play with. It's your chance to make some money while you're at work.

THEFT OF OFFICE SUPPLIES

Office supplies are an important part of your total compensation package. If God didn't want people to steal office supplies he wouldn't have given us briefcases, purses, and pockets. In fact, no major religion specifically bans the pilfering of office supplies.°

The only downside is the risk of being caught, disgraced, and imprisoned. But if you compare that to your current work situation I think you'll agree that it's not such a big deal.

The secret is to avoid getting too greedy. Office supplies are like compound interest—a little bit per day adds up over time. If you want some yellow sticky notes, don't take the whole box at once. Instead, use several sheets per day as page markers on documents that you're taking home. Later, carefully remove them and reassemble them into pads.

You can steal an unlimited amount of pens and pencils, but avoid the rookie mistake of continually asking the department secretary for the key to the supply closet. That attracts suspicion. Instead, steal supplies directly from your co-workers. Casually "borrow" their writing tools during meetings and never return them. Act naturally, and remember you can always laugh and claim it was a "reflex" if you get caught putting their stuff in your pocket.

°Some religious scholars will debate my interpretation. But ultimately it's a matter of faith.

Your co-workers will be trying to swipe your writing implements too. Defend your pens and pencils by conspicuously chewing on them during meetings. I've found that a few teeth marks are more effective than The Club in preventing theft.

If you have a home computer, say good-bye to purchasing your own diskettes. Stolen diskettes look exactly like work-related diskettes that are being taken home so you can "do a little work at night." The only practical limit on the number of diskettes you can steal is the net worth of the company you're stealing from. Your company will go broke if you steal too many diskettes. Nobody wins when that happens. That's why moderation is the key. After you have enough diskettes to back up your hard drive, and maybe shingle your house, think about cutting back.

USE COMPUTERS TO LOOK BUSY

Any time you use a computer it looks like "work" to the casual observer. You can send and receive personal e-mail, download pornography from the Internet, calculate your finances, and generally have a blast without doing anything remotely related to work. These aren't exactly the societal benefits that everybody expected from the computer revolution, but they're not bad either.

When you get caught by your boss—and you will get caught—your best defense is to claim you're teaching yourself to use the new software, thus saving valuable training dollars. You're not a loafer, you're a self-starter. Offer to show your boss what you learned. That will make your boss scurry away like a frightened salamander.°

°In laboratory tests, three out of four frightened salamanders were mistaken for supervisors.

WAITING FOR INFORMATION FROM CO-WORKERS

Hardly any task can be done without first getting help from other people in the company. Luckily you'll never get that help because the other people are busy trying to get help from other people too.

This situation is good news for everybody. Nobody does any real work and you can all blame your woes on some worthless bastard in another department. Simply make phone calls and wait for help that never comes. At the weekly status meeting you can legitimately claim that you've done everything you can do for now.

Boss: "Did you finish your product designs?"

You: "I made phone calls but nobody called me back."

Boss: "That's no excuse."

You: "What do you suggest?"

Boss: "Get me involved earlier if you're not getting support."

You: "I tried but you didn't call me back."

Boss: "I'm involved now. After the meeting, tell me who's not giving you proper support and I'll take care of it."

You: "I'll call you."

VOICE MAIL

Voice mail has freed more employees from work than any other innovation. Prior to voice mail, people answered the phone personally and often found themselves doing more work because of it. Now you can just let it ring until the call rolls over to voice mail. This has a triple advantage: You can (1) escape immediate work, (2) screen messages to avoid future work, and (3) create the impression that you're overworked!

Sample Voice Mail Message

"This is Scott Adams. I can't take your call because I am a martyr doing the job of several people. Although I am dying from exhaustion I'm sure that the reason you called is highly important and worthy of my attention. Please leave a detailed message so I can evaluate your importance in relation to the six hundred other messages I will get today."

7

PERFORMANCE REVIEWS

THE PURPOSE OF THE PERFORMANCE REVIEW

One of the most frightening and degrading experiences in every employee's life is the annual Performance Review.

In theory, the Performance Review process can be thought of as a positive interaction between a "coach" and an employee, working together to achieve maximum performance. In reality, it's more like finding a dead squirrel in your backyard and realizing the best solution is to fling it onto your neighbor's roof. Then your obnoxious neighbor takes it off the roof and flings it back, as if he had the right to do that. Ultimately, nobody's happy, least of all the squirrel.

Theory aside, your manager's real objectives for the Performance Review are:

- Make you work like a Roman orchard slave.*

- Obtain a signed confession of your crimes against productivity.

- Justify your low salary.

Your objective as an employee is to bilk as much unearned money as possible out of the cold, oppressive entity that masquerades as an employer while it sucks the life-force out of your body.

Luckily for you, I'm on your side.

This chapter will teach you how to glide through the Performance Review process while lining your pockets with the money that rightfully belongs to your more productive co-workers. (If your co-workers have a problem with that, let 'em buy their own helpful book.)

*I don't know if there were any such things as Roman orchard slaves. But if there were, the job probably involved climbing rickety ladders where anybody could look up your toga.

The key to your manager's strategy is tricking you into confessing your shortcomings. Your boss will latch on to those shortcomings like a pit bull on a trespasser's buttocks. Once documented, your "flaws" will be passed on to each new boss you ever have, serving as justification for low raises for the rest of your life. Here are two examples of employees who wandered into that trap:

From E-mail . . .

From: (name withheld)
To: scottadams@aol.com

Scott,

At my company we have to fill out evaluation forms. One has a number of categories (creativity, initiative, teamwork, etc.) with spaces for you to indicate "strengths" and "growth opportunities."

I'm new and didn't know better, so I filled it out honestly, and tried to identify some good growth opportunities. But a co-worker stopped me and said any "growth opportunities" are then automatically spit back to employees by management as examples of poor performance. I don't need any of that, since I'm already the United Way campaigner, and we know what that means.

From: (name withheld)
To: scottadams@aol.com

Scott,

I used to work for [company] doing project management. As a part of that job, I was asked, "What do you think of pie charts?" to which I responded, "Personally, I hate them." I was asked this, in this way, several times by various "superiors."

When I got my next review, I got several negative comments about how I "refused to do pie charts." I pointed out to my boss that I had never been ASKED to do pie charts, merely about my opinion of them. This of course made no difference in my review—"refused to do pie charts" is PART OF MY PERMANENT RECORD!

Your only defense against your boss's "development trap" is to identify development needs in yourself that don't sound so bad:

- "I need to become less attractive so co-workers are not constantly distracted."

- "In the interest of teamwork, I need to learn to control my immense intelligence in the presence of less gifted co-workers."

- "I need to learn how to relax instead of working my typical nineteen-hour days."

- "I need to make contact with an alien civilization, since their technology is the only thing I don't already understand."

STRATEGY FOR PERFORMANCE REVIEWS

You know you deserve more money than you're getting, based on two undeniable facts:

1. You show up most of the time.

2. See number one.

Your manager might not see it that way (the bastard!). Luckily you have several things working in your favor: (1) Your manager is probably too lazy to write your Performance Review without your "input," and (2) your manager fears that you might cry publicly or resort to violence. Those advantages provide enough traction to pull the "performance train" in your direction.

WRITING YOUR OWN PERFORMANCE REVIEW

Your boss will ask you to document your accomplishments as input for your Performance Review. To the unprepared employee, this might seem like being forced to dig one's own grave. But after studying this chapter you will come to view it more like a jewelry store fantasy.

JEWELRY STORE FANTASY

Imagine your boss as a wealthy but clueless jewelry store owner. He gives you these instructions before leaving for a long vacation. "When nobody's around, count up how many rubies are in that huge sack in the back. I've wondered about that for years."

Performance Reviews can be like a big bag of uncounted rubies. It doesn't matter how many rubies were originally in the bag; what matters is the number you report to your boss. Follow that simple philosophy when describing your accomplishments.

TIPS ON DESCRIBING YOUR ACCOMPLISHMENTS

1. Some people will foolishly limit their list of accomplishments to projects that they've actually worked on. This is a mistake. Don't forget the intangible benefit of "thinking about" a project.

2. No matter how badly your project screwed up, focus on how much money would have been lost if you'd done something even stupider. Then count the difference between the failure you cre-

ated and the even bigger failure you *could* have created as a "cost avoidance."

3. Acronyms are your allies. They sound impressive while conveying no information. Use them liberally.

   Boss: "What was your contribution to the project?"

   You: "Mostly QA. I was also an SME for the BUs."

   Boss: "Um . . . okay. Excellent work."

4. If all you did this year was sit in your cubicle and masturbate, dress it up with the latest buzzwords. Say you're a self-starter who proactively reengineered your personal inventory with Total Quality, conforming to all EEO, OSHA, and ISO 9000 requirements. Stress your commitment to continue this good work into the next fiscal year.

5. Include testimonials from unverifiable sources. Your manager is far too lazy to verify your sources. And since your employee file is confidential, the person you quote doesn't need to know about it either.

6. For this year's accomplishments include everything you did last year and everything you plan to do next year. Bosses don't have a keen grasp of time. If they did, they wouldn't ask you to do six months of work in two weeks. This is your chance to use that curious time-awareness deficiency of your boss to your advantage.

7. Include as your accomplishments anything done by an employee who has a similar name or similar appearance to you. It's worth a shot, and if you're discovered just say, "I always get us confused" and quickly change the subject.

SETTING THE STAGE

You can set the stage for your Performance Review by talking about your accomplishments in glowing terms at every opportunity. Follow this model:

SURROUND YOURSELF WITH LOSERS

Make sure you work in a group with losers. Losers are the ones who will get low raises, thus leaving ample budget funds for you. The worst mistake you could make is to work in a group with highly qualified people. That's a no-win situation for all of you. Losers are your friends (figuratively speaking). If you don't have any losers in your group, help your boss recruit some, preferably in areas that don't affect your life. You want the losers to be within the same general budget area, but not close enough to annoy you on a daily basis.

I remember many joyous occasions after a reorganization at companies where I worked. I would run to get a copy of the new organization chart, almost skipping with joy at the prospect of identifying the co-workers who would "fund" my next raise. Discovering an incompetent co-worker in your group is like finding a gold nugget in your flower garden. It's free money without the burden of additional work.

So if you think the only value that morons provide to the world is to support the commemorative plate industry, you're wrong; they also help pay your salary. You have to respect that.

360-DEGREE REVIEW

If you're lucky enough to have a "360-degree review" process at your company, this is your chance to threaten your boss with "mutually assured destruction." Under this type of system each employee gets to review subordinates, co-workers, and (here's the best part) devil-spawned bosses.

The secret to making this system work for you is to be sure you're the *last* person to complete your review forms. Carry the forms with you wherever you go, occasionally taking them out and saying things like "That reminds me . . ." in the most ominous voice you can muster.

And don't forget to hammer your co-workers too. Every dollar that goes to a co-worker is a dollar that's not available in the budget for you. You might feel selfish doing this, but remember, your co-workers will just blow the money on stupid stuff like education and health care, whereas you would stimulate the economy by spending it on clothes. You have to look at the big picture when you decide how your co-workers "performed."

WRITING YOUR OWN ACCOMPLISHMENTS

Your boss will mentally scale back whatever wild claims you make about yourself on your input to the Performance Review. Fortunately your boss is "flying blind" with no way of knowing how much to scale back.

Therefore, logically, your best strategy is to lie like a shoe salesman with a foot fetish.°

Here are some recommended phrases that I've used as the input for my Performance Reviews over the years, grouped by trendy category. These are written for the boss's signature, thus removing the need for your boss to do any thinking whatsoever.

Does employee demonstrate teamwork?

Scott loves his peers like he loves himself, except without the intense physical attraction. If there's a team, Scott's on it, even if only in spirit or simply taking credit. That's the kind of team player he is.

Does employee have communication skills?

Scott is fluent in seventeen languages including the African one with the clicking sound, which he combines with Morse code in order to multi-task.

Does employee demonstrate customer focus?

Nobody focuses on customers more intensely than Scott. Sometimes it makes the customers nervous, especially the women, but we think they like it.

Does employee demonstrate leadership skills?

Scott is a natural leader. People follow him everywhere he goes, and they watch him too. Some people say Scott is paranoid, but no, that's leadership.

°I believe that all shoe sales people have foot fetishes, for the simple economic reason that they'd be willing to work for less pay than somebody who hates feet. That explains why they often "forget" your foot measurement and insist on doing it again.

Does employee model and foster ethical behavior?

Oh yeah. Big time. For example, he would never exaggerate his accomplishments in an attempt to unethically inflate his salary to the level of "market comparables" that he keeps hearing about.

Does employee set high expectations and standards?

Scott's standards are so high that he despises the worthless laggards around him—the so-called co-workers. He thinks even less of the customers, who apparently haven't taken the time to do any comparison shopping.

Scott's expectations are very high. He has often expressed his goal of evolving into pure energy and becoming the supreme overlord of the universe. He's got a long way to go, but his hair loss is a sure sign of some sort of rapid acceleration.

Does employee involve and empower others?

Scott empowers those around him by giving them his work whenever his co-workers are not—in his opinion—busy enough. Sometimes he gives all his work away and has to make up a few things just so everybody gets something. His co-workers couldn't be happier about it because they feel empowered.

Does employee set priorities?

Scott knows his priorities. When I (his feeble and unattractive boss) asked him to work on this Performance Review he hung up the phone on his primary customer and sprang to the keyboard like a panther.

Does employee understand the company vision?

Scott is the only person who has actually "seen" the company vision. He claims it appeared to him one night in the forest and it's "difficult to explain" but he knows it when he sees it. He also came back with some "commandments" from God carved on a flat rock.

(On an unrelated note, Scott has excellent penmanship, based on the observation that it is almost exactly like God's!)

Performance Summary

Scott is my role model. It is my dream to be more like him. Sometimes I follow him around and buy the same clothes. Once in a while I rummage through his trash.

I once observed Scott walking across a lake to heal an injured swan.

He is love.

CONCLUSION

If all else fails, try a subscription to *Soldier of Fortune* magazine and have it delivered to the office. You don't have to read it, just leave it prominently on your desk. Add to your boss's nervousness by asking for "time off to work through a few personal problems."

If you follow my advice, it is my opinion that your next Performance Review will result in a larger raise than you could possibly be worth.

8

PRETENDING TO WORK

When it comes to avoiding work, it's fair to say I studied with the masters. After nine years at Pacific Bell I learned just about everything there was to know about *looking* busy without actually *being* busy. During that time the stock price of Pacific Bell climbed steadily, so I think I can conclude that my avoidance of work was in the best interest of the company and something to be proud of.

Here for the first time ever I am revealing my secrets for Pretending to Work. It's your ticket to freedom.

Your boss is the biggest obstacle to workday leisure. He will try to make you work right up to—but not beyond—the point of death. This may seem like an unfair generalization, because obviously it's more economical for him to push the people who are approaching retirement age a little bit harder.

As an employee, you need a strategy for survival. You need to develop your ability to appear productive without actually expending time or energy. Your very life is at stake.

Based on my painstaking research* I have concluded that there are three types of employees:

1. Those who work hard regardless of the compensation (Idiots).

2. Those who avoid work, thus appearing lazy (Idiots).

3. Those who avoid work while somehow appearing to be productive (Contented Employees).

The rest of this chapter outlines specific strategies for becoming a Contented Employee at the expense of your employer who doesn't deserve somebody as nice as you anyway.

BE A CONSULTANT ON A TEAM

If you can't be a manager, the next best way to avoid real work is to be an "adviser" to people who are doing real work. You might need to develop

*There wasn't much of it, but it hurt.

some actual expertise to become an adviser, but don't go overboard with it. You only need to know one percent more than the people you're advising and then you'll be indistinguishable from Marilyn vos Savant.*

To demonstrate my point, consider this hypothetical situation: You're having a conversation with Albert Einstein and he suddenly gets struck by lightning. This freak accident makes him instantly twice as smart. Could you tell the difference?

Once a person is smarter than you, it doesn't matter if he's one percent smarter or one thousand percent smarter. You can't tell the difference. Don't waste your time acquiring a bunch of knowledge that will do nothing to elevate your perceived value.

The best areas in which to become an expert are those areas that are vital to many projects, shallow in substance, and spectacularly uninteresting. Select an area that is so dry that when the average person is exposed to it he'll want to drill a hole in his head to let the boredom out. Some suggested areas that fit this description:

1. Facilities management

2. Database administration

3. Tax law

WAITING FOR SOMETHING

Seek out assignments that depend heavily on the input of incompetent co-workers, overworked managers, and lying vendors. If any one of them screws up, you won't have the resources you need to do your job. You'll have no choice but to wait around. You can encourage these failures on the part of other people by asking for the things that are least likely to happen:

---

*Marilyn vos Savant has the highest recorded IQ of any human. She once solved a Rubik's Cube just by scaring it into alignment.

- Ask illiterate "outdoorsy" managers to review huge documents in detail.

- Place orders for "vaporware" products that will be "available soon" according to the vendor.

- Ask for meetings with co-workers who have poor time-management skills.

These activities have the unmistakable air of being necessary while at the same time providing you with all the free time you'd ever want.

CHANGE JOBS FREQUENTLY

Job descriptions are hideously cumulative. The longer you stay in one job, the more work you'll be asked to do. That's because people will figure out what you do and they'll know how to find you. Worse yet, you will become competent over time, and that's as good as begging for more work.

Change jobs as often as possible. That clears the deck of all the pesky people who have your phone number. You can then reinvent yourself in a less busy role as an "adviser" to something. Two years is the most you should ever spend in the same job.

COMPLAIN CONSTANTLY ABOUT YOUR WORKLOAD

Take every opportunity to complain about the unreasonable demands that are being placed on you. Reinforce your message during every interaction with a co-worker or manager. Here are some time-tested phrases that you should insert into every conversation:

"I'm up to my ass in alligators."
"I've been putting out fires all day."
"I had fifteen hundred voice mail messages today. Typical."
"It looks like I'll be here on the weekend *again*."

Over time, these messages will work themselves into the subconscious of everybody around you and they will come to think of you as a hard worker without ever seeing a scrap of physical evidence to support the theory.

In other words, don't be this guy:

VOICE MAIL

Never answer your phone if you have voice mail. People don't call you just because they want to give you something for nothing—they call because they want *you* to do work for *them*. That's no way to live. Screen all your calls through voice mail.

If somebody leaves a voice mail message for you and it sounds like impending work, respond during your lunch hour when you know the caller won't be there. That sends a signal that you're hardworking and conscientious even though you're being a devious weasel.

If you diligently employ the method of screening incoming calls and then returning calls when nobody is there you greatly increase the odds that the caller will give up or look for a solution that doesn't involve you. The sweetest voice mail message you can ever hear is "Ignore my last message. I took care of it."

If your voice mailbox has a limit on the number of messages it can hold, make sure you reach that limit frequently. One way to do that is to never erase any incoming messages. If that takes too long, send yourself a few messages. Your callers will hear a recorded message that says "Sorry, this mailbox is full"—a sure sign that you are a hardworking employee in high demand.

If you wake up in the middle of the night to heed nature's call, take a moment to leave a voice mail message for your boss. Your message will automatically leave a recorded time-stamp, thus reinforcing the illusion that you work around the clock. This is a big improvement over reality—that you chugged a beer before going to bed.

Some voice mail systems will activate your pager automatically when a message is left for you. And some voice mail systems will let you schedule a message to be sent at a future time. (I'll bet you know where this is going.) If you have a useless meeting coming up, program the voice mail system to send yourself a voice mail message during the meeting, thus activating your pager. Leave the pager on "beep" instead of vibrate so everybody knows you're being paged. Get a look of horror on your face as you check the incoming number on the pager, then excuse yourself rapidly. Mumble "Ohmygod . . ." on the way out.

ARRIVING AND LEAVING

Always arrive for work before your boss arrives. If you can't do that, leave work after your boss leaves. If you get to work before your boss does you can claim you got there at four A.M. and there's no way to disprove it. If you leave after your boss leaves you can claim you worked until midnight.

Your co-workers are the only ones who can bust you. That's why it's important to let them know that you're watching their arrival and departure times too. That's how you keep one another "honest."

MESSY DESK

Executives can get away with having a clean desk. For the rest of us, it looks like you're not working hard enough. Build huge piles of documents around your work space. To the observer, last year's work looks the same as today's work; it's volume that counts. Pile them high and wide. If you know somebody is coming to your cubicle, bury the document you'll need halfway down in an existing stack and rummage for it when she arrives.

ARRIVAL AND DEPARTURE AT MEETINGS

Come to meetings late and leave early. This leaves the impression that you
are so busy you can't do everything. The first part of a meeting is useless
and the last part of a meeting is when the assignments are handed out.
That is wasted time for a busy person such as yourself.

STUDY THINGS

Get a job that lets you "analyze" or "evaluate" something as opposed to actually "doing" something. When you evaluate something you get to criticize
the work of others. If you "do" something, other people get to criticize *you*.

Often there are no clear performance standards for the job of analyzing
something. You can take your time, savoring the mistakes of those people
who were foolish enough to "do" something.

WORK ON LONG-RANGE PROJECTS

You can easily hide your laziness when you're associated with a long-range
project. There's always another day to do the stuff you don't do today. And
realistically, the project will probably get canceled or altered beyond
recognition before it's completed anyway—so there's no harm done if you
don't do your part.

Avoid short-term projects at all costs. They're trouble. People expect
results and they expect you to work late to meet deadlines. You don't need
that hassle.

LOOKING INCOMPETENT

Nothing is more effective for deflecting work than sheer incompetence.
The more incompetent you seem, the less work you'll be asked to do. This
is not without its risks, as you might imagine. For example, you might be
recognized as an imbecile and promoted into a management job. But short
of that risk, it's a pretty safe strategy.

AVOIDING MEANINGLESS ASSIGNMENTS

The average boss generates many meaningless tasks for the employees. Most of the meaningless assignments go to people who are unfortunate enough to fall into one of these categories:

- The person who sits closest to the boss's office.

- The first person who asks a related question.

- The next person who enters the boss's office.

You should never under any circumstances inquire about something that is not part of your job description. Your questions will be interpreted as interest in taking on new work. By virtue of asking the question you become elevated to the position "most appropriate" for any meaningless assignment in that area.

In the boss's eyes, the hapless subordinate whose office is closest will appear like a huge "out basket." Avoid the "out basket" office location even if you have to sleep with the facilities planner to do it.* It's a prison sentence. Every time you hear footsteps you'll have to pretend you're working. Every piddling task ends up on your chair with a little yellow sticky note from the boss. Your value to the corporation will become associated with a stream of unimportant assignments. Your career can never recover from a bad office location.

Never enter the boss's office unless it's absolutely necessary. Every boss saves one corner of the desk for useless assignments that are doled out like Halloween candy to each visitor. Conduct all your business with your boss by voice mail or e-mail, thereby avoiding the "treats" afforded to less clever visitors.

STRATEGIC VACATION PLANNING

Lastly, save some of your vacation for a time when you can use it strategically.

*This is another excellent reason for entering the facilities management profession.

9

SWEARING

THE KEY TO SUCCESS FOR WOMEN

For men, swearing can help them bond with other men. But this contributes in only a tiny way to business success. Men are expected to swear, so it means little when they do. There is no shock value.

For example, if a man comes to the office of another man and offers to show him a report, a typical response might be "Ah, shove it up your ass and die."

Then both men laugh and spit and make passing references to "hooters," thus creating a lifelong bond that cannot be broken.* It's not pretty, but swearing has its place among men, albeit a minor one.

For women it's very different. Swearing can be shocking and attention-grabbing. It is a sign of female power and a disregard for boundaries. And it is the second most important factor for success.

*Unless hooters are involved.

Female Success Factors

1. Who you know

2. Swearing

3. Education

4. What you do

I have reached this conclusion after observing an admittedly small sample of successful female executives who swear like wounded* pirates.

But it's not my fault that the sample size was small. I blame the "glass ceiling." And I take no personal responsibility for the glass ceiling, having spent all of my corporate career under the "glass carpet." Don't get me started.

To understand how swearing can help women, consider the following hypothetical situations:

Scenario #1 (Without Swearing)

A man comes to a woman's office and offers to show her a report. The woman responds by saying, "Well, I'm a bit busy right now." Undeterred by this mild rebuff, the man will pull up a chair and proceed to chew up an hour of the woman's valuable time. Eventually the woman's productivity will be devoured by an endless parade of men who would rather talk to her than do work. Her career will begin a death spiral, until eventually she becomes a bag lady. And if she doesn't learn to swear, she won't be much of a bag lady either.

Now let's assume that this same woman was adept at the business art of swearing. The scenario might go like this:

*And I'm not talking about a flesh wound. I'm talking about the kind where you start shopping for the peg leg and you have to kill your parrot because he won't stop doing Woody Woodpecker jokes.

SCENARIO #2 (WITH SWEARING)

A man comes to a woman's office and offers to show her a report. The woman responds by saying, "Ah, shove it up your ass and die."

The man will be momentarily stunned. It is unlikely that he will pull up a chair. Nor will he experience any bonding. He will probably back slowly out the door. The woman's productivity will skyrocket.

But what about repercussions? The woman might someday need a favor from the man she has just verbally abused. Fortunately for her, all men are trained at birth to accept verbal abuse from women and get over it rather quickly.

And in the unlikely event that the man shows some hesitation to be helpful in the future, the situation can be smoothed over with the simple communication technique of saying, "Do it now or I'll rip off your nuts and shove them down your throat."

There are three scenarios I've left out, but they can be discussed easily:

ACTION	RESULT
Man swears at woman	Six-year prison sentence
Woman swears at woman	How would I know?
Person swears at computer	Improved operation

1 0

HOW TO GET YOUR WAY

This chapter contains strategies to help you get your way. These aren't the kinds of strategies that will propel you to the top of the corporate pig pile, but if you use them you might get some small satisfaction from thwarting the dolts who surround you.

The good thing about dolts is that they can be easily duped. I'll address that issue in more detail in the sequel to this book, titled *Hey, Why'd I Buy Another One of These Books?*

Winning isn't the most important thing in business. You also have to get rich, otherwise there isn't much point to the whole thing. If wealth is all you care about, I recommend becoming a butler for an aging millionaire who has lost his cognitive abilities but not his penmanship. But if you can't be rich, the next best thing is to be smug and cynical. That's where these strategies can help.

THE FINAL SUGGESTION MANEUVER

For years I employed the "Final Suggestion Maneuver" in meetings in which I knew that opinions would vary and that only my own opinion had any value. In other words, I used it in every meeting I ever attended. The success rate of this approach is nothing short of astonishing. And it's a good thing, because the "less than astonishing" zone contains a lot of strategies you don't want to try.

Less Than Astonishing Strategies

- Pretend to be a wax statue.
- Make your own neckties out of toilet seat protectors.
- Use racial epithets to "get people's attention."
- Practice chiropractic arts in your cubicle.

In contrast to those "go nowhere" strategies, the Final Suggestion Maneuver can work for you. It works like this.

Final Suggestion Maneuver

1. Let everybody else make moronic suggestions.

2. Stay uninvolved while the participants shred each other's suggestions like crisp cabbage in a Cuisinart. Watch as they develop intense personal dislikes that will last their entire careers.

3. Toward the end of the allotted meeting time, when patience is thin and bladders are full, offer your suggestion. Describe it as a logical result of the good thoughts you've heard at the meeting, no matter how ridiculous that might be.

If you time it right, all the participants will be feeling a sense of incredible frustration and physical discomfort and will realize that your suggestion is the fastest way to end the horror of the meeting. By disguising your suggestion as a composite of the participants' thoughts you minimize their need to attack you to defend their hard-argued positions.

You'll look like the rational deal-maker while the other participants look like partisan whiners. The only downside is that you won't be singularly identified with the idea if it works. But that's typically not a problem, since most ideas don't work. And your boss takes credit for the ones that do.

USE SARCASM TO GET YOUR WAY

By definition, people with bad ideas cannot be swayed by logic. If they were logical they wouldn't have bad ideas in the first place—unless the ideas were based on bad data. That leaves you with two possible strategies for thwarting an illogical idea and getting your way:

- Argue with data. Do exhaustive research to demonstrate the flaws in the person's assumptions.

- Use sarcasm to mock the idea and make the person look like a dolt.

If the "exhaustive research" option looks good to you, you have way too much time on your hands. Plus, it can only work if you're dealing with a co-worker who is logical and willing to admit error. And while you're at it, why not find a co-worker who is an omnipotent supermodel. (Note the clever use of sarcasm to show the folly of this approach.)

Option two—sarcasm—is more flexible. It works whether the person you wish to manipulate has bad data or a bad brain. Appeal to the person's sense of fear and insecurity. Use sarcasm to point out the potential for future ridicule.

An example will be useful. Let's say that your idiot boss has just suggested that hardworking employees should be rewarded with a certificate of appreciation. Here's how you can use sarcasm to make him change his plans.

EXAMPLE OF THE POWER OF SARCASM

You: "I used to think that all of the problems with our company were caused by poor management and an inadequate compensation system."

Boss: "That's a common misperception."

You: "Now I realize that we were suffering from a shortage of certificates."

Boss: "Um . . ."

You: "The part I like most is that for every person who gets a certificate there will be fifty people who don't—and that spells "extra effort"!"

Boss: "I think I see what you're trying to—"

You: *"I want to earn that certificate! I'll stop at nothing!"*

Boss: "Okay, point made . . ."

You: "Would it be okay if I stayed late tonight and waxed the tables in the conference rooms with my hair?"

THE BIG PICTURE MANEUVER

The theory behind the Big Picture Maneuver is that all white-collar workers are striving to be the one who can see the "big picture" while all those around them are myopic losers. Your co-workers will try to one-up any "big picture" scenario that you lay out. You can manipulate them by taking advantage of that impulse.

Let's say you've just blown a million dollars on a project that went down harder than a drunken ninety-year-old woman with a broken hip. You're sitting in a meeting with a bunch of vultures who would like to spend the entire meeting rubbing your face in the fiscal entrails. Your mission is to escape this fate, and—with luck—even enhance your position. Here's where the Big Picture Maneuver is indispensable.

The conversation might go something like this:

You: "I spent a million dollars but the project didn't work out."

Wally: "You blew a *million dollars*!!"

Alice: "What were you thinking?"

Ted: "Helloooo!!! Wasn't *anybody* managing that thing???"

You: (Coolly looking at the big picture) "A million dollars is just "noise" when you consider the entire Research and Development budget. We're in a risky business."
(At this point the other meeting participants will realize they have been flanked by the Big Picture Maneuver and they will scramble to compensate.)

Wally: "For only a million dollars, we learned a great deal."

Alice: "Compared to the total domestic GNP, it's a rounding error."

Ted: "Can we talk about something *important* now?"

DINOSAUR STRATEGY

The Dinosaur Strategy involves ignoring all new management directives while lumbering along doing things the same way you've always done them.

What makes this strategy successful is that it usually takes six months for your boss to notice your rebellion and get mad about it. Coincidentally, that's about the length of time any boss stays in the same job.

The average life of an organization chart is six months. You can safely ignore any order from your boss that would take six months to complete. In other words, the environment will change before you have to do anything. You can just keep chewing leaves and scampering in the volcanic ash while new bosses come and go.

If you wait long enough, any bad idea will become extinct. And most good ideas too. So if you have time to master only one strategy, this is the one for you.

Example of the Dinosaur Strategy

From: (name withheld)
To: scottadams@aol.com

Scott,

Management, when faced with a management problem, having no clue what to do, but feeling that they should be doing SOMETHING, always seems to resort to the dreaded DATABASE. Of course, they have no strategic plans for actually USING the database, but the activity of putting one together seems to keep them occupied and out of the engineers' hair (for a while).

The first memo explains how the new database will solve all our problems.

The next memo explains that the database is a major corporate undertaking and will require the cooperation of everyone to "shape the vision of the future."

The next few memos explain that the database is still in progress and is looking better and better.

The next memos provide example outputs of what the database will provide, with a disclaimer noting that the data are not yet complete enough to provide meaningful results.

More memos explain that the data collection is taking longer than expected, because the engineers are not providing their inputs in a timely manner.

The engineers continue to ignore all the memos and chastising.

Eventually, all goes quiet and the DATABASE fades into the sunset.

MARKETING AND COMMUNICATIONS

I can speak with some authority on the subject of marketing because I once took a marketing class. Moreover, I have purchased many items.

To an outsider, the entire discipline of marketing might seem like it could be summarized by the following concept:

> If you lower the price you can sell more units.

But this is a gross oversimplification that insults marketing professionals and ignores hundreds of years of cumulative understanding about the subtle intricacies of the marketing arts. Those subtle intricacies are:

- If you raise the price you will sell fewer units.

- How do I look in this outfit?

The Marketing Department uses many advanced techniques to match products and buyers in a way that maximizes profits. For example, they give away keychains.

But that's not all. For your convenience I have summarized the major concepts of marketing so you won't have to sit through a marketing class as I did. You're welcome.

MARKET SEGMENTATION

Every customer wants to get the best product at the lowest price. Fortunately, many customers can't tell the difference between fine Asian silk and Bounty paper towels. No matter how pathetic your product is, there's always somebody who can't tell the difference or won't have access to the alternatives. The job of marketing is to identify these "segments," stick a vacuum pump in their pockets, and suck until all you get is lint.

Market segmentation might sound like a complicated thing, but it's the same process you used as a child to select players for a team. Each potential player is evaluated on objective characteristics, such as speed, skill, and power. If those characteristics don't produce a conclusive choice, then the group is further segmented by their levels of acne and popularity. The children who rate high in the preferred characteristics are placed in the "team segment" and those who rate lowest become the market segment most likely to grow up and purchase inflatable women. It's that simple.

The most important market segment is known as the "Stupid Rich," so named because of their tendency to buy anything that's new regardless of the cost or usefulness. If you can sell enough units to the Stupid Rich, your production costs per unit will decrease. Then you can lower your prices and sell to the Stupid Poor—that's where the real volume is.

It's never a good idea to design your product for the Smart Poor or the Smart Rich. The Smart Poor will figure out a way to steal your product. The Smart Rich will buy your whole company and fire your ass. As a rule, smart people are an undesirable market segment. Fortunately, they don't exist.

PRODUCT DIFFERENTIATION

The best way to differentiate your product is by making it the best one in its class. But there can be only one best product in every class, and if you're reading this book you probably don't work for that company. So we don't need to get into that strategy.

Suppose you sell a product that is exactly like other products on the market, for example, long distance phone service, insurance, credit cards, or home mortgages. You can make your product look special by disguising the true costs and then claiming it's more economical than the alternatives.

Some good techniques for disguising the true cost of your product include:

Disguising Costs

- Link payments to exotic interest rates, such as the Zambian Floating Q Bond.

- Offer discount plans so confusing that even Nostradamus would throw up his hands and say, "I dunno. You tell me."

- Give coupons that are redeemable for prizes through an impossibly inconvenient process that combines the worst elements of scavenger hunts, tax preparation, and recycling.

- Compare your lowest cost plan with the competitor's highest cost plan.

- Offer lease options to people who are bad at math.

- Assess gigantic penalties for customers who miss payments. Once a year, forget to mail the customer a bill.

- Offer steep discounts for initial payments, followed by obscene price increases. Make it difficult for customers to wiggle out after they're caught in your web.

- Sell the product without any of the features that could make it useful, for example, computers without keyboards and RAM.

THE WIN-LOSE SCENARIO OF MARKETING

Sometimes your company has a bad product at a high price. That's when the real magic of marketing comes into play. The focus changes from educating the consumer to thoroughly screwing the consumer.

If you experience any ethical problems in this situation, remember the Marketing Professional's Motto:

"We're not screwing the customers. All we're doing is holding them down while the salespeople screw them."

Thank goodness for the ignorance of your customers. Confusion is your friend. Take advantage of the goodwill created by your competitors and create products that are eerily similar but much worse.

Examples

Somy Walkman
Honduh Accord
Porch 911
Harry Davidson motorcycles
Popsi Cola

ADVERTISING

Good advertising can make people buy your product even if it sucks. That's important, because it takes the pressure off you to make good products. A dollar spent on brainwashing is more cost-effective than a dollar spent on product improvement.

Obviously there's a minimum quality that every product has to achieve. It should be able to withstand the shipping process without becoming unrecognizable. But after the minimums are achieved, it's advertising that makes the big difference.

A good advertising campaign is engineered to fit a precise audience. In particular, there is a huge distinction between what message works for men and what message works for women.

Males are predictable creatures. That makes it easy to craft a marketing message that appeals to them. All successful advertising campaigns that target men include one of these two messages:

1. This product will help you get dates with bikini models.

2. This product will save you time and money, which you'll need if you want to date bikini models.

Compared to simpleminded, brutish men, women are much more intricate and complex. Your advertising message must appeal to women's greater range of intellectual interests and aesthetic preferences. Specifically, your message has to say this:

1. If you buy this product you'll be a bikini model.

Reinforce your message of "quality" by quoting experts who say good things about your product. Some experts will insist on looking at your product before commenting on it; steer clear of those people. You want the type of expert who can be swayed by a free lunch and a pamphlet.

Don't knock yourself out trying to get your expert to give you the ideal quote. In advertising, as in journalism, you can reword people's quotes for readability. In fact, you can create entirely new sentences using any word the expert has ever spoken. Technically, that's still a quote. Many of your finer publications use this method. You can use it too.

Original Literal Quote

"The lack of quality and complete disregard for the market are evident in this product."

Edited Quote

"The quality are evident in regard of dis product."

UNDERSTANDING THE CUSTOMER

It's essential that you understand the customer. It won't change anything about your product—since those decisions are driven by internal politics—but it's necessary if you want to exhibit an "I'm-more-customer-focused-than-thou" attitude in meetings.

The process for understanding customers primarily involves sitting around with other marketing people and talking about what you would do if you were dumb enough to be a customer. It sounds like this:

Marketer #1: "You and I might prefer beef in our hamburgers, but the average consumer isn't that discriminating."

Marketer #2: "I heard of a guy who eats light bulbs and nails."

Marketer #1: "Exactly. They don't care what they eat."

Marketer #2: "So we could fill our burgers with lawn clippings and toenails and that kind of [expletive deleted] and they'd never know the difference."

Marketer #1: "They might even thank us for saving them money."

Marketer #2: "I'm exhausted from all of this market analysis. You want to get a steak?"

Marketer #1: "I'm a vegetarian."

If you've ever actually met a customer, generalize about the behavior of all customers from that one example. If you haven't met a customer, retell the story you heard from somebody who has met a customer, adding your own little twists when absolutely necessary.

Over time, the one customer anecdote will be retold and altered just enough to become "common knowledge" about customer preferences.

True story: A customer for a large phone company complained because he didn't have a way to test his equipment on the public data network unless he paid for the service first. With each telling of this customer's complaint it became obvious that "many customers" needed to test equipment. One manager frequently referred to the "stack of requests" on his desk. Eventually the customer demand became so great that a low-ranking employee was assigned the project of building a multimillion-dollar lab facility to solve the problem. But every time he tried to verify the huge customer demand, each story traced back to the one original guy, who had long since solved his problem. The employee was ordered to build the lab anyway under the theory that there must be more customers like the one guy who asked for it. The project was eventually killed for political reasons. The low-ranking employee eventually left the phone company and became a syndicated cartoonist.

You can use Focus Groups to narrow the range of your research. Focus Groups are people who are selected on the basis of their inexplicable free time and their common love of free sandwiches. They are put in a room and led through a series of questions by a trained moderator.

For many of these people it will be the first time they've ever been fed and listened to in the same day. This can cause some strange behavior. They will begin to complain vehemently about things that never really bothered them before. Then they will suggest product features that they would never buy.

Person #1: "If my toothbrush had a dog brush on the other end I could clean my teeth and brush my Chihuahua at the same time. Now that's a product I'd buy."

Person #2: "Yes, yes! And it could have a third prong for waxing your car at the same time. I'd buy that. If I had a car."

Person #3: "Whoa whoa whoa! What if the toothbrush could also start your car? Or better yet, somebody else's car?"

In time, heady from the thrill of free sandwiches and all the attention, the Focus Group participants will offer breakthrough suggestions that will alter the course of your company forever. Unless you get a bad batch of Focus Group people, in which case they'll eat your sandwiches, bitch about you, and leave.

Now you're ready for market research.

MARKET RESEARCH

In more primitive times, businesses had to use trial and error to find out what customers wanted. That was before market research was invented, thus turning this hodgepodge of guesswork and natural selection into a finely tuned scientific process.

MARKETING

Market research was made possible by the discovery that consumers make rational, well-reasoned buying decisions. That being the case, all you need to do is craft an unbiased survey and ask a statistically valid subset of them what they want.

Here are some of the more successful market research surveys that led directly to the creation of wildly successful products and services that would not have been possible otherwise.

HISTORICAL USES OF MARKET SURVEYS

AIRLINE SURVEY (1920)

If you had to travel a long distance, would you rather:

A. Drive a car.

B. Take a train.

C. Allow yourself to be strapped into a huge metal container that weighs more than your house and be propelled through space by exploding chemicals while knowing that any one of a thousand different human, mechanical, or weather problems would cause you to be incinerated in a spectacular ball of flame.

If you answered "C" would you mind if we stomped on your luggage and sent it to another city?

VCR Survey (1965)

If you could purchase a device that displayed recorded movies on your television, how much would you be willing to pay for it?

A. $200.

B. $500.

C. $2,500 because it will be well worth it if I can rent filthy movies and masturbate like a wild monkey.

Online Computing Survey (1985)

If you could connect your computer to a vast network of information, how would you use this service?

A. Gather valuable scientific information.

B. Improve my education.

C. Demonstrate my complete lack of personality by spending countless hours typing inane and often obscene sentence fragments that can be viewed by people just like me in "real time."

If you answered "C" above, what should that service be called?

A. Computer Chat.

B. I'm a Moron and I'll Prove It!

C. Good-bye Savings Account.

MARKET REQUIREMENTS

After you have your market research it's time to design the product. Your engineers will ask you to specify what the product needs to do. That can be a lot of work and it will set you up to take the blame if nobody buys the product later. Avoid specifying market requirements at all costs. If the Engineering Department keeps asking for market requirements, take one of these approaches:

1. Insist that you've already specified the requirements when you said it should be "high quality and low cost." Complain to the engineer's boss that the engineer is stalling.

2. Ask the engineer to tell you all the things that are possible plus the associated cost so you can choose the best solution. Complain to the engineer's boss that the engineer is uncooperative.

3. Specify market requirements that are either technically or logically impossible. Complain to the engineer's boss that the engineer is not being a can-do person.

CREATING A MARKET

If there's no market for your product, sometimes you can create one. This involves inventing a problem and then providing the solution. The most effective methods for creating a market include:

PROBLEM YOU CREATE	MARKET OPPORTUNITY
Write bad software	Sell upgrades
Build undependable products	Sell service warranties
Tell people they stink	Sell deodorant

NATURAL ENEMIES

Engineers are the natural enemies of marketing people, always trying to inject their unwanted logic and knowledge into every situation. Often they will make unreasonable demands that a product have some use. Sometimes they'll whine endlessly because the product maims customers. If it's not one thing it's another. You can minimize the problem by not inviting them to meetings.

Engineers can be most dangerous when they take advantage of marketing people's tendency to believe whatever they hear, as in these examples:

MARKETING ILLUSTRATED

Marketing Antics Reported by E-mail

From: (name withheld)
To: scottadams@aol.com

Scott,

Here's a mind-boggling stupid idea from our Marketing Department that you might be able to use.

We make [type of machine]. A new version of our product is both cheaper and faster. A great breakthrough, right?

Well, Marketing wants Engineering to slow the unit down so they have a low-cost unit to sell. Then sell them upgrades to full speed at an enormous price. These would be physically identical, just one would have the code messed up on purpose to run slow.

From: (name withheld)
To: scottadams@aol.com

Scott,

We asked the Marketing Division to give us some numbers in regard to how many of each product they want to sell.

Their reply: We need "X" number of dollars. You figure out how many of each product you need to produce to meet that figure.

Our conclusion: Marketing has no idea how to do its job; Marketing does not want to do its job; Marketing and related vital business activities (such as forecasting) are all figments of our imagination.

From: (name withheld)
To: scottadams@aol.com

Scott,

Before I started at [company] two years ago, they had completed their base-level product. On the verge of making a couple of sales, Marketing decided to divulge some of the details of
the "next-generation system" to the potential customers. They
all liked the sound of it so much that they decided to *not* buy
the current system and wait for the new one. [Company's]
potential customers are looking for a system that will be put in
place and expected to last as much as twenty-five years, so they
are not going to rush into a purchase.

Three years later the "next-generation" system is almost
done. Customers are impressed with demo units, but express
some reservations.

"Not to worry," says Marketing, "in two years we will have a
'high-performance system' completed which will take care of
your concerns."

Once again, the customers have decided to wait. In the mean-
time, [company] has run out of $$$, and the much-advertised
"high-performance system" is only in the early planning stages.
All the production people have been laid off, but most of the
managers and all of the marketers are still employed. The final
system may never become a reality.

1 2

MANAGEMENT CONSULTANTS

If the employees of your company are incompetent you might want to get some consultants. A consultant is a person who takes your money and annoys your employees while tirelessly searching for the best way to extend the consulting contract.

Consultants will hold a seemingly endless series of meetings to test various hypotheses and assumptions. These exercises are a vital step toward tricking managers into revealing the recommendation that is most likely to generate repeat consulting business.

After the "correct" recommendation is discovered, it must be justified by a lengthy analysis. The consultants begin working like crazed beavers in a coffee lake. Reams of paper will disappear. You'll actually be able to hear the screams of old-growth forests dying as the consultants churn out page after page of backup charts and assumptions. The analysis will be cleverly designed to be as confusing as possible, thus discouraging any second-guessing by sniping staff members who are afraid of appearing dense.

When consultants are added to a department they change the balance and chemistry of the group. You need a new process to take advantage of the consultants' skills. The most efficient process is to use the dullard employees as data gatherers to feed the massive brains of the consultants. This keeps the employees busy and makes them feel involved while the consultants hold meetings with senior managers of the company to complain about the support they're getting and to pitch new projects.

Consultants use a standard set of decision tools that involve creating "alternative scenarios" based on different "assumptions." Any pesky assumptions that don't support the predetermined recommendation are quickly discounted as being uneconomical—for the consultants.

The remaining assumptions are objectively validated by sending employees off to obtain information that is not available. Later, the assumptions are transformed into near-facts through the process of sitting around arguing about what is "most likely."

Consultants will ultimately recommend that you do whatever you're *not* doing now. Centralize whatever is decentralized. Flatten whatever is vertical. Diversify whatever is concentrated and divest everything that is not "core" to the business. You'll hardly ever find a consultant who recommends that you keep everything the same and stop wasting money on consultants. And consultants will rarely deal with the root cause of your company's problems, since that's probably the person who hired them. Instead, they'll look for ways to improve the "strategy" and the "process."

Consultants don't need much experience in an industry in order to be experts. They learn quickly. If your twenty-six-year-old consultant drives past the Egghead software outlet on the way to an assignment, that would qualify as experience in the software industry. If Egghead has a sale on modems that day: hardware experience. This type of experience is unavailable to the regular staff members who have worked in the industry for twenty years but still use yellow sticky notes to identify their various excretory openings.

Aside from their massive intellects, consultants bring many advantages to your company that regular employees can't match.

- Consultants have credibility because they are not dumb enough to be regular employees at your company.

- Consultants eventually leave, which makes them excellent scapegoats for major management blunders.

- Consultants can schedule time on your boss's calendar because they don't have your reputation as a whiny little troublemaker who constantly brings up unsolvable "issues."

- Consultants are often more attractive than your regular employees. This is not always true, but if you get a batch of homely ones you can always replace them in a month.

- Consultants will return your calls, because it's all billable time to them.

- Consultants work preposterously long hours, thus making the regular staff feel like worthless toads for working only sixty hours a week.

CONSULTANTS ILLUSTRATED

TALES OF CONSULTANTS

From: (name withheld)
To: scottadams@aol.com

Scott,

Here's one that happened at a company I worked for. . . .

President of the company ignores suggestions by employees on how to improve operations. He hires a consultant to come in and make suggestions. Consultant talks to employees, gets their same suggestions, and presents them to president, who says they are "good ideas" and implements them.

Quite irritating, it was. . . .

From: (name withheld)
To: scottadams@aol.com

Scott,

I used to work at a large company that made nuclear weapons and MRI scanners. They hired a consulting group to come in and tell them how they should change the business.

The consultants said that [company name] was the company to be like. That company started a bike business from nothing and had grown to become some huge presence in a very short time.

When you ordered your bike, they measured you and made a bike to your size and painted it the color you wanted. You had it within two weeks. The theme here was customizing to the customer.

We made very large expensive MRI scanners. We weren't sure if that meant we had to paint them different colors.

The middle managers were all toeing the company line and trying to whip us into agreement. At the same time, I was looking for a bike and I thought it would be neat to have one measured for me. I went looking for a [company name] bike, but I couldn't find any. Bicycle shops told me that the bike manufacturer went out of business.

The next day I mentioned it to my manager. He informed me I was naive (I was) and that I must be wrong (I wasn't).

It really pissed me off, so I called some of the shops that had ads with [company name] brand names and got their regional contact. The regional contact said they no longer were in the business and gave me the national contact.

When I called the national contact I got the division that handles "massage and bath products" for [company name]. He said they hadn't been in that business for at least six months and if there was anything left it was sold to [another company name].

I documented all my facts and contacts and phone numbers and went back to confront my manager. (I told you I was naive.) I guess he took it to his manager and that was the last we heard of that.

I bet they never called the numbers.

From: (name withheld)
To: scottadams@aol.com

Scott,

About four months ago, my company [a copy center] hired a very expensive consultant to teach us all about the new "Q Program," the basic upshot of which is that we aren't allowed to make mistakes anymore. Naturally, we raised the question of the possibility of such perfection, and his arguments went something like this:

(A) If you can go for ten seconds without making any mistakes, you can go for a minute without making any mistakes. And if you can go for a minute, you can go for sixty perfect minutes. And so on and so forth.

(B) You're saying it's okay for [company] to make mistakes? How many are okay? One in a hundred? Yes? What if doctors dropped one in a hundred babies on their heads? What if one out of a hundred planes crashed into the side of a mountain?

Yes, the man actually drew a parallel between copying errors and the deaths of thousands.

BUSINESS PLANS

Somewhere between the hallucinations of senior management and the cold reality of the market lies something called a business plan. There are two major steps to building a business plan:

1. Gather information.

2. Ignore it.

In the information-gathering phase, each area of the company is asked to predict its revenues and expenses for the coming years. As you might expect, the predictions will be "padded" to make them easy to achieve. For example, if a business unit sold a million units last year it might submit less aggressive targets for the coming year.

SALES ESTIMATE FOR NEXT YEAR

"Sales will be negative for the year. We expect that many shoplifters will take our product off the shelf and bring it to the cashier for a refund using only gum wrappers as receipts. Medical expenses will be up thirty percent because the few customers who actually pay for our products will return them by throwing them at employees."

Senior management will look at the aggregated lies of the individual business units and adjust them to where they "know they should be." This can cause a fairly large gap between what the employees think they can do and what senior management tells them they must do. This gap can be closed by adjusting the assumptions.

First, assume that any positive trends will continue forever and any negative trends will turn around soon. Then run the numbers through a computer spreadsheet. The result is the future. (Later, if you turn out to be wrong, blame it on the global economy.)

Some companies change what they're doing to get the future they want. This is a waste of time. You can get the same result by adjusting the assumptions in your business plan. Remember, the future depends on assumptions and the assumptions are just stuff you make up. No sense in knocking yourself out.

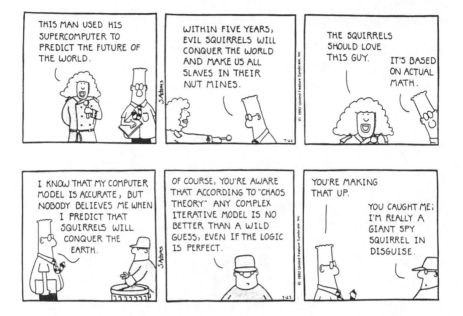

It is never a good idea to be constrained by reality when you craft your assumptions for the business case. Reality is very unpopular and it is not fun to read. If you've never seen any reality written down, here are some examples to illustrate how unmotivating it can be.

Assumptions Based on Reality (Avoid)

The project team leader is a nitwit. Our best case scenario is that he won't run with tools in his hands and hurt someone.

The project team will need additional people. Management will respond by increasing the frequency of status reports.

Our market research was apparently conducted at a mental health clinic. Either that or there really is a robust market demand by people named Moses.

On the surface it might seem unethical to build a business plan that intentionally avoids any contact with reality. I say "pish tosh" to that, not because it means anything, but just because it's fun to say.*

Everybody knows that business plans are created after decisions have been made by the executives of your company. Therefore, nobody believes your assumptions anyway. So you're not being unethical when you use ludicrous assumptions, you're just lying to keep your job. People will respect you for that.

It's not always easy to craft assumptions that support the result your executives want. But I'm here to help. Here are some valuable tips for getting the "right" answers in your analyses.

* Go ahead, try it. You'll find yourself saying pish tosh often and liking it.

Irrational Comparisons

If there's a better solution than the one your executives want you to justify, avoid it like a William Shatner poetry festival. Make no mention of the better alternative and hope nobody notices. Instead, focus on the hideously stupid alternatives that make the recommended approach look good in comparison.

Bad Alternatives That Make Yours Look Good

1. Upgrade obsolete equipment.

2. Hire hordes of troublemaking, union-inclined workers.

3. Do nothing and watch the business crumble while your nimble competitors reap obscene profits, live in big houses, and use your relatives as servants.

UNREALISTIC REVENUE PROJECTIONS

If only one percent of the world buys your product, that's fifty million customers!

Some variation of that "analysis" has been used successfully by every company that ever launched a product. It's a compelling argument for launching a new product because everybody knows that the general population breaks down this way:

60%	People who don't need your product
30%	People who have no money
5%	People who are nuts
5%	People who will buy any damn thing

That leaves a neat ten percent of the population who can be considered likely customers for your product, and that's more than enough to support a business plan. If somebody questions your market projections, simply point out that your target market is "People who are nuts" and "People who will buy any damn thing." Nobody is going to tell you there aren't enough of those people to go around.

WRITING THE COMPANY BUSINESS PLAN

Employees want to feel that they participated in the formation of the business plan. This scam is called "buy-in," and it's essential for reminding the employees that if anything goes wrong it's their fault.

These are the important steps to achieving buy-in for a company business plan.

1. Executives set the company direction with useful statements such
   as "Become the market leader in fabric softener and satellite communications."

   This direction is essential, because employees can easily be misled into believing that the goal of the company is to go out of business. Or worse, a driver for a delivery truck might become confused by the absence of direction and start designing microchip
   circuits instead of hauling fabric softener.

2. Employees are asked to objectively rank the value of their activities in supporting the company's objectives.

3. Employees rank every activity as a top priority, critical to the very
   existence of the company. They support their claims with indeci-
   pherable, acronym-laden bullet points.

4. The employees' input is collected into large binders.

5. The Budget Department uses the input from the employees as the
   basis for lengthy discussions about the relative stupidity and
   worthlessness of each department.

   Eventually, budget recommendations are made on the basis of
   several weighted factors:

   10% Which project acronyms are most familiar to the Budget
        Department.
   10% Fourth-hand anecdotes they've heard that would indicate
        executive support for a particular project.
   80% What department the budget people would like to eventu-
        ally work in if only they could find a way to get out of
        doing budgets.

6. A technical writer is called in to accept the blame for the fact that
   the various components of the plan make no sense and important
   projects are unfunded. Feeling bitter and cynical, but secure in

the knowledge that nobody will ever see the plan, the technical writer cobbles a document together and then resigns in disgust after erasing the source file.

7. The plan is locked up in a secure place because it is too proprietary to share with the employees.

14

ENGINEERS, SCIENTISTS, PROGRAMMERS, AND OTHER ODD PEOPLE

People who work in the fields of science and technology are not like other people. This can be frustrating to the nontechnical people who have to deal with them. The secret to coping with technology-oriented people is to understand their motivations. This chapter will teach you everything you need to know.

All technical professionals share a common set of traits. For convenience, I will focus primarily on engineers. It is safe to generalize to the other science and technology professions.

For the record, I'm not an engineer by training. But I spent ten years working with engineers and programmers in a variety of jobs. I learned their customs and mannerisms by observing them, much the way Jane Goodall learned about the great apes, but without the hassle of grooming.

In time, I came to respect and appreciate the ways of engineers. Eventually I found myself adopting their beautiful yet functional philosophies about life. It was too late for me to go back to school and become a real engineer but at least I could pretend to be one and enjoy the obvious benefits of elevated sexual appeal. So far I think it's working.

Engineering is so trendy these days that everybody wants to be one. The word "engineer" is greatly overused. If there's somebody in your life who you think is trying to pass as an engineer, give him this test to discern the truth.

ENGINEER IDENTIFICATION TEST

You walk into a room and notice that a picture is hanging crooked. You . . .

A. Straighten it.

B. Ignore it.

C. Buy a CAD system and spend the next six months designing a solar-powered, self-adjusting picture frame while often stating aloud your belief that the inventor of the nail was a total moron.

The correct answer is "C" but partial credit can be given to anybody who writes "It depends" in the margin of the test or simply blames the whole stupid thing on "Marketing."

My contribution to the understanding of engineers will be to try to explain the noble, well-reasoned motives behind what the so-called normal people perceive as odd behaviors.

SOCIAL SKILLS

It's totally unfair to suggest—as many have—that engineers are socially inept. Engineers simply have different objectives when it comes to social interaction.

"Normal" people expect to accomplish several unrealistic things from social interaction:

- Stimulating and thought-provoking conversation

- Important social contacts

- A feeling of connectedness with other humans

These goals are irrational and stupid. Experience shows that most conversations degenerate into discussions about parking spaces, weather patterns, elapsed time since you last exercised, and—God forbid—"feelings." These topics hardly qualify as stimulating and thought-provoking. Nor are they useful.

Engineers realize that making personal contacts is not valuable in their occupation. For them it's not "who you know" that matters, it's "who knows less than you do" that counts.

Nor is there much tangible value in feeling "connected" with other humans. That stuff is best left to the poets and the multilevel marketing organization. To an engineer, most "normal" people are intellectually indistinguishable from Mexican jumping beans with faces.* Feeling "connected" with carbon-based dolts holds all the joy of being handcuffed to a dead zebra—it sounds special, but it can get old fast.

In contrast to "normal" people, engineers have rational objectives for social interactions:

- Get it over with as soon as possible.

- Avoid getting invited to something unpleasant.

- Demonstrate mental superiority and mastery of all subjects.

These are sensible goals and ones that can produce great joy. The social skill of an engineer must be evaluated on the basis of these rational objectives, not on the basis of bizarre and nonsensical societal standards. Viewed in this light, I think you'll agree that engineers are very effective in their social interactions. It's the "normal" people who are nuts.

FASCINATION WITH GADGETS

To the engineer, all matter in the universe can be placed into one of two categories: (1) things that need to be fixed, and (2) things that will need to be fixed after you've had a few minutes to play with them. Engineers like to solve problems. If there are no problems handily available, they will create their own problems. Normal people don't understand this concept; they believe that if it ain't broke, don't fix it. Engineers believe that if it ain't broke, it doesn't have enough features yet.

No engineer looks at a television remote control without wondering what it would take to turn it into a stun gun. No engineer can take a shower without wondering if some sort of Teflon coating would make

---

*If you think it's easy to come up with great analogies let's see you do it.

showering unnecessary. To the engineer, the world is a toy box full of sub-optimized and feature-poor toys.

That's a good thing, society-wise.

If not for the compulsions of engineers, mankind would have never seen the wheel, settling instead for the trapezoid because some Neanderthal in Marketing convinced everybody it had great braking ability. And there would be no fire, because some middle-manager cave person would point out that if fire was such a good idea the other cave people would already be using it.

From E-mail . . .

From: (name withheld)
To: scottadams@aol.com

Scott,

I work for [company] as a tech-rep, providing on-site service to a variety of clients. Once, I answered a call at an engineering firm. They said the copier was jamming. When I got there I discovered a huge pile of copier components, nuts, bolts, etc. and a stripped copier frame.

The head engineer had compiled a two-volume set of notes listing real, false, and perceived faults with the copier. They had recorded time of day, job conditions (one-sided copies, two-sided copies, document handler selected/nonselected, paper weight, etc.), and line voltage fluctuations. I asked them why they had disassembled it, and they replied, "So it would take you less time to fix it."

It took four days (I am not kidding or exaggerating in the least!) to reassemble and set up page after page of meticulous, tedious adjustments.

And do you know what the problem was? They had put developer in the ink receptacle! From a tech-rep's point of view the easiest thing in the world to diagnose, takes thirty minutes to fix (on that particular product).

FASHION AND APPEARANCE

Clothes are the lowest priority for an engineer, assuming the basic thresholds for temperature and decency have been satisfied. If no appendages are freezing or sticking together, and if no genitalia or mammary glands are swinging around in plain view, then the objective of clothing has been met. Anything else is a waste.

If you think about it logically, you are the only person who doesn't have to look at yourself, not counting the brief moments you look in the mirror. Engineers understand that their appearance only bothers other people and therefore it is not worth optimizing.

Another plus: Bad fashion can discourage normal people from interacting with the engineer and talking about the cute things their children do.

LOVE OF "STAR TREK"

Engineers love all of the "Star Trek" television shows and movies. It's a small wonder, since the engineers on the starship *Enterprise* are portrayed as heroes, occasionally even having sex with aliens. Every engineer dreams about saving the universe and having sex with aliens. This is much more glamorous than the real life of an engineer, which consists of hiding from the universe and having sex without the participation of other life forms. Consequently, ratings for "Star Trek" will remain high as long as they stay away from any realism.

DATING AND SOCIAL LIFE

Dating is never easy for engineers. A normal person will employ various indirect and duplicitous methods to create a false impression of attractiveness. Engineers are incapable of placing appearance above function.

For society, it's probably a good thing that engineers value function over appearance. For example, you wouldn't want engineers to build nuclear power plants that only *look* like they would keep all the radiation inside. You have to consider the global perspective. But the engineer's emphasis on function over form is a big disadvantage for dating, where the goal is to act phony until the other person loves you for the person that you are.

Engineers don't like to make small talk because no useful information is exchanged. It is more useful to explain complicated technology issues to any human who will stand still. That way at least some information is exchanged and the encounter is not wasted. Unfortunately, it seems that a normal person would rather have a bushel of pine cones rammed up the nose° than listen to a story about technology. But that's no reason to stop imparting valuable knowledge to a person who doesn't want it.

Sometimes normal people will try to use body language to end an encounter with an engineer. But engineers ignore body language because

---

°In controlled lab tests, nineteen out of twenty subjects preferred to have pine cones rammed up their noses. The other subject preferred to have the engineer rammed up his nose. He'll be missed.

it is an imprecise science at best. For example, it's almost impossible to tell the difference between a comatose stare and an expression of interest.

Fortunately, engineers have an ace in the hole. They are widely recognized as superior marriage material: intelligent, dependable, employed, honest, and handy around the house. While it's true that many normal people would prefer not to *date* an engineer, most normal people harbor an intense desire to *mate* with them, thus producing engineerlike children who will have high-paying jobs long before losing their virginity.

Male engineers reach their peak of sexual attractiveness later than normal men, becoming irresistible erotic dynamos in their mid thirties to late forties. Just look at these examples of sexually irresistible men in technical professions:

- Bill Gates.

- MacGyver.

- Etcetera.

Female engineers become irresistible at the age of consent and remain that way until about thirty minutes after their clinical death. Longer if it's a warm day.

BATTLING UNFAIR STEREOTYPES

Engineers are often stereotyped in the media. It is horribly unfair to assign a set of common traits to an entire group of people. There is some talk that I have been guilty of doing this myself, but I contend I've been framed.

To set the record straight, I have interviewed thousands of engineers and determined that the stereotypes do *not* fit them all. Here are the exceptions I found:

ENGINEER	EXCEPTION TO STEREOTYPE
Elmer Moline, Calgary, Canada	Had a second date at age twenty-three
Herb Blinthem, San Jose, California	Enjoyed *Bridges of Madison County*
Anita Fluman, Dublin, California	Has rhythm
Hugh Hunkelbein, Schaumburg, Illinois	Doesn't care how his television remote control works as long as it does

HONESTY

For humans, honesty is a matter of degree. Engineers are always honest in matters of technology and human relationships. That's why it's a good idea to keep engineers away from customers, romantic interests, and other people who can't handle the truth.

Engineers sometimes bend the truth to avoid work. But thanks to the concept of "common usage" this is not technically dishonest in the modern workplace.

Sometimes engineers say things that sound like lies but technically are not because nobody could be expected to believe them. The complete list of engineer lies is listed below.

"I won't change anything without asking you first."

"I'll return your hard-to-find cable tomorrow."

"I *have* to have new equipment to do my job."

"I'm not jealous of your new computer."

FRUGALITY

Engineers are notoriously frugal. This is not because of cheapness or mean spirit; it is simply because every spending situation is simply a problem in optimization, that is, "How can I escape this situation while retaining the greatest amount of cash?"

ADVICE

Engineers are always delighted to share wisdom, even in areas in which they have no experience whatsoever. Their logic provides them with inherent insight into any field of expertise. This can be a problem when dealing with the illogical people who believe that knowledge can only be derived through experience, as in this case:

EXPLAINING ENGINEERING

Most people don't know what it means to be an engineer. There are many types of engineers and they do many fascinating things during the workday. However, the excitement and pure adrenaline rush of the engineer's life is sometimes lost when it is explained to other people.

POWERS OF CONCENTRATION

If there is one trait that best defines an engineer it is the ability to concentrate on one subject to the complete exclusion of everything else in the environment. This sometimes causes engineers to be pronounced dead prematurely.

There are numerous reports* of engineers who were halfway through the embalming process before they sat up and shouted something like

*I can't remember where I saw these reports, but when I think of it I'll mail you copies.

"I've got it—all it needs is a backup relay circuit!!!" Some funeral homes in high-tech areas have started checking résumés before processing the bodies. Anybody with a degree in electrical engineering or experience in computer programming is propped up in the lounge for a few days just to see if he or she snaps out of it.

RISK

Engineers hate risk. They try to eliminate it whenever they can. This is understandable, given that when an engineer makes one little mistake the media will treat it like it's a big deal or something.

EXAMPLES OF BAD PRESS FOR ENGINEERS

- *Hindenberg.*

- Space Shuttle *Challenger.*

- Hubble space telescope.

- *Apollo 13.*

- *Titanic.*

- Ford Pinto.

- Corvair.

The risk/reward calculation for engineers looks something like this:

RISK

Public humiliation and the death of thousands of innocent people

REWARD

A certificate of appreciation in a handsome plastic frame

Being practical people, engineers evaluate this balance of risks and rewards and decide that risk is not a good thing. The best way to avoid risk is by advising that any activity is technically impossible for reasons that are far too complicated to explain.

If that approach is not sufficient to halt a project, then the engineer will fall back to a second line of defense:

"It's technically possible but it will cost too much."

The quickest way to make a project uneconomical is by doubling the resources needed and using the cover story that you need to prevent failures.

EGO

Ego-wise, two things are important to engineers:

- How smart they are.

- How many cool devices they own.

The fastest way to get an engineer to solve a problem is to declare that the problem is unsolvable. No engineer can walk away from an unsolvable problem until it's solved. No illness or distraction is sufficient to get the engineer off the case. These types of challenges quickly become personal—a battle between the engineer and the laws of nature.

Engineers will go without food and hygiene for days to solve a problem. (Other times just because they forgot.) And when they succeed in solving the problem they will experience an ego rush that is better than sex—and I'm including the kind of sex where other people are involved. Not only is it better at the moment, but it lasts for as long as people will listen to the engineer's tale of conquest.

Nothing is more threatening to the engineer than the suggestion that somebody has more technical skill. Normal people sometimes use that knowledge as a lever to extract more work from the engineer. When an engineer says that something can't be done (a code phrase that means it's not fun to do), some clever normal people have learned to glance at the engineer with a look of compassion and pity and say something along these lines:

"I'll ask Bob to figure it out. He knows how to solve difficult technical problems."

At that point it is a good idea for the normal person to not stand between the engineer and the problem. The engineer will set upon the problem like a starved Chihuahua on a pork chop.

Engineers can actually hear machines talk to them. The rattle in the car's engine teases softly, "I'll bet you can't find me." The computer hums an approving tune when the engineer writes an especially brilliant piece of computer code. The toaster says "Not yet, not yet, not yet" until the toast pops out. An engineer who is surrounded by machines is never lonely and never judged by appearance. These are friends.

So it should be no surprise that engineers invest much of their ego in what kind of "friends" they have.

ENGINEERS ILLUSTRATED

1 5

CHANGE

"Change" was a very ordinary thing for many eons. But thanks to consultants, "change" has been elevated to an important business concept. It all started with downsizing.

Many managers lost their jobs because of downsizing. These ex-managers wisely called themselves "consultants," because that sounded far sexier than "street urchins."

As the consultants applied their skills, the phrase they used most often was "Spare change?" It began as a plaintive mumble, but over time the consultants became more aggressive, shouting *"Spare change!"* to passersby, almost as if it were a command. Over time the phrase was shortened to "change" and it developed into a thriving consulting practice. (I might have some of the details wrong, but I know the story involves consultants asking for money.)

The best thing about change consulting is that it can be sold to just about any company. Businesses are experiencing more changes than a bunch of babies in a beer-drinking contest.*

The consultant's sales pitch works like this:

Consultant: "So, are you planning to change anything?"

Manager: "Well . . . yeah, I suppose."

Consultant: "Do you have a change management plan in place?"

Manager: "What's that?"

Consultant: *"You're doomed!!!* Give me money, quick!"

---

*Yes, this analogy is uncalled for and it adds no value to the chapter. But I worked all morning on it and I'm not willing to throw it out.

FEAR OF CHANGE

People hate change, and with good reason. Change makes us stupider, relatively speaking. Change adds new information to the universe; information that we don't know. Our knowledge—as a percentage of all the things that can be known—goes down a tick every time something changes.

And frankly, if we're talking about a percentage of the total knowledge in the universe, most of us aren't that many basis points superior to our furniture to begin with. I hate to wake up in the morning only to find that the intellectual gap between me and my credenza has narrowed. That's no way to start the day.

On the other hand, change is good for the people who are causing the change. They understand the new information that is being added to the universe. They grow smarter in comparison to the rest of us. This is reason enough to sabotage their efforts. I recommend sarcasm with a faint suggestion of threat.

Changer: "I hope I can count on your support."

You: "No problem. I'll be delighted to jeopardize my short-term goals to help you accomplish your career objectives."

Changer: "That's not exactly—"

You: "I don't mind feeling like a confused rodent and working long hours, especially if the payoff is a new system that I vigorously argued against."

The goal of change management is to dupe slow-witted employees into thinking change is good for them by appealing to their sense of adventure and love of challenge. This is like convincing a trout to leap out of a stream to experience the adventure of getting deboned. (Trout are not team players.)

To overcome the natural reluctance of the victims, consultants have developed a battery of advanced management techniques that I have summarized below for your convenience.

CONTENT-FREE COMMUNICATIONS

Faced with change, employees have one question: "What's going to happen to me?" A successful change management communication program will avoid that question.

Rarely does a business change result in everybody being happy and nobody getting the shaft. That can be a problem because change requires the participation of all parties, including the eventual shaftees. For management, the trick is to string everybody along until the change is complete and the losers can be weeded out for shaftage.

Communication about change is a lot like a wooden hamburger. (Work with me here.) If you put enough garnish on it, somebody is going to swallow it. Not coincidentally, the same people who might eat a wooden hamburger (let's call them the "ungifted" people) are the ones singled out for victimization after a major change.

You can fool the ungifted wood-eaters by having plenty of meetings, e-mail messages, newsletters, and voice mail broadcasts that speak of good things ahead without addressing specific people. The eventual victims will start to believe they are part of the golden future. With luck, they might even be duped into becoming "Change Masters."

CHANGE MASTERS

Employees are told that if they embrace change they will be hailed as "Change Masters" instead of hapless victims. This is the adult equivalent of being a Mighty Morphin Power Ranger except without the cool outfits and action figures. Given the choice of being a Change Master or not, I'd certainly want to be one, just on the off chance it would give me X-ray vision.

The cynical employees who prefer to stay uninvolved while baiting the Change Masters have a name too. They are called the "Change Master Baiters." But that's another book.

PERPETUAL MOTION

Change is caused by consultants. Then you need consultants to tell you how to handle the change. When you're done changing you need consultants to tell you that the environment has changed and you'd better change again.

It's a neat little perpetual motion machine. That's the problem when you pay consultants by the hour. In some small towns there is a rule that consultants can't serve as volunteer firemen. The fear is that they'd drive around setting fire to the town.

1 6

BUDGETING

The budget process was invented by an alien race of sadistic beings who resemble large cats. The cat aliens taught budgeting to the Egyptian pharaohs, who used it as punishment during the construction of the pyramids. That explains how twenty-ton slabs of rock were carried for miles by as few as three people.

The diabolical plan of the cat aliens was to torment large segments of the human population at once, then come back later and chow down. Tragically, the cat people parked their mother ship in a warm spot of the galaxy, curled up to take naps, and ended up getting sucked into the sun.

Over the years the true purpose of the budget process was lost. Now, due to an unfortunate misinterpretation* of hieroglyphics, budgeting is seen as a method of controlling spending at big companies. Ironically, this goal has been accomplished primarily by removing managers from the productive flow—where they would otherwise be tempted to spend money—and trapping them in meetings that can last for months.

Contrary to what you might expect from the word "budget," it is not a fixed amount. It will change many times throughout the year to take advantage of the principle of "Budget Uncertainty":

*The hieroglyphic for "meeting" is very similar to the symbol for "*Ouch!!* A sphinx sat on my leg!"

If you change the budget often enough, the employees will begin acting like gophers on a rifle range, afraid to do anything that draws attention. And where there is fear there is low spending. And where there is low spending there are huge stock options for senior management, followed by an eventual death spiral of the corporation.

I had a point when I started all that, but I suspect it was not a compelling one.

PADDING YOUR BUDGET

You can guarantee that you get your fair share of the budget pie by exaggerating your value and your requirements. While it's true that every single manager has used this technique since the first caveman requested two burnt sticks to scratch on the cave wall, it can still work for you.

Your boss will expect you to come in with a high number that will then be whittled down in the time-honored battle between the clueless and the dishonest.

Some employees make the naive mistake of asking for twice as much as they need. The boss will see right through that clumsy maneuver and cut the request in half. (Bosses aren't as dumb as they look!)

The solution—which seems obvious to me—is to ask for several billion dollars more than you need. If, for example, you need three personal computers for your department, you could ask for $50 billion. This will be met with angry stares, sometimes even profanity. But if you only end up with, say, twenty percent of what you requested, that's still a cool $10 billion. And that means an end to "out of memory" error messages forever.

DEFENDING YOUR BUDGET

Management will try to trim the budget by sending an army of low-ranking, clueless budget analysts to interview you and ask insightful questions such as: "What could you do if you had half the budget you have now?"

Your first impulse might be to toss your head back and laugh in that mocking, self-righteous tone that you reserve for the "special" clueless.

Don't follow that impulse.

It's best to humor budget analysts. They make recommendations to management about budget cuts. Pretend to be interested in them personally (as if you would have a friend who spends all day doing budget work). People who work in budget departments do not have any real friends so they have no frame of reference to determine if you're just yanking their chains. Sometimes you can protect millions of dollars in your budget simply by buying a bag of cookies, dropping it on the budget analyst's desk, and saying something deeply personal such as "How was your weekend, big guy?"

When you are forced to defend your budget there are two techniques to keep in mind (1) lying and (2) lying.

You might feel some ethical discomfort about lying. The feeling will go away after the first time you tell the truth and discover that your budget

has been cleaned out like the last bag of potato chips at a Grateful Dead*
concert. In the worst case, you'll get used to lying. Eventually, you'll
develop a strong preference for it.

Lying does not come easily to some people. Study these examples to get
a better feel for the technique:

Wrong

"Well, since ninety percent of everything we do is a failure, and nobody on
the team thinks a customer would buy the product anyway, I'd say you
could put my whole department in a burlap bag, drown us in the river, and
come out ahead of the game."

Correct

"Good Lord, man!!! Are you Satan's spawn?? Don't you realize that if you
cut even one dollar from our budget it will set off a chain reaction that
could alter the rotation of the planet, melt the polar ice caps, and con-
demn us all to a frosty death!!!??"

Wrong

"Okay, you caught me. We don't need all of this money. It was just a ploy
to puff up my personal empire and get me promoted so I can have an
attractive executive assistant to take with me on trips."

Correct

"Aaaagh!!!! How can you even think such a thing! I'm operating on a shoe-
string. I'm chipping in my own money. But that's okay, because I believe in
this project, unlike the bloated, overfunded 'Project Unicorn' down the
hall. And if you talk to them, tell them I said you do not look like a Mister
Potato Head."

*This analogy was written prior to the untimely demise of Jerry Garcia. But I like it so much I
decided to keep it as a reminder of the importance of preserving our rain forests.

Always provide confusing charts and spreadsheets to support your budget requests. There's no such thing as too much information when it comes to defending your budget. Boredom and confusion are your allies in the budget fight.

Your budget charts and spreadsheets should look complicated enough to convey two messages:

1. "I have researched my budget requirements thoroughly."

2. "Smart people would understand this chart. Don't you be one of the 'other' people."

SPEND IT ALL

Whatever you do, don't leave any money in your budget at the end of the year. This is perceived by your management as a sign of failure and weakness, not to mention poor forecasting. Your budget for next year will be decreased accordingly as punishment.

Your management wouldn't give you all that money if it didn't want you to spend it. However, it might be necessary to loosen your definition of what types of expenses are vital to the health of the company. I recommend ordering large cargo containers of paper towels to make up whatever budget underruns you have. Paper products are always useful and they have the advantage of being completely flushable if you need to make room in the storage area later.

BUDGETING ILLUSTRATED

TRUE TALES OF ACCOUNTING

From: (name withheld)
To: scottadams@aol.com

Scott,

A few years ago the local management turned off the down escalators to save some money, no kidding. This was soon ended after the manager who was responsible gave a presentation to the visiting CEO, using this as an example of how creative he was in saving money.

From: (name withheld)
To: scottadams@aol.com

Scott,

Our company solicited ideas for cost cutting. Someone decided that we could save "X" amount of dollars by eliminating feminine hygiene products in the women's bathrooms. Our new gung-ho personnel director decided this was really neat, and announced the new proclamation to the whole company via e-mail.

Needless to say, the women in the company flamed this guy to a well-done crisp. The amount of estimated savings was close to the total amount that we pay the janitorial service, which provides these products for no extra cost.

The e-mail got hotter: "The idea is sexist," "We should get rid of the coffee machines," "Eliminate executive bonuses . . . "

What finally shut everyone up and got the procedure reversed was e-mail from a manager who told about a female sales exec he knows. When she is involved in a deal with a prospective client, she always checks the feminine hygiene supplies in that company's bathrooms. If the supplies are missing, she knows the company is going down the tube.

RELATED STORY OF MY OWN

A Pacific Bell co-worker of mine determined that the janitor service was removing the used rolls of toilet paper from the stalls well before the final square was used. To him, this was a huge waste and maybe even some sort of elaborate janitorial scam.

I talked him out of the conspiracy theory, but he was convinced that action was needed. He spent the afternoon crafting an elaborate memo on this problem, complete with calculations of costs, and sent it to the Facilities Department for action.

He's still waiting for a reply.

SALES

NEXT WEEK, A DOCTOR WITH A FLASHLIGHT SHOWS US WHERE SALES PROJECTIONS COME FROM.

If your company's products are overpriced and defective you can compensate by having a good sales incentive plan. No problem is so great that it cannot be overcome by a salesperson who has the proper motivation.

For example, it is well-documented that a frightened ninety-pound woman can generate enough adrenaline to lift a Chrysler minivan that has parked on her foot. Experiments have also shown that after the third time you park the minivan on her foot she will slay the researchers with a mechanical pencil and scream something like "DON'T EVER ASK ME TO BE A TEMPORARY SECRETARY AT THIS HELLHOLE AGAIN!!!" The strange thing about it is that the woman will scream in all capital letters. And that's my point: People can do almost anything if they have the proper incentive.

If sales at your company are low, it's because the sales force does not have the proper incentives. This situation is easily remedied. All you have to do is raise the sales quotas until the sales force must choose between two lifestyles:

A. A life of deception and treachery.

B. A life in a trailer park.

Salespeople can only survive for about three minutes in a trailer park. That's how long it takes the other residents to hunt them down and kill them. (Trailer park residents tend to have bitter memories of the salespeople who convinced them that metal is a good material for keeping summer heat out.)

Smart salespeople will choose option number one—a life of deception and treachery. That's something they can get used to, and with patience and practice, they can learn to enjoy it. There are few pleasures greater than selling defective products to obnoxious customers. It's not something you'd brag about to the grandkids, but it feels better than a good sneeze in the forest.

Selling isn't easy. Sure, anybody can sell high-quality products at reasonable prices. There's no trick to that. The real art of selling comes in when your product sucks compared to the competition. Your company's Marketing Department can only go so far in closing that gap. (See Chapter 11 on marketing.) The sales force must do the rest. Here are some tips for becoming a world-class sales professional:

Avoid Discussing Costs

Never discuss the true cost of your product with customers. It only encourages them to make rational decisions. Focus on the many "intangible" economic benefits your company offers. And remember that confusion is your friend in sales.

Example:

"If you bank with us, your money will accrue tax-free inflation from the first day!"

Irrelevant Comparisons

Prey on the natural stupidity of the average customer. Most people wouldn't know the difference between a logical argument and a porcupine strapped to their forehead.* Steer the customer toward silly and irrelevant comparisons.

Example:

"Well, sure, maybe forty-eight miles per hour isn't an impressive peak speed for a sports car, but you have to compare that to hopping."

Be a "Partner"

Become a "partner" with your customer, not just a vendor. The distinction is important. A vendor simply takes the customer's money and provides a product. A partner takes the customer's money and provides a "solution" that looks suspiciously like a "product" except it costs more.

A partner works with customers to help them define their requirements. This can be a problem if the only thing that makes your product

---

*At last, an analogy that isn't "pointless."

distinctive is its flaws. For example, in the case of the sports car that has a peak speed of forty-eight miles per hour, you can emphasize safety as a major advantage.

Example:

"If you don't count starvation, nobody has ever died in one of these sports cars. That's gotta be your top concern."

Attitude

Optimism is contagious. A professional salesperson will avoid negative phrases and use only positive-sounding words.

DON'T SAY	DO SAY
Old technology	Backward compatible
Overpriced	Premium
Unavailable	Can't keep it on the shelf
Piece of shit	Stands alone
Incompatible	Proprietary

Find the Decision-Makers

A sales professional should always try to find the decision-makers in the organization. The decision-makers have the least knowledge of the situation and are therefore more likely to believe whatever the salesperson says.

One reliable way to know if you have found the decision-maker is to examine the office and furnishings of the person in question. Decision-makers are rarely found in anything that resembles a large cardboard box, that is, a "cubicle." And you will never see any of the signs shown below on the wall of an important decision-maker:

"What part of NO didn't you understand?"
"On time. No defects. Pick one."
"Cubicle Sweet Cubicle."

But don't be fooled by an impressive office with a door. Non-decision-makers have offices too. You can test a person's importance in the organization by asking how much RAM his computer has. Anybody who knows the answer to that question is not a decision-maker.

Salespeople can set up meetings with executives of client companies anytime. Employees can't do that. The only way the average employee can speak to an executive is by taking a second job as a golf caddie. Executives hate talking to employees because they always bring up a bunch of unsolvable "issues." Salespeople just buy the executives lunch. It's no contest.

A salesperson can use this access to the executives as a threat to the low-level, cubicle-dwelling, dumb-sign-hanging "recommenders" of the company. Employees live in fear that the executives will hear something bad about them. And rest assured the executives *will* hear something bad about any employee who recommends buying something other than the salesperson's product.

SALES ILLUSTRATED

MEETINGS

If you're new to the business world, you might mistakenly think that meetings are a boring, sadistic hell, populated by galactic-level morons. I had that same misperception when I joined the working world. Now I understand that meetings are a type of performance art, with each actor taking on one of these challenging roles:

- Master of the Obvious

- Well-Intentioned Sadist

- Whining Martyr

- Rambling Man

- Sleeper

Once you understand the true nature of meetings you can begin to hone your acting skill and create your own character. In this chapter I will describe some of the classic roles, but feel free to combine characters and come up with your own interpretations.

MASTER OF THE OBVIOUS

The Master of the Obvious believes that while he was studying the writings of Plato, Sir Isaac Newton, and Peter Drucker, the rest of the planet was watching "Three's Company" and eating Oreos. The "Master" feels a responsibility to share his wisdom at every opportunity. He knows that any concept—no matter how mundane it might seem to him—will be a cosmic revelation to the raisin-brains around him.

The favored lines of the Master of the Obvious (delivered with great conviction) include:

- "You need customers in order to have revenue!"

- "*Profit* is the difference between *Income* and *Expense*."

- "Training is essential."

- "There is competition in the industry."

- "It's important to retain your good employees."

- "We want a win-win solution."

The secret to being a convincing Master of the Obvious is to combine condescension with sincerity. Your audience must believe that you genuinely wonder how other people can manage to dress themselves and make it to work every day on the first try. And it must seem as though you care.

You can practice for this role while you're alone. All you need is a common table lamp. Lean toward the lamp and repeatedly explain why "electricity is essential" to the illumination process. Continue to restate the thought in different ways. Try to develop a stammer or at least an annoying habit of pausing to think of the right word. Keep practicing until you can make a bulb burn out just by talking to it.

WELL-INTENTIONED SADIST

The Well-Intentioned Sadist believes that meetings should hurt. This is essentially the same attitude taken by the more successful serial killers. In fact, they have the same motto:

"Does this hurt? How about now?"

The Well-Intentioned Sadist has several tools at his disposal for causing discomfort in others. These techniques may be used alone or in any combination:

- Schedule excessively long meetings regardless of the topic.

- Have no clear purpose.

- Have no bathroom breaks (best when combined with coffee).

- Schedule meetings for Friday afternoons or lunchtimes.

This role must be played with a combination of sincerity, dedication, and, most of all, a sociopathic disregard for the lives of other people. You can get in the right mood by continually watching movies in which the star's family gets massacred and later his dog dies while taking a bullet for him. (Look for titles that feature exceptionally bad actors who are good at martial arts.)

WHINING MARTYR

Whining Martyrs get a lot of stage time. That's why there is so much competition for the role. People will detest you for being a Whining Martyr, but that can fuel your creative fires. With performance art, the audience is part of the show.

As a Whining Martyr, you should craft your complaints into tales that illustrate how valuable and intelligent you are compared to the obstructionist dolts who surround you. Imagine that your co-workers are trying to stymie your every move, now add a dash of self-pity, and voilà—you have the perfect Whining Martyr attitude.

Recommended Whines

"It looks like I'll have to sit in for the boss *again*."

"Don't worry about taking the last of the coffee. I'll just use my pen to scrape some of the residue off the inside of the pot and chew on it during the meeting."

"I can't believe the CEO wants *another* meeting with me."

"[Sigh] . . . Yes, I can do that for you . . . I'll have time on Saturday night, as usual. It's no problem, since my spouse left me and took the kids."

"Boy, I'd *love* to be able to take sick days like you people who don't have work to do."

"Another meeting? There goes the last lunch break I could have taken this fiscal year."

RAMBLING MAN

Most of the major roles at a meeting can be played by a male or a female. But the part of "Rambling Man" can only be played by a male. Women sometimes try to take on this role, but it always comes across as "babbling"* instead of true "rambling."

The Rambling Man's role is to redirect any topic toward an unrelated event in which he participated. The unrelated event might have a humorous climax, but more often than not it's just a way to let everybody know how clever he is.

The Master of the Obvious can be an accomplice to the Rambling Man, occasionally saying things like "It gets cold in Minnesota during the winter." These comments are construed as encouragement to continue and can make the entire scene last for hours.

Rambling Man is usually a cameo role and not a recurring character in regularly scheduled meetings. That's because even the Well-Intentioned Sadist and the Whining Martyr tire of this character. (And they *enjoy* pain.)

The Rambling Man clicks best when combined with the Sleeper, described below.

---

*Unlike rambling, babbling is related to the topic, yet somehow it lasts a long time without conveying any useful information. Men and women can both babble, but only men are successful ramblers.

SLEEPER

The Sleeper is essentially a stage prop. There are no lines involved in this role. You are expected to dress fashionably, but not so flamboyantly that you detract attention from the actors who have speaking parts.

It is acceptable to nod the head gently when the other actors are speaking. This suggests the gentle swaying of a tree in the wind. You may also eat pastries and drink coffee. If trapped into responding verbally, as a last resort you can use one of these phrases:

- "Uh huh."

- "Nothing new to report."

- "Same ol' same ol'"

- "You got that right" (said with slight hillbilly accent).

1 9

PROJECTS

If you're not on a "project," then you probably have a thankless, boring, repetitive job. You're like an ant carrying crumbs back to the ant hole over and over again.

But if you *are* working on a project, life is very different. You're still an ant carrying crumbs, of course, but there's a Russian Squat-Dancing* festival between you and the anthill. And you spend much of your waking hours fantasizing about how great it would be to have a thankless, boring, repetitive job.

---

*Yeah, I'm sure there's another name for it. But they *should* call it Squat-Dancing.

This chapter is for the benefit of those of you who are considering being on a project.

Executive summary: RUN AWAY!! RUN AWAY!!

There are several distinct stages to every project, regardless of the purpose of the project. I will discuss each of them separately, because if I discussed them all at the same time it would look somewhat random. Can't have that.

NAMING THE PROJECT

The success of any project depends primarily on two things:

1.   Luck

2.   A great project name

There's nothing you can do about luck, except maybe rub garlic on a penny and keep it in your sock. That's what I do. It's not an ancient tradition or anything like that; I just like the way it makes me feel. And who knows, maybe that's how ancient traditions get started. Somebody has to go first.

If you're doing all you can do in the luck department, the next most important task is picking a winning project name. You want a name that conveys strength and confidence. It must be distinct yet easy to remember.

This is the normal process for selecting a winning project name:

1.   The project team brainstorms about names.

2.   A "multivote" process is used to narrow the choices.

3.   The top choice is presented to senior management for approval.

4.   A vice president names the project after his favorite Muppet.

TEAM LEADER

The job of Team Leader is often viewed as a stepping stone to a management position. That's because anybody who is gullible enough to take on extra work without extra pay is assumed to have the "right stuff" for management. Given the negative stigma of the job, it's difficult to find somebody willing to volunteer to be a Team Leader. Management is generally forced to conscript a Team Leader based on these qualifications:

- Candidate must know how to make viewgraphs.

- Candidate must be a carbon-based life form.

The Team Leader is typically a person who has no special talent. This characteristic serves the Team Leader well during long meetings. While all the skilled people are squirming around wishing they were out applying their skills, the Team Leader can sit serenely, content in the knowledge that no personal talent is going to waste.

The word "leader" might be debatable in this context, since the job of a Team Leader involves asking people what they should be doing, then asking them how they're doing, then blaming them for not doing it. But leadership takes many forms, and sometimes just being annoying is exactly what the situation requires.

REQUIREMENTS

At some point in the project somebody will start whining about the need to determine the project "requirements." This involves interviewing people who don't know what they want but, curiously, know exactly when they need it. These people are called "end users" or simply "pinheads."

Research has shown that there is nothing on this planet dumber than an "end user." The study below ranks the relative intelligence of some common household items this way:

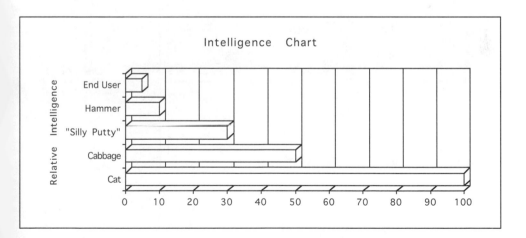

The project team will continue to gather requirements until one of these two conditions is met:

1. The end users forget to breathe, which causes them to die in their sleep.*

2. The project team decides that requirements aren't as important as once thought.

*It's a bigger problem than you'd think.

MANAGEMENT SUPPORT

No project can succeed without management support. The best sort of management support is the kind in which management doesn't find out about the project until it's a market success. If management notices a project too soon it'll support it in the following ways:

- Demand frequent status reports to explain why the team doesn't have enough time to meet deadlines.

- Demand explanations of how the project is different from all the projects that have similar acronyms.

- Ask the team what it could do if it had only half as much funding.

- Appoint an Oversight Committee whose members are always on trips.

To put it another way, managers understand that their role is to remove obstacles from the project team. They could probably do that, with the help of Dr. Kervorkian, but most managers are not such good sports. Therefore, coincidentally, the biggest obstacle to the success of any project is management itself.

SCHEDULING

   The scheduling phase of the project involves asking people how long it will take them to do work. It usually goes like this:

Project Leader: "How long will it take to select a vendor?"

Team Member: "Between a day and a year."

Project Leader: "You need to be more specific."

Team Member: "Okay, three years."

Project Leader: "Um, three years is longer than a year."

Team Member: "Fine. You're the expert, *you* pick a time. I quit."

Project Leader: "How about if we say two years?"

Team Member: "Sure, and why don't you pick the vendor while you're at it, since quality obviously means nothing to you."

   Eventually this constructive process of give and take will produce an accurate time line for your project. The time line will be transferred onto a complicated chart and hung on the wall of a conference room where it can be conveniently ignored until some external factor determines the actual project due date.

For large projects, Team Leaders use sophisticated project management software to keep track of who's doing what. The software collects the lies and guesses of the project team and organizes them into instantly outdated charts that are too boring to look at closely. This is called "planning."

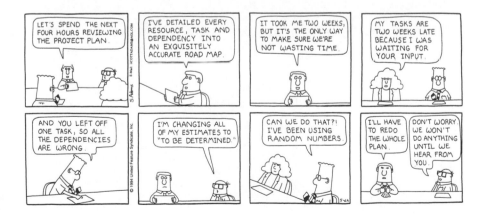

COMPLETING THE PROJECT

PROJECTS ILLUSTRATED

20

ISO 9000

If your company is not involved in something called "ISO 9000" you probably have no idea what it is. If your company *is* involved in ISO 9000 then you definitely have no idea what it is. Don't ask me what it is; I can't figure it out either. But I have pieced together enough evidence to form a working theory.

My theory: A group of bored Europeans had a few too many Heinekens and decided to play an elaborate prank on the big companies of the world. This prank came to be known as ISO 9000, so named because of the number of beers that were consumed that night. (The phrase "ISO" is either an unintelligible phrase or possibly one of the four hundred European slang words meaning "Is that my beer?")

The inebriated Europeans correctly figured that any silly-ass management technique could become an international craze if they could only keep a straight face when telling people about it. Their "idea" was that if companies documented every process and job description in the organization, this could solve a big problem that businesses have, that is, what to do with all that spare time.

As predicted by the pranksters, customers began hearing about the benefits of ISO 9000 and started demanding that their suppliers get with it. If you aren't ISO 9000 compliant, they reasoned, who knows what you're doing with all that spare time?

Managers at big companies everywhere began documenting everything they did and labeling every tool they used. It was a frenzy of labeling and documenting, labeling and documenting. Slow-moving employees would go home at night and soak in the bathtub to remove the labels slapped on their bodies by overzealous co-workers. It was ugly.

But the effort was not without reward—for consultants. Consultants who were having a tough time selling "Quality" programs quickly reinvented themselves as ISO 9000 experts. To the untrained eye it might seem as though Quality programs and ISO 9000 are not related. I was confused too until one consultant explained it to me this way: "ISO 9000 is closely related to Quality because everything you do is Quality and ISO 9000 documents everything you do, therefore give us money."

I don't think any of us can argue with that.

ISO 9000 ILLUSTRATED

21

DOWNSIZING

When I entered the workforce in 1979 the word "downsize" hadn't been invented yet. A new employee could burrow into the bureaucracy and make a little nest that would last for decades. I felt like a happy little termite living in a Victorian mansion that was always adding another room. I gnawed on the beams, paycheck after paycheck, and nobody ever noticed my tiny teeth marks.

I remember my first "staff" job in a big bank in San Francisco. It was 1980. My partner Dean and I were plucked from the management training program and put on a "special project."

The term "special project" means "All the real jobs are filled by people who, at first glance, don't appear nearly as incompetent as you." That was certainly true in my case. Dean was actually pretty good at appearing competent, but he theorized that he was being punished for something he said to somebody.

Our job was to build a computer information system for the branch banks. We were the perfect people for the job: Dean had seen a computer once, and I had heard Dean talk about it.

Our office was an unused storage room in the basement just off the parking garage, big enough to hold two beat-up desks and some squeaky chairs. It had bare white walls, an uncarpeted floor, no windows, and an annoying echo. It was like a prison cell, but without access to a library and free weights.

Sometimes I would try to call other people in the company to get important information for our project. The response was always the same: "Who are you and why do you want to know?"

I would try to sound important by invoking the first name of the senior vice president and describing how the fate of the free world depended on this vital transfer of information. For example, "Bill needs it . . . to keep our great nation independent."

But somehow they always figured out I was a twenty-two-year-old guy with a bad haircut and a cheap suit sitting in a storage room just off the parking garage. If I was especially charismatic that day, they would have the courtesy to swear at me before hanging up.

Eventually Dean and I degenerated into a pattern of sitting in our little bare room gossiping about co-workers, balancing our checkbooks, and fantasizing about whether the sun was out that day. When we got bored we would hypothesize about the information we needed, talking about it for hours until we were both pretty sure we knew what it "should" be. Then we packaged it up as "user requirements" and gave it to a woman named Barbara who programmed the system in about two weeks. The whole project took about a year, because it's not the type of thing you want to rush.

When it was done, the results of the system were notoriously inaccurate. But our manager assured us that it was okay because he only used the numbers that supported his personal opinion anyway.

It was during this year that I realized the world would run smoothly if companies employed far fewer people like me. In the years that followed, managers all over the world reached the same realization. It was the dawn of downsizing.

The first round of downsizing erased people like Dean and me*—people in jobs that sound good in concept but provide no legitimate value to anybody. The company improved its earnings and nobody worked harder because of it.

The second round of downsizing was tougher. The employees who remained had to work harder to pick up the duties of the departing workers. But in many cases these were "exempt" employees, meaning they would work extra hours without squawking too much about extra pay. Result: The companies improved their earnings. They knew they had a winning strategy here.

For the third round of downsizing, essential jobs were eliminated in huge numbers, but mostly in areas where the impact wouldn't be noticed for at least a year. That includes areas like research, new systems development, business expansion, and training. Result: The companies improved their earnings. There didn't seem to be any bottom to this downsizing well.

The bold companies that are contemplating the fourth round of down-

*Dean and I survived the downsizings by anticipating where they'd happen and slithering into more protected areas.

sizing are relying on the promises of "reengineering" to free up some more human charcoal to fuel the downsizing barbecue. (For a scholarly discussion of reengineering, see Chapter 23.)

The secret to making downsizing work is for managers to recognize the psychological impact. Experiments on laboratory animals show that if you apply continuous electrical shocks to a captive dog, eventually your utility bill will be so high that you'll feel angry at the dog. Companies apply this same medical theory to downsizing. The first rounds of downsizing usually get the people that nobody likes anyway. Those are easy. By the later rounds, managers begin to genuinely hate the remaining employees. They'll become cold-hearted enough to fire family members while humming show tunes. That's when the real savings start.

From E-mail . . .

From: (name withheld)
To: scottadams@aol.com

Scott,

Here's a new one:
You know all about companies trying to get "lean and mean." A friend says her company has now transcended lean and mean. Now it's "skinny and pissed."

MY OWN EXPERIENCES WITH DOWNSIZING

During the banking phase of my career I had the opportunity to work in a variety of jobs for which I was thoroughly unqualified. Fortunately, none of these jobs added value to the company so my incompetence didn't do much damage to the local economy.

At one point I was working as a commercial loan approver for "Professional Loans" (business loans to doctors) even though I had never made a loan or taken a class in lending. Veteran lending officers were instructed to submit their loan proposals to our department for approval. Each loan package was reviewed by all five members of the group (in case anybody missed anything) and then we took it to our boss for the "real" approval.

Although I had no formal training, I learned much on the job:

- Doctors are bad customers because they can prescribe drugs for themselves.

- According to my ex-boss, all Chinese customers cheat on their taxes, thus providing excellent cash flow for repaying loans. (Later I learned this was an unfair generalization.)

- If your co-worker brings his coffee mug to the men's room every day to wash it, you can tell people he goes in there to sit in a stall and drink coffee.

When the downsizing began it didn't hurt much. Instead of five non-value-added people we had four, then three, then eventually only me. I let everybody know that I was "doing the work of five people." I got no sympathy because everybody was "doing the work of five people" if you believed what you heard.

Eventually I left the job. For the past thirteen years, zero people have been doing the work of five people but there were no complaints. This was a fairly clear indication that downsizing had a future.

BRIGHTSIZING

Pessimists point out that the first people to flee a shrinking company are the bright people who can take the "buy-out" packages and immediately get better jobs elsewhere. The dullard employees who remain produce low-quality work, but they compensate by working long hours and producing more low-quality work per person than ever before. The pessimists would have us believe this is a bad thing.

I was one of the people who survived all the early rounds of downsizing, so I know that the pessimists are wrong. Contrary to their gloomy little "logic" I was not producing large volumes of low-quality work after the downsizing. In fact, I moved to a strategy job in which I produced no work whatsoever.

After all the bright people fled, companies realized they had to make downsizing sound like more of a positive development in order to keep morale high.* This was accomplished through a creative process of inventing happier-sounding phrases that all meant essentially the same thing:

"You're fired." (1980)
"You're laid off." (1985)
"You're downsized." (1990)
"You're rightsized." (1992)

*For some reason, morale was low for the employees who realized their workload had tripled, their salaries remained unchanged, and they were still there after all the "good people" had left.

I expect the trend to continue. You'll see the following phrases used within the next five years:

"You're happysized!"
"You're splendidsized!"
"You're orgasmsized!"

From E-mail . . .

From: (name withheld)
To: scottadams@aol.com

Scott,

Here at [company] they have come up with a new way to tell you that you are about to be laid off: It's called "put in the mobility pool."

DOWNSIZING ILLUSTRATED

COMPANIES THAT STILL HAVE TOO MANY EMPLOYEES

From: (name withheld)
To: scottadams@aol.com

Scott,

I spent Friday morning at [company's] quarterly all-hands meeting. I was willing to sacrifice a morning of my life for a T-shirt, in this case a very nice one.

Anyway, they gave out a "Process" award.

The award for best new process was awarded to the group who made up the process for awarding awards.

From: (name withheld)
To: scottadams@aol.com

Scott,

At my company we have a coordinator's committee for the five task forces that are working on office climate issues.

The mission of the committee is to coordinate the work of the task forces. The task of the task forces is to gather information and make recommendations on a process for creating a plan to address office climate issues . . .

I'm not making this up, as you obviously know!!

From: (name withheld)
To: scottadams@aol.com

Scott,

Last week, one of our managers called a meeting for all of the female personnel at one of our offices to say that someone has been stealing toilet paper from the women's room and that it has to stop.

Isn't that ludicrous? I mean, imagine the costs of this manager trying to monitor the toilet paper supply, and the costs of having several people attend this meeting when they could be working more productively. I'm sure the costs of this toilet paper policing and enforcement exceeds the costs of the few "stolen" rolls!

Well, it's not all for naught; this toilet paper scenario has somehow sparked some creative juices that our otherwise rule-laden, bureaucratic environment never does. In good humor, some people have started writing anonymous messages about it and someone has gone about the business of setting up another to be blamed for the stealing by placing a roll of toilet paper in another woman's desk drawer, and having a telltale end of it sticking out of the open drawer and rolled out onto the carpet and extending out of her cubicle! And of course all sorts of puns have emerged about wiping out the problem, etc.

From: (name withheld)
To: scottadams@aol.com

Scott,

I am not making this up.

At our company, our middle managers (two levels up) were all formed into an enormous committee to address areas of concern voiced by employees in one of our recent employee surveys.

There are about one hundred middle managers. They came up with many hilarious suggestions. This is the best one:

They formed a subcommittee to detect and excise "deadwood." Totally missing the fact that the definition of deadwood is "the other guy," they produced two suggestions:

(1) The Deadwood Hotline. Any employee could accuse any other employee of being "deadwood," upon which an investigation would be immediately launched. Paranoia.

(2) Groups of middle managers would "roam the halls," searching for deadwood. I call this the "Deadwood Posse." I have no idea how they intended this to work.

They failed the laugh test in front of the Executive Council, I'm happy to report.

From: (name withheld)
To: scottadams@aol.com

Scott,

Here's a copy of a REAL (no kidding!) memo which was sent out just a few days ago.

—Memo—

Over the past few months, the cost of our monthly donut meeting has been extremely high. Much of this cost is due to the fact that more and more donuts are needed at each meeting.

It's not that we have more people month to month, but because we are experiencing a lack of fairness when it comes to these donuts. For those employees who get to the meeting first, they are taking three or four donuts at a time, thus leaving nothing for the people who arrive a little later, therefore forcing the cafeteria to serve even more. In addition to this problem, there are people who normally do not attend the meeting just coming in for a donut or two. This needs to change.

Therefore, effective with the February meeting, and all subsequent meetings thereafter, we will be issuing a "Donut Ticket." This ticket will entitle the bearer to one twelve-ounce coffee or soda, and one piece of fresh fruit or a donut. We believe this will help eliminate excessiveness by our employees, and of course, keep our monthly cost down.

Our meetings are set for February 13th, 14th, and 15th– Before that time, please stop by the front desk to pick up your tickets for distribution to your departments. These tickets are to be distributed to the employees just before their meeting time. These tickets are not to be duplicated. These tickets are good for the "February Donut meeting only." One ticket per person, per meeting.

I appreciate your assistance in this matter. Should you have any questions, please do not hesitate to contact me.

—End of memo—

From: (name withheld)
To: scottadams@aol.com

Scott,

One delightful experience which you missed involved the critical strategies we incorporated in the Phase Group reports to the officers.

Clerical people transcribed the wonderful thoughts which group members scribed up on butcher paper taped to the wall. Some scribes didn't write all that clearly. A critical strategy was, "DON'T SELL PAST THE CLOSE." The transcription came out, "DON'T

SELL PLASTIC CLOTHES." We left it in the report. I think one intermediate-level manager picked up on it and questioned it. He let us leave it in.

From: (name withheld)
To: scottadams@aol.com

Scott,

Here is some fodder for you.

A programmer from the MIS Department wrote a useful program for Department A. Department A had a meeting with the MIS Department to have the program documented and enhanced. The MIS Department said the project could not be done.

Department A replied that the program already existed!

The next day Department A found that the program in question had been deleted from their computers.

The project was never done.

HOW DOWNSIZING IS ARTFULLY BEING HANDLED

From: (name withheld)
To: scottadams@aol.com

Scott,

I just got a company mailing saying that we'll have a "Special Day" where the people who are leaving the company for the Voluntary Force Reduction are supposed to sit in the cafeteria with name tags on and have the other employees wander around and look at them.

There's also supposed to be a bake sale. I'm not sure what the point is, but maybe if we make enough on the bake sale some of them could be rehired or something. I can't quite put my finger on why this seems kind of bizarre in a *Soylent Green* kind of way.

From: (name withheld)
To: scottadams@aol.com

Scott,

The large company I work for recently published guidelines for its new "Career Transition Plan" a.k.a. layoff policy.

This document has been sent to everyone in the company, which greatly boosted morale.

Among the "highlights and advantages" of this plan are that it is "competitive." This led me to think, "Hmmm. Is a competitive advantage of this company its Career Transition Plan? Should this layoff policy be included in recruiting interviews as an advantage of working here?"

From: (name withheld)
To: scottadams@aol.com

Scott,

I recently learned that in one of our executive meetings the vice
president of the company made a presentation on the upcoming
year's forecast. In the course of his speech he mentioned that the
company would no longer have the position of marketing director.

You guessed it! The next person's turn to make a presentation was
the director of marketing, and this was the way he was informed.
Two weeks later he was gone.

I hope that didn't affect his presentation.

From: (name withheld)
To: scottadams@aol.com

Scott,

I had an abject lesson in corporate humiliation today. A whole slew
of us here at [company] had to call a phone number to see if we were
still employed. Management e-mailed a phone number, we called
it—and got the elemental "thumbs up" or "you're meat."

Big yucks huh? Well, many folks commented on it all being remi-
niscent of Dilbert . . . In fact, my variant is: Boss sends out the
1–800-GOTJOB? number, *but* jobs are only available (in classic DJ
style) to the seventh caller or whatever . . .

From: (name withheld)
To: scottadams@aol.com

Scott,

Morale is so bad in my department that they sent the "corporate shrink" down from [city]. He appeared to be depressed, probably because HIS job was being reengineered, and he didn't expect to keep his job another year.

He did a presentation to the work groups about things being tough all over . . . etc., but the gist of his message was: "Well if you think you've got it bad, listen to my story."

With a little bit of probing I found that the company insurance has no programs for other counseling—just the corporate shrink.

HOW TO TELL IF YOUR COMPANY IS DOOMED

You might be working for a company that is doomed. Check for the presence of any of these deadly factors:

HARBINGERS OF DOOM

- Cubicles

- Teamwork

- Presentations to management

- Reorganizations

- Processes

CUBICLES

Assuming your computer hasn't made you sterile, someday your descendants will look back and be amazed that people of our generation worked in things called "cubicles." They will view our lives much the way we now view the workers from the Industrial Revolution who (I've heard) worked twenty-three hours a day making steel products using nothing but their foreheads.

Imagine our descendants' disbelief when they read stories about how we were forced to sit in big boxes all day, enduring a stream of annoying noises, odors, and interruptions. They might think it was the product of some cruel experiment.

Scientist: "Whenever you start to concentrate, this device on the desk will make a loud ringing sound to stop you."

Employee: "Um. Okay."

Scientist: "If your stress levels begin to normalize we'll have your boss pop in and give you an assignment that sat on his desk until it was overdue."

Employee: "What exactly is this research supposed to discover?"

Scientist: "Nothing, really. We like to do this sort of thing to people during our lunch break."

The widespread use of cubicles is a direct result of early laboratory tests on rats.

In the early 1960s, rats were placed in a scale-model cubicle environment and given a set of unreasonable objectives. At first the rats scurried around excitedly looking for cheese. Eventually they realized that their efforts were not rewarded. The rats fell into a pattern of attending meetings and complaining about a lack of training. The researchers labeled these rats "poor team players" and ignored them. Many of the rats died or escaped, thus reducing headcount. Companies heard of this new method for reducing headcount and began moving employees into cubicles.*

If your company already has cubicles that doesn't necessarily mean it's doomed. But if the direction of the company is toward smaller cubicles or more people in each cubicle, you're doomed.

*Some companies kept the rats on the payroll, typically for jobs in auditing and Quality Assurance. If you suspect that your co-worker is a rat, observe his interaction with the computer mouse. If he is using it to manipulate the cursor, he's human. If he's trying to mate with it, he might be a holdover from earlier testing. If he's using it as a foot pedal, he's your boss.

TEAMWORK

If you hear a lot of talk about teamwork at your company, you're doomed.

The whole concept of "teamwork" changed when it migrated from the world of sports to the world of business. In basketball, a good team player is somebody who passes the ball. If you put a businessperson on a basketball team he'd follow the player with the ball, saying things like "What do you plan to do with that? Can we talk about it first?"

Teamwork is the opposite of good time management. You can't do a good job managing your time unless you can blow off your co-workers. They will try to convince you to abandon your priorities in favor of their priorities. They are selfish and evil.

When you're a team player you look like a big ol' pile of birdseed in an aviary. Every co-worker will swoop in for a beak full of your resources and leave you a little "present" that has limited resale value. Anywhere you see teamwork you'll see people with lots of beak wounds on their heads.

All companies experience some degree of teamwork, but they're not all doomed. An easy way to determine if you have enough teamwork to be doomed is simply to measure how long it takes from the time you decide to go to lunch together until the time you actually eat.

TIME IT TAKES TO GET TO LUNCH	TEAMWORK RATING
Five minutes	Teamwork is annoying but not yet dangerous
Fifteen minutes	Danger, Red Alert
Sixty minutes	Teamwork has reached critical mass; company doomed

PRESENTATIONS TO MANAGEMENT

Your company is doomed if your primary product is overhead transparencies. A typical company has just enough resources to do one of the following:

1. Accomplish something.

2. Prepare elaborate presentations that lie about how much is being accomplished.

The rational employee will divert all available resources away from accomplishing things and toward the more highly compensated process of lying about accomplishments. It's the same amount of work, but only one has a payoff.

REORGANIZATIONS

Managers are like cats in a litter box. They instinctively shuffle things around to conceal what they've done. In the business world this process is called "reorganizing." A normal manager will reorganize often, as long as he's fed.

You can tell that you've reorganized too often—and are therefore doomed—if you hear your co-workers asking any of these questions in the hallways:

"If I had to live in a dumpster, how bad would that be?"

"Where do street people shower?"

"Is tuberculosis fatal?"

PROCESSES

If your company is staffed with a bunch of boneheads, you are doomed. This situation is usually referred to indirectly as a need for "process improvement." If you notice a lot of attention being given to process improvement it's a sure sign that all the smart employees have left the company and those who remain are desperately trying to find a "process" that is so simple that the boneheads who remain can handle it.

At this point it would be very funny to close your eyes and imagine a public address system at your office with the following announcement: "Marilyn vos Savant has left the building."

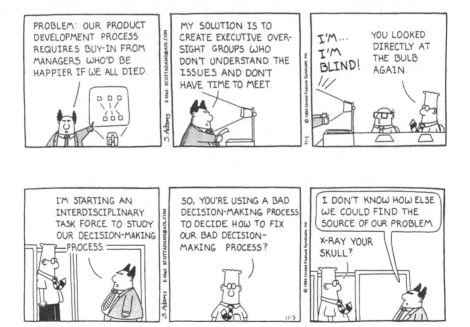

REENGINEERING

Reengineering was invented by Dr. Jonas Salk as a cure for Quality programs.

Just kidding.

The acknowledged parents of reengineering are Michael Hammer and James Champy. When I say they're the "parents" I don't mean they had sex—and I apologize for making you think about it. I mean they wrote the best-selling business book *Reengineering the Corporation,* which was published in 1993.

Businesses flocked to reengineering like frat boys to a drunken cheerleader. (This analogy wasn't necessary, but I'm trying to get my mind off that Hammer and Champy thing.)

Reengineering involves finding radical new approaches to your current business processes. On paper, this compares favorably with the "Quality" approach, which involves becoming more efficient at the things you shouldn't be doing.

But there is a dark side to reengineering. There's a risk that whatever natural incompetence is present in the company can be unleashed in epic scale instead of doled out in puny "Quality" portions. This can be dangerous if—as I've often stated—we're all a bunch of idiots.

Hammer noted this risk and cleverly followed up with another book in 1995, *The Reengineering Revolution*. It describes all the boneheaded things that managers did to screw up his recipe for reengineering.

Example of How to Screw Up Reengineering

CEO: "Underling, go reengineer the company."

Underling: "I'll need $2 million."

CEO: "For what?"

Underling: "I need it to reengineer the company."

CEO: "You fool—reengineering *saves* money."

Underling: "Um . . . I'll get right on it."

CEO: "Let me know when you're done."

Reengineering has a tendency to reduce the number of employees needed to perform a function. That unfortunate side effect causes fear and mistrust in the employees whose participation is vital to making reengineering a success. You might think fear and mistrust would sabotage the effort, but that doesn't have to be the case. There are many examples of processes that work just fine even when there's plenty of fear and mistrust. Examples:

- Capital punishment

- Presidential elections

- Multilevel marketing

From E-mail . . .

From: (name withheld)
To: scottadams@aol.com

Scott,

In an executive washroom the other day I overheard this
exchange:
"Hey, how's it going? I haven't seen you in a while."
"I got reengineered."
"Hey, too bad."

Pity the poor slob who is assigned the task of reengineering the company; insufficient management support from above, treachery from below. It's possible to succeed, but the odds are against it.*

Here are some of the specific obstacles to reengineering.

SILVER BULLET DEFENSE

Managers are often asked to donate employees from their groups to the company's reengineering effort. This is an opportunity for managers to unload their most incompetent workers, all in the name of "teamwork." These incompetent employees act as "Silver Bullets" to destroy the reengineering project while leaving the existing organizations intact.

Once the "Silver Bullets" are assembled it's time to have some meetings and brainstorm about radical reengineering options:

Silver Bullet #1: "Does anybody have any radical reengineering ideas?"

Silver Bullet #2: "Why don't we pre-lick all our envelopes?"

---

*The odds are approximately the same as if you bet on a race horse who has not won on a muddy track and it suddenly starts pouring rain. And the horse has a cast on two legs. And it's dead.

Silver Bullet #1: "That's more like an incremental "quality" idea than a radical "reengineering" idea."
(Long silence)

Silver Bullet #2: "We could downsize some people we don't know, thus saving money."

Silver Bullet #3: "Who would do their work?"
(Another long silence)

Silver Bullet #2: "Other people that we don't know?"

Silver Bullet #1: "I like those numbers!"

CAMOUFLAGE DEFENSE

Mid-level managers who are threatened by reengineering will make clever defensive adjustments. They quickly redefine whatever they're already doing as reengineering. Suddenly your "Customer Service Project" gets renamed to "Customer Service Reengineering Project." You're not getting a haircut, you're "reengineering your head." You're not going to lunch, you're "reengineering your intestines." Pretty soon there's so much reengineering going on that it's hard to find anything that *isn't* reengineering, at least in name.

Then comes budget time.

Senior executives know they should be funding something called "reengineering" or else they'll look like troglodytes. Reengineering is "in" and it's happening. The cheapest way to fund reengineering is by calling the stuff you're already funding "reengineering." (Senior managers were once middle managers; they know how to manage a budget.)

The executives might throw a bone to the one "real" reengineering project by giving it some money to do a small trial.

REENGINEERING TRIAL

A reengineering trial is a small-scale test of a proposed new "reengineered" process. Typically, none of the technology or resources that are proposed for the large-scale reengineering project is available for the trial. So planning for the trial goes like this:

Team Member #1: "We'll need distributed workstations, all connected by a worldwide satellite network system."

Team Member #2: "All we have is this pot of decaf coffee that was left here from the meeting before ours."

Team Member #3: "Let's use it. We can interpolate the results."

Team Member #1: "Are you nuts? That's *decaf.*"

CONCLUSION

Reengineering a company is a bit like performing an appendectomy on yourself. It hurts quite a bit, you might not know exactly how to do it, and there's a good chance you won't survive it. But if it does work, you'll gain enough confidence to go after some of the more vital organs, such as that big red pumping thing.

24

TEAM-BUILDING
EXERCISES

If the employees in your company are a bunch of independent, antisocial psychopaths, you might need some team-building exercises. Team-building exercises come in many forms but they all trace their roots back to the prison system. In your typical team-building exercise the employees are subjected to a variety of unpleasant situations until they become either a cohesive team or a ring of car jackers.

On two occasions during my cubicle career I had the thrill of participating in a "Ropes" course with my talented and trusted co-workers. I learned so much in the first experience that the second Ropes course was much easier. In particular, I learned that if you fake a hand injury you can be exempt from activities that might kill you.

Our first "learning" during my second Ropes course experience was a trust-building exercise. We were randomly paired; one person would stand stiffly upright and fall backward, protected by the trusted partner who would break the fall. That seemed to work smoothly for most of the pairs in my group. But my partner (let's call her Margie) chose the path of least resistance and let gravity run its course. When quizzed about this later, Margie explained that she figured my wiry five-foot-eight-inch body would be "too heavy" so it was best to get out of the way.

I knew that later we would be expected to dangle from high trees protected only by the vigilance of our trusted co-workers who would be holding ropes to protect us. Sadly, my old hand injury flared up and I had to pass on that portion of event.

However, not all was lost in the experience. I did get to wear an incredibly dorky helmet and stand around watching my co-workers do things that aren't generally done by people who are—shall we say—smart enough to get out of jury duty. I felt quite majestic in my helmet, all outdoorsy, bonding with my teammates. Until somebody pointed out to the assembled crowd that my helmet was on backward. Another co-worker ran to get a camera because I "looked so funny" in my shorts and dorky helmet. That was the day I realized that if I ever tunneled out of that corporate prison hell I'd be sure to fill in the hole before sprinting for town.

The highlight of the experience for me was an exercise in which we had to move our entire team across a field, stepping only on log stumps that were placed too far apart for leaping. The trick was to use planks to build temporary bridges in just the right sequence to move the team without leaving any planks or people behind. Partway through this exercise our fearless district manager realized that listening to the opinions of the group was a losing strategy, so he "took control" and started barking directions. We followed his directions, even though they seemed to be somewhat suboptimal. But by then we trusted him—and of course there was always the "retribution thing" to worry about—so we readily accepted his leadership. The exercise ended with all of us except our leader safely on the other end of the field. He was stranded many stumps back trying to balance two planks in his arms. I think he's still there.

Everything else you need to know about team building and teamwork is in the cartoons and e-mail messages that follow.

TEAM WORK ILLUSTRATED

TALES OF TEAMWORK

From: (name withheld)
To: scottadams@aol.com

Scott,

At [company], a lot of business is done in the hallway. Getting dragged into these ad hoc meetings can be a huge time-waster; however, it's hard to avoid them because the participants always seem to want everyone's opinion.

I have taken to either excusing myself to the rest room to get out of them, or carrying ice back to my office from the kitchen by hand. That way, when I get caught in a meeting, I can say, "See, this ice is melting and my hand is cold. I must go now." They let me out, and nobody seems to question the utility or business case for my ferrying ice around all day.

From: (name withheld)
To: scottadams@aol.com

Scott,

So the team is hiring a new engineer, and we had a cube with furniture reserved for her. She's starting next week. But a guy on the team [Co-Worker #1] decided he'd rather have *that* cube than *his* cube, so he recruits some other team members to help him move in.

I come over to see what the fuss was about and they are just moving the new hire's furniture out. I sez to myself, "That furniture is better than my furniture," so I got the guys to move the new hire's furniture into my cube and take my furniture . . . well, actually my furniture ended up in [Co-Worker #1's] new cube, and his old furniture stayed where it was, which is now the new hire's cube.

As they're moving my desk, which is identical to [Co-Worker #1's] desk, out of my cube, another engineer [Co-Worker #2] comes by to see what the fuss was about, and happens to mention that that desk is better than *his* desk (because he hasn't got a desk, just a table).

So by the time the new hire shows up, I figure she'll have roughly two broken file cabinets, a four-by-four table, and a guest chair, and she'll be in the cube next to the conference area.

Plus, none of us worked at all this morning, and a couple people got pretty concerned that maybe one of us was leaving the team, what with our furniture being moved and all.

From: (name withheld)
To: scottadams@aol.com

Scott,

Here's a funny disaster scenario, a true situation that happened at a company I worked at. The president of our company decided we needed an off-site. He decided that an ideal off-site was a bike ride. He chose a thirty-mile route and handed out hand-drawn maps.

Half the company didn't have bikes and rented them. Nobody was in shape. The route turned out to be fairly hilly (and thirty miles is a long ride even in flat terrain for someone who doesn't ride regularly). The map was wrong and nobody had real maps. Several people got lost and never made it to lunch. One person ended up in the hospital (he collapsed due to low blood sugar while biking up a hill). The planned discussions and activities for the day never happened. And the president didn't understand until days later how much of a disaster the day had been. After all, he'd enjoyed his ride.

2 5

LEADERS

DEFINITION OF A LEADER

Leadership is an intangible quality with no clear definition. That's probably a good thing, because if the people being led knew the definition, they would hunt down their leaders and kill them.

Some cynics might say that a "leader" is a someone who gets people to do things that benefit the leader. But that can't be a good definition because there are so many exceptions, as you well know.*

---

*Please tell me what those exceptions are; I'm starting to get cynical.

ORIGIN OF THE WORD "LEADER"

The word "leader" is derived from the word "lead," as in the material that bullets are made out of. The term "leader" was popularized at about the same time as the invention of firearms. It grew out of the observation that the person in charge of every organization was the person whom everyone wanted to fill with hot lead.

I don't recommend this; it's just a point of historical interest.

LEADERSHIP VISION

Leaders spend their time concentrating on "visions" of the future. This can involve having lunch with other leaders, attending golf events, or even reading a book. It can take many forms, as long as nothing tangible is produced during the process. Through these activities the leader hopes to convince the employees of the following things:

1. The leader knows the future and has agreed to share it with the company instead of using this awesome power to make a fortune gambling.

2. The chosen direction is somehow not as "obvious" as you think, so you're lucky to have the leader at any price.

3. There are intangible benefits to being an employee. These intangible benefits compensate for the low pay and poor working conditions. The nature of these intangible benefits will be revealed to you at some future time, unless you have a bad attitude.

Obviously, any good leader operates under the assumption that the people being led are astonishingly gullible. This has proven to be a fair assumption throughout history, as demonstrated by the fact that many leaders have *not* been assassinated.

LEADER SURVIVAL SKILLS

The most important skill for any leader is the ability to take credit for things that happen on their own. In primitive times, tribal chieftains would claim credit for the change in seasons and the fact that wood floats. They had the great advantage of the ignorance of the masses working in their favor. But television has largely filled the "knowledge gap," so the modern leader must take credit for more subtle happenings.

For example, if the company accountants predict that profits are going up because of a change in international currency rates, the good leader will create a company-wide "Quality Initiative," thus having a program in place to take credit for the profit increase. The employees play along with the illusion in hopes that the leader will be noticed by another company and hired away. Everybody wins when the leader is successful.

WHERE DO LEADERS COME FROM?

It's an age-old question: Are leaders born or made? And if they're made can we return them under warranty?

Leaders are people who can pursue a path that is seemingly nonsensical or even dangerous to everybody else. Common sense tells us that nobody needs a leader to take the path that's intuitive; people would do that on their own. Therefore, since the leader recommends a path that is seemingly illogical to the "average" person, we can conclude that a leader must be either:

1.   So smart that nobody can share the vision

Or . . .

2.   A nitwit

To divine the answer to the "visionary or nitwit" question we can review some of the great acts of leadership and determine, after the fact, whether they were the work of the mentally incompetent or of great visionaries. If a pattern emerges, we have our answer.

GREAT WALL OF CHINA EXAMPLE

Take the Great Wall of China. It took literally dozens of Chinese people working overtime to build this wall that stretches for many miles across the Chinese nation. It's so large you can see it from outer space, although frankly it's not worth it because you'd have to hold your breath a long time and you'd probably burn up on reentry.

The Great Wall's purpose was to keep out invading armies. But invading armies soon realized that the gatekeepers along the Great Wall could easily be bribed. Thanks to unreasonable taxation by the Chinese rulers, the average gatekeeper's net worth was a crust of bread and a few shiny stones. This made the gatekeepers somewhat vulnerable to bribery.

Any invading general would pull his army up to the wall, toss a couple of sandals to the gatekeeper, and wait for the door to fling open. Then the general would kill the gatekeeper because there's no point in wasting good sandals.

Conclusion

The leaders who built the Great Wall were nitwits.

Secondary Conclusion

But they were smarter than gatekeepers.

GREAT PYRAMIDS EXAMPLE

Let's examine the great pyramids of Egypt. I've never actually watched an entire PBS show about the pyramids, so I can't speak authoritatively. But I think the purpose of the pyramids was to honor the leaders and maybe help them in the afterlife. It looked good on papyrus.

But it didn't turn out the way they planned. I once paid $12 to peer at the box that held King Tutankhamen's little bandage-covered midget corpse at the De Young Museum in San Francisco. I remember thinking how pleased he'd be about the way things turned out in his afterlife.

Conclusion

The leaders who built the pyramids were nitwits.

GENGHIS KHAN EXAMPLE

Many years ago, on a desperately cold evening on the tundra, Genghis Khan ordered his Mongol hordes to "mount their horses" and do a ride-by "mooning" of the neighboring village. There was no real reason for this except that he wanted some peace and quiet while he sat in his tent designing various fashion items made out of dead animals.

Some of the Mongols were later embarrassed to admit that they misinterpreted the order to "mount their horses." This made for a good laugh back at the camp.

Later, through a series of creative retellings, this whole Genghis Khan legend got blown up into a much bigger deal than it was. But you have to remember, there were maybe two dozen people on the planet at the time, so everything seemed important. And everybody agreed it was probably best to embellish the story a bit so the Mongol hordes wouldn't look bad in business books later on.

Conclusion

Genghis Khan was a nitwit as a leader, but he was a pretty fair designer of fur fashions.

MODERN EXAMPLES OF LEADERSHIP

One cannot reach a conclusion on the basis of a few historical examples, even if they do seem pretty darned persuasive. Let us turn instead to the words of some people who are being led in companies around the globe. I think you'll see a pattern emerge.

> From: (name withheld)
> To: scottadams@aol.com
>
> Scott,
>
> This is a true story:
> Our overworked Accounting Department recently put in twenty straight days of work to close the books for the year, working through weekends and the 4th of July holiday. When it was over, one of the managers approached the big boss about possible comp time or money bonus. The boss replied, "Didn't you read the 'Red Badge of Courage'?" That was his full response.

From: (name withheld)
To: scottadams@aol.com

Scott,

Just when I thought management couldn't get any more clueless . . .

A friend of mine here at [company] just turned in her resignation letter today. Management red-penned it, and sent it back to her for a rewrite (they thoughtfully provided her with a copy of the resignation letter of her closest peer, who resigned last week, as a model of what they liked to see).

By the way, both people mentioned "clueless management" as one of the reasons they were leaving. They were challenged to provide examples.

Duh . . .

From: (name withheld)
To: scottadams@aol.com

Scott,

A few years ago, the VPs of [company] visited a number of other companies, with the purpose of discovering what management practices accounted for their success. One of the companies was Federal Express.

After weeks and weeks of these visits, what did they come back with? Well, it seems FedEx employees are called "associates," not employees. That must be why FedEx does so well!

So it was announced to us with great fanfare that henceforth we would all be called "associates," not employees. *All* of us would be called associates, too—nice and egalitarian. This was supposed to increase our efficiency and productivity. Some weeks later, the VP of human resources announced that now there would be "associates," "leaders" (i.e., supervisors and middle managers), and "senior leaders" (i.e., senior management).

This was the most visible (and the most effective) result of the VP's visits to see how to emulate well-run companies.

From: (name withheld)
To: scottadams@aol.com

Scott,

A recent work situation left me feeling totally Dilbert:

(1) Boss asks me what I think of a proposal he has because it impacts my department.

(2) I reply that I don't think it will work.

(3) Countless meetings, conference calls, and e-mails on the proposal.

(4) Consensus is that this is not a worthwhile proposal.

(5) Boss decides to implement proposal.

(6) Boss's boss e-mails boss asking why this proposal was implemented. It doesn't make sense.

(7) Boss forwards e-mail to me asking why we implemented proposal and to prepare a response!

From: (name withheld)
To: scottadams@aol.com

Scott,

Here's a true-life story.

I am working on a project in cooperation with [large company]. In this project we need to come up with a name of a [product]. They've had a lot of trouble deciding on a name.

Today we learned that they have made some real progress toward determining a name. Their management team explained that they have created a team of managers who will by next Monday identify another individual whose responsibility will be to produce a schedule for determining the name of the device.

And to think we were worried they weren't doing anything . . .

From: (name withheld)
To: scottadams@aol.com

Scott,

A newly appointed VP of my company, in an interview printed in the internal company news rag, made the following comment when asked whether existing employees would be relocated if the company won an upcoming contract, or if the company would instead hire local people:

"Engineers are basically a commodity. It doesn't make economic sense for the company to pay for moves when we can buy the same commodity on site."

Naturally, this disturbed some individuals in the workforce and a number of them showed up at an all-hands meeting held by this VP a few days later and sat in the front row plastered with signs labeling themselves as "Bananas," "Pork Bellies," etc.

The VP made a valiant effort to tap dance around his statements but didn't make many converts.

From: (name withheld)
To: scottadams@aol.com

Scott,

Look out, Newt . . .

My division has decided to inspire employees in true Republican style by giving each engineer a three-by-five-inch plastic card with the ten-point "[Division Name] Contract." According to a letter distributed with the contract:

"Someone once said that you know your strategy is sound if you can say 'no' to a request. Use this card in that way. If you're asked to do something not related to the contract, challenge its importance and sustain the focus we require to set ourselves up for a great future of opportunity, growth, and profit."

First of all, wasn't it *Dogbert* who noted the difference between a company with a strategy and one without a strategy?

Maybe life did imitate art in this case. You make the call. Take a look at this cartoon from a book published in 1991:

THE IMPORTANCE OF STRATEGIES

ALL COMPANIES NEED A STRATEGY SO THE EMPLOYEES WILL KNOW WHAT THEY DON'T DO.

COMPANY WITH NO STRATEGY

UH-OH...WHAT SHOULD I DO?

RRRRING

COMPANY WITH A STRATEGY

WE DON'T DO THAT.

BUILD A BETTER LIFE BY STEALING OFFICE SUPPLIES Dogbert's Big Book of Business 101

From: (name withheld)
To: scottadams@aol.com

Scott,

This story is from a friend of mine who works for [company name].

Two senior-level VPs are scheduled to visit the lab. Of course all productive work is stopped for a week while the floors are buffed, the lab rearranged, and the bathrooms cleaned. (At least some good is coming out of this.)

One of the managers took it upon herself to label all of the equipment in the lab. She labeled everything short of the pencil sharpener. My friend actually removed some of the labels because at some point it was insulting.

Thank heavens there was a "Logic Analyzer" label covering the

HP Logic Analyzer logo. I think the label "Buffed Floor" wouldn't stick because of the new wax. The absurdity doesn't end here though.

A local VP takes a preview tour of the lab, shakes his head, and says, "Jesus, I wanted a lab tour not a trade show" and leaves. This creates a murmur in the powers-that-be:

"He didn't want a trade show." "He didn't want a trade show."

The final insult occurred as he was leaving and they were putting new sod down around the entrance in some of the more bare spots.

Another half day is lost while they rearrange the lab again.

I've got visions of an entourage including one guy to drop sod in front of these VPs lest someone's foot touch sand. I wonder how many people it takes to hold these guys off the toilet seats and how they fit them all into the stall???

From: (name withheld)
To: scottadams@aol.com

Scott,

The stupidest thing my boss ever did for our group was institute a point system. We all had checklists, and we checked off what we did during the day, and we got points.

Not a bright guy.

From: (name withheld)
To: scottadams@aol.com

Scott,

True story:
When we were down in the dumps one year, our newish CEO decided that we needed a motivational meeting, complete with professional corporate motivation video. The video featured the "try again until success" attitude of balloonist Maxie Anderson and was coordinated with a personal letter from the famed balloonist.

(Maxie had been killed three years earlier in a ballooning accident.)

From: (name withheld)
To: scottadams@aol.com

Scott,

True story:
One day at a meeting one of the big deals was daydreaming and chewing on the side of his pen. The pen started leaking and no one in the room bothered telling this guy that he had blue ink gathering at the side of his lip and dripping on his shirt. Here they are trying to keep a straight face and he has blue dripping down his face.

They let him go the whole meeting that way.

From: (name withheld)
To: scottadams@aol.com

Scott,

Certain specific engineering disciplines are in demand around here so experienced staff have been leaving for other companies to make up to fifteen percent more money for about half the work.

Management calls a meeting of the remaining engineers.

There is some anticipation by these engineers that management will announce some correction in their salaries or workload.

The meeting is held—management hands out T-shirts and basically says, "Have a nice day."

The engineers are seen in their offices dancing on the T-shirts.

From: (name withheld)
To: scottadams@aol.com

Scott,

You may not believe this; I didn't at first, but it is true.

A program here at [company] is requiring five hours per week overtime. We do not get paid for the first five hours of overtime each week. Anyway, a woman working on the program took two weeks of vacation. When she returned she was told that she owed ten hours of overtime for the time she did not put in while on vacation.

She told them they could fire her ass. I thought she was far too nice about it.

From: (name withheld)
To: scottadams@aol.com

Scott,

Apparently, the Technical Division has sent around the new [company] Mission Statement and is requiring all the employees to sign it to indicate their support of it.

When you sign off on the Mission Statement, you get a special pin that you're supposed to wear. Then (here's the *best* part), if you see someone else wearing the special pin, you're supposed to give them the "secret salute." This "secret salute" consists of touching your hand to the pin and then giving the "thumbs up." We figured it would probably be easier to just give the Nazi salute.

Yours in Wonderland

From: (name withheld)
To: scottadams@aol.com

Scott,

We have a "Team Leader" here that also is one of those people (idiots) who comes into a meeting fifteen minutes late and insists on bringing up every topic that's already been discussed.

Over the holidays there wasn't much going on and he didn't have anything to do. He actually came into a meeting that had nothing to do with him or his department. He sat down and said he just didn't feel like he was "working" unless he could attend a meeting. Since this was the only meeting going on in the building that day, he decided to join it.

We agreed that he could sit there if he really felt the need, but only if he would keep quiet. Of course he couldn't, and brought up irrelevant points that we had already discussed.

From: (name withheld)
To: scottadams@aol.com

Scott,

Our company's eight-year "anniversary" was approaching. A bunch of employees got together to organize a party in the courtyard behind our building. When the boss found out he insisted on giving a speech during the festivities.

Well, everything went according to plan. Over a hundred employees showed up to eat fajitas and imbibe large amounts of margaritas. The boss then proceeds to get on his soapbox and give his speech, which consisted of "we may be a new company, but we will continue to become a better company by hopefully hiring better employees than we have now."

The amusing thing is that this man never realized he just insulted every employee in the company. We talk about the "infamous speech" to this day.

From: (name withheld)
To: scottadams@aol.com

Scott,

Is management at your company *this* inspired?
From the front page of [company's] Total Quality newsletter:
"The single factor that separates winning companies from their unsuccessful counterparts is the ability to stay competitive in an incredibly competitive world! . . . "

Does management have a firm grasp of the obvious or what . . . ??

From: (name withheld)
To: scottadams@aol.com

Scott,

Our director general gave an all-staff pep talk just before Christmas, at which he defined our mission as "being the company of choice for customers, partners, and employees," whereupon in February he resigned to go head up the competition.

Well, he certainly made his choice.

From: (name withheld)
To: scottadams@aol.com

Scott,

I was sitting here finishing my uncut raisin bagel and took the second to last bite . . . as I noticed a co-worker across the hall in the other cubicle saying something about "corporate executives" and not "walking the walk" . . . it occurred to me how perfectly the chunk of bagel in my hand would bounce off his head if I threw it full force across the cubes . . .

From: (name withheld)
To: scottadams@aol.com

Scott,

The story:
I created a graph a couple of years ago, showing a problem with a circuit that we had designed, and were using in most of our products. I had a meeting with our VP of Engineering, and during the meeting I told him that we had a problem, and I showed him the graph.

He took the graph, looked at it, and said, "Wow."

I thought he was seeing the same thing I was: There was a problem with the circuit, and we would have to fix it in a substantial part of our product line.

"Wow," he said again, "How did you make this graph?"

Over the next two weeks, I spent most of my time creating graphs for our VP of Engineering to use in his Corporate Management Committee meetings, where he was finally able to upstage all the marketing bozos (other VPs) with their Mac graphics that their secretaries had spent a week working on.

If I had drawn the graph on a piece of engineering paper, then he might have seen the problem, and we might have fixed it. As it was, though, I did not work on the problem until a year later, when our customers finally tracked down a problem they were having, and found that it was in our chip (the same problem), and demanded that we fix it.

Oddly enough (or maybe not), I then got credit not for finding the problem before our customers had trouble with the part, but for fixing it after the customers found it.

From: (name withheld)
To: scottadams@aol.com

Scott,

A manager suggested a way to keep meetings on time:
For every minute late to a meeting the tardy person has to contribute $1 for every person present and kept waiting.
($ = persons x minutes).
This did not last long as soon as the instigator of this policy arrived forty minutes late to a meeting with thirty people!

From: (name withheld)
To: scottadams@aol.com

Scott,

In our company, we were required to account for our time on our time cards in °°SIX MINUTE INCREMENTS°°. Mind you, we were supposedly "salaried" employees.

The reason for this pickiness is that some years ago, division potentates were caught messing with the books. The cure for this was not to particularly punish the princes, but rather to flog the peasants by harassing them about every detail of their time charges (we have eleven-digit charge numbers).

A while back, one of our people was caught in a sneak audit. Questions like, "What are you working on? What is your charge number? Have you ever committed fraud?" (Not kidding about the last. They DO ask!!)

But the interview lasted longer than six minutes . . . (just seven minutes, to be exact). So later on he was called on the carpet for charging the interview time to his project!! The worker had to write a memo saying he was sorry, the supervisor had to write a memo saying it would never happen again, and the "cognizant VP" (an evident oxymoron) wrote a memo saying heads would roll if this flagrant misbehavior continued. . . .

Things are improving, though: They relaxed the rules so we now only have to account for our time in fifteen-minute intervals . . .

From: (name withheld)
To: scottadams@aol.com

Scott,

Recently, a human resources manager was telling me about an employee that was having trouble with repetitive stress syndrome and it was related to using a mouse. I suggested that person be given a $150 pen and tablet to replace the mouse and alleviate pain while restoring productivity.

The manager's response was, "Shhhh, don't tell anyone about this. If they find out that they can avoid pain and suffering, everyone will want one of these things!"

From: (name withheld)
To: scottadams@aol.com

Scott,

During a particularly vicious interoffice war, when everyone was sweating for their jobs, the director walks into the weekly staff meeting, places a tape recorder on the table, and turns it on. Everyone sits up, glances right and left. Expressions go carefully vacant.

The director berates the attendees for not speaking up in meetings and for being "too stressed out."

Then the director's hench-person passes out copies of a form labeled "STRESS-O-METER." The form has seven boxes, each labeled with a degree of stress. The names went all the way from "don't care about anything" (zero stress) to "ready to explode" (number seven stress).

Each form had to be filled out, signed, and returned.

The STRESS-O-METERS were collected, totaled, averaged, and the number posted on an office wall.

"Stress at 4.3 this week!"

Next week, "Stress at 4.2, good work!"

Of course, all the "confidential" forms were taped to the coffee room wall, so everyone tried to figure out who was ready to explode and who was sleeping in their office.

From: (name withheld)
To: scottadams@aol.com

Scott,

So here's the latest from my company:

Our systems organization has recently gone through a series of layoffs, each supposedly final. Whole groups have been outsourced, but only after lengthy and public debate of how their detailed technical knowledge is "non-value-added." There is an ongoing "Bullet Team" to try to implement the "Indian Initiative." We have just reorganized, and half of the management has been appointed very obviously on the basis of their ability to suck up to the guy in charge of that half.

Morale is just a wee bit low.

Now, surprisingly enough, the morale problem has been acknowledged. (I think they're a little worried that people are starting to leave without being laid off first.) A "Work-Out" was called to address the issue. Alternatives discussed at the Work-Out included:

- Recognizing and rewarding technical expertise.
- Getting a pay scale close to market value.
- Communicating outsourcing plans and guidelines.
- Retraining folks with those less "value-added" skills.

After all those alternatives (and many more) were discussed, the outcome of lengthy deliberation was . . . The FUN Team!!! Employee morale is low. We need more picnics and bowling. If we just socialize more, all our problems will go away.

If I had just gone to more leadership classes, I'm sure I'd understand all this. . . .

THE IMPORTANCE OF HAIR FOR MALE LEADERS

Lastly, no discussion of leadership can be complete without considering hair. For women, it's sufficient just to have hair. But for men, the quality of hair is an essential leadership component.

The hair-leadership correlation is something I first noticed while working at Crocker Bank and then later at Pacific Bell. Over time I realized it couldn't be a coincidence.

At the top of the executive heap you consistently find men with thick, medium-length, parted-at-the-side hair. It's the kind of hair that turns silver with time, never thinning. Perma hair. Jack Kemp hair. Newt Gingrich hair. Hair that will not die. Hair that can deflect a bullet. Hair that would protect a space vehicle on reentry.*

---

*In case you want to go look at the Great Wall of China.

There are exceptions, of course. Sometimes a highly capable bald executive like Barry Diller will slip through, like a dolphin evading a tuna net. But this is rare and I attribute it mostly to the fact that these executives are part dolphin. (If you look closely at Barry Diller you'll see a little blow hole right on the top of his head.) The executives who are part dolphin can be identified by two striking characteristics:

1. They lack hair.

2. They ask you to write a "porpoise statement."

CONCLUSION

I don't mean for this chapter to imply that leadership is the same as a con job. The differences are substantial, in the sense that leadership pays much more and doesn't require quick wits. I recommend it as a career path to all of you.

LEADERSHIP ILLUSTRATED

26

NEW COMPANY MODEL: OA5

In this chapter you will find a variety of untested suggestions from an author who has never successfully managed anything but his cats. (And now that I think of it, I haven't seen the gray one for two days.)

Some people think that because I cleverly mock current management methods I must have some excellent ideas that I am selfishly keeping to myself. Over time, I have begun to believe this myself. (If this doesn't prove my central thesis—that we're all idiots—then nothing will.)

I doubt that anything you read here will improve your life, but I'm fairly confident that it won't hurt you either, and that's better than a lot of the things you're doing now.

If any of you are gullible enough to take my recommendations, don't say you weren't warned. That said, I think you'll find some interesting ideas here.

FUNDAMENTALS

The key to good management is knowing what's fundamental to success and what's not. Here's my grand insight about company fundamentals:

Companies with effective employees and good products usually do well.

Ta-daa!!

That might seem like a blinding flash of the obvious, but look around your company and see how many activities are at least one level removed from something that improves either the effectiveness of the people or the quality of the product.* (Note: If you're in one of those jobs, you might want to update your résumé.)

Any activity that is one level removed from your people or your product will ultimately fail or have little benefit. It won't seem like that when you're doing it, but it's a consistent pattern.

It's hard to define what I mean by being "one level removed" but you know it when you see it. Examples help:

- If you're writing code for a new software release, that's fundamental, because you're improving the product. But if you're creating a policy about writing software then you're one level removed.

- If you're testing a better way to assemble a product, that's fundamental. But if you're working on a task force to develop a suggestion system then you're one level removed.

- If you're talking *to* a customer, that's fundamental. If you're talking *about* customers you're probably one level removed.

- If you're involved in anything on the list below, you're one level removed from the fundamentals of your company and you will not be missed if you are abducted by aliens.

<u>NOT FUNDAMENTAL</u>

Quality Faire
Process Improvement Team

*When I refer to "product" I mean the entire product experience from the customer's perspective, including the delivery, image, and channel.

Recognition Committee
Employee satisfaction survey
Suggestion system
ISO 9000
Standards
Policy improvement
Reorganization
Budget process
Writing Vision Statements
Writing Mission Statements
Writing an "approved equipment list"

These "one off" activities are irresistible. You can make a convincing argument for all of them. You couldn't run a company, for example, without a budget process. I'm not suggesting you try. But I think you can focus more of your energy on the fundamentals (people and product) by following a simple rule for all the "one off" activities.

Rule for "one off" activities: consistency. Resist the urge to tinker. It's always tempting to "improve" the organizational structure, or to rewrite the company policy to address a new situation, or to create committees to improve employee morale. Individually, all those things seem to make sense. But experience shows that you generally end up with something that is no more effective that what you started with.

For example, companies tinker endlessly with the formula for employee compensation. Rarely does this result in happier and more productive employees. The employees redirect their energies toward griping and preparing résumés, the managers redirect their energies toward explaining and justifying the new system.

The rule of consistency would direct you toward keeping your current compensation plan—warts and all—unless it's a true abomination. The company that focuses on fundamentals will generate enough income to make any compensation plan seem adequate.

The best example of a fruitless, "one off" activity that seems like a good idea is the reorganization. Have you ever seen an internal company reorganization that dramatically improved either the effectiveness of the employees or the quality of the product?

Sometimes there are indirect benefits because a reorganization is a good excuse for weeding out the ninnies, but that hardly justifies the disruption. The rule of consistency would say it's best to keep the organization as it is, unless there's a fundamental shift in the business. Add or subtract people as needed, but leave the framework alone. Let the employees spend time on something besides reordering business cards.

Many of the "one off" activities start taking care of themselves if you're doing a good job with your people and your products. A company with a good product rarely needs a Mission Statement. Effective employees will suggest improvements without being on a Quality Team. Nobody will miss the Employee Recognition Committee if the managers are effective and routinely recognize good performance. The budget process will suddenly look very simple if you're making money (by focusing on your products).

As far as consistency goes, I would make an exception for changes that are radical enough to qualify as "reengineering" a process. It's the fiddling I object to, not elimination or major streamlining.

If you buy my argument that too much energy is being spent on the "one off" activities, the next question is how to focus on the fundamentals of making your people more effective and your products more desirable.

I'm here to help.

OUT AT FIVE

I developed a conceptual model for a perfect company. The primary objective of this company is to make the employees as effective as possible. I figure the best products usually come from the most effective employees, so employee effectiveness is the most fundamental of the fundamentals.

The goal of my hypothetical company is to get the best work out of the employees and make sure they leave work by five o'clock. Finishing by five o'clock is so central to everything that follows that I named the company OA5 (Out at Five) to reinforce the point. If you let this part of the concept slip, the rest of it falls apart. You'll see why.

In today's corporate environment the employee who walks out the door at five P.M. is held in lower regard than a Michael Jackson Day Care Center. The goal of OA5 is to change that—to guarantee that the employee who leaves at five P.M. has done a full share of work and everybody realizes it. For that to happen, the OA5 company has to do things differently than an ordinary company.

Companies use a lot of energy trying to increase employee satisfaction. That's very nice of them, but let's face it—work sucks. If people liked work they'd do it for free. The reason we have to pay people to work is that work is inherently unpleasant compared to the alternatives. At OA5 we recognize that the best way to make employees satisfied about their work is to help them get away from it as much as possible.

An OA5 company isn't willing to settle for less productivity from the employees, just less time. The underlying assumptions for OA5 are:

- Happy employees are more productive and creative than unhappy ones.

- There's a limit to how much happiness you can get while you're at work. Big gains in happiness can only be made by spending more time away from work.

- The average person is only mentally productive a few hours a day no matter how many hours are "worked."

- People know how to compress their activities to fit a reduced time. Doing so increases both their energy and their interest. The payoff is direct and personal—they go home early.

- A company *can't* do much to stimulate happiness and creativity, but it can do a lot to kill them. The trick for the company is to stay out of the way. When companies try to encourage creativity it's like a bear dancing with an ant. Sooner or later the ant will realize it's a bad idea, although the bear might not.

STAYING OUT OF THE WAY

Most people are creative by nature and happy by default. It doesn't seem that way because modern management is designed to squash those impulses. An OA5 company is designed to stay out of the way and let the good things happen. Here's how:

1. Let the employees dress any way they want, decorate their work spaces any way they want, format memos any way they want. Nobody has ever demonstrated that these areas have an impact on productivity. But when you "manage" those things you send a clear signal that conformity is valued above either efficiency or creativity. It's better to get out of the way and reinforce the message that you expect people to focus on what is important.

   I stop short of recommending that employees should use any kind of computer that they want. Every situation is different, but there can be overriding efficiency considerations for keeping a standard computer type. Efficiency has to be a higher principle than creativity, otherwise you have chaos.

2. Eliminate any artificial "creativity" processes in the company, such as the Employee Suggestion Plan or Quality Teams. Creativity comes naturally when you've done everything else right. If you have a good e-mail system, a stable organization chart, and an unstressed workplace the good ideas will get to the right person without any help. The main thing is to let people know that creativity is okay and get out of the way.

WHAT DOES AN OA5 MANAGER DO?

"Staying out of the way" isn't much of a job description for a manager. So if you want to be a manager in an OA5 company you'll need to do some actual work too. Here are the most useful activities I can think of for a manager.

1. Eliminate the assholes. Nothing can drain the life-force out of your employees as much as a few sadistic assholes who seem to exist for the sole purpose of making life hard for others.

Sadly, assholes often have important job skills that you'd like to keep. My advice is that it's never worth the tradeoff. In an OA5 company if you're making your co-workers unhappy, then you're incompetent by definition. It's okay to be "tough" and it's okay to be "aggressive" and it's okay to disagree—even shout. That's not necessarily being an asshole. Some conflict is healthy. But if you do it with disrespect, or you seem to be enjoying it, or you do it in every situation, guess what—you're an asshole. And you're gone.

2. Make sure your employees are learning something every day. Ideally, they should learn things that directly help on the job, but learning anything at all should be encouraged. The more you know, the more connections form in your brain, and the easier every task becomes. Learning creates job satisfaction and supports a person's ego and energy level. As an OA5 manager you need to make sure every person is learning something every day. Here are some ways you can ensure that people are learning daily:

- Support requests for training even when not directly job related.

- Share your own knowledge freely and ask others to do the same, ideally in small digestible chunks.

- Make trade magazines and newspapers available.

- If the budget allows, try to keep employees in current computers and software. Make Internet connections available.

- Support experimentation sometimes even when you know it's doomed (if the cost is low).

- Make "teaching" a part of everybody's job description. Reward employees who do a good job of communicating useful information to co-workers.

3. Collectively all the little things create an environment that supports curiosity and learning. Imagine a job where after you've screwed up your boss says "What did you learn?" instead of "What the hell were you thinking?"

4. Teach employees how to be efficient. Lead by example, but also continuously reinforce the following behaviors in others:

- Do creative work in the morning and do routine, brainless work in the afternoon. For example, staff meetings should be held in the afternoon (if at all). This can have a huge impact on people's actual and perceived effectiveness.

- Keep meetings short. Get to the point and get on. Make it clear that brevity and clarity are prized. The reward for brevity is the ability to leave at five o'clock with a clear conscience. Every company says brevity is good but only an OA5 company rewards it directly.

- Blow off low-priority activities and make it clear why. Don't be sucked into an activity because it's the polite thing to do. If it's a "one off" activity, say no. Say why you're saying no. Be direct.

- Respectfully interrupt people who talk too long without getting to the point. At first it will seem rude. Eventually it gives everybody permission to do the same, and that's a tradeoff that can be appreciated. Remember, there's a reward—you get out at five.

- Be efficient in the little things. For example, rather than have some Byzantine process for doling out office supplies, add $25 a month to each employee's paycheck as a "supply stipend" and let employees buy whatever they need from their local store. If they spend less, they keep the difference.

- If you create an internal memo with a typo, just line it out and send it. Never reprint it. Better yet, stick with e-mail.

THE BIG FINISH

A culture of efficiency starts with the everyday things that you can directly control: clothes, meeting lengths, conversations with co-workers, and the like. The way you approach these everyday activities establishes the culture that will drive your fundamental activities.

What message does a company send when it huddles its managers together for several days to produce a Mission Statement that sounds something like this:

"We design integrated world-class solutions on a worldwide basis."

Answer: It sends a message that the managers can't write, can't think, and can't identify priorities.

Managers are obsessed with the "big picture." They look for the big picture in Vision Statements and Mission Statements and Quality Programs. I think the big picture is hiding in the details. It's in the clothes, the office supplies, the casual comments, and the coffee. I'm all for working on the big picture, if you know where to find it.

Finally—and this is the last time I'm going to say it—we're all idiots and we're going to make mistakes. That's not necessarily bad. I have a saying: "Creativity is allowing yourself to make mistakes. Art is knowing which ones to keep."

Keep your people fresh, happy, and efficient. Set a target, then get out of the way. Let art happen. Sometimes idiots can accomplish wonderful things.

TALES OF COMPANIES THAT TURN ON THEMSELVES

Here are some of my favorite stories of employees who need to be weeded out.

From: (name withheld)
To: scottadams@aol.com

Scott,

Let me relate an incident that typifies a bizarre trait of the "squirrel" human condition.

Desperate to resolve a bad customer problem with a dead system, the techie finally isolates the cause and needs a replacement widget.

It is after hours. Using every informal channel he knows, he finally tracks down the emergency store man who, surprisingly, isn't too miffed about the late-night call. They read the runes (microfiche), find the right part number, check the stores database, and find one in a depot close by.

"Great—that's a relief!"

"Whoa—I can't let you have THAT."

"Why not!?" (Mounting hysteria . . .)

"That's the last one—if I let you have that, I'd be out of stock!"

. . . agonized scream cut short by dial tone . . .

From: (name withheld)
To: scottadams@aol.com

Scott,

I have yet to convince anyone that the following actually happened.

Shortly after taking my first job, I submitted a trip report and expense account only to have it returned to my desk because one item "violated company policy." Being a concerned employee, I immediately contacted the soon-to-be-retired career bureaucrat in charge, expressed my contrition, and requested a copy of the company policies so as to avoid another violation. The bureaucrat informed me that company policies were secret and not for general distribution, as then "everyone would know them."

After a moment of silent contemplation, I slunk back to my desk, realizing that I was clearly outclassed.

From: (name withheld)
To: scottadams@aol.com

Scott,

The MIS manager, who doesn't know anything about computers, buys computers one at a time so he can purchase them on his personal credit card. He then files for reimbursement on his expense account. Why does he do this? To acquire frequent flyer miles given by his credit card company. Therefore, it takes an entire year to buy twenty computers.

From: (name withheld)
To: scottadams@aol.com

Scott,

This happened to one of my cubie-mates.

He uses a Daytimer to keep track of appointments, deadlines, etc. This being December, he went (as he has each previous December) to the "Supply Sergeant" (our director's secretary) to get his refill. She informed him that she had only ordered for "management" (of which he was not) and a few others. Obviously, he was not on that list either.

However, he was told that if he were to bring his old one ('94) to her (in order to prove that he does use it), she would give him a new insert.

His response . . . "Thanks anyway, I'll find some other way to keep my notes and appointments." Being the inventive software engineer that he is, he now has numerous paper towels (from the rest room) hanging from his desk bookshelf.

From: (name withheld)
To: scottadams@aol.com

Scott,

   I'm currently a senior software engineer at [company]. I'm rather young (twenty-four), so am looked down upon by one of our more "experienced" engineers.
   During a design meeting I was running, this guy stood up and started saying I was completely off base and what I was proposing would never work. When asked for an alternative he went barreling off into a confused discussion of a different topic. He finally declared that we had to do things his way even though "his way" was a rather unclear concept, and did not address our design problem.
   When asked to justify his position, the man replied, "I have years of experience." When pressed for a more descriptive justification he clarified things a bit. "I have years of experience—you wouldn't understand."
   Needless to say he wasn't invited to future meetings.

From: (name withheld)
To: scottadams@aol.com

Scott,

   True story:
   A customer requests a product and we order it for him. The guy in shipping says okay and enters them into his database. After a few days, the customer calls to ask where his order is. We call to shipping and the shipper guy says, "Oh yeah, I couldn't find the customer in my database so I canceled the order." (Of course, without telling any-

body.) So we ask the shipping guy to search his database right now for the ORDER NUMBER he gave us. He responds, "Nope, I can't find that customer's name in my database." So then we ask him "Okay, now try searching on the ORDER NUMBER you gave us." He says, "Oh, here it is–yeah, it says I canceled that order because I couldn't find them in the database." Hmmm.

From: (name withheld)
To: scottadams@aol.com

Scott,

   Our company is so bad we actually have an engineers union. During our latest negotiations the company representative told the union that one of their demands is to reduce our lunch hour from the present forty-two minutes (yes— exactly forty-two minutes— even a buzzer rings)—to thirty minutes. When asked why, the company representative said that it's because not enough people are using the cafeteria—if the lunch hour is only thirty minutes, no one will be able to go out to lunch; therefore they will have to use the cafeteria. It seems that they are losing money!! (By the way, the food really stinks there.)

From: (name withheld)
To: scottadams@aol.com

Scott,

   A few weeks ago, I overheard a discussion in the hall about a new, company-wide software QA manual. I listened in and heard it mentioned that the preamble decreed that all employees developing or using software for sensitive work are obliged to conform to the procedures described in the manual. This is essentially everything that I do. Kind of odd that I only found out about it by overhearing a conversation.

So, I head off to the documents people and ask for a copy. The guy there says, "I can't give you a copy of that, it's protected."

"Well, how do I get one?"

"You need this form filled out with all of these managers' signatures."

"But it says right at the front of this document that I am obliged to do what it says, or else!"

He looked up at me suspiciously and asked, "How do you know that?"

I gave up and took a copy of the form.

From: (name withheld)
To: scottadams@aol.com

Scott,

This really happened:

We recently moved into a new building. Since all companies are worried about showing a profit, it's no longer automatic just to order lots of supplies or all of the chairs, cabinets, and things everyone wants. Nothing is ordered if it isn't requested.

Our modular furniture had been delivered and assembled. Shortly after, the "white boards" were delivered and mounted on the walls. At an executive staff meeting the question was asked "Will we be getting board markers and erasers?"

The response from the manager responsible for supplies was,

"Well, I don't think so . . . it seems to me the boards get written on once and then never erased."

After seeing the expression on everyone's face, he added, "Maybe I should rethink that one."

From: (name withheld)
To: scottadams@aol.com

Scott,

One of the things I like most about my current job is that I haven't felt impelled to scream, "I'm living in a Dilbert cartoon!" every five minutes, unlike I was in my previous job.

Well, that was something I used to like. Until now.

I will describe [company] Soda Situation to you in hopes that you'll find something amusing in our misery, something that you can use to torture Dilbert and Wally.

We have until recently been a little startup company. Like most startup companies, our company does everything it can to keep us here working. Continuously. It does its best to make sure we don't leave our desks. It trucks in food, juice, soda, espresso machines, video games, and all the comforts of home. Or it used to, anyway.

The food was the first to go. We were told it was being "evaluated," which is apparently shorthand for "suspended, and we hope you'll forget about it soon and not hassle us." Next, we were told that we'd be charged $3 to get replacement access cards, because "people were 'losing' them too often."

The quotes around "losing" in the e-mail infuriated a lot of people. What, we're losing our cards *on purpose*????? Is there some kind of black market in access cards? Huh?

The free juice and soda seemed unassailable, until now.

We noticed two weeks ago that the refrigerators were looking a little empty. Popular soda types were gone, the milk for the espresso machines was just a distant memory, and the juice bottles were looking pretty scant.

Things continued like this for days, getting slowly worse as people moved on from the good sodas to consume the yucky sodas. Eventually, the fridges were totally emptied, and people started sending e-mail to our facilities people.

This is the answer they got, sent to the whole company, with the name of the culprit deleted:

Hello all:

We are currently going through a cost-cutting "experiment" with coffee, beverages, kitchen supplies, and office supplies. We have temporarily asked our vendors to cut down on our usual weekly inventory.

During this experiment, we hope to determine what kind of beverages and coffee are consumed more than others. We hope to find out what flavors of juices/Calistoga water/sodas we can eliminate, so that we can make sure that we'll never be understocked of those more popular items or overstocked on those that are less popular.

The very same goes for office supplies. We're trying to determine how many different kinds of pens/paper/envelopes/etc. we really need to stock.

We'll continue to order special items that you request. All we ask is to keep the cost down. A $15 Rolodex will do the same as a $50 one. Please use good judgment.

So please bear with us. I will be monitoring both beverage and coffee inventory as well as office supplies during this experiment. If we are low or out of coffee/water/soda/milk/etc., please keep me informed. The same goes for office supplies. In the meantime, please check our other kitchens and supply rooms on other floors to get what you're looking for. It would also be appreciated and beneficial if you would use each product to its fullest. Which means finishing your can of soda before grabbing another one or using some of our used binders before grabbing a new one.

You can also help us by keeping our kitchens and supply rooms clean as you would in your own home.

Thanks for your help. I will inform you as soon as this experiment is complete.

-K

I think the rest of the story should be allowed to tell itself. Here are some responses to that e-mail, and the mysterious K's replies.

Reply and response pair one:

K:

We're not sure how cutting down on beverage inventory will help determine usage. With reduced inventory our preferred drinks run out and we're forced to consume inferior beverages.

For example, I prefer to drink Coke. The building is now out of Coke, so I drink root beer instead. The problem is, I hate root beer. I drink it only because I need caffeine and root beer is better than any of the other alternatives. However, since I'm drinking root beer, you will think there is a demand for it and will order even more. Furthermore, since I'm drinking root beer more than Coke, you'll think I like it and will order more root beer than Coke in the future.

Yikes!

It seems that an effective way to monitor consumption would be to order large, equal amounts of each beverage, wait a week, and then see how much of each beverage is left.

-T

―――-

T:

Excellent point! But, if you are an avid Coke drinker like you say you are, then you'll be willing to go to different floors to find your Coke. I know we have Coke here on the first floor. It's a bit inconvenient, but you may find it to be worth the trip. I myself am an avid Diet Coke drinker. I do like root beer, Mountain Dew, as well as Coke, but I prefer Diet Coke. So I'm willing to check other floors first before I go to my alternate choice. But that's just me.

-K

―――-

Reply and response pair two:

―――-

K, forgive me for sounding rude, but this is ridiculous. I am not willing to interrupt the important work I'm doing here on the third floor to wander around the other two floors checking to see whether or not there is any of the drink I prefer. Wandering like this is a serious drain on my productivity, and will just make me mad if I don't find what I'm looking for on some other floor. Having some drinks sometimes available on some floors is not a reasonable alternative.

If your goal is to determine which drinks people prefer, then the scheme of ordering fewer of all drinks will definitely lead to skewed results, as T pointed out. People will drink things that are not their preference, simply because their preference is not available.

I have been drinking only apple juice recently. Several times in the last few weeks, there has been no apple juice, so I didn't drink anything and was in a bad mood instead. I'm not sure how this helps your experiment but maybe it's data you want to know.

—J

——-

J:

Thanks for your data!

—K

——-

Reply and response pair three:

——-

K:

The shortage of juice is making me very angry. There is no juice at all in the third-floor refrigerator. I don't drink carbonated things, so the Veryfine juice is the only thing provided by the company that I will drink.

Our old ration of juice was already small enough that we usually ran out of juice before the refrigerator got restocked. Now it seems that we have even less juice and we're out even in the morning.

I started eating lunch before noticing the lack of juice. I am very thirsty, annoyed, and have a lot of work to do. I am now going to have to visit all the other floors to find out if there's anything I can drink in the building.

Did you change the drink order to create an artificial shortage? Why?

This is really inconvenient for me!!

—D

——-

D:
>Did you change the drink order to create an artificial shortage?
YES!
>Why?
A DECISION THAT WAS NOT MINE. AGAIN, IT'S ONLY IN
ITS EXPERIMENTAL STAGE AND WILL BE INCREASED
SHORTLY.
>This is really inconvenient for me!!
I APOLOGIZE. I'M ONLY DOING WHAT I WAS TOLD.
—K

———

Is K channeling Catbert?
I think they'd have outraged fewer people if they just started
charging for soda. Meanwhile, we continue to purchase expensive
[equipment] and pay useless employees. I think we should just pay
for the soda by taking just one employee out back and shooting
him/her. I suggested that we choose the employee by a company-
wide vote. Nobody's yet told me I'm insane.

THERE'S HOPE

Last, here's my favorite e-mail message of all time. It gives me hope that
our species has a chance of surviving.

From: (name withheld)
To: scottadams@aol.com

Scott,

When I was younger, I made a trip to Chicago. When I got out of a cab, my umbrella fell on the street and got run over before I could retrieve it. When I submitted my expense report, I put in $15 for my umbrella. Naturally the accountant disallowed it. Next time I put in an expense report, at the bottom I wrote, "Now find the umbrella!"

THE
DILBERT™
FUTURE

THE
DILBERT™
FUTURE

Thriving on Business Stupidity in
the 21st Century

SCOTT ADAMS

HarperBusiness
A Division of HarperCollins*Publishers*

A hardcover edition of this book was published in 1997 by HarperBusiness, a division of HarperCollins Publishers.

First paperback edition published 1998.

Designed by Nancy Singer

The Library of Congress has catalogued the hardcover edition as follows:

Adams, Scott, 1957–
    The Dilbert future : thriving on stupidity in the 21st
century / by Scott Adams. — 1st ed.
      p. cm.
   ISBN 0-88730-866-X
   1. American wit and humor. I. Title.
PN6162.A345 1997
741.5'973—dc21   97-7137

ISBN 0-88730-910-0 (pbk.)

98 99 00 01 02 ❖/RRD 10 9 8 7 6 5 4 3 2 1

Dedicated to my parents,
Paul and Virginia Adams,
so they won't be too mad that
I made jokes about them

CONTENTS

FOREWORD   xi

INTRODUCTION   1

1   HOW TO PREDICT THE FUTURE   5

Adams's Rule of the Unexpected 5
Adams's Rule of Self-Defeating Prophecies 6
Adams's Rule of Logical Limits 6

2   AGING   9

Retirement 11
Genetically Engineered Children 11
Children Are Our Future 12

3   TECHNOLOGY PREDICTIONS   17

Life Will Not Be Like *Star Trek* 17
Technology to Avoid Work 26
The Future of the Internet 29
Clothing of the Future 31
The Network Computer versus the Personal Computer 33
ISDN 40
The Bozo Filter 46
Censorship on the Internet 50
Technology Makes Us Less Productive 53
Energy Sources 56
Technology as the Leading Cause of Death 58

Men Who Use Computers—The New Sex Symbols 65

4   LIFE ON OTHER PLANETS   **71**

5   THE WORLD GETS MORE COMPLICATED   **75**

The Incompetence Line .80
Your Busy Life 89
Household Services 89

6   THE FUTURE OF DEMOCRACY AND CAPITALISM   **93**

The Future of Voting 96
Vote Deflation 99
The Rise of the Hairy Reasoners 101

7   THE FUTURE OF GENDER RELATIONS   **105**

Sex in the Future 105
Women in Charge 107
Technology to Free Men 115

8   THE FUTURE OF WORK   **119**

The Future of Managers 119
Employee Motivation 123
The Revenge of the Downsized 126
The Job Search in the Future 129
Outsourcing 134
The Job Model of the Future 136
The Future of Telecommuting 143
The Future of Office Workstations 149
Acronyms Shortages 155
Industrial Espionage .158

9 MARKETING IN THE FUTURE   159

Spiderweb Marketing Strategy 166
Markets of the Future .170

10 GOOD AND BAD JOBS OF THE FUTURE   173

Mothers, Don't Let Your Children Grow Up to Be Vendors. . .178
Procurement 180
Temp 181
Accounting, Auditing, and Dentistry 183
Venture Capitalist 186
Records Retention 188
Get Paid to Criticize Others 189

11 SOCIAL STUFF   191

Poverty 191
The Age of Consent 192
Crime 193
News in the Future 199
Parent Licenses 204
Euthanasia 206
Privacy 208
Pet Services 211
Food in the Future 213

12 ENDANGERED SPECIES   217

13 SOME THINGS WON'T IMPROVE   221

Airlines 221
Bicycle Seats 222

14 A NEW VIEW OF THE FUTURE   **225**

The Double Slit Experiment .231
Objects Move 235
Gravity Exists 236
Cause and Effect 240
Chaos Theory 244
Affirmations 246

POSTSCRIPT TO CHAPTER 14: MORE WEIRD STUFF   **255**

Gravity Rebuttals 255
Revenge of the Skeptics 258
More on Skeptics (Pun Intended) 260
My Unified Field Theory 264

APPENDIX A: AFFIRMATIONS TECHNIQUE   **269**

APPENDIX B: DISCLAIMERS OF ORIGINALITY   **273**

FOREWORD

In the brief period since *The Dilbert Future* appeared in hardcover, several of my predictions have already come true. This has not always been a good thing.

My prediction 51 stated, "In the future, the media will kill famous people to generate news that people will care about." That prediction was published just a few months before Princess Di's tragic death. Many readers noticed the spooky accuracy of my prediction and wondered if I might have been driving the mystery car in the tunnel. For the record, I was home inking cartoons that night. Yes, I was legally drunk, but I find that it helps me maintain the level of artistic expression that *Dilbert* is known for.

My prediction 30 was a bull's-eye too. I said, "Most scientific and technical breakthroughs in the next century will be created by men and directed at finding replacements for women." The biggest science story of the year was the cloning of Dolly the sheep. Do you think scientists are perfecting cloning so they can have more wool? I don't think so. I'll bet that within ten years you'll see supermodels selling bits of their own DNA to offshore corporations who will grow mail-order brides and sell them to grotesque millionaires in other countries.

My prediction 49 is also shaping up the way I predicted. I said, "In the future, new technology will allow police to solve 100 percent of all crimes. The bad news is that we'll realize 100 percent of the population are criminals, including the police." Consider the Kenneth Starr Whitewater investigations. Practically every person that his investigators talk to—including the witnesses—ends up being accused of a crime by someone. The investigators have kicked up everything from illegal billing of law clients to obstruction of justice to illegal taping of conversations to perjury to bigamy to you-name-it. Even some Arkansas state troopers are accused of lying. As

I predicted, the police are no more law-abiding than anyone else. With the possible exceptions of you and me, everyone in the world seems to be a lying, law-breaking weasel.

Lastly, in number 18 I predicted, "In the future, computer-using men will be the sexiest males." Many computer-using males wrote to tell me they weren't seeing the signs of that yet. Be patient. As you can see, my track record is very good. But in the unlikely event that I'm wrong, you computer-using males might want to start saving your money for a supermodel clone. They should be shipping in about twenty years.

INTRODUCTION

There are two types of people in the world: the bright and attractive people like yourself who read *Dilbert* books, and the 6 billion idiots who get in our way. Since we're outnumbered, it's a good idea not to refer to them as idiots to their faces. A devious *Dilbert* reader suggested calling them "Induh-viduals" instead. The advantage to this word is that you can insult someone without risk of physical harm. Example:

You: You're quite an Induhvidual, Tim.

Tim: Thank you.

If you're not already surrounded by Induhviduals, you will be soon. New ones are being born every minute, despite the complexity involved in breeding. Frankly, I think much of the procreation of Induhviduals happens purely by accident when two of them are trying to do something complicated—like jump-start a car—and they suddenly get confused. Whatever causes the breeding—and I truly don't want to know the details—it's safe to assume there will be more of it.

The way I see it, you have three good strategies for thriving in a future full of Induhviduals:

1. Wear loose clothing and pretend your car battery is dead.

2. Keep Induhviduals in your car so you can use the car-pool lane.

3. Harness the stupidity of Induhviduals for your own financial gain.

Option one is dangerous. I recommend that you stay away from anything that involves Induhviduals, electricity, and sex. It's just common sense.

Option two requires you to be in your car with Induhviduals for long periods of time. There is a real risk that they will attempt to make conversation. That would negate any benefits you get from avoiding traffic congestion. And if you accidentally leave them in the car and forget to crack the window open, they'll die. You'll need more than one of those little Christmas-tree air fresheners to solve that problem.

I recommend option three: Harness the stupidity of Induhviduals for your own financial gain. In order to do that, you'll need to be able to anticipate their moves well in advance. This can be difficult, because the average Induhvidual does not anticipate his own moves in advance.

If you asked the average Induhvidual about his plans, he'd say he has no plans. But if you yanked the eight-track tape player out of that Induhvidual's Pinto and then repeatedly hit that average Induhvidual with it, you could make him confess that he has some plans, even if those plans are not very exciting:

Average Induhvidual's Plans

- Become shorter and more crotchety over time.

- Lose all appreciation of popular music.

- Cultivate ear hair.

- Get a new eight-track player.

Clearly, with a world full of people who have goals like that, most of the things that happen in the future will not be the result of good planning. That makes the future difficult to predict. That's why you need this book.

I have compiled my predictions here so you won't have any unpleasant surprises during the next millennium. Any morning you're wondering whether it would be better to drown yourself in your cereal bowl or face 6 billion Induhviduals again, at least you'll be making an informed decision.

This book is an exhaustive analysis of the future, in the sense that if you held the book above your head for several hours, you would become exhausted. I recommend you do just that before reading it so you'll be groggy and won't notice that the paragraphs don't all fit together—like this next one.

I'm more of a sprinter than a marathoner when it comes to many aspects of life. For example, when I'm running. Over short distances—up to two yards—I can run faster than cheap panty hose on an itchy porcupine. But over long distances, I'm not so impressive.

I try to compensate for my lack of long-distance endurance by having good form. I'm told that my running style is quite majestic. That's probably because I learned to run by watching nature films in which leopards chased frightened zebras. Now when I run, I open my eyes real wide and let my tongue slap the side of my face. If you saw it, you'd be saying, "That's very majestic." And then you'd run like a frightened zebra. That's why my homeowners association voted to ask me to do my jogging with a pillowcase over my head.

If you think none of this is relevant to the future, you'd be oh-so-wrong, because it leads quite neatly to my first prediction:

PREDICTION 1

In the future, authors will take a long time to get to the point.
That way the book looks thicker.

There are many methods for predicting the future. For example, you can read horoscopes, tea leaves, tarot cards, or crystal balls. Collectively, these methods are known as "nutty methods." Or you can put well-researched facts into sophisticated computer models, more commonly referred to as "a complete waste of time." While these approaches have their advantages, none are appropriate for this book, because they require more work than sitting in front of my computer and typing. Instead, I will use these far-more-efficient methods to divine the future:

Methods for Divining the Future

1. My awesome powers of logic.

2. My crystal-clear observations.

3. My almost frightening intuition.

4. My total lack of guilt.

The future is an excellent topic for any author. By the time you realize I was wrong about everything I predicted, I will be dead. Business schools refer to that phenomenon as the "time value of money," or more colloquially as "GOOD LUCK GETTING A REFUND NOW!!"

Books about the future also have a nice upside potential. For example, let's say most of civilization is destroyed by some huge calamity. (That's not the good part.) And let's say a copy of this book somehow gets encased in amber and trapped in a tar pit. (It happens more often than you'd think. It happened to my brother. He makes a great conversation piece.) Eons from now, when our descendants find it (the book, not my brother), they will read my predictions and believe I was a wise holy man. I think I'll like that, except for the part about being dead.

As with my previous books, I will say a lot of obvious things that you already agree with, thereby making me look like a genius. But in a departure from the past, I will also say as many controversial and inflammatory things as I can (i.e., pretending to have actual opinions). If lots of gullible Induhviduals get mad at me, it might generate enough publicity to get me invited as a guest on *Larry King Live*. That's really the goal here. So if you see something that makes you mad, don't just sit there, organize a protest. I'll chip in for the poster boards and Magic Markers.

Throughout this book, I will delve into many areas in which I am thoroughly incompetent, including politics, history, economics, physiology, and particle physics. My intellectual shortcomings will manifest themselves as inaccuracies, misconceptions, and logical flaws. I recommend that you read it quickly so you won't notice.

ONE

HOW TO PREDICT THE FUTURE

Some people try to predict the future by assuming current trends will continue. This is a bad method. For example, if you applied that forecasting method to a puppy, you'd predict that the puppy would continue growing larger and larger until one day—in a fit of uncontrolled happiness—its wagging tail would destroy a major metropolitan area. But that rarely happens, thanks to the National Guard.

The future never follows trends, because of three rules I have named after myself in order to puff up my importance.

ADAMS'S RULE OF THE UNEXPECTED

Something unexpected always happens to wreck any good trend. Here are some examples to prove my point:

GOOD TREND	UNEXPECTED BAD THING
Computers allow us to work 100 percent faster.	Computers generate 300 percent more work.
Women get more political power.	Women are as dumb as men.
Popular music continues to get better.	I get old.

ADAMS'S RULE OF SELF-DEFEATING PROPHECIES

Whenever humans notice a bad trend, they try to change it. The prediction of doom causes people to do things differently and avoid the doom. Any doom that can be predicted won't happen.

Here are some examples of dooms that people predicted and how the indomitable human spirit rose to the challenge and thwarted the prediction:

PREDICTION OF DOOM	HUMAN RESPONSE
Population will grow faster than food supply.	Scientists realize you can call just about anything a "meat patty."
Petroleum reserves will be depleted in twenty years.	Scientists discover oil in their own hair.
Communism will spread to the rest of the world.	All Communists become ballerinas and defect.

I might have some of the details wrong; I'm working from memory here. But the point is that none of those predictions came true once we started worrying about them. That's the way it always works.

ADAMS'S RULE OF LOGICAL LIMITS

All trends have logical limits. For example, computers continue to shrink in size, but that trend will stop as soon as you hear this report on CNN:

This just in. A computer systems administrator sneezed, and his spray destroyed the entire military computing hardware of North America, leading to the conquest of the United States by Haitian bellhops. More on that later, but first our report on the healing powers of herbal tea.

At that point, we'll say, "Hey, maybe those computers were too small." That will be the end of the shrinking computer trend.

If all trends end, what can we look at to predict the future? There are some things in life so consistent that they are like immutable laws of human nature. You can predict most of the future by looking at these immutable laws and applying logic.

Immutable Laws of Human Nature

- Stupidity

- Selfishness

- Horniness

Those are the things that will never change, no matter what else does. People don't change their basic nature, they just accumulate more stuff upon which they can apply their stupidity, selfishness, and horniness. From this perspective, the future isn't hard to predict.

I realize that by telling you my secrets I'm not only opening my kimono, but I'm also doing jumping jacks in front of your picture window, if you catch my visual gist. But I'm not worried about you learning my secrets, because I'll always be one step ahead of you.

PREDICTION 2

In the future, you will wish I had never put the image in your head of me doing jumping jacks in an open kimono.

TWO

AGING

Human life expectancies increase every year. This is not necessarily a good thing.

PREDICTION 3

On average, Induhviduals who are alive today will experience 80 years of complaint-free living. Unfortunately, they'll live to 160.

The aging of Induhviduals will create some big challenges for businesses. Senior citizens are never in a hurry, and they're not willing to put up with any crap. The average retail transaction will take up to three days. It won't even be that quick unless stores start accepting as legal tender whatever elderly Induhviduals find in their pockets. Merchants will be forced to accept hard candy, tissues, and bird seed as payment. But that's okay. The merchants will handle it the same way they handle Canadian pennies and Kennedy fifty-cent pieces—by giving them to timid customers as change.

I make fun of senior citizens, but obviously I aspire to be one of them, the alternative being what it is. Unfortunately, not all older people will be pleasant, intelligent, and reasonable—the way I plan to be. Many will be Induhviduals who somehow managed to survive for years without ever eating anything from a container with a skull on it. This means trouble, because the only thing worse than being surrounded by Induhviduals is being surrounded by senior citizen Induhviduals.

Young Induhviduals sometimes feel pressure to keep their thoughts to themselves, but that impulse goes away over time. Eventually, we'll have several billion senior citizen Induhviduals who will feel the need to complain loudly about things they don't understand, which, as you can guess, will include just about everything. The cumulative noise from all that whining will cause planet-wide deafness in small animals.

However, there is a solution. It's called cryogenic freezing. The theory is that when someone has an incurable illness, you can freeze their bodies and then thaw them out in the future when scientists have invented a cure. This seems like a perfect solution, assuming we have enough storage space.

Cryogenic freezing has several advantages:

1. The Induhvidual pays for it himself.

2. Technically, it's not murder.

3. There's no gooey stuff to clean up.

4. You can convince their relatives to kiss them and watch the fun as their lips get frozen stuck.

All you have to do is convince the Induhviduals around you that they have incurable illnesses and cryogenics is their only hope. You'd get the hypochondriacs first. They'd be the easiest. You could get a few million more Induhviduals to sign up for the plan by sending them a computer virus through the Internet. You'd be surprised how many Induhviduals think they can get viruses from their computers.

For the rest of the Induhviduals, you'd need accomplices in the medical community. But I don't think it will be a problem because unlike retailers, doctors won't put up with being paid in hard candy, tissues, and bird seed.

RETIREMENT

Most people are not saving enough money for retirement. If you're one of them, I suggest you start exercising vigorously so that later in life you can bully your frail peers and take their stuff when you need it.

I often see senior citizens in the park practicing Tai Chi Chuan. The *alleged* purpose is to increase balance and energy or some such baloney. What ever happened to TAKING A WALK?

You don't need to learn lethal skills to increase balance and energy. It's obvious to me that those senior citizens are preparing to slap the bejeezus out of the rest of us and take our stuff. They're just biding their time and waiting for us to realize there isn't enough retirement money for everyone.

Many of you are saving money instead of exercising. It seems like a smart thing to do, but later you'll be cursing yourselves as you watch the Tai Chi experts carry your stuff away in huge boxes.

PREDICTION 4

The people who are studying Tai Chi Chuan instead of saving money are planning to beat us up and take our stuff when we're retired.

Don't say I didn't warn you.

GENETICALLY ENGINEERED CHILDREN

At some point—probably in your lifetime—we'll have the technology to make all children tall, lean, and muscular. They'll have smooth skin, perfect hair, good teeth, and 20/20 vision. All genetic abnormalities will be spotted and corrected in the womb. This is very good news for the people born in the future.

It is very bad news for those of you reading this book. We'll look like a hideous Quasimodo society to the perfect generation that will follow us. We'll not only be old, we'll have a whole range of physical imperfections that will make us appear repulsive to the young. They'll look like the cast of *Baywatch* and we'll look like extras on *The X-Files*.

PREDICTION 5

The people who are alive today will appear grotesque to the perfectly engineered children of the future.

This situation will cause an even greater rift between the older and younger generations. But it will also ease our guilt about plundering the planet and leaving our garbage and debt to those ungrateful little Barbie and Ken dolls. So it's not entirely bad.

CHILDREN ARE OUR FUTURE

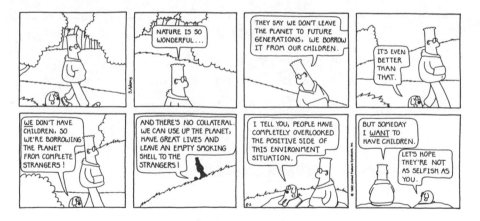

True Story

The scene is a grocery store. A father studies a can of chili. His ten-year-old son stands nearby. His mother is at the far end of the aisle picking up another item. I am one of a dozen other shoppers in this aisle. The father says to his son, "Ask your mother if Hormel chili is okay." The son turns and yells at the top of his lungs, "HEY MOM! IS HORMEL CHILI OKAY?!"

The children are our future. And that is why, ultimately, we're screwed unless we do something about it. If you haven't noticed, the children who are our future are good-looking, but they aren't all that bright. As dense as they might be, they will eventually notice that adults have spent all the money, spread disease, and turned the planet into a smoky, filthy ball of death. We're raising an entire generation of dumb, pissed-off kids who know where the handguns are kept. This is not a good recipe for a happy future.

Fortunately, there's a solution: Brainwashing.

PREDICTION 6

In the future, we will accelerate our successful practice of brainwashing children so they'll be nice to us while we plunder their planet.

Brainwashing the children is the only logical solution to our problems. The alternative is for adults to stop running up debts, polluting, and having reckless sex. For this to happen, several billion Induhviduals would have to become less stupid, selfish, and horny. This is not likely.

The path of least resistance is brainwashing the kids. We do it already in lots of ways and it works well. Obviously, we'll have to use a different word than "brainwashing." I suggest calling it "lessons in right and wrong," just as our parents did.

Children's brains are like fresh mashed potatoes that you can push around with your fork, making a little bowl to hold your gravy. If you get to them early, you create little citizens who grow up to enthusiastically volunteer for amazingly dangerous tasks—such as killing people in other countries.

I know you can't always tell when I'm kidding. So to be perfectly clear:

I'm *totally in favor of brainwashing*. Brainwashing works, which is why there will be a lot more of it in the future.

There are some forms of brainwashing that most of us will agree are good. This will form the baseline requirements for all kids in the future, just as it does today:

Acceptable Brainwashing

- Respect your elders.

- Worship God.

- Democracy is the best system.

- Just say no to drugs.

- Low-paying jobs are "honest work."

- Buy *Dilbert* products.

We'll need to add a few new brainwashing themes to prepare for the future.

Additional Brainwashing

- It is an honor to give your money to old, ugly people.

- It is a privilege to experience the pollution of previous generations.

- Wrinkles are sexy.

- Forgetfulness is a sign of wisdom.

- God likes it when you use all your money to pay interest on your parents' debts.

- Baldness, huge thighs, and potbellies are all signs of intelligence and sexual potency.

Some might say this view of the future is too cynical. They might say adults can learn to change their behavior and reverse the damage they're causing the planet, thus protecting the world for future generations. My response to this argument is, "There's no such thing as being TOO cynical."

THREE

TECHNOLOGY PREDICTIONS

LIFE WILL NOT BE LIKE *STAR TREK*

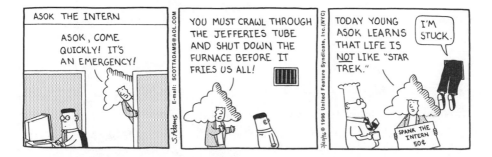

There are so many *Star Trek* spin-offs that it's easy to fool yourself into thinking that the *Star Trek* vision is an accurate vision of the future. Sadly, *Star Trek* does not take into account the stupidity, selfishness, and horniness of the average human being. In this chapter, I will explore some of the flaws in the *Star Trek* vision of the future.

PREDICTION 7

Life in the future will *not* be like *Star Trek*.

Medical Technology

On *Star Trek*, the doctors have handheld devices that instantly close any openings in the skin. Imagine that sort of device in the hands of your unscrupulous friends. They would sneak up behind you and seal your ass shut as a practical joke. The devices would be sold in novelty stores instead of medical outlets. All things considered, I'm happy that it's not easy to close other peoples' orifices.

Transporter

It would be great to be able to beam your molecules across space and then reassemble them. The only problem is that you have to trust your co-worker to operate the transporter. These are the same people who won't add paper to the photocopier or make a new pot of coffee after taking the last drop. I don't think they'll be double-checking the transporter coordinates. They'll be accidentally beaming people into walls, pets, and furniture. People will spend all their time apologizing for having inanimate objects protruding from parts of their bodies.

"Pay no attention to the knickknacks; I got beamed into a hutch yesterday."

If I could beam things from one place to another, I'd never leave the house. I'd sit in a big comfy chair and just start beaming groceries, stereo equipment, cheerleaders, and anything else I wanted right into my house. I'm fairly certain I would abuse this power. If anybody came to arrest me, I'd beam them into space. If I wanted some paintings for my walls, I'd beam the contents of the Louvre over to my place, pick out the good stuff, and beam the rest into my neighbor's garage.

If I were watching the news on television and didn't like what I heard, I would beam the anchorman into my living room during the commercial break, give him a vicious wedgie, and beam him back before anybody noticed.

I'd never worry about "keeping up with the Joneses," because as soon as they got something nice, it would disappear right out of their hands. My neighbors would have to use milk crates for furniture. And that's only after I had all the milk crates I would ever need for the rest of my life.

There's only one thing that could keep me from spending all my time wreaking havoc with the transporter: the holodeck.

Holodeck

For those of you who only watched the "old" *Star Trek*, the holodeck can create simulated worlds that look and feel just like the real thing. The characters on *Star Trek* use the holodeck for recreation during breaks from work. This is somewhat unrealistic. If I had a holodeck, I'd close the door and never come out until I died of exhaustion. It would be hard to convince me I should be anywhere but in the holodeck, getting my oil massage from Cindy Crawford and her simulated twin sister.

Holodecks would be very addicting. If there weren't enough holodecks to go around, I'd get the names of all the people who had reservations ahead of me and beam them into concrete walls. I'd feel tense about it, but that's exactly why I'd need a massage.

I'm afraid the holodeck will be society's last invention.

Sex with Aliens

According to *Star Trek,* there are many alien races populated with creatures who would like to have sex with humans. This would open up a lot of anatomical possibilities, but imagine the confusion. It's hard enough to have sex with human beings, much less humanoids. One wrong move and you're suddenly transported naked to the Gamma Quadrant to stand trial for who-knows-what. This could only add to performance anxiety. You would never be quite sure what moves would be sensual and what moves would be a galactic-sized mistake.

Me Trying to Have Sex with an Alien

Me: May I touch that?

Alien: That is not an erogenous zone. It is a separate corporeal being that has been attached to my body for six hundred years.

Me: It's cute. I wonder if it would let me have sex with it.

Alien: That's exactly what I said six hundred years ago.

The best part about having sex with aliens, according to the *Star Trek* model, is that the alien always dies a tragic death soon afterward. I don't have to tell you how many problems that would solve. Realistically, the future won't be that convenient.

Phasers

I would love to have a device that would stun people into unconsciousness without killing them. I would use it ten times a day. If I got bad service at the convenience store, I'd zap the clerk. If somebody with big hair sat in front of me at the theater, *zap*!

On *Star Trek*, there are no penalties for stunning people with phasers. It happens all the time. All you have to do is claim you were possessed by an alien entity. Apparently, that is viewed as a credible defense in the *Star*

Trek future. Imagine real criminals in a world where the "alien possession" defense is credible.

> **Criminal:** Yes, officer, I did steal that vehicle, and I did kill the occupants, but I was possessed by an evil alien entity.
>
> **Officer:** Well, okay. Move along.

I wish I had a phaser right now. My neighbor's dog likes to stand under my bedroom window on the other side of the fence and bark for hours at a time. My neighbor has employed the bold defense that he believes it might be another neighbor's dog, despite the fact that I am standing there looking at him barking only twenty feet away. In a situation like this, a phaser is really the best approach. I could squeeze off a clean shot through the willow tree. A phaser doesn't make much noise, so it wouldn't disturb anyone. Then the unhappy little dog and I could both get some sleep. If the neighbor complains, I'll explain that the phaser was fired by the other neighbor's dog, a known troublemaker who is said to be invisible.

And if that doesn't work, a photon torpedo is clearly indicated.

Cyborgs

Given the choice, I would rather be a cyborg instead of 100 percent human. I like the thought of technology becoming part of my body. As a human, I am constantly running to the toolbox in my garage to get a tool to deal with some new household malfunction. If I were a cyborg, I might have an electric drill on my arm, plus a metric socket set. That would save a lot of trips. From what I've seen, the cyborg concept is a modular design, so you can add whatever tools you think you'd use most.

I'd love to see crosshairs appear in my viewfinder every time I looked at someone. It would make me feel menacing, and I'd like that. I'd program myself so that anytime I saw a car salesman, a little message would appear in my viewfinder that said "Target Locked On."

It would also be great to have my computer built into my skull. That way I could surf the Net during useless periods of life, such as when people talk to me. All I'd have to do is initiate a head-nodding subroutine during boring conversations and I could amuse myself in my head all day long.

I think that if anyone could become a cyborg, there would be a huge rush of people getting in line for the conversion. Kids would like it for the look. Adults would like it for its utility. Cyborg technology has something for everyone. So, unlike *Star Trek*, I can imagine everyone wanting to be a cyborg.

The only downside I can see is that when the human part dies and you're at the funeral, the cyborg part will try to claw its way out of the casket and slay all the mourners. But that risk can be minimized by saying you have an important business meeting, so you can't make it to the service.

Shields

I wish I had an invisible force field. I'd use it all the time, especially around people who spit when they talk or get too close to my personal space. In fact, I'd probably need a shield quite a bit if I also had a phaser to play with.

I wouldn't need a big shield system like the one they use to protect the *Enterprise*, maybe just a belt-clip device for personal use. I could insult dangerous people without fear of retribution. Whatever crumbs of personality I now have would be completely unnecessary in the future. On the plus side, it would make shopping much more fun.

Shopping with Shields Up

Me: Ring this up for me, you unpleasant cretin.

Saleswoman: I oughta slug you!

Me: Try it. My shields are up.

Saleswoman: Damn!

Me: There's nothing you can do to harm me.

Saleswoman: I guess you're right. Would you like to open a charge account? Our interest rates are very reasonable.

Me: Nice try.

Tractor Beam

On *Star Trek,* they use tractor beams to retrieve damaged shuttle crafts. I think if that technology were available today, it would be used primarily by boring people to keep their victims within range. I'm glad there are no tractor beams.

Long-Range Sensors

If people had long-range sensors, they would rarely use them to scan for new signs of life. I think they would use them to avoid work. You could run a continuous scan for your boss and then quickly transport yourself out of the area when he came near. If your manager died in his office, you would know minutes before the authorities discovered him, and that means extra break time.

Vulcan Shoulder Massage

Before all you Trekkies write to correct me, I know there is no such thing as a Vulcan Death Grip even in *Star Trek*. But I wish there were. That would have come in handy many times. It would be easy to make the Vulcan Death Grip look like an accident.

"I was just straightening his collar and he collapsed."

I think the only thing that keeps most people from randomly killing other citizens is the bloody mess it makes and the high likelihood of getting caught. With the Vulcan Death Grip, it would be clean and virtually undetectable. Everybody would be killing people left and right. You wouldn't be able to have a decent conversation at the office over the sound of dead co-workers hitting the carpet. The most common sounds in corporate America would be, "I'm sorry I couldn't give you a bigger raise, but . . . erk!"

And that's why the future won't be like *Star Trek*.

TECHNOLOGY TO AVOID WORK

Much has been written—too much, really—about the technology for making workers more productive. What we really need is technology for helping workers goof off without detection. There's a much bigger market for that. Look at the numbers. For every boss who wants to make you work harder, there are a dozen employees who want to prevent it.

PREDICTION 8

In the future, there will be a huge market for technology products that help workers goof off and still get paid.

Naturally, most of the new goofing off technology will be disguised as productivity tools, just as the current ones are. Employees today goof off with the telephone, e-mail, Internet connections, and their computers. It all looks like work to the unsuspecting employer.

Managers will try to stop employees from any unsanctioned enjoyment at work. They know that enjoyment can lead to high morale and any number of other harmful things. Companies have a variety of technologies for preventing enjoyment. For example, bosses can check logs of phone calls, block access to fun Internet sites, and even snoop on your e-mail. This enjoyment-blocking technology is improving every day.

Companies will give employees ID badges that can be tracked anywhere in the building, so managers can tell how much time you spend reading the newspaper in the restroom, wandering the halls, and hanging out in the cafeteria.

The flaw with the locator-badge concept is that within a month of introduction, an underground market in counterfeit ID badges will spring up. Employees will lock their locator badges in desk drawers and roam freely wearing the fakes. They will not only be free, they will have the added psychological thrill of feeling like they're getting away with something.

It won't be difficult to thwart the locator-badge concept, but employees will need outside help to battle other forms of management-induced evil. That's why you'll see the emergence of a new industry dedicated to helping employees avoid work. I think you'll see advertisements like these in the near future:

Excuse 9000™

The patented Excuse 9000 device will add selected background noise to any phone conversation, giving you the perfect alibi for not being at work. Need a flat tire alibi? No problem. Just set the Excuse 9000 for "Highway Noise" and leave your boss a voice-mail message from the comfort of your own bed. Other noises in the basic starter pack include: airliner going down, deep-lung coughing, and armed intruder.

WorkSurfer™

Is your evil employer monitoring which web sites you visit during the day? Is it getting harder to satisfy your daily requirement of online comics, sports news, and pornography while pretending to work? We've got the answer in the WorkSurfer. We'll e-mail you the web pages you specify every day from a new, untraceable address. WorkSurfer costs only $20 per month, and our invoice lists the service as "Three Ring Binders," so you can hide it on a voucher and make your boss pay!

BuzzCut™

This advanced software will strip the buzzwords out of any e-mail you receive from your boss and give you what you need to know.

Example:

Boss's e-mail: We must facilitate the redesign of our core processes to optimize customer satisfaction.

BuzzCut Translation: Hey, I wrote a memo!

THE FUTURE OF THE INTERNET

Experts predict the Internet will slow down or blow up because of increasing traffic. They're all wrong. I know this because I'm a guy.

I remember the joy when my cartoon syndicate, United Media, told me they were upgrading the Dilbert Zone web site from a T1 link to a DS3. (DS3 is a very fast speed—a "big pipe" as they say in the business.)

When I told other people about the new DS3 pipe, I found myself sniffing smugly, yanking up my pants, taking a deep breath, and actually talking in a hillbilly drawl:

"Yup, we got us a DS3 now. Whatcha runnin' on yers?"

When I described my telecommunications superiority, I felt manly and powerful. Colors seemed more vivid. I felt alive, albeit alive as a hillbilly.

There are millions of people like me—males who care a great deal about the speed of the Internet. They want speed. They need it. They'll find a way to get it.

PREDICTION 9

In the future, Internet capacity will increase indefinitely to keep up with the egos of the people using it. Cost will not be an issue.

Obviously, there are millions of women using and building the Internet, too, but on average they don't care the same way men do. For women, the Internet is a tool. For men, it's personal. Men are obsessed about the size of their pipes, whereas women claim it "doesn't matter."

It won't be economical for companies to keep buying equipment to meet the growing Internet demand. At first glance, that would seem to be a big problem, but that economic gap can be filled through a common business process called "lying like a filthy weasel."

As I write this, technical professionals around the world are writing proposals for Internet funding and trying not to laugh so hard that they get spittle on the final hard copy. These proposals will make their way to high-ranking executives (mostly males) who will skim the document, become thoroughly boggled, and come away with just one message:

Your pipe is very small.

The frightened male executives will immediately approve funding for bigger pipes. Then they will sniff smugly, yank up their pants, take deep breaths, and begin talking with hillbilly drawls. It won't be pretty.

All of the technical professionals who created these lies will switch jobs with other professionals in their industry and begin implementing their predecessors' plans. Later, they'll all blame "the last guy" for lying about the true costs. This is how the Internet will be funded indefinitely.

CLOTHING OF THE FUTURE

My clothes don't do enough for me. All they do is cover my naughty parts and keep me warm. And they don't even do that right, because in the summer I'm too warm. My clothes are Induhviduals. I want smarter clothes.

PREDICTION 10

In the future, your clothes will be smarter than you.

I have great expectations for clothes of the future. I want my clothes to keep me at the perfect temperature all day. I want my clothes to tickle me when I'm sad. My clothes should sense danger and electrically stimulate my leg muscles so I run away before I even know what the problem is.

I want transmitters in my clothes to tell my house what room I'm in at all times. I will walk from room to room like Moses parting the Red Sea, the lighting and temperature adjusting to suit my personal preferences. The people who are already in those rooms won't like it one bit, but I'm sure Moses had his critics, too. You can't let the opinions of other people get to you.

I want my clothes to have a fake Batman-like muscular torso and head cover. That way I'll look more like a studly superhero and less like a little bald guy.

And I want a cellular phone built into the head cover so I have yet another way to insult gullible Induhviduals to their faces without fear of retribution.

> **Me:**   You're the most gullible imbecile I've ever met.
>
> **Induhvidual:**   What did you call me?
>
> **Me:**   Shhh! I'm on the phone.
>
> **Induhvidual:**   Oh, sorry.

I want my clothes to have stealth technology so I can avoid all the people who ask for my help. I want stealth technology that is so good, I can walk into a car dealer's lot carrying a tub full of cash and not draw any attention. I want to absorb radar so I can speed without getting caught. I want to leer at attractive women without detection. I want to sneeze on the buffet and blame the guy behind me.

I want clothes that have a nonstick surface so food stains slide off. I want clothes that can be cleaned by taking them outside and shaking them vigorously. (You'll be naked when you go outside because you'll only have one of these expensive garments. But it won't matter that much because the neighbors will think the person who lives in your house has much better torso muscles, so you must be a visitor.)

The clothes of the future will create some new risks. They'll be so valuable that muggers will steal your clothes and leave your wallet. Crooks will be frolicking around town in your jumpsuit making long distance calls with the built-in phone while you're hiding naked in an alley. And you won't be able to find help, because the other pedestrians will have the stealth feature of their own clothes turned on so people like you can't locate them.

It won't necessarily be a good thing to be the first person in your town to have the clothes of the future. For example, if someone wants to use your phone, you'll have to say no, because your only phone will be built into your clothes. If they insist, you'll have to let them wear your jumpsuit. When you try to get your clothes back, they'll turn on the stealth feature and disappear for days. Your friends will be taking joyrides in your jumpsuit while you're sitting around the house naked. That's why I don't make friends.

THE NETWORK COMPUTER VERSUS THE PERSONAL COMPUTER

Many technology forecasters are wondering whether the new breed of Network Computers (NCs) will replace Personal Computers (PCs). On the off chance that you are not familiar with the NC versus PC debate, allow me to provide some background:

> The NC is blah, blah, blah, Java, blah, blah, trying to screw Microsoft, blah, blah, no hard disk, blah, blah, Larry Ellison.

Those are the pertinent points. I'd give more details, but frankly, if you haven't heard of Network Computers already, you'll probably just skim this section looking for naughty words.

If you don't understand all of the technical issues, don't worry that you are an ignoramus. I will compensate by typing this section slowly. And you really don't need to know the technical differences between NCs and PCs in order to drink fully of the beauty and elegance of my arguments that follow.

You do need to know that an NC is essentially a PC with no hard drive (or a tiny one). An NC downloads software from the Internet and executes it on an as-needed basis. The main advantage of the NC is that it will be cheaper and easier to use than a PC—but it will do less.

The driving force behind the NC is the belief that the companies who brought us things like Unix, relational databases, and Windows can make an appliance that is inexpensive and easy to use if they choose to do that. This is a bit like hiring Doctor Kevorkian to be the physician at your day care center, but I'm getting ahead of my point here.

There have been many spirited and stimulating debates about the relative technical merits of the NC versus the PC. This debate is an important one primarily because technology magazines can't sell advertisements if the rest of the magazine is empty. The NC has filled that important void.

A brilliant futurist such as myself doesn't need to wallow around in the technical differences between the NC and the PC in order to make spookily accurate predictions. Let us instead find relevant parallels in history on which to base our prediction.

First, look at the arguments put forth by the proponents of the NC.

PRO-NC ARGUMENT	**COUNTERARGUMENT**
Many people will prefer a low-cost solution, even if it means giving up some functionality and prestige.	One word: Yugo.
The NC will be much easier to use than full-blown PCs, thus guaranteeing a dominant market share.	One word: Macintosh.
This new computing paradigm will neuter Microsoft's stranglehold on the PC industry.	One word: Bill.

Some people will argue that Bill Gates and Microsoft aren't smart enough to stop NC's threat to the PC market. But don't forget, Bill Gates is the guy who turned Apple Computer into a no-cost Microsoft R&D center and made everyone believe it was a separate company, thus reducing antitrust complaints. Then he launched Windows 95 to make it seem like he couldn't possibly be that smart.

How smart is he really? Smart enough not to let you know how smart he is. Or to put it another way, if he ever decides to slay a family member, I don't think you'll find his bloody glove at the scene.

Now let's say, for argument, that the NC started to become a big threat to Microsoft. Would Bill Gates watch the value of his $20 billion in Microsoft stock shrink to zero, or would he make one of the following strategic moves:

Potential Strategic Moves

1. Bundle a free NC with every copy of Windows 95.

2. Create strategic alliances with the NC companies and act "helpful."

I think you can see that either of these choices would work. So Microsoft should come out of this okay.

No matter what happens in the overall market, there will certainly be plenty of demand for NCs in places like prisons, libraries, and airports, but the home market will be hard to crack. The companies who make NCs will have to do some sophisticated market segmentation analysis. Or they can just read the sophisticated analysis that I include here for your convenience:

CUSTOMER PROFILE	LIKELY TO BUY
This person always wants the latest computer, no matter how complicated or expensive.	Personal Computer (PC) based on Intel chip and Windows software.
Same as above, but supports public television. Dreams of quitting job and becoming an artist. Might have a goatee.	Macintosh computer.
Same as first profile, but enjoys pain and has no friends. Might be portly and wear suspenders.	Unix workstation.
This person thinks that a computer would look lovely with the furniture and wants to "check out that Internet" someday to do some shopping and maybe book airline tickets. Might work in senior management.	Network Computer (NC).

This NC-buying group won't be able to handle too much complexity in a computer. The NC manufacturers know that, of course, but I predict they will still vastly overestimate the intelligence of the target market.

To illustrate my point, I heard this story about a computer technician who services corporate PCs:

True Story

> When the technician enters the office of especially clueless-looking managers, he gives them this computing advice: "Once in a while, you have to stretch the computer cables out straight. That's because the data is digital, which means it's all ones and zeroes. The zeroes can make it through the bent cable okay, because they have smooth edges, but the ones can get stuck."

I'll bet there are still managers throughout this technician's territory who straighten their cables on a regular basis. I'm guessing some even put binders beneath their PCs so the data will run downhill.

Do you need more convincing? A *Dilbert* reader recently told me this story.

True Story

> The copy machine was near a thermostat control box on the wall. An office prankster put a sign over the thermostat box with instructions to speak into the microphone to control the

copier with voice commands. There was much merriment when one member of the staff inserted his document in the copy machine, walked to the thermostat, and said, "Two copies, no staple."

Most new NC customers will take it out of the box and try to randomly plug the cables into whatever orifices they can find around the house, hoping to get lucky. If you see your neighbor's dog growling and scooting its tail on the ground, you can be sure its owner just got an NC.

Then there's the complex issue of whether the power needs to be turned on in order for the NC to function properly. That might seem silly to you Brainiacs who are smart enough to read *Dilbert* books, but believe me, many people are routinely stumped by this question.

If you call the tech support number for your computer and tell them that your printer is not working, the first question they will ask is, "Is it turned on?" If you pass that portion of the intelligence test they will ask, "Is it connected to your computer?"

They don't ask these questions simply to belittle you and insult your intelligence, although it's obvious they enjoy that aspect of the transaction, too. No, they ask because experience shows they can solve many problems with those two questions. You can never underestimate the stupidity of the general public.

I contend that the term "easy-to-use computer" is an oxymoron. The NC will be the physical proof. It will provide the final answer to the question, "Just how dumb are people, anyway?"

Despite the fact that the typical NC customer will be thoroughly unable to operate the device, I predict a healthy market demand. This prediction is based on an in-depth analysis of the kinds of products most similar to the NC: home exercise equipment.

I recently bought one of those trendy new exercise devices—the kind that builds muscles that are useful only for mowing your lawn and pulling on tight panty hose, neither of which I do. (I pay a guy to come over once a week to pull my tight panty hose on for me.)

When I first saw a picture of that fiendish-looking exercise device, I thought that it would be boring, painful, and annoying to use. But I was greatly influenced by the television commercial, which featured attractive women who do unrelated kinds of exercises in order to look the way they do. When I saw the ad, I said, "That's good enough for me!" and I dialed the 800 number immediately. After all, if you can't believe paid models, who can you believe? The exercise machine is in my garage under some boxes.

People will buy NCs for the same reason they buy exercise machines: an irrational need. People who buy exercise machines believe it will make them healthy and thin. People who will buy NCs will believe they will make them technically sophisticated and knowledgeable about the Web.

When I worked at Pacific Bell, one of my jobs was giving demonstrations of our fast digital telephone lines (ISDN, actually) to helpless, trapped customers who didn't know why they were there. We would lure them into the lab to watch stimulating technical displays such as "file transfers" and "digital telephony."

The customers' eyes would glaze over. Although we were showing them useful and valuable services, the demonstrations acted like verbal lobotomies. The poor, pathetic customers would sit there as though shot by boredom-filled darts. If we wanted to, I'm sure we could have put them into cages, loaded them into Range Rovers, and transported them to a remote forest for release. (We only did that once, and we caught hell for it.)

Toward the end of the demonstration, just before the customers' souls could abandon their cold, lifeless shells, I would fire up a demonstration of a new thing (it was new then) called the World Wide Web. The only thing you could do with the Web at the time was call up twelve dinosaur pictures and maybe look at some precious gems from the Smithsonian collection, unless their server wasn't working, which it usually wasn't. The Web was slow, unreliable, and totally void of useful information, but the customers' eyes would widen when they saw it. They would stand up and demand permission to use the mouse and click on this "Internet thing" themselves. Then they would start grilling me about what they needed to buy. They wanted to be able to look at dinosaurs and gems themselves. And they wanted it bad.

I witnessed pure technology lust. The customers were literally having a physical response to the Web. It was like a drug to them. And it happened to every type of customer we brought to the lab. It defied explanation. People became instantly irrational. They became immune to issues of value, cost, and complexity. All they knew is that they wanted it.

This experience convinced me that any analysis of the NC's merits is a waste of time. People will buy them. They will buy lots of them. Many will choose it over the PC simply because it costs less. They won't care that it has less functionality, because they are immune to the question of its value.

PREDICTION 11

In the future, Network Computers will be purchased and used with the same enthusiasm as home exercise equipment.

Or, as I like to say, "If you build it, they will be dumb."

ISDN

There are two things that any company needs in order to bring a bold new technology to market:

1. Stupidity.

2. See 1.

Whenever bold new technologies are created, the poor bastards who create them find out the market isn't ready or the technology isn't refined enough. The innovator rarely makes money. Then some clever company comes in and sees what went wrong, corrects the bone-headed mistakes, and makes it all work. In general, it is always better to be a clever company than a poor bastard.

So why would any company ever introduce a new technology knowing that the odds are stacked against them? They do it because they have just the right mix of stupidity and stock options. Thank goodness for that. Otherwise, civilization would never advance. We'd be sitting around in leaf beds picking bugs out of each other's fur. And frankly, I don't want to touch your fur.

Speaking of bugs in fur, let's talk about ISDN, a subject I know from my days as an employee at Pacific Bell. If you're not familiar with ISDN, the letters represent four words that don't mean anything useful when you string them all together. This is a perfect metaphor for ISDN, and, in retrospect, I'm certain it's what the developers intended.

The basic idea with ISDN is that your local phone company can convert your existing telephone wires into a nifty high-speed digital path from you to anyplace else. You can use ISDN lines for everything from phone calls to video conferencing. Most people use ISDN to connect to the Internet at speeds up to 128 kilobits per second. This improves productivity, because it allows you to view online *Dilbert* cartoons without cutting into your work time. The phone companies don't spell that out in the brochures, but I think we all know what they mean.

According to the telephone companies, ISDN is very "flexible," meaning it can do many things. According to the customers, ISDN is a "frustrating piece of crap," because it can do many things, thereby making it nearly impossible to figure out how to make it do any one particular thing.

Calling ISDN "flexible" is like saying a drowning victim has moist skin. It's technically true, but you're not impressed. There is such a thing as too much of a good thing. That's the problem with ISDN.

I worked in Pacific Bell's ISDN lab for a few years and got to see many people try to make an ISDN connection work. I have yet to see anybody succeed on the first try, even by luck.

The odds are impossibly stacked against the unwitting ISDN customer. ISDN equipment can have a thousand possible options with unfathomable names like "SPID" and "TEI." Even if you figure out what the acronyms mean, no amount of common sense can help you sort out what goes where. (Many new Induhviduals were procreated during ISDN testing. Refer to Chapter 1.)

With some technology, you get the feeling that the designers weren't fully considering its ease of use. With ISDN, you get the feeling that the designers hate your friggin' guts. I'm not saying they *do* actually hate you, but I never saw anything to disprove the theory.

If somehow you set all the options correctly on the ISDN equipment on your desk, you still have to deal with the options on the ISDN line itself. Those are set by the phone company per your instructions. There are a thousand possible settings, depending on how you plan to use it and what kind of equipment the phone company uses for your neighborhood. That adds another thousand things to go wrong. Then you have to select a long-distance phone service for your ISDN connection. That adds a few more options that can be set wrong.

When you order an ISDN line, the phone company will ask how you want the options set on the line. But how do you know? The company that sold you your ISDN equipment won't tell you what you need. If the information is in their documentation, it's spread across multiple chapters. You have a better chance of finding Jimmy Hoffa in your documentation than you have of finding the information you need to order an ISDN line.

All I've talked about so far is the confusion on one end of the ISDN connection. There has to be something on the other end of the connection or it's somewhat pointless. The other end generally has a different set of equipment and often a different flavor of ISDN service from the phone company. That's another several thousand potential problems.

I'm exaggerating a bit, but let's say your odds of getting ISDN to work on the first try are a billion to one against you. This is higher than the real number, but not by a meaningful margin. The question is, Why would the phone companies think they could sell something like that?

It's my fault.

Prior to working in Pacific Bell's ISDN lab, I worked on ISDN strategy. It was my job to recommend whether the company should go hog-wild and make ISDN available all over California or just slink away from it in shame. Here's my story.

The way I see it, there are three possible paths for every major corporate recommendation:

1. The right way.

2. The wrong way.

3. The weasel way.

The right way would require too much honesty for you to keep your job. The wrong way would require lying, and that would be bad, especially if you got caught. The path I chose—the weasel way—allows you to be completely honest, but in a way that puts the blame on someone else when everything goes to hell.

I studied the market for ISDN and calculated all of its costs. I found that it was a great technology with no immediate competition, and it probably had a large market potential. The only thing that could limit its success was complete incompetence on the part of all the phone companies, colossal stupidity by every single ISDN hardware vendor, and complete idiocy on the part of the regulatory oversight bodies.

It was obvious to me that ISDN was doomed.

Since ISDN had been around for years already without making money, it attracted more than its share of slugs, malcontents, and blithering Induhviduals who couldn't get meaningful work elsewhere. There was a smattering of bright, well-meaning people working with ISDN, but they were outnumbered and rendered totally harmless.

This situation made it difficult to present my findings in an objective fashion. I couldn't stand in front of the senior executives of Pacific Bell and say, "All of the problems with ISDN are caused by the most amazing collection of morons that history has ever known. I expect the bad news to continue unabated. Let's run like frightened rabbits."

Instead, when it came time to make my presentation, I carefully described the economic opportunity that could spring from a hypothetical future of well-designed ISDN equipment and superlative operational support. I pointed out that all of the current problems were human-created and human-solvable. All it would take was the intelligence and professionalism of employees and vendors working as a team. I recommended full steam ahead.

The executives asked some probing questions to test my analysis, questions like, "Why is the expense line bumpy?" I bobbed and weaved and made it out of the meeting without ever telling a lie.

ISDN was studied many more times by employees and consultants who had the same dilemma that I had. I assume they took the weasel way too, since Pacific Bell has been deploying ISDN like crazy. No doubt the other phone companies noticed the enthusiasm that Pacific Bell displayed for ISDN and assigned their own people to study it more thoroughly, creating the same weasel way results.

The big question everyone asks about ISDN is whether it has a future. Will the average person use it for fast connections to the Internet or will they use some future service through their cable television company? I can answer that question with the same analytical skill that brought you ISDN in the first place. But first, some background.

Cable companies have what appears to be a huge technical advantage— a big coaxial cable into your house that can carry far more information than a phone line with ISDN service. Most pundits argue that this advantage will be enough for the cable companies to trounce ISDN in the market of the future. This argument misses one important fact:

Cable companies are staffed with people who couldn't get jobs
at telephone companies.

No matter how many technical advantages the cable companies start with, it's a huge hairy deal to change their networks for two-way communications. The technology exists, but making it work will require the intelligence and professionalism of thousands of cable company employees and vendors working as a team. Obviously, cable companies are doomed.

When cable companies add the departments needed to support a two-way transmission service, they will become tangled and bloated. Their resources will be devoured by "technical standards meetings," "quality initiatives," and continuous pointless reorganizations.

Every time their technical people build a test network, the marketing requirements will change. Every time they test a new set-top box for the home, a newer and better one will become available. Meanwhile, cable company employees are giving weasel way presentations to their own management and recommending full steam ahead.

Telephone companies had a running start with ISDN—they already knew how to provide two-way phone services—and it has still taken them ten years to improve from total incompetence with ISDN to mild incompetence. Meanwhile, the cable companies are painting targets on their shoes, cleaning their guns, and laughing like tickled hermits over the fact that their cables are thicker. Poor bastards.

I predict the cable companies will flounder for at least ten years in their attempts to offer two-way data service to the home. You'll see hundreds of trials and dozens of small-scale overhyped services, but nothing substantial. By then, ISDN will be simpler to use and widely available.

ISDN works great after you figure out how to set the options. The only thing that stands between ISDN and market success is ease of use, and that has improved each year. In effect, the phone companies will be both the poor bastards who developed ISDN—and failed—and the clever companies who figured out what went wrong and fixed it.

Technology is impossible to predict, but stupidity is a known constant. ISDN service has experienced the highest saturation of stupidity of any service you can think of. And it survived. That's what I call robust. That makes ISDN a good bet.

The cable companies are still at the beginning of their stupidity saturation phase. They have to pass through the poor bastard failure before they can become a threat to ISDN. In the near term, the best we can hope for is that we won't lose our television reception completely.

PREDICTION 12

In the future, ISDN services will improve to the point where you can mention it in a crowd without generating laughter.

THE BOZO FILTER

One of my biggest problems in life is the constant stream of complaints, dumb questions, and inane opinions that other people burden me with. I don't want new ways to communicate, I want new ways to stop the people who are trying to communicate with me. I know I'm not alone, even though I wish I were.

Every day, I get e-mail from someone who says something like, "How do you get ideas? Please tell me how you do it so I can get ideas, too."

I do not know how to answer that inquiry without insulting the person. I don't want to say, "I'm sorry to report that if your brain does not create any ideas, you are dead. This is hell."

And I can't say, "Everyone gets ideas. If you're getting bad ones, it must be because your brain is defective."

And I can't say, "I'm far too busy to be bothered with your insignificant and ludicrous question. Thank you for writing. Please pick up the latest *Dilbert* book."

And I can't say the truth—that I look at Garfield and change the cat jokes to fit Dogbert, add a few corporate buzzwords, and pass it off as original.

There's really no graceful way out. So I find myself wishing I had never gotten the question in the first place. I wish I had—to borrow a phrase from Guy Kawasaki at Apple Computers—a "Bozo Filter." I mean no disrespect to Bozo the Clown when I say this. I would enjoy getting a message from the real Bozo. You expect a famous clown to be able to send funny e-mail messages, unless he just doesn't care anymore.

The Bozo Filter would be software that checks incoming e-mail and weeds out the ones that are worthless. The worthless ones always have tell-tale signs. The filter would easily find them.

For example, when I get an e-mail message that has fifty other addressees and the phrase "I thought you might be interested in this," I want my software to delete that message immediately. And I want the originator of that message to be added to my list of people who are forever banned from my electronic kingdom.

About three times a day, different people forward the same e-mail messages to me about an alleged incident involving Neiman-Marcus and their secret cookie recipe. This is a famous urban legend. The gist of it is that someone supposedly asked for cookies at Neiman-Marcus and then, through a misunderstanding, was charged a bundle for their secret cookie recipe instead. The alleged angry customer is now getting revenge by spreading the alleged secret recipe all over the net. I want my Bozo Filter to look for the words "Neiman-Marcus" and "cookies" and reject those messages. And I want a mild electric shock sent back through the Internet to whomever thought I needed to see that.

Once or twice a day, I get an e-mail message with the phrase "cup holder" in it. This is another urban legend that several hundred people have told me has happened to them or a friend. This story involves a computer user who calls technical support to report a broken cup holder on the computer. The cup holder turns out to be the CD-ROM drive tray. I want my Bozo Filter to prevent me from ever seeing this message again. And I want the lying weasels who say they took that tech support phone call to be locked in a room and forced to fight it out until there is really only one left. This might be more than the software can deliver, but I can dream.

PREDICTION 13

In the future, we'll all use sophisticated Bozo Filters to prevent idiots from communicating with us.

The Bozo Filter will definitely be available for e-mail. America Online already lets you block certain e-mail addresses. And if you use Claris Emailer software, for example, you can search for keywords in incoming software and have them prioritized or filed automatically. I want the filters to extend to the telephone system, too.

I want my voice-mail system to compensate for the Induhviduals who leave messages. In particular, I want these features:

Auctioneer Mode: Speeds up messages left by people who speak too slowly.

First Ten/Last Ten: Deletes everything except the first and last ten seconds of a message. The stuff in the middle is never worth listening to anyway.

Rambler's Nudge: A rude voice that interrupts callers who are leaving overly long messages and says, "Just leave your stinkin' phone number, will ya? I HAVE A LIFE!"

Number Watcher: Voice recognition system that listens to see if the caller mumbles an unintelligible return phone number. If so, a voice will break in and say, "What language is that—Mumblican? Spit out your sandwich and try it again."

My telephone system should also have a voice-stress analyzer to filter out Induhviduals before the phone even rings.

Bozo Filter:	This is Scott Adams's Bozo Filter. Please answer yes or no. Will this phone call benefit Scott Adams in any way?
Caller:	Um . . . yes. Yes, it will.
Bozo Filter:	Liar! *Click.*

If I can't shut out all the Induhviduals in my life, I think I should be compensated for listening to them. That's only fair. When our Bozo Filters become good enough to prevent Induhviduals from getting freebies, they will certainly be willing to pay us to listen.

CENSORSHIP ON THE INTERNET

When I meet people, I can tell immediately whether they were harmed by exposure to dirty pictures when they were kids. The people who viewed dirty pictures tend to be cynical and sarcastic. More often than not they are syndicated cartoonists. But those who were lucky enough to be sheltered from the effects of obscene pictures are monks now. I'm overgeneralizing, of course. There's lots of gray area. For example, some people looked at pictures of themselves naked and they become gay monks, but these are the exceptions and not the rule.

In the future, greater efforts will be made to protect young people from pornography on the information superhighway. I'm totally in favor of that. Those kids should get their pornography the same way the kids of my generation did—by shoplifting. Granted, my generation suffered some ill effects from exposure to pornography, but at least we were learning a trade in the process of getting it. Kids today don't have to leave the house. They can fire up the computer and fill their hard drives with free pornography. At least that's what I've been told.

While researching this chapter, I tried to find obscene pictures on the Internet that didn't require a credit card to view. I fired up an Internet "search engine" and input several words that are too disgusting to mention. I hoped it would tell me where to find all the pornography.

And did it ever. Whoo hoo! I tried one location after another and found that the servers were all too overloaded with traffic to be viewable. I concluded from this experience that the Internet is already safe for children.

Kids have shorter attention spans than adults. They would never sit in front of a blank screen for hours on the slight chance that they might see something naughty at some undetermined time in the future. It's not a competitive use of time. In terms of arousal per second, there's a much better payoff from flipping through your mom's Victoria's Secret catalogs. Remember, we're talking about kids here—mostly boys—and if they're anything like I was, all it takes is a commercial for *Wheel of Fortune* and you're off to the races. Hello Vanna! The Internet is overkill when you're thirteen years old.

By my estimate, you'd have to be at least twenty-one years old before you'd be willing to sit in front of a blank screen for several minutes waiting for pictures of naked people. There's a natural protection built into the Internet, because people get more patient with age; and the nastier the pictures on the Internet, the longer you have to wait to see them. Logically then, all sexually explicit Internet sites will be jammed with traffic from horny adults (and authors doing research), because these people have the most patience.

PREDICTION 14

In the future, kids won't have access to online pornography, because the X-rated Internet sites will be clogged by horny adults who have more patience.

Companies will still be able to make a fortune selling products that block minors from pornography, but technical solutions can only go so far. In my opinion, we don't need more technology to block sexually oriented Internet sites; we need more horny old people to jam them with traffic. This is a very good use for horny old people. Frankly, it's the only one I can think of. And since these horny old people are usually parents, you get the added bonus of parental involvement.

TECHNOLOGY MAKES US LESS PRODUCTIVE

I love computers. To me, computers are like tangerines, in the sense that I can't make a good analogy about either one of them right now. But if I could, it would involve a clever point about how computers are fun even though they create a lot of work. Here are some of my favorite cartoons on that point.

PREDICTION 15

In the future, technology will continue to make our lives harder and many of us will be delighted about it

---

ENERGY SOURCES

Scientists will eventually stop flailing around with solar power and focus their efforts on harnessing the only truly unlimited source of energy on the planet: stupidity.

PREDICTION 16

In the future, scientists will learn how to convert
stupidity into clean fuel.

The challenge will be in figuring out how to control this bountiful resource. I predict that the energy companies will place huge hamster wheels outside of convenience stores and offer free lottery tickets to people who spend five minutes running in them. The hamster wheels will be connected to power generators. This plan will produce an unlimited supply of cheap power.

I predict that wind power will finally become a viable large-scale energy source, but not because of better windmill technology. We will discover more wind—the flapping of people's mouths.

All that's needed to harness this wind is a critical mass of people and a controversial topic. I predict you'll see windmills near Macintosh-user group meetings. A representative from the power utility company will be planted in the audience. At a strategic time during each meeting, he will stand up and say, "The Windows platform seems just as good as the Macintosh. Why don't we all just switch?"

An accomplice will quickly open the door facing the row of windmills and get out of the way.

TECHNOLOGY AS THE LEADING CAUSE OF DEATH

At the moment, the leading cause of death is heart disease. That will change in the future, not because we'll cure heart disease, but because we'll come up with many more ways to accidentally kill healthy people.

PREDICTION 17

In the future, technology will become the leading cause of death.

If you think about it, human beings are the worst possible creatures to have access to powerful technology. It would be much better for everyone if, for example, fish were the ones with all the technology. They wouldn't be able to push the buttons with their little fins. No humans would get hurt, and the fish would be able to brag about their great stuff until eventually it all turned into protective barrier reefs.

But it's not a perfect world, and fish don't own all the technology. Humans do. That's bad, because technology magnifies the ability of one person to have a big impact on other people. If that doesn't scare you, then the next time you see professional wrestling on television, look at the crowd shots and ask yourself if you'd like those people to have a bigger impact on your life.

There's no required safety testing for technology. I think that's because the danger doesn't seem obvious to the casual observer. That's what futurists like myself are for—to scare the bejeezus out of you for no useful purpose whatsoever.

Let's get on with that important work.

Television is our biggest threat as a species, but not because of the sex and violence. It's because Hollywood pipes an endless stream of impossibly attractive people into our consciousness.

It's awfully hard to get naked in front of someone who has just watched *Body Shaping* on ESPN . . . especially if your partner points the remote control at you and starts clicking it desperately. Nobody needs that.

If television doesn't ruin our ability to mate, the conversations about technology will. For the first time in history, it's possible to have a conversation with someone who speaks the same language and yet have no idea what the topic is. The problem is mostly with men. Women are better conversationalists, and they tend to contain their talk about technology. Men have less verbal awareness. We'll keep yammering about things like sub-second response times, CPU cycles, and bandwidth until there's bloodshed.

Technology allows us to put more of our lives in the hands of engineers every day. This might not scare those of you who work in nonengineering companies, but personally, it's enough to make me wake up screaming every night. I know a lot of engineers.

We all know that big companies make economic decisions about the trade-offs between price and safety. That's understandable. It only gets scary when you realize that engineers are the ones who are making those calculations. And engineers don't like people. In my nightmares, just before I wake up screaming, I hear the engineers talking:

Engineer #1:   This solution will work, but it will be more dangerous.

Engineer #2:   How much more dangerous?

Engineer #1:   I figure a thousand people would die. And most of them would be strangers.

Engineer #2:   Is there any way we could modify it . . . you know, to kill more strangers?

Engineer #1:   Wow, you hate strangers, too?

Engineer #2:   Who doesn't? Plus, I figure there's a good chance that you'd be killed doing the modifications.

Sometimes I fear that I will forget all of my passwords and my secret codes and some large organization will keep all of my money because I can't prove it ever belonged to me. My driver's license and passport will be useless, because toddlers will have the technology to forge that kind of thing on their little "Forge-n-Learn" toys.

So one day I'll find myself in a heated argument with a banking representative in which I try to explain that I really am stupid enough to forget all of my secret codes. I won't know whether I should make an eloquent argument, thus jeopardizing my claim of stupidity, or a really stupid argument, thus proving that I'm correct about how stupid I am. It will all be terribly confusing and frustrating.

Eventually, I'll become a pathetic homeless guy, wandering around muttering, "Was it gb7k99 or was it gB7k99. I'm sure the 'B' is capitalized!"

Technology also allows us to get very angry and abusive with people who can't punch us in the nose at that very minute. That is bound to be a dangerous situation, especially for scrawny vegetarians like myself. I never hesitate to question someone's parentage or offer obscene dining suggestions by e-mail. I cleverly calculate the precise amount of insult that will make someone *think* about tracking me down and beating me up, but not mad enough to actually do it. The trouble is, it's a fine line between being almost hunted down and actually hunted down. That's why I sleep in the attic most of the time and leave a dummy in my bed. (I don't call her dummy to her face. I mumble so it sounds like "honey.")

Kidding!

When it comes to physical toughness, there are two types of people:

There are people like me . . . and then there are people who can beat the crap out of people like me. The latter have always been bullies. As children, it was their responsibility to administer the wedgies and noogies to all of the other children. This taught the bullies responsibility. They learned to control their power.

Those of us who were on the receiving end of the wedgies and noogies never learned to control our power, because we didn't have any. Until now. E-mail allows us to lash out at the people we consider stupid while leaving plenty of time to run away if things get out of hand.

One of the biggest unreported sources of potential violence is a direct result of technology. Quite accidentally, technology has become so important that the people who control it have great power over the rest of us. Sadly, in the real world you hardly ever hear the sentence, "Not only is he great with technology, but he's a friendly person and helpful, too!" Instead, you get this guy:

There's also a growing threat from smaller countries who have access to more technology than they can handle. I'm not just talking about nuclear devices. Undeveloped countries are interested in lots of technologies that could blow up or possibly fall on your head if you do something stupid. Imagine a world where hundreds of countries have inexpensive technology to launch huge payloads into low Earth orbits, but don't have any compelling reason to do so. This could be very dangerous.

"Hey, Borpney, what should we do with this old broken truck?"

"Let's launch it into space. (Hee hee. Snort.)"

If every little pissant country like France, for example, starts sending rockets into space, it won't be safe to come out of your basement. You'll take two steps onto your lawn and a booster rocket will crush your skull. That's no way to live.

MEN WHO USE COMPUTERS—THE NEW SEX SYMBOLS

I wrote this article for the May 1995 edition of *Windows* magazine. It is reprinted here with some minor modifications. *Windows* magazine had asked me to write a column of either 700 or 1,100 words. Then they made the mistake of telling me they would pay me per word. This is what they got.

I get about 350 e-mail messages a day from readers of my comic strip *Dilbert*. Most are from disgruntled office workers, psychopaths, stalkers, comic fans—that sort of person. But a growing number are from women who write to say they think Dilbert is sexy. Some women say they already married a "Dilbert" and couldn't be happier. They gush about the virtues of their very own Dilbert.

If you're not familiar with Dilbert, he's an electrical engineer who spends most of his time with his computer. He's a nice guy, but not exactly Kevin Costner. (I'm talking about the old Kevin Costner who had good hair.)

A few years ago, I drew a *Dilbert* comic where his dog, Dogbert, put up a billboard advertising "Date a Dilbert—quantities are limited." It needed a phone number, so I used the number for my home fax, which I temporarily equipped with an answering machine in case anybody tried to call.

I got 650 calls.

Most of the calls were from men who wondered if Dilbert had a sister. Other callers wanted to fix their dog up with Dogbert. But many callers were women who said they thought Dilbert was sexy. This puzzled me.

Okay, Dilbert is polite, honest, employed, and educated. And he stays home. These are good traits, but they don't explain the incredible sex appeal.

So what's the attraction?

I think it's a Darwinian thing. We're attracted to the people who have the best ability to survive and thrive. In the old days, it was important to be able to run down an antelope and kill it with a single blow to the forehead. But that skill is becoming less important every year.

Now it only matters if you can install your own Ethernet card without having to confess your inadequacies to a disgruntled tech support person.

It's obvious that the world has three distinct classes of people, each with its own evolutionary destiny:

1. Knowledgeable computer users who will eventually evolve into godlike non-corporeal beings who rule the Universe.

2. Computer owners who try to "pass" as knowledgeable but secretly use a hand calculator to add totals for their Excel spreadsheets. This group will gravitate toward jobs as high school principals and operators of pet crematoriums. Eventually, they will become extinct.

3. Non–computer users who will eventually grow tails, sit in zoos, and fling dung at tourists.

PREDICTION 18

In the future, computer-using men will be the sexiest males.

Obviously, if you're a woman and you're trying to decide which evolutionary track you want your offspring to take, you don't want to put them on the luge ride to the dung-flinging Olympics. You want a real man. You want a knowledgeable computer user with evolutionary potential.

And women prefer men who are good listeners. Computer users are excellent listeners, because they can look at you for long periods of time without saying anything. Granted, early on in a relationship it's better if the guy actually talks, but men are not deep. We use up all the stories we'll ever have after six months. If a woman marries a guy who's in, let's say, a retail sales career, she'll get repeat stories starting in the seventh month and lasting forever. But if she marries an engineer, she gets a great listener for the next seventy years.

With the ozone layer evaporating, it's good strategy to mate with somebody who has an indoor hobby. Outdoorsy men are applying suntan lotion with SPF 10,000 and yet, by the age of thirty, they still look like dried chili peppers with pants. Compare that with the healthy glow of a man who spends twelve hours a day in front of a video screen.

And it's a well-established fact that computer users are better lovers. I know this is true, because I heard an actual anecdote from somebody who knew a woman who married a computer user. They reportedly had sex many times. I realize this isn't statistically valid, but you have to admit it's the most persuasive thing I've written so far.

If there's still any doubt in your mind about male computer users being sexier, consider their hair. Male computer users tend to have two kinds of hair:

1. Male pattern baldness—a sign of elevated testosterone.

2. Unkempt jungle hair—the kind you only see on people who have just finished a frenzied bout of lovemaking.

If this were a trial, I think we could reach a verdict on the strong circumstantial evidence alone.

I realize there are a lot of skeptics out there. They'll delight in pointing out the number of computer users who wear wrist braces, and they'll suggest it isn't the repetitive use of the keyboard that causes the problem. That's okay. Someday those skeptics will be flinging dung at tourists. Then who's laughing? (Answer to rhetorical question: everybody but the tourists.)

Henry Kissinger said power is the ultimate aphrodisiac. (This was much catchier than his original motto: "Thick glasses are the ultimate aphrodisiac.") And Bill Clinton once said that knowledge is power. Therefore, logically, according to the government of the United States, knowledge of computers is the ultimate aphrodisiac. You could argue with me—I'm just a cartoonist—but it's hard to argue with the government. Remember, they run the Bureau of Alcohol, Tobacco, and Firearms, so they must know a thing or two about satisfying women.

You might think this is enough evidence to convince anybody that men who use computers are sexy, but look at it from my point of view—I'm getting paid by the word for this article. I'm not done with you yet. Don't be so selfish.

In less enlightened times, the best way to impress women was to own a hot car. But women wised up and figured out it was better to buy their own hot cars and then they wouldn't have to ride around with jerks.

Subsequently, technology has replaced hot cars as the new symbol of robust manhood. Men instinctively know that unless they're seriously considering getting a digital line to the Internet, no woman is going to look at them twice.

And it's getting worse. In the not-too-distant future, anybody who doesn't have their own home page on the World Wide Web will probably qualify for a government subsidy for the home-pageless. And nobody likes a man who takes money from the government, except maybe Marilyn Monroe, which is why the CIA killed her. And if you think that sounds stupid, I've got about a hundred words to go.

And there's the issue of mood lighting. Good lighting is important for bringing out a person's sex appeal. And nothing looks sexier than a man in boxer shorts illuminated only by the light of a fifteen-inch SVGA monitor. Now, if we can agree that this is every woman's dream scenario, then I think we can also agree that it's best if the guy knows how to use the computer he's sitting in front of. I mean, otherwise he'll just look like a loser sitting in front of a PC in his underwear.

FOUR

LIFE ON OTHER PLANETS

There has been much speculation about whether there is life on other planets. In particular, we wonder if life on those planets is so boring that they're willing to travel thousands of light-years to stick various objects into the body holes of earthlings.

You wouldn't think a highly advanced race of beings would find that entertaining. But *we're* an advanced civilization, and there are lots of people who think cow-tipping* is a sport. Maybe we're not being visited by the cream of the alien crop, if you know what I mean. The aliens that come our way probably aren't the same bunch of aliens who invented space travel on their planets. Just look at the people driving past you on the highway; how many of them could have invented the automobile? Maybe the aliens who visit us are alien Induhviduals.

Let's not jump to any conclusions. I will use my uncanny powers of logic to ferret out the truth about UFOs and alien abductions. There's plenty of evidence to piece it all together. I don't know why no one has tried it before.

Every year, thousands of Induhviduals report sightings of flying saucers. Some of the Induhviduals have captured grainy images of these unexplained ships on video cameras. All of the alien ships filmed by Induhviduals look exactly like ashtrays or the tops of garbage pails. But what are the odds there would be that many ashtrays and garbage pail lids

---

*For you city dwellers, cow-tipping involves sneaking up on sleepy cows on hills and pushing them over so they roll down the hill. This is very bad for the cow, and it is even worse for anyone who is tired of hearing "milkshake" puns.

flying around? That seems far less likely than the explanation that the skies are filled with unidentified flying spacecrafts.

I think we can logically conclude from the video evidence that the accounts of unidentified "visitors" are true. The question is, Where did they come from?

The popular view is that the strange creatures travel from a distant planet. This assumes three things about these creatures:

1. They are capable of intergalactic travel.

2. They are capable of finding us in the vastness of space.

3. Their stealth technology makes video images of their ships look like grainy pictures of ashtrays and garbage pail lids.

This seems plausible to me, but you must compare this theory to the only logical alternative: The strange creatures live on Earth, but they are hiding most of the time.

Ask yourself this: Is it easier to build a spaceship capable of intergalactic travel or hide behind some trees? I think you can see where I'm heading with this. If not, let me back up and put it all together for you.

You might have noticed that the world is full of people who are much smarter than other people. For example, the average IQ in the general population is 100. If you remove from the sample all of the people reading this book, the average drops to maybe 40 or 45, tops. On the other end of the spectrum, Marilyn vos Savant's IQ is well over 200.

Just how big a difference is there between Marilyn vos Savant and the "average" person? Let me put it this way. Imagine that a true/false test is administered to three creatures: Marilyn vos Savant, her dog, and an average Induhvidual. Now imagine that the questions are so hard that you need an IQ of 180 or higher to do well.

Marilyn's score would be 100 percent. The Induhvidual's score would be 50 percent, assuming normal luck in guessing. Marilyn's dog would also score 50 percent, because his strategy would be no more effective than the Induhvidual's.

From Marilyn's perspective, there's not a big difference between the average Induhvidual and the dog, except the dog is cuter. Who do you think she'd rather spend time with?

There's a point coming, albeit slowly.

Throughout history, there have always been super-smart people born to the general population. I'm guessing they wouldn't want to hang around with the rest of us. Being super-smart, they'd find an alternative. They'd figure out where they could go live with each other and they'd create an elaborate cover story to keep the Induhviduals away.

If such a place existed on Earth, we could identify it with some good investigative work. All we would have to do is look for a place where all the problems caused by stupid people don't exist. I think that land would look like this:

How Super-Smart Land Would Be

> They would be neutral in all wars.
> Their clocks would be very, very accurate.
> They would have the highest standard of living.
> They would have excellent chocolate.
> Their pocketknives would be extraordinary.

Obviously, the super-smart people created their own country long ago and called it Switzerland. Every weekend, they take the hovercrafts out and look for Induhviduals who have video cameras. It's a game with them. After years of inbreeding, the super-smart people have evolved into skinny, gray creatures with huge eyes. They wear makeup to look like stern Germans when tourists are around.

PREDICTION 19

In the future, we'll realize that the creatures we thought were from other planets are actually smart people who live in Switzerland.

You might think I'm jumping to conclusions here, but have you ever met anyone from Switzerland? Neither have I.

That's my theory, and in the future you will see that I am right.

FIVE

THE WORLD GETS MORE COMPLICATED

It seems like everything I own is broken. Here is a sample of the things that are defective at the time of this writing:

Defective Things in My Home

- My online service says "try again later."
- My television won't let me look at channel 2.
- My TV remote control is broken.
- None of my telephones work.
- My stereo is blinking wildly for no reason.
- My headphones are broken.
- My computer freezes up several times a day.
- My laptop computer is broken.
- My pager only shows the tops of numbers.
- My fax line is dead.
- The timer on the water sprinkler is broken.

- My outside lights are broken.

- My roof is leaking.

- My vacuum cleaner is broken.

- My furnace is broken.

- My toilets require handle-jiggling.

- My cat needs to visit the vet.

This is not an unusual day for me. My car stopped working recently, so I bought a new one. The new one lasted approximately sixty seconds before its first major malfunction—the climate control computer failed as I pulled out of the dealer's lot. I was surprised, because I expected to make it all the way to the intersection before something like that happened.

Now, only a few weeks later, I have a new car problem. A light on the dashboard says, "Check Engine." What does that mean? I looked under the hood, and the engine is still there. That wasn't enough to make the light go out. I need another hint.

I feel helpless around all of my broken stuff. I can't fix *anything* myself. There's a blown lightbulb at the highest point of my ceiling. I can't figure out how to change it. I don't have a ladder that goes that high. Even if I did, I wouldn't want to risk my life to change a lightbulb. I'd hate to die changing a lightbulb, because that's how everyone would remember me. Nobody would say, "I'll miss him." They'd say, "How many cartoonists does it take to change a lightbulb? Ha ha ha!" If I'm going to die in a household accident, I want it to be one that doesn't involve lightbulbs.

The hardware store has a device for changing lightbulbs. It's a long pole with a lightbulb grabber on the end. It says on the instructions that it only works if you had originally put the lightbulb in with that sort of device. How should I know what the previous owner used to put that lightbulb in with? He could have used a trained monkey taped to a broom, for all I know. If I buy this bulb-changer device, I will end up beating the lightbulb senseless, getting amazingly frustrated, and gaining nothing in terms of illumination. And it will take the entire afternoon to fail at this task.

I can't solve the lightbulb problem myself. How do I find someone who changes lightbulbs for a living? Do I check the Yellow Pages under the letter "T" for "Tall Guy Who Changes Lightbulbs"? Or how about "S" for "Someone Who Isn't a Total Loser Like Me"?

I am totally stumped by this lightbulb dilemma. I use my flashlight if I want to see anything at night in that room. I plan to move my broken stereo in there, because the blinking lights will act like a night-light. If that's not enough, I always have the sound of my running toilets to act as a homing beacon.

I live in a crumbling and defective world. I'm too busy or too clueless to fix any of it. It wouldn't help anyway. As soon as I fixed one thing, another thing would sense the void and plunge into spontaneous disrepair. At least with my method—the "Active Neglect" method—I can show off my nice things to friends and still be free from the maintenance.

"That's my stereo in that dark room over there. No, you can't listen to it, but you can see it when it blinks."

Other futurists predict the world will become increasingly polarized into technology "haves" and "have-nots." The part they get wrong is that the "have-nots" will be the lucky ones.

The "have-nots" won't spend hours a day trying to keep their stuff working. They'll be sitting on the porch sipping lemonade and whittling little animals to give away as gifts. Meanwhile, I'll be trying to figure out why I can't get five peripherals to work on my SCSI chain. And I'll be doing it in the dark.

We techno-buried people will envy the rocking chairs of the simple people. We'll thirst for their lemonade. And we'll hate the little carved animals they keep giving us on special occasions (although I won't mind them too much if I can burn them for heat and light).

This movement toward simplification has already started, but it won't get huge until the simple-life people have their own magazine called *LoafWeek* with a bunch of blank pages. They will have their own television show featuring a guy sitting in a chair doing nothing. The show won't be broadcast in the traditional sense, since none of the target audience will own televisions, but people will enjoy knowing there's a guy sitting in a chair someplace at the same time every week.

People who cling to their complicated lifestyles will be willing to pay anything to have other people do the things they don't have the time or skill to do themselves. Many people already pay for housecleaning, cooking (at restaurants), changing the oil in the car, and mowing the lawn.

PREDICTION 20

In the future, the trend of "personal services" will continue until busy people are handling almost none of their routine bodily functions themselves.

I saw a glimpse of the future recently when I had a cameo appearance on the TV show *NewsRadio*. Between takes, a makeup expert would swoop in and dab some makeup on my shiny forehead and wet down the only scrap of hair I have, which tragically happens to be a cowlick. How great it would be to have people swoop in and straighten you up during the day. They could shadow you from morning to night, always ready to charge in and knock an eyelash off your cheek or zip up your pants if you forgot.

A professional photographer was nice enough to send me some photos from a public talk I did recently. The photos clearly showed a huge chunk of food stuck in my teeth during my presentation. I wish someone had swooped in and saved me from that embarrassment. I would have paid a lot for that service. Ideally, this person would be someone petite whom I could tape to a broomstick to change my lightbulbs. But that's just dreaming.

THE INCOMPETENCE LINE

Every year, it takes more brains to navigate this complicated world. More people are falling below what I call the "incompetence line," through no fault of their own.

I fell below the incompetence line this year. I use airline travel as my benchmark. Air travel has become amazingly complicated. The percentage of the population that is too dumb to fly gets bigger every day.

Imagine if you had never traveled by air and you had to figure it out without asking anyone for help. You would have many questions that do not have intuitive answers:

Nonintuitive Air Travel Questions

- Should you put your arms around the person in front of you and lean into the curves?
- How much should you tip the flight attendants?
- How many times can you go through the metal detector before you become sterile?

- Are the skycaps authorized to do strip searches or are they just kidding about that?

I used to think I had all of the air travel questions figured out. I felt like quite the accomplished traveler. I learned that I have to order my vegetarian meals twenty-four hours in advance so they have more time to forget it. I learned to avoid the last row on the plane, because the seat doesn't lean back. I know just how much reading material to bring for the flight. I even got luggage with built-in wheels so I don't have to prove to the world that I haven't been to the gym lately. For a while, I was comfortably above the incompetence line for air travel.

Then the frequent flyer programs started kicking in. Suddenly, the airlines began sending weekly envelopes stuffed full of offers for hotels, luggage, rental cars, and free trips. All I had to do was use their airline and then figure out how their reward program worked. I would be awash in free stuff. Woo-hoo!

But it didn't work out that way. Instead, my spare bedroom and three file cabinets are packed full of complicated literature from the airlines. I keep telling myself I'll look at it closely and figure it all out "in my free time," but every day a truck pulls up to my house and dumps another load of airline literature on my lawn. It has miles of fine print about things like black-out periods and award levels and expiration dates and special offers. According to the airlines, I'm an executive something and a gold something and a frequent something, all of which gives me many rights and privileges—if I just had time to figure out what they are.

Then the airlines started ganging up with hotels and credit card companies to increase the complexity. I believe I have millions of dollars worth of unclaimed prizes now, if only I could figure out where they are and how to claim them.

So I am now officially below the incompetence line when it comes to flying. I can still figure out how to fly from one place to the next, but I'm sure I'm doing it wrong. By wrong, I mean that I'm spending more money and getting less free stuff than I could if I were smarter. But I don't have time to be smarter. I can't dedicate my life to my airline reward programs. The airlines have defeated me. I am buried under mounds of good news from them. They have pushed me below the incompetence line for their service and I don't like it one bit.

I don't think I'm alone. Other people must be getting forced below the incompetence line every day. Some people don't have so far to go. I get especially scared when the flight attendant is reading the safety instructions and I glance at the Induhviduals sitting in the escape-door aisles. I'm quite certain that if the plane had an emergency, these people would grab the headphones out of the seat-back pockets, hold them to their mouths, and try to breathe. Other people would run into the rest rooms and try to flush themselves to safety. If you could put on special goggles that allowed you to identify which people around you are below the incompetence line already, it would be truly frightening, especially if you were near a reflective surface.

This all brings me to my prediction.

PREDICTION 21

Lack of education will not be the biggest problem in the future. The problem will be an excess of stupidity as more people fall below the incompetence line.

I don't want to come off sounding like one of those conspiracy nuts, but I'm fairly sure everything in my house was designed by someone who is intentionally trying to kill me or make me feel stupid.

I think it might be this guy:

When I was a kid, I had a little black-and-white Sears television set that was very easy to use. There were only three steps:

1. Turn on power.

2. Select channel.

3. Wrap a long string to the horizontal hold knob on the side of the television so I could continually adjust it from across the room by pulling the string with my feet.

Those simple days are gone. Now I have a home entertainment center. It has six remote controls. If I want to watch television using the satellite dish as a source, I follow these steps:

1. Hire Sherpa guides.

2. Mount expedition to locate the AVR 80 remote control.

3. Press the "Main Power" button. (If nothing happens, unplug and replug TV set.)

4. Press the "LD" button. (LD stands for "satellite dish." Don't ask why.)

5. Press the "Source Power" button.

6.   Switch to RCA remote control.

7.   Press "Guide" button.

8.   Scroll to movie *Broken Arrow*.

9.   Press "Display."

10. Press "Menu-Select."

There are lots of other buttons on my remote controls. They have names like Fetch, Matrix, DISC DECK ANT, FAV•INPUT, and MEMO. I don't trust myself with this much power. I'm afraid I'll hit the wrong button and turn off the life support systems on the Russian space station. I don't want that on my conscience, so I leave those buttons alone.

The satellite dish has added a lot to my viewing pleasure. For example, I can watch the movie *Broken Arrow* at just about any time of day for only three dollars. I've seen it 700 times so far. There are other movies, too, but they don't interest me. I don't want to feel like the system is a waste of money, so I watch *Broken Arrow* whenever I can.

You can also watch sports from all over the country, with the exception of your local teams, which are blacked out. This is handy if you're traveling, but only if you're willing to take your dish with you and install it in your hotel room. That's the only way you're going to see your favorite team, no matter where you are.

You can't beat the picture clarity on a satellite system. It won't help you with any of the network television shows, because you can't get those on the dish, for some legal reason, unless you live in the wilderness. But you can watch the *Howard Stern* radio show on E! channel. I think it's important to have full digital clarity when you're watching a radio show. I already forget how I lived without it.

I used to know how to record television shows on my VCR. I had a success rate of well over 60 percent, which I believe put me in the ninety-fifth percentile of the general population. But that was when I had a television set, not a home entertainment center. Now I can't figure out how to record anything. My success rate is 0 percent and holding. I have fallen below the incompetence line in entertainment. I am now literally too dumb to entertain myself.

All day long, my television set powers itself on and off randomly. It does this to tease me. I believe it is on the verge of becoming a sentient life-form. ("Sentient" is a word I learned from watching *Star Trek* episodes back when I knew how to use the television, before my *Broken Arrow* days.)

It's tempting to think we can compensate for the complexity of modern life by improving the educational system, but it won't help me unless there's an evening degree program in watching television. Education isn't the fix-all solution everyone wants it to be. There are only two types of educations:

1. Useful.

2. Useless.

If you're foolish enough to get one of those useful educations, such as an engineering degree, everything you learn will be obsolete in five years. The rest of what you learn for the remainder of your life will come from reading brochures from vendors.

That's why I majored in economics. With economics, you never have to worry that your degree will become less relevant over time. I mean, how the hell could it?

I tried to use my economics training at my first job out of college. I was a bank teller. I soon found my knowledge more of a burden than an advantage. My co-workers were happily taking deposits and earning money for the bank. Meanwhile, I would be explaining to my customers how they should empty their passbook savings accounts and invest in small cap mutual funds through a discount brokerage company. Ironically, the more I displayed my knowledge of economics, the less money I earned in raises.

My economics degree wasn't enough to help me as a bank teller. Stupidity is immune to education. We're being buried by the growing complexity of the world—which makes us stupider every day—and we have no strategy for survival.

Our only hope in the future is that a charismatic figure will emerge and rid the world of creeping, sadistic complexity before it's too late. Maybe it will be Dogbert.

YOUR BUSY LIFE

What's the future look like? I'll tell you: It's about tough choices. For example, this morning I noticed that my electric razor had spilled its entire collection of whiskers all over the inside of my fashionable leather toiletry bag. I had two choices. I could laboriously remove those whiskers, individually cleaning each of the other contents of the bag, thus missing at least an hour of useful work, or I could say to myself, "If I didn't mind having those whiskers on my face, why should I mind them on my little traveling aspirin bottle?"

I chose the latter. After all, I already got used to the toothpaste all over everything in that bag. How bad could a few hairs be?

That's what the future looks like—a bag filled with toothpaste, whiskers, and unidentified containers. We're entering an age when the things we need to do and want to do are absorbed and overwhelmed by other things we need to do and want to do. We'll make random, often stupid choices, because we don't have the brains or time to do better.

Our only hope is that the marketplace will work its magic and provide the services that busy people need to get by. That seems to be happening.

PREDICTION 22

In the future, there will be a huge increase in the number of "household services" to compensate for the pathetic incompetence of the average person.

HOUSEHOLD SERVICES

Every year, I'm becoming a bit more helpless when it comes to maintaining my house. I depend on "service people" to come over and do two vital things in my house:

1. Fix something.

2. Make me feel like a complete loser.

Household Service people use even more confusing language than people who work in big companies. At least the jargon in big companies is a language that can be understood by a few people in the department. Service people, on the other hand, seem to develop their unique language while driving around in their trucks all alone. As far as I can tell, the language is some combination of traffic noises, bodily emanations, and snippets from talk radio all rolled into one. I had a service person install some telephone wiring in my house recently, and a conversation with him went like this:

Wire guy:	The line loops to the outside patch then goes live from the cable to the scromet.
Me:	What's a scromet? And which line are you talking about?
Wire guy:	That's what patches into the live cable wire from the blue wires, unless you want it to be the orange ones. It's up to you.
Me:	Why would I care what color the wire is? And what the hell is a scromet?
Wire guy:	Okay, we'll go with the blue. But don't complain later when you wish you'd said orange.
Me:	Why? Why orange? What's the difference? And what's a scromet?
Wire guy:	The scromet is connected to the orange directly. That's my point.

Me: YOUR *POINT*?! I DON'T UNDERSTAND A
                 WORD YOU'RE SAYING. WHAT POINT??

Wire guy: So, we'll go with the blue wire. I'm sure you
                 know best.

So now my scromet is wired to something or other and all I know is that every time the phone rings my shower comes on. I'd call the wire guy back to have it fixed, but I can't go through that experience again.

SIX

THE FUTURE OF DEMOCRACY AND CAPITALISM

On election day, I always perform my civic duty by not voting. Believe me, the country is better off if I stay away from the polls. I am far too ignorant to add anything but randomness to the outcome. I say this despite the fact that I read as many bumper stickers as I can, thus making me more informed than the average voter.

Even if I were uncaring enough to participate in elections, I wouldn't know how to register without exposing myself to unnecessary risk. Someone told me I can go to the post office to register, but I'm afraid they'll throw my application in the wrong bag and I'll end up in the military. The next thing I know, I'm a Navy SEAL. I'm fairly certain I would be killed by my own squad in order to put an end to my incessant seal puns.

I realize it's a small risk, but when I compare it to the statistical likelihood that my vote will improve the efficiency of our government, I think it's a fair assessment. And when you factor in the odds of being hit by a stray bullet while standing in line at the post office, voting seems downright reckless. My cats need me alive, despite any outward signs to the contrary, such as dragging me into the litter box and covering me with sand.

When it comes to voting, I'm just barely smart enough to know that I'm a total idiot. This might sound self-deprecating, but on the intelligence scale, it puts me comfortably ahead of all the Induhviduals who actually vote.

To understand how voting became a futile exercise, let me give you a refresher course on early American history. A few hundred years ago in early America, a bunch of intelligent, hard-working landowners set out to design a new form of government that emphasized fairness. They came up with a system that favored intelligent, hard-working landowners. There were bonus points for being a "dorky white male."

There was a heated discussion among the Founding Fathers about the wisdom of openly discriminating against everyone else, especially the stupid white males (let's call them, collectively, the pre-Induhviduals). There were so many of them, and they all had weapons. This fear was allayed when Benjamin Franklin pointed out, "Hey, they're pre-Induhviduals. The worst thing that could happen is they'll get mad at us and try to attack France." Everyone laughed so hard the floor was covered with wooden dentures. It took hours to sort it out.

During the cocktail hour afterward, some of the Founding Fathers questioned Ben about his use of the phrase "pre-Induhviduals," pointing out that the term "Induhviduals" hadn't been created yet. Ben just smiled and mumbled something about being ahead of his time. Then he got in his car and drove home.

Declaring independence wasn't enough. There was still the small matter of breaking free from England. The Founding Fathers created a fighting force of pre-Induhviduals and ordered them to kill everyone in the British army. We have no information about the Induhvidualness of the British soldiers except that they wore bright red uniforms and marched on unprotected roads in good lighting while singing the British fight song that goes like this: "Shoot me . . . shoot me . . . shoot me." (For a more complete discussion of this phenomenon, refer to Charles Darwin's *The Origin of Species*.) Eventually, this tedious war was over and America was born.

Long after the Founding Fathers laughed themselves to death, the original intent of the Constitution was forgotten and the bonus points for being a dorky white guy were removed from the law. But the core of the system—giving the shaft to lazy and stupid people who have no land (or "capital")—remained intact, forming the basis of our capitalist system. It has worked very well so far.

Any kind of system will tend to discriminate against one group or another. The beauty of our current system of capitalism is that it legally discriminates against the two groups who are least likely to complain: stupid people, AKA Induhviduals, because they don't realize they're getting screwed; and lazy people, because protesting is like work. Unlike other forms of discrimination that are rightly outlawed, almost everyone agrees it's fair to discriminate against lazy and stupid people. It's a very stable system.

PREDICTION 23

Democracy and capitalism will continue to give the shaft to lazy and stupid people. Neither group will complain.

Despite their many shortcomings, Induhviduals and lazy people often end up with large amounts of money through a variety of nonproductive activities, including inheritance, marriage, lotteries, crime, and middle management. In the future, you can expect rapid growth in any business that seeks to take money from Induhviduals and lazy people. Here are some good industries for investment:

- Television.

- Hair growth shampoos.

- Stretch pants.

- Home exercise equipment.

THE FUTURE OF VOTING

In the early days of the United States, it made sense to let ordinary people vote. The issues were relatively simple ones that anyone could understand.

Example of Simple Political Issue from the Past

"Do you think our national bird should be the bald eagle or the turkey?"

Anyone could have an informed opinion on that issue. You could be the kind of guy who's out in the barn trying to milk the chickens and you'd still have all the brainpower needed to cast a meaningful vote on the national bird question.

Thankfully, the voters chose wisely on the national bird issue. Otherwise we'd have to insult people by calling them eagles. Boy Scouts would aspire to be Turkeys. I wouldn't want to live in that country.

Lately, the issues have become so complicated that the average voter is totally baffled. There aren't any simple bird-related questions anymore. It's all complicated stuff like economic policies, strategic alliances, and national health care. The average citizen can't possibly spend enough time to have informed opinions on those subjects, but the country hums right along anyway, because a total lack of comprehension doesn't stop people from having strong opinions and "voting their conscience."

If you think I'm overstating the case, try this exercise. Keep a completely straight face and ask several registered voters this question.

Voter Comprehension Question

"Do you think the Federal Reserve should increase the money supply or should they be required to wear school uniforms?"

The question makes no sense, but I'll bet you can find someone who has a strong opinion about it. Humans have become so accustomed to forming opinions about things they don't understand that it's almost a reflex.

You might be thinking that I'm being overly dismissive of the average person's ability to grasp complicated issues. Here is a true story about an average person, sent to me by a *Dilbert* reader:

True Story of an Average Person

> A secretary was asked to order paper for the office fax machine. The need was immediate, and she didn't want to wait for the next-day delivery. Thinking "outside the box," she called the office supply store and asked if they would fax her some paper to hold them over until the delivery came.

How much should we cut taxes to stimulate the economy without causing inflation? Let's ask the secretary who's waiting for some paper to be faxed to her!

The worst invention in the democratic world is something called referendums. That's where the voters get to vote directly for something. The proponents of most referendums are either intentionally trying to mislead the voters or too stupid to explain the issues clearly. Take a look at this recent true example I received by e-mail:

> From: (name deleted)
> To: scottadams@aol.com
>
> Last month the South Carolina ballot contained a referendum question so that each county could decide whether their "blue laws" should be abolished. These are the laws that control when businesses may open on Sundays. Charleston and Greenville had already abol-

ished their Sunday blue laws, but other counties had not.

The exact wording of the referendum follows.

"Shall the prohibition on Sunday work continue in this county subject to an employee's right to elect not to work on Sunday if the prohibition is not continued after certification of the result of this referendum to the Secretary of State?"

In the case of Greenville County voters, a "no" vote meant they wanted Greenville County to be exempt from the blue laws (which it already was), and a "yes" vote meant they wanted to put the blue laws back into effect in Greenville County.

So many voters misinterpreted what "continue" and "continued" meant in the question that they voted "yes." The blue laws will probably be reinstated here in Greenville County.

If voters have opinions but don't have knowledge or comprehension of the issues, what are they basing their opinions on?

You don't want to know.

Nineteen of the last twenty-six U.S. presidential elections were won by the taller candidate. I know that's true, because I heard it on television. In the few cases where the short candidate won, he tended to have the best hair (Kennedy versus Nixon, for example). Actually, I don't know if the hair correlation is true—I just made it up—but I'd bet on it.

Prior to the Republican convention in 1996, Bob Dole was trailing Bill Clinton in the polls by double digits. Immediately following the convention, the candidates were only a few points apart. Yet the convention generated no new information for voters. No new policies were introduced. No new arguments were made. Apparently, many voters were influenced by SOMETHING other than information.

Look at the effectiveness of television campaign ads. Every voter knows that campaign ads are intentionally misleading, yet campaign ads are very effective. Often they determine the outcome of the election. Here again, people allow themselves to be influenced by something that can't be considered "information" by any stretch of the imagination.

Then there's party loyalty. No matter what information is available about the candidates, most people end up voting for the party they belong to. They remain loyal even if their party's track record and platform change. I'm convinced that if one of the major parties nominated a bag of lettuce for president, the lettuce would get 25 percent of the popular vote. This 25 percent would rationalize their decision by saying things like:

- "Well, at least that lettuce has principles!"
- "It can't be any worse than the other guy."
- "I just think it's time for a change."

Of all the things that influence elections, it appears that information is the least significant. Elections are won by the candidate whose staff members are the most skilled at manipulating the voters. That's not necessarily a bad thing, because you have to be quite smart to figure out the best way to manipulate millions of Induhviduals into marching in the same direction. And if we get tall presidents with good hair who hire smart staff members, that's not the worst thing that could happen.

PREDICTION 24

In the future, most democratic countries will be led by tall people with good hair and smart staff members.

VOTE DEFLATION

Two hundred years ago, there were only sixteen people in the whole United States who voted in the presidential election. (This is an approximation based on the assumption that I don't want to look up the real number.) If you were one of the sixteen people, your vote counted as 6.25 percent of the total votes.

If you voted in the most recent election, your vote was watered down by tens of millions of dolts who think the Speaker of the House is part of their Surround Sound stereo system. Every time a new Induhvidual is registered, the value of your vote is diluted.

PREDICTION 25

In the future, the value of your vote will become less than zero. That happens when the amount you pay in taxes to have your own vote counted is greater than the value you get from the vote itself.

The crossover point is rapidly approaching. It will be much worse when technology makes it easier to register and vote.

Eventually, you will be able to vote over the Internet using your television set and remote control. This raises the frightening specter of millions of people watching *Beavis and Butt-head* and voting during the commercials. The easier it is to vote, the lower the average intelligence of the voters will be. I can't prove this, but under the current system, I have to think a lot of voters get lost on the way to the polling booth. That weeds a lot of Induhviduals out. In the future, you'll never be too drunk or too stupid to vote.

A Phrase You'll Hear in the Future

"I might be too drunk to find the polling place, but I can still help determine the future of the free world!"

Will election results be worse when we have dumber average voters? Let me walk you through a hypothetical situation. Imagine that somehow you find the 100 smartest humans on earth (Hint: look in Switzerland). You ask them to vote on an issue in which the general public is evenly divided.

There are two potential outcomes:

1. The smart people will be just as divided as the general public. That means intelligence is irrelevant to democracy. Ouch.

2. The smart people would all vote for the same side of the issue. That would indicate that intelligence is *very* relevant, but democracy erases its impact. Ouch again.

In either case, you'd find out something you really don't want to know. The scariest result would be to find out that intelligence made a big difference, because tomorrow the super-smart people will be back in Switzerland and the real elections will instead be determined by huge numbers of Induhviduals.

Given all these problems with democracy, the question for any good citizen is clear: How can I make some money out of this? It's easy.

Months before a presidential election, you will hear predictions about stocks that will be helped if a particular national candidate gets elected. For example, if one candidate opposes restrictions on tobacco companies, you might expect tobacco stocks to go up if that candidate gets elected. Having read this book, you are at an advantage compared to other investors. You know there is a 76 percent chance that the tallest candidate will be elected president. And if the tallest candidate also has the best hair, it's a mortal lock. You know which way those tobacco stocks are heading months ahead of the ignorant investors who are studying the so-called "fundamentals."

THE RISE OF THE HAIRY REASONERS

Today, if you're a stunned and confused citizen—and who isn't—you have two choices regarding voting:

Current Voting Choices

1. Make uninformed choices because it's all too confusing.

2. Be a bad citizen.

I think everyone has a nagging feeling that democracy has some bugs, but there's a complete vacuum of ideas about how to fix it. Fortunately, nature abhors a vacuum, which I assume is the reason my vacuum cleaner doesn't work. (Ironically, it does not suck.) I predict the vacuum will be filled by what I call the "Hairy Reasoners."

In the future, voters will wish that some well-informed smart person would just tell them who and what to vote for. That way citizens won't feel like their vote is a waste of time. I predict that this need will be filled with what I will call Hairy Reasoners, so called because I imagine them as people with good reasoning skills and bad hair. (People with good reasoning skills tend to have bad hair. Nobody knows why.)

PREDICTION 26

In the future, voters will be so baffled that they'll want smart people with bad hair to tell them what to do.

I expect the first Hairy Reasoners will be professors, lawyers, and judges—people who are trained to explain things logically even when it differs from their personal opinions. The Hairy Reasoners will have the rare ability to explain complex issues with logic and simple common sense.

It's tempting to think voters can be educated to make better decisions on their own, but some of the dumbest things ever spoken have come out of the mouths of educated people. Well-informed, educated people need Hairy Reasoners, too.

Consider the debate about whether repeat criminals should be locked up for life. I've heard educated people argue that crime does not decrease if you keep the people who commit the crimes in jail. The people who have this opinion need someone like a Hairy Reasoner to explain the situation slowly:

"People . . . who . . . are . . . in . . . prison . . . are . . . not . . . elsewhere . . . at . . . the . . . same . . . time . . . committing . . . crimes. It's a physical law. It's math. This is not a gray area. The real issues are cost and justice."

With the rise of Hairy Reasoners, democracies will experience a decade in which good judgment and informed opinions influence government. People will feel that their vote has regained its lost value. But after a few years of that nonsense, large companies will realize that it doesn't take much money to bribe a Hairy Reasoner. Then we'll see Hairy Reasoners wearing beer company shirts and explaining why it's a good idea for every citizen to smoke three packs of cigarettes a day. But it will be nice until then.

SEVEN

THE FUTURE OF GENDER RELATIONS

SEX IN THE FUTURE

Scientists tend to put the most energy into the areas that interest them personally. That makes it easy to predict one upcoming scientific breakthrough:

PREDICTION 27

In the future, scientists will create a powerful and legal aphrodisiac.

I base this prediction on the fact that most scientists are horny, heterosexual men. What do *you* think they're working on?

Arousal is a function of chemicals in the body. Scientists are getting very good at controlling those chemicals. Before long, we'll have a good idea exactly which chemicals cause which reactions. And since horniness is a naturally occurring condition, it will have no side effects, except for high online service charges.

The scientists will be clever enough to disguise their discovery so it can be approved by the FDA and become widely available. I predict that the new aphrodisiac will be marketed as an antidepressant. That's not too much of a stretch, because it's difficult to be horny and sad at the same time.

The beauty of calling the aphrodisiac drug an antidepressant is that anyone can act depressed, thus qualifying for the drug. It's not as if your doctor is going to tickle you to see if you're lying. And if she does, you might want to see if her diploma is signed.

The warning on the antidepressant drug's label will say something like, "Might cause amazingly high levels of arousal. Avoid alcohol, vacuum cleaners, and farm animals."

No other marketing will be necessary.

Unfortunately, new sexually transmitted diseases will keep springing up every year. We'll have a population of incredibly horny people who are afraid to have sex with one another.

The solution is virtual reality.

Virtual reality technology is also being developed primarily by horny males. You might notice a pattern in these technical developments. Historically, the true purpose of every invention is disguised.

INVENTION	REAL PURPOSE
Club	Seduce women
Fire	Stay warm while seducing women
Printing press	Print Bibles in order to impress women
Automobile	Go on dates with women
Television	Look at women who are prettier than the ones in your house
VCR	Watch other people seduce women
Virtual reality	Imagine what it's like to seduce women

Women are largely oblivious to this scientific motivation, and that's probably a good thing. It gives women more time to run the world. That leads to my next subject, almost by coincidence.

WOMEN IN CHARGE

PREDICTION 28

In the future, women will run the world in all democratic countries.

I base this prediction on two facts that cannot be disputed:

1. Women already control the world.

2. Who's going to stop them?

Men live in a fantasy world. I know this because I am one, and I actually receive my mail there. We men like to think we're in charge because most of the top jobs in business and government are held by men, but I have a shocking statistical insight for you men—THOSE ARE *OTHER* MEN. The total percentage of men in those top spots is roughly .0000001 percent of the male population. I'm not one of them. I just draw cartoons and write these stupid books. Chances are, if you're a man reading this, you're not running the world, either.

I have about as much in common with the CEO of a Fortune 500 company as I have with my cat. It's not logical to say that I, as a man, run the world based on the fact that total strangers with similar chromosomes have excellent jobs. Yet that is exactly what many people believe.

When the Joint Chiefs of Staff are deciding whether to go to war, they do not call my house and say, "We're calling all the men who run the world to ask for their input." Believe it or not, they make those decisions without consulting me. That's probably a good thing, because I favor air strikes against all countries whose names are difficult to pronounce. It's not a "policy" in the strictest sense of the word, but it would sure make it easier to discuss world events.

Furthermore, tiny countries should have short names so the mapmakers can fit it all in. I think that would stimulate the economy somehow. But these excellent ideas are wasted under the current system of global decision-making.

Someone might argue that men have access to the top jobs whereas women do not. There's some truth to that, but the mathematical fact is, 99.9999999 percent of all men can't get those top jobs, either. There aren't enough of those jobs to go around. The rest of us men live in a world that is ruled by women, as I will explain for those of you who hadn't noticed.

What evidence do I have that women rule the world? Take a look at the world and ask yourself how it would be different if men were REALLY in charge. Look at the things that men want most, then check to see if the world is organized to *provide* those things or to *limit* them. Logically, if men made the rules, the world would be organized to provide them with the things they want most.

Men want sex. If men ruled the world, they could get sex anywhere, anytime. Restaurants would give you sex instead of breath mints on the way out. Gas stations would give sex with every fill-up. Banks would give sex to anyone who opened a checking account.

But it doesn't work that way, at least not at my bank. (Having your own "personal banker" isn't all it's cracked up to be.)

Instead, for the most part, sex is provided by women if they feel like it, which they usually don't. If a heterosexual guy wants sex, he has to hold doors, buy flowers, act polite, lift heavy objects, kill spiders, pretend to be interested in boring things, and generally act like a complete wuss. Can anyone think men designed *that* system?

If men were smart enough to figure out what's going on, they might be tempted to use their superior size and strength to dominate women. But women are too clever to let that happen. Thousands of years ago, women figured out they could disguise their preferences as "religion" and control gullible men that way. In one part of the world, I imagine the conversation went like this:

Husband:	I'll be back in an hour. I'm going to go covet my neighbor's wife.
Wife:	You can't do that.
Husband:	Why not?
Wife (thinking fast):	Um . . . God said so. He's an omnipotent being. If you don't obey him you'll burn in hell.
Husband:	Whoa, that was a close one. Thanks for warning me . . . How about if I kill her husband first?
Wife:	Ooh, bad news on that, too.

PREDICTION 29

In the future, religious groups will get mad at me, thus
boosting my book sales.

Religion is only one of the ways women control men. It runs much deeper than that. I'll explain it all in this next section.

Manners

Our lives are guided by annoying little rules called "manners." The rules kick in whenever there are other people around, which is most of the time. That means whoever invented these manners is controlling our behavior most of the time without even being there.

Do you think men invented manners?

Manners would be a lot different if men created them. For example, the Swiss Army Knife would be the right utensil for any occasion, including holidays and weddings. If you're wearing clothes, you have all you need in the napkin department. It's that simple.

The best evidence that women invented manners is the fact that formal dinners have many forks. This multiple-fork situation must have been invented by people who really, really *like* forks. There's no other explanation. I have never seen a man comment on the quality or beauty of a fork. No man ever said, "This fork is terrific. I wish I had several of them for this meal. We can use one to eat food and the other to . . . um . . . eat more food."

If men had invented forks there would be no prohibition about using one in each hand at the same time. Obviously, women are the driving force behind the proliferation of forks, and, by logical extension, they must be responsible for all manner of manners.

We can test this assumption by looking at some of the major categories of manners and asking how likely it is that men were involved in their design.

Elbows on Table

People who have good manners don't put their elbows on the dinner table. Clearly this is not a male idea. That table is EXACTLY WHERE THE ELBOWS SHOULD GO. It makes no sense to put a table in front of a person at elbow-height if it's just going to tease. Your lap will hold a plate, but your lap won't rest your elbows. There must be some reason tables were invented. When I look at the tables in my house, they are covered with flower centerpiece thingies, but no elbows. Whose idea do you think that was? If you ask me, flowers belong in the ground and elbows belong on the table. But nobody asked.

Covering Your Sneeze

Do you think men came up with the concept of covering your mouth with your hand when you sneeze? I can't imagine a man sitting around saying, "You know, the very best place to sneeze is on part of my own body."

I don't think so. Sneezing on your own body is the very worst place you could possibly sneeze. Even your family pet knows to sneeze on a family member instead of its own paw.

Swearing

Certain words are considered impolite. Can you imagine a smoke-filled room where silver-haired men discuss which words will be considered impolite?

Smoke-Filled Room Fantasy Scene

"The next word for consideration is 'pud.'"

A collective gasp fills the room. A man in the front faints. The group wisely decides to add it to their forbidden list.

No, I can't imagine it either.

Courtship

Under our current system of courtship, men do most of the date-asking and women get to squish men's fragile egos like Fudgsicles on a Los Angeles freeway. I'm reasonably certain that men did not invent this system.

If it were up to men, all women would be equipped with special hormonal monitors to tell men such vital information as when it's a cry-free time of the month and when arousal is highest. Then we'd know when it's a good time for courting and when it's a better idea to run some errands. This would be a huge time-saver for everyone, but obviously nobody consulted men about how courtship should work.

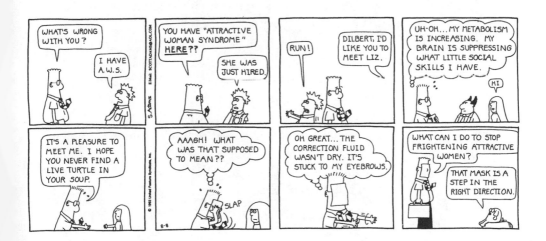

Fun

Nothing annoys women more than watching men have fun when there are heavy items in need of being moved to other places. If men ruled the world, all of those heavy objects would be in the right place to begin with, no matter where they were. But they aren't. Oh, no, everything is in the wrong place and must be moved now, not after your favorite television show is over.

Money

On average, men get paid more money than women. Most people think that is unfair, but let's look at it another way. Given a choice, most people would rather spend money than earn money. And who is doing all the spending?

If you don't believe that women spend most of the money, just walk into any Sears store and see what they're selling. If you're a male, you see maybe two things you might want—a second cordless drill (so you have a spare in the car) and a trickle charger, because you like how they look in the garage. That's all you want in the whole store. But SOMEONE is buying all that other stuff in there or Sears wouldn't be in business. Someone is buying those fuzzy toilet seat covers. Someone is buying decorative covers for tissue boxes. Someone is buying place mats.

Who could it be?

Kids don't have money. Pets aren't allowed in Sears. By the process of elimination, we can conclude that women must be buying all that other stuff. Women are spending most of the money.

If you were from another planet, such as Switzerland, and you only knew these two facts—1) Men earn most of the money, and 2) Women spend most of the money—what would you assume about who is holding whom by the whatchamacallits and swinging the person who owns the whatchamacallits around in the air while yelling, "I AM WOMAN, HEAR ME ROAR!"?

It's a rhetorical question.

Fashion

If men controlled fashion, they'd convince women to wear uncomfortable, pointy-heeled shoes that made legs look attractive. They'd promote bras that lifted the breasts upward for no apparent reason. The standard business attire for women would be skirts that display lots of leg. Men, on the other hand, would be able to get away with wearing a dull gray suit or jeans every single day.

Actually, I guess that's the way it is. Obviously, men control fashion. But that's the only thing men control.

In the short term, I predict women will try to tighten their grip on the world. We'll have more knickknacks and doilies than at any time in history. But that's in the near term. In the long term, technology will provide freedom for men, as I'll explain in the next section.

TECHNOLOGY TO FREE MEN

Scientists, most of them men, will continue to develop technologies that can provide men with freedom from the women who control every aspect of their lives except fashion.

PREDICTION 30

Most scientific and technical breakthroughs in the next century will be created by men and directed at finding replacements for women.

If you're looking to invest in the future, put your money in those areas that hold the most promise for replicating the roles of women:

- Genetic engineering.

- Virtual reality.

- Artificial intelligence.

- Internet.

- Robotics.

- Voice mail.

Those technologies that hold no promise as female replacements will stagnate. A good example of dead-end technology is air travel. It's essentially the same as it was thirty years ago—same cramped seats, same peanuts. The headphone technology has advanced all the way to "the hollow plastic tube." I'm not sure how ancient the flight control radar is, but I think it involves interns standing on top of the flight tower yelling, "Turn right! Turn right!" (More on this topic later.)

In contrast, during this extended period of airline technology stagnation, the nation's phone system has developed substantially. Your telephone has turned into a ubiquitous female presence through the widespread use of voice mail and audiotex systems that feature primarily feminine voices.

The "official" reason given for using female voices is that they are easier to hear, but I think it's obvious that the male technologists who promoted this technology wanted to have something on their desks that would sound like a woman and ask to be touched.

"Press one if you'd like to leave a message. Press two if it's the only action you'll get this month."

EIGHT

THE FUTURE OF WORK

THE FUTURE OF MANAGERS

In an earlier book, *The Dilbert Principle*, I explained why incompetent employees are systematically identified and promoted to management. I will reiterate it here, in case you didn't read my earlier book, or you were drunk, or you refuse to listen, or you are not very bright, or you enjoy reading the same stuff twice. Your reasons are your own. I'm just trying to meet you halfway.

The underlying fact that prompted me to write *The Dilbert Principle* is that it takes less brains to be a manager than to be the people who are managed. For example, it takes a big ol' brain to write a computer program with a revolutionary new data encryption algorithm. A much smaller brain is needed to command that programmer to write status reports justifying his value.

If you're a surgeon, it takes a great deal of skill and intelligence to perform an organ transplant. It is much less challenging to write a mission statement for the hospital that explains your deep desire to avoid killing patients accidentally.

Middle management is becoming a dumping ground for professionals who have no special skills. It's the safest place to put them. You don't want one of them performing heart bypass surgery on you. There are already millions of highly skilled employees being managed by people who aren't nearly as bright, and this is not a stable situation.

Alleged True Story

The CEO of a small company decided they needed a motto to commemorate their longevity in the industry. This is what he came up with:

"Our innovation makes us first—our quality makes us last!"

The predictable result of the Dilbert Principle is that skilled professionals won't put up with the indignity of being "managed" by idiots.

PREDICTION 31

In the future, skilled professionals will flee their corporate jobs and become their own bosses in ever-increasing numbers. They'll become entrepreneurs, consultants, contractors, prostitutes, and cartoonists.

Recently, an executive of a well-known magazine told me that he couldn't find any writers who were willing to join the company as employees. Several good writers were willing to work on a contractual basis, but none of them wanted a boss and a cubicle. Nor would they fall for the trick of agreeing to an exclusive contract. I predict you'll see a lot more of this in the future— the smartest professionals will avoid becoming either managers or employees. They'll have clients instead of bosses. They will be blissfully independent.

True Story

Yesterday at the airport I ran into an ex-coworker from my days at Pacific Bell. She quit the cubicle world two years ago to start her own consulting business. This week she hired her seventy-fifth employee.

We didn't have time to talk, because she was rushing off to exercise with her personal trainer.

The gutsiest professionals are already quitting their jobs and going it alone, but they're the exception. Most professionals are like sheep. (That's why so many business suits are made of wool, in case you wondered.) Employees have been conditioned by their employers to be timid and frightened. The sheepish employees will have to make the transition the way I did—by launching a new career from the security of a cubicle while still wearing a little wool outfit.

People often ask me how they can put energy into building a second career when they are already giving 100 percent to their current one. This would be a big problem if your salary and job security were somehow related to your performance. But that's living in the past. In the future, financial security will come primarily from your ability to divert company resources toward your new start-up business. I call it "employer financing." That way it doesn't sound so much like stealing. This is similar to when your boss refers to mandatory unpaid overtime as "being competitive."

Some people would say employer financing is unethical, maybe even illegal. That viewpoint is important to remember, because you'll want to remind people what they said later when they come to your new company and ask for a job.

EMPLOYEE MOTIVATION

The current method of motivating employees involves frightening them until their arteries harden, then trying to make it all better by giving them inexpensive gifts bearing the company logo. Employees routinely trade their health for T-shirts, movie tickets, and framed certificates of accomplishments. To an objective observer—i.e., someone who doesn't care about you (i.e., your boss)—it would seem that employees are not very bright. But it wasn't always like this.

There was a time, years ago, when companies rewarded employees with a thing called "money." But after the "Dawn of Downsizing," the balance of power shifted completely to the employer. Companies didn't have to give away their hard-earned money to retain employees. They had too many workers already. What were the disgruntled employees going to do, quit?

This was a problem for middle managers. They were being paid to motivate the employees, but they didn't have the two tools that had always been effective in the past—money and the promise of job security. Managers needed new ways to dupe employees into working harder— ways that didn't cost anything.

With the help of highly paid consultants (i.e., people who had already been downsized), the managers hatched a wide range of "recognition" schemes that involved giving away things that come out of a laser printer instead of the U.S. Treasury.

This e-mail message describes one person's experience with a recognition award.

Subject: ataboys
From: (anonymous)
To: scottadams@aol.com

I just received an "ataboy" in the form of a time-off award. The letter I received described the events leading to the award and then it had this paragraph:

The above contributions resulted in a nonmeasurable benefit of small value and limited application. Therefore, four hours time off will be awarded to the employee.

Some "ataboy," eh?

Employees responded to the new recognition systems by staying at work for longer hours than ever. Most of that extra time was spent writing résumés and making long-distance calls from the fax room. But managers observed the employees staying in the office for longer hours and declared the recognition programs to be brilliant substitutes for money.

Somewhere right now I'm sure there is a manager sticking a bent paper clip into an eraser and wondering if he can pass it off as the "Excalibur Award for Excellence." He's thinking to himself that it's the recognition that counts, not the value of the gift. Any employee would be delighted to be recognized as a person who works eighty hours per week in return for a bent paper clip stuck in an eraser. That's exactly the kind of recognition employees crave—recognition as suckers.

Employees who don't appreciate "recognition" programs don't want to complain, because another downsizing could be around the corner.

Complaining during downsizing is like playing with a pogo stick in a fox-hole. It feels good, but it doesn't last.

THE REVENGE OF THE DOWNSIZED

Working for a big company was a great deal until the nineties. If you could get hired, it was practically impossible to get fired. The biggest risk was that you'd cram too many office supplies in your pants and blow out a pocket.

Then the era of downsizing came. Employees were shoveled out the door faster than a pile of dead chipmunks at a cotillion. (And that's pretty darned fast even if I don't know what it means.) But many of the down-sizees had been avoiding real work by taking company-sponsored training courses for years. They were capable of doing excellent work if anybody had thought to ask. Suddenly, they were unemployed. Out of necessity, they reinvented themselves as "self-employed" people and scrambled to create new careers that would use the skills they learned while avoiding work.

Time passed. Then a funny thing happened. Downsized companies dis-covered they couldn't run a multinational company with just a CEO and a

Diversity Director. They needed employees. But it was too late to get their old employees back on the same basis. Companies couldn't offer job security without laughing. All they had was money. The balance of power had shifted. It became a seller's market for the most highly skilled workers.

PREDICTION 32

In the future, the balance of employment power will change.
We'll witness the revenge of the downsized.

It's not unusual to find companies where one-third of the technical staff are consultants and contract employees, some earning over $100 per hour. Unemployment pays very well if you do it right. Now everyone wants to get in the act.

More people are discovering the joys of self-employment every year. Before long, they'll band together to get discounts on insurance, office equipment, training, and travel. They'll have their own magazines and conventions. They'll share information and blackball certain employers, cutting them off from the top talent. The self-employed will have power. Then the real fun begins.

The old-fashioned "job interview" will be a relic. Instead of the employer tormenting the helpless wannabe employee, you'll have the contract employees interviewing the employer.

Old Job Interview Process

Employer: I see that your name is Carl, but I'll call you pimple boy. Is that okay with you?

Job Seeker: Yes sir. You are very observant.

Employer: What is your biggest weakness, aside from your appearance, your lack of education, and your irrelevant experience?

Job Seeker: When I tongue-washed your car this morning, I forgot to move the car one foot ahead so I could wash the part of the tire that was on the ground.

Employer: INCOMPETENT FOOL! GET OUT OF MY OFFICE!

Future Job Interview Process

Employer: What can I do to convince you to accept obscene amounts of money to work here on a short-term contract basis? I'm begging. Please.

Contractor: Well . . . I always wanted to have a pony.

Employer: I'll get you a pony!

Contractor: No, I want you to *be* my pony.

PREDICTION 33

In the future, highly qualified people will go on job interviews
purely for recreation.

This new balance of power will be loads of fun for the contract employees, especially the bitter ones who were downsized. But despite the fun of
being a contract employee, there will still be lots of regular employees.
Their balance of power will also change, but in a totally different way. That
leads me to the next topic.

THE JOB SEARCH IN THE FUTURE

Most people end up in their jobs by luck. For every person who planned a
career, there are twenty who have stories that sound a lot like this one that
I just made up:

Not a True Story

Well, one day I was riding my bike and a huge dog bit me and left me for dead. On the way to the hospital, a tanker truck ran a red light and collided with my ambulance, creating a gigantic explosion that propelled me across the street and onto a table at a sidewalk cafe. I started screaming, "WAA-OOO-AAHHH!" One of the patrons at the cafe was a music producer. He signed me to a five-record deal and drove me to the hospital. That's where I met my drummer.

Most people won't admit how they got their current jobs unless you push them up against a built-in wall unit and punch them in the stomach until they spill their drink and start yelling, "I'LL NEVER INVITE YOU TO ONE OF MY PARTIES AGAIN, YOU DRUNKEN FOOL!" I think the reason these annoying people won't tell me how they got their jobs is because they are embarrassed to admit luck was involved. I can't blame them. Typically, the pre-luck part of their careers involved doing something enormously pathetic.

Take me, for example. I'm a successful cartoonist and author because I'm a complete failure at being an employee of the local phone company. Despite the fact that my co-workers were so lifeless they were often mistaken for mannequins, I was not streaking past them on my way up the career ladder. I didn't have the hair or height to succeed in management. Instead, I spent my time mocking successful managers and accidentally preparing for my future career.

I learned to draw when I was a kid because the alternative forms of entertainment were limited. I didn't grow up in what you'd call "a town with intellectually stimulating people." I suppose I could have made friends with the kids my age who were fascinated with the interaction of firecrackers and frogs, but science didn't interest me at the time.

We had a television, but we only received one channel clearly. It required some ingenuity to do any channel surfing, especially since we didn't have a remote control. I would wait until my little sister wandered by and then yell, "Cindy, change the channel while you're up." This was very funny until the millionth time, after which she broke my jaw with a hassock.

My only other choices for entertainment were drawing cartoons or playing Scrabble with Mom. Mom took her Scrabble very seriously. She was a brutal competitor. In fact, she didn't teach me any language skills until I reached the age of six, because she figured that would give her an edge in Scrabble later on. I was in college before I figured out that Webster didn't really make any last-minute handwritten additions to the dictionary. To this day I still wonder about her claim that head-butting is allowed in Scrabble.

So I ended up drawing cartoons alone in my room because it didn't require any language skills and I wouldn't have to watch my Mom do that damned victory dance on the kitchen table. If I wrote a completely accurate résumé for myself right now, I'd have to say something like, "Leveraged my inadequacies into a career that involves making fun of people who are more successful in business than I am."

There are some exceptions to the career luck rule. For example, lawyers and doctors study for years to prepare for their professions, diligently acquiring valuable information that they can use later in lieu of personalities. But the rest of us don't have a clear career path. If we're lucky, we're bitten by large dogs and propelled into sidewalk cafes where something lucky happens.

It's a good thing that career luck happens so often. It's more effective than the alternative—lying on your résumé and hoping you get an interview with someone who has poor perception.

The current job-filling process has been a wonderful thing for unqualified people. I was a major beneficiary of the system in my corporate past. I could always count on moving to a new job within the company, assisted by the fact that the hiring manager didn't have a good system for finding a better candidate. My employer's lack of alternatives was my gain.

But what happens when every job opening and every résumé is on the Internet? Surely that will happen. You'll suddenly find yourself competing against *thousands* of candidates for every low- and medium-skill job. You won't be able to rely on the inefficiency of the job search process anymore.

Companies will be able to find a candidate who not only fits a job perfectly without training, but might be willing to do it for *less* than the normal salary for that position. For example, someone in a godforsaken hellhole like North Dakota might want to move to California and be willing to accept a low salary to do it. In fact, they might be willing to do it without demanding that their relocation costs be paid. In fact, they might be willing to strap their livestock to their backs and walk to California. (Note: If you are a resident of the godforsaken hellhole of North Dakota, the only thing I actually know about your state is that you don't buy many *Dilbert* books. The conclusion that it is a hellhole follows logically. If this bothers you, I suggest that you move to South Dakota where you can get some respect.)

For the first time in history, companies will have an abundance of good applicants for every job opening in the "medium-skill" level. That means salaries for medium-skilled jobs will go down, unless the government gets involved. If the government notices what's happening to salaries, they will step in and do what governments always do for the powerless—they'll raise their taxes. So it's bad news all around.

PREDICTION 34

In the future, salaries will go down for people in medium-skilled jobs, thanks to the godforsaken hellhole called North Dakota.

It's happy days ahead for the highly skilled laborer. The job market will start to look like the NBA. Top technical people will command amazingly obscene salaries. The employee who is 1 percent better in a high-skill area is worth a hundred times as much as someone who is just "pretty good." That 1 percent might be the difference between winning and losing in the marketplace—just as it is in sports.

Professional sports is a good model for how the rest of the economy will look in the future. Pro sports is an industry where there is almost complete information about who has what skills and who has what openings. It's a fairly efficient job market.

In the NBA, you end up with amazingly rich athletes on one end of the scale and everyone else who works for the club has job descriptions like, "Guy who wipes perspiration off the court during time-outs." There are a few executives in the middle to hold it all together, but they aren't terribly important.

That's what the job market will look like in the future—rich superstar professionals on one end of the spectrum, perspiration wipers on the other, and a few managers in the middle. Everything else will be done by consultants or outsourcing firms.

PREDICTION 35

In the future, employees will either be superstars or perspiration wipers. Those who aren't qualified to do either will become managers.

OUTSOURCING

My mother always told me to beware of strangers. But over time, I've noticed that strangers are consistently nicer than the people I know. I don't think it's a coincidence. I have to conclude that all of the insightful, talented, and generous people in the world are in fact strangers.

Many companies have reached the same conclusion. They know that it's a waste of time to have their own bumbling employees perform important functions. It's better to trust those functions to the people who have our best interests in mind (i.e., complete strangers in distant lands). This is the concept behind "outsourcing," and it's a good one.

I use outsourcing in my job, too. My cats were my in-house legal department until I discovered they were coughing up hairballs and recording the time as billable hours. Now I pay a human being in another city to handle my legal stuff. He still coughs up hairballs, but he has the professional courtesy to call it "phone conversation" when he lists it on the invoice.

When you're trying to outsource work, always select the low-cost provider. Quality isn't important, because you can always fix that later by learning the native tongue of your supplier and making threatening phone calls in the middle of the night. The only risk is that the electrical impulses from your telephone network won't travel across the baling twine used as a phone network in your supplier's country. Sometimes you can compensate by yelling.

PREDICTION 36

In the future, all work will be outsourced, until all the work on the
planet is being done by one guy.

In the future, all companies will outsource their work to other companies who will subcontract their work to yet other companies. Eventually,
there will be one guy doing all the work on Earth. This will all be well and
good until one day he calls in sick and the entire economy of the planet is
plunged into a depression. Until that happens, there's no real downside.

If you want to thrive in an era of outsourcing, try to avoid being that one
guy who does everyone's work. He'll make a lot of money in the short run,
but you know he's going to take the blame when things go terribly wrong.

THE JOB MODEL OF THE FUTURE

I'm convinced that my job situation is a model of the future. This chapter
is being written as I sit alone in my home office in my pajamas. (They're
red flannel, just so you can picture it.) The only noise is the whir of my
hard disk and the sound of my cat, Sarah, chewing through my modem
cables.

I have no employees at the moment, yet the *Dilbert* business is generating record sales and reaching 140 million readers every day. My relationship with the hundreds of professionals who bring *Dilbert* to the market is
contractual. I am blissful in my non-boss environment.

I've noticed that when people have contracts, they do what the contract
says. Full-time employees have fuzzier objectives. They often feel underpaid and abused. They don't have much incentive to do the right thing,
especially since big raises and promotions are mostly history.

In those rare situations where employees have clear objectives and good
intentions, their efforts are blocked by various mandatory productivity-
thwarting activities:

Productivity-Thwarting Activities

- Mandatory dress code.

- Mandatory safety training.

- Mandatory sexual harassment training.

- Mandatory diversity training.

- Mandatory United Way kick-off meeting.

- Mandatory staff meetings.

When you work alone, everything is optional, including clothes. I can do dangerous things if I want to. I can do dangerous things naked if I want to. I can sexually harass myself while doing dangerous things naked. And I can insult myself for doing it. Best yet, I can do it during the time I've scheduled for my own staff meeting. I try to do all of those things as often as possible.

If you're an employee of a big company, you've probably spent hours contributing to the creation of your department's mission statement. I also have a mission statement, but I didn't have to consider the inane opinions of any co-workers when I wrote it. My entire mission statement took twelve seconds to write. It goes like this:

Scott Adams's Mission Statement

"Rub my bald spot once a day."

My mission statement doesn't help me make more money. It doesn't even make sense. But I've never seen a mission statement that met either of those tests. At least I didn't spend much time writing mine. That's more than you can say if you work for a big company.

Here is a selection of cartoons that best describe the productivity and effectiveness of the typical office environment. If you haven't already decided to work for yourself, this should push you over the edge.

PREDICTION 37

In the future, more people will work for themselves, creating a huge
market for bizarre products.

Obviously, with a work environment like Dilbert's, a growing number of
people will choose to work at home. There's a huge market opportunity for
anyone who can figure out what products to sell to people who work at
home. Three ideas come to mind:

Products Needed for the Work-at-Home Market

- Smell-o-meter to remind you when to bathe.

- Anti-cat guard for your computer keyboard.

- Pants with special holsters for holding bananas. (I like to snack
  during the day and I resent the trips to the kitchen.)

I also want a fake "call-waiting" feature for my phone. That would be a
huge time-saver, because my friends think that just because I'm sitting
around in my pajamas rubbing my bald spot, I'm not working. They don't
know that is exactly what my mission statement says I should be doing. I'd
like to be able to tell the people who call me, "Ooh, It sounds like I have
another call. Would you mind hanging up and never calling again?" I
already say that to people, but I think some are catching on that I'm making the call-waiting sound by whistling.

THE FUTURE OF TELECOMMUTING

A growing number of workers—those who are more clever than industri-
ous—have already discovered the unbridled joy of sitting at home and getting paid for sleeping, eating, masturbating, and watching television. This

technique—sometimes called telecommuting—has all the financial advantages of being employed with none of the stigma of being a filthy, perverted hobo.

PREDICTION 38

In the future, filthy, perverted hobos will refer to themselves as telecommuters, until someone points out that they aren't being paid.

Telecommuting is much better than the alternative of going into the office and having your co-workers peck you to death like a flock of chickens on a tissue-paper bag full of corn. (Please take a moment to savor that analogy. If you close your eyes, you can almost hear the chickens clucking.)

Those of you who are foolish enough to transport your bodies to the office are faced with the daily horror of what some people have begun calling "negative work."

NEGATIVE WORK FORMULA

Real Work + Negative Work = Zero Work

For example, let's say you need some vital information from a co-worker in order to do "real work." Your co-worker is likely to generate enough "negative work" to cancel your productivity for the day.

Example of Negative Work in Action

You: Please give me that vital information that you alone possess.

Co-worker: Sure, but while I've got you here, why don't you attend my project meeting?

You: Um . . . what does your project have to do with me?

Co-worker: It's an important project. You should be there to provide your valuable input.

You: I don't even know what your project is about.

Co-worker: Of course not! You haven't attended any of the meetings. It starts in ten minutes. I'll give you the vital information right afterward. Heck, we might even discuss the vital information during the meeting. You don't want to miss that, do you?

(At this point in the conversation, you realize you will never get help from this co-worker again unless you cave in to this ludicrous request.)

You:	Well, okay, I guess.
Co-worker:	Great. Oh, and bring a pad. It's your turn to take the minutes.

The result of this is negative work.

Productivity in the modern office can be scored like golf, as in "I'm three under for the day." For every unit of work, there is at least one off-setting unit of negative work created by your Induhvidual co-workers.

It's worse for women, of course, because male Induhviduals know that flirting with female co-workers looks exactly like work. Males naturally want to talk to as many women as possible during the day. This maximizes their enjoyment and income while trading off nothing except shareholder value—and that belongs to people who should know better than to invest in your company. So it's hard to feel sorry for them.

The lonelier the guy and the more attractive the woman, the greater the amount of negative work that will be generated. For lonely guys, a business meeting with attractive co-workers is like a date, except at the end of the meeting, the women give you correct phone numbers. Speaking as a guy who has dated, this is a big improvement.

I realize it's unwise to go deeper into this topic during times of great sensitivity about diversity in the workplace, but there's something that all women need to know about men in order to understand what's behind much of the negative work. Here it is. The secret that all males in the workplace don't want women to know is:

WE'RE THINKING ABOUT HAVING SEX WITH YOU!

If you're a woman, you're thinking, "Duh." You already knew that. The part you probably don't know is *when* men think it and how often.

The "how often" part is whenever you're talking. Men can only do one thing at a time. We're notorious single-taskers. We can't speak a sentence and hold a good fantasy at the same time, so when *we're* talking, we're *not* fantasizing. But when a woman is talking to a man, the man has two choices:

1. Listen.

2. Fantasize about having sex with the woman who is generating all that noise.

This explains the common complaint that women have about men—we don't listen. It's not because we don't *want* to listen to what you have to say, but that we can't do two things at once. Listening never gets higher than the number-two priority. (Okay, maybe that's the same as saying we don't *want* to listen. But let's not get all caught up in semantics.)

The reason I can safely reveal this secret is that men already know it and women won't believe it. Women are multitaskers. I'll bet women can mix a fantasy with their conversation without missing a beat. Women probably think men are like that, too—capable of entertaining mild fantasies throughout the day without losing focus or drifting in and out of comas. Well, we can't. When you're talking, we're thinking intensely about having sex with you. If you're unattractive, we're focusing on the woman just over your shoulder. It's not something we're proud of. It's just the way we're wired.

If there are any women who think I'm overgeneralizing, I'll be happy to meet with you to listen to your point of view. But please bring a cute friend as an emergency backup in case you're wrong.

Telecommuting isn't for everyone. It takes a certain kind of person to be able to work alone. I recommend trying telecommuting for one week and then taking this quiz to see if you have what it takes to enjoy it.

Telecommuting Enjoyment Test

- Did you at any time open the refrigerator and start shoveling anything that wasn't stuck to the shelf toward the big hole in your face?

- Did you at any time take a conference call in the nude and experience an intense guilty pleasure?

- Did you at any time curse at an inanimate object and later apologize to it?

- Did you at any time engage in solo sex and yell out, "I'M GETTING PAID FOR THIS! HA HA HA HA HA!"?

If you said yes to any of those questions, you should be telecommuting more often.

THE FUTURE OF OFFICE WORKSTATIONS

When I first joined the work force in 1979, anybody with a body temperature over eighty degrees qualified for a private office with a door. Those were glorious, carefree days. I was working for a huge California bank. Every day, I would close the door to my private office and spend hours making personal phone calls, balancing my checkbook, and flirting with attractive female co-workers. Sometimes I flirted with unattractive female co-workers, but in my defense, I considered it "practice."

Thousands of my co-workers were doing similar things behind their own closed doors, except for the handful of attractive co-workers who were forced to roam from office to office to keep the system working.

Eventually, my company was purchased by its competitor for the price of $12 plus some postage stamps (I forget the exact figure), and most of my co-workers were fired. I escaped their fate by calling upon my most valuable professional resource—luck—which allowed me to attach myself in a barnacle-like fashion to another big company in the nick of time. I even got a large undeserved salary increase too.

Although I successfully leveraged my incompetence into a better job, I still looked back with bitterness, dismay, and yes, sometimes laughter. The laughter part was usually when my ex–co-workers called to ask if there were any openings at my company. I found 100 different ways to tell them that my new company had much higher standards, and it wasn't really an option they should be considering.

Although I was out of banking, I couldn't stop wondering what the victorious bank had that my old vanquished bank didn't have. Why could one company triumph where one had failed? In time, I uncovered their secret: cubicles.

The bank discovered that when employees were taken out of private offices and put in tiny, fabric-covered containers, they became competitive dynamos. These cubicle-bound titans used less real estate, heating, and cooling. And the sleek, doorless design cut way back on the flirting and personal calls. Those workers became unstoppable, productive juggernauts capable of squashing any sissified office-dwelling company.

Employee communication increased significantly. With the open-cubicle design, they could hear not only the conversations directed at themselves, but also the conversations directed at anyone else. And they weren't limited to audio inputs. They could read the body language of everyone in the office who waddled past the cubicles all day long.

That bank hasn't rested on its laurels. They're still innovating. Recently, they improved the restrooms by removing all the stalls and adding windows to the hallway. Result: Nobody goes in there to read the sports section anymore. Profits have zoomed. It looks like another good year for the stockholders.

But what of the future of office workstations? Nothing ever stays the same. It's safe to predict that cubicles are not the ultimate answer for office space. So let's follow the logic and see where it leads.

Cubicles are more competitive than private offices, but they still have a lot of wasted room. A fully occupied cubicle is 70 percent air. That waste has not escaped the notice of workstation designers. Most of the unused airspace will be driven out of the design of future work areas. This is already happening at many companies, albeit gradually, as they replace larger cubicles with ever-smaller versions. This practice even has a name at some companies: "densification." But it won't end there.

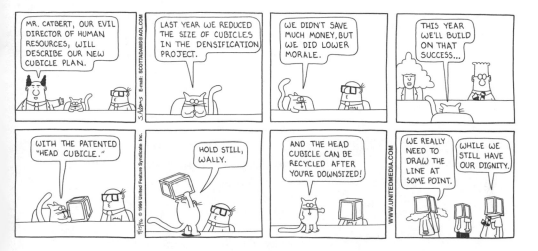

I see the workstation of the future looking like a high-tech hairdresser's chair. You'll have your computer built into the base of the chair and the keyboard swinging onto your lap from the side. No desk surface will be needed. An oversized helmet-like device (let's call it a "head cubicle") will be attached to the back of your chair and cover your head for privacy. On the inside of the head cubicle will be a display screen, speakers, and a microphone. Every unit will be wired to the Internet and the public phone system. These workstations will be lined up side by side in warehouse-like office spaces in dangerous neighborhoods. You'll be able to shout and sing and moan in your head cubicle without disturbing your co-worker who is two feet away. And you won't hear his annoying cries for help after sustaining a bullet wound on the way to work.

PREDICTION 39

In the future, aggressive companies will replace standard cubicles with head cubicles.

New technology will allow managers to monitor the unproductive activities of each employee as never before. Sensors will detect your pulse and breathing rates to determine whether you're downloading pornography from the Internet or doing anything else that is fun or stimulating. Monitors will detect REM patterns and beep whenever an employee nods off. Employees will learn to stay in a narrow range of joyless existence between happiness (which shouldn't be compensated) and sleep (which is unproductive). Let's call that the "Compensated Work Zone," or CWZ for short. I don't plan to use the phrase ever again for the rest of my life, but I think we can all admit we like acronyms and leave it at that.

You won't need conference rooms, because everyone will be able to attend virtual meetings without leaving the chair. Visitors from the outside will get their own special chairs in the lobby so they never have to see the employees in person.

The virtual meetings won't use video conferencing technology in the way most people imagine. There's one huge drawback to video conferencing: Many employees are ugly. Logically, it is a waste of bandwidth to transmit an image of something you'd be better off not looking at. If you think about it, there are very few of your co-workers who have faces you'd like to see more often. I've never met anyone who kept pictures of their co-workers on their desk in little frames. It's rare to find anyone carrying a picture of a co-worker in their wallet. So then why on Earth would we want to transmit their ugly faces across the network and have them appear two feet from our noses?

The obvious solution—and inevitable by any reasoned opinion—is that people will send digitally enhanced images to represent themselves at meetings. This will solve the ugliness *and* the dress code problem at the same time.

Every employee will have a chance to create their own digital representative. There will be corporate guidelines of course, which I imagine will look something like this:

Corporate Guidelines for Digital Representatives (DR)

1. Your DR may not be a nudist.

2. Your DR may not resemble our CEO in leather chaps.

3. Your DR's head and buttocks must be clearly differentiated.

4. Your DR may not be visibly aroused.

ACRONYMS SHORTAGES

There are only twenty-six letters in the alphabet. Eventually, all of the good acronyms that are less than four letters will be used up. This will be a major problem for businesses.

We'll also start running out of new company names and logo designs. The first sign of trouble—and we're already seeing it—is when major companies begin using coffee stains for logos.°

We're already starting to scrape the bottom of the name barrel.

°After the Brown Ring of Quality strips were published in the newspaper, I got many e-mail messages from people who assumed I was referring to AT&T's Lucent spin-off. Many other people wrote to say it reminded them of their own logos. Apparently, the coffee stain concept was a popular one.

PREDICTION 40

In the future, your only choices for new project names will be ones
that sound undignified.

True Story

At one technology company, the senior management became angered that two important projects had been named Ren and Stimpy, after famous cartoon characters. They declared that henceforth there would be a master namer who would approve the names of all future projects. The master namer would choose from a list of famous river names to ensure appropriate and dignified names.

The process worked well until engineers presented the status of projects Ubangi and Volga. Senior management was livid until someone explained that those are the names of rivers.

INDUSTRIAL ESPIONAGE

Industrial espionage sounds like a great concept on paper. The theory is that your competitors know something important that you should also know.

PREDICTION 41

In the future, it will become increasingly obvious that your competitors are just as clueless as you are.

NINE

MARKETING IN THE FUTURE

In the past, every successful company had some sort of "barrier to entry" that kept other companies from swooping in and stealing their customers.

PREDICTION 42

In the future, all barriers to entry will go away and companies will be forced to form what I call "confusopolies."

Confusopoly: A group of companies with similar products who intentionally confuse customers instead of competing on price.

All the things that used to be barriers to entry are disappearing, thanks to huge improvements in technology, capital markets, transportation, and communication. Any company can enter any other business by buying the parts they need and putting them together. You can buy the people, the knowledge, the equipment, and the market research. In theory, every company in the future will be able to figure out exactly what the customer wants and then buy the resources needed to produce it. Even patents are becoming less of a barrier, because there is always a way to engineer around them. Without exception, all the things that have been traditional barriers to entry are diminishing in importance.

A hundred years ago, it was only practical to have one major phone company serving the United States. Today, there are lots of choices and more on the way. They all provide nearly identical service. You would think this would create a price war and drive the prices down to the cost of providing it (that's what I learned between naps in my economics classes), but it isn't happening. The companies are forming efficient confusopolies so customers can't tell who has the lowest prices. Companies have learned to use the complexities of life as an economic tool.

A few short years ago, a tiny software startup called Netscape Communications built an Internet browser that threatened to dethrone Microsoft's stranglehold on computer software. Within a year, Microsoft was able to buy all the talent and resources it needed to build a similar product that didn't violate any patents or copyrights. That's the model of the future: Any new product can be rapidly matched by a determined competitor. Browser software is just complicated enough that I can't tell which one would be better for the things I might be doing in the future. Netscape and Microsoft have formed a confusopoly, thus guaranteeing that both will survive and prosper.

Several other industries are already dominated by confusopolies:

Existing Confusopolies

- Telephone service.

- Insurance.

- Mortgage loans.

- Banking.

- Financial services.

Those types of companies are natural confusopolies, because they offer products that would be indistinguishable to the customer except for the great care taken to make them intentionally confusing.

Companies form confusopolies to make it impossible for the average Induhvidual to determine who has the lowest price. This way each major company gets a share of the pie, the size of which depends on how skillfully they can dupe ignorant customers with advertisements. That will be the primary job of marketing professionals in the future—disguising the true cost of your product in order to be a successful confusopolist.

I recently had a conversation with a top executive for an energy company. He told me that in the near future I would be able to specify which company I wanted to provide electricity to my house. My local power utility will handle all of the physical connections and billing, but I will be able to specify which company actually produces the electricity I buy. Uh-oh.

This means—lord help us all—that power companies will soon form confusopolies and fill the advertising channels with information about the quality of their electricity. They will accuse the competitors of having defective electricity. Celebrities will be hired as electricity spokespersons. People will want to use the electricity that Michael Jordan uses, because it will be so much better.

You'll see magazine ads featuring toast made with the competitor's electricity, all spotty and burnt, compared to perfect toast made with the advertiser's electricity.

Eventually, word will get around that electricity is pretty much the same regardless of who makes it. So marketing will begin to focus on confusing people about the true price. Each power company will have different electricity pricing models that claim to be the cheapest.

Electricity Advertisements

- Only a dime per watt!

- Lease your electricity, don't buy!

- Huge discounts on off-peak usage!

- Big savings for frequent microwavers!

The vast array of confusing choices will anger you as a consumer, but you will have to pick one—unless you crave the Unabomber lifestyle (which looks more rational every day). You'll choose your power company by using sophisticated analytical methods, such as looking at the names of each company and trying to decide which one sounds like they have "good people."

In a future where confusion is the most important competitive asset, the successful companies are the ones who do it best. Dogbert would make an excellent entrepreneur in that environment.

In the future, if all products and services are essentially the same, only the effectiveness of advertisements will set them apart.

PREDICTION 43

In the future, the science of advertising will improve to the point where buying what you see in an advertisement is no longer optional.

Every human skill improves over time. Athletes are faster and stronger every year. Medicine saves more lives. Teachers learn better teaching techniques. Logically, advertising skills will also continue to improve.

Hundreds of years ago, advertisements were created to generate awareness. Then they improved to the point of being persuasive. Now they're downright manipulative. The next step—and we're almost there—is where advertisements are so effective that you will be compelled to buy whatever they tell you to buy.

The only choices you'll be able to make is where you choose to see the advertisements. If you tune your radio to KFOG, you end up buying a Ford. If you tune your radio to K101, you buy a Honda. Your purchasing decisions will be limited to your choice of radio stations. The radio sponsors will decide what car you buy. When you run out of money, you'll close the blinds, turn off the electricity to your house, and wait for the next paycheck to arrive. Your only defense will be to hide from the ads.

Everyone has a weak spot when it comes to advertisements. For example, I'll buy anything that Cindy Crawford is selling. I have a garage full of Revlon products, and I built a nice toolshed out of lipstick containers. I don't paint my house anymore; I give it a powder base and then add rouge. You have a weak spot, too. Advertisers will figure out how to identify your weak spot and target it. Gullibility will reach heights we never dreamed possible.

In the future, it will be totally unnecessary to have an actual product in order to sell it. Good advertisements will whip people into a buying frenzy. All you need is a good demo and a complete absence of social conscience.

SPIDERWEB MARKETING STRATEGY

When customers find out that a product is terrible they try to avoid paying for it. This can be a real problem for the companies who are trying to sell terrible products. That's why smart companies who provide terrible products have found ways to force you to continue to pay for things you don't want. I call it the "spiderweb marketing strategy." Once they get your credit card number, they have you. The spiderweb technique involves making it so difficult to cancel the product or service that it's easier to just keep it. These are the most effective spiderweb tricks.

How to Prevent Customers from Canceling Your Product or Service

- Have poor phone support so it takes hours to reach a human being who will process the cancellation.

- Print no phone number on your bills or user manual.

- Have penalties for early withdrawal.

- Require the customer to mail the item back before a certain time or else they have to pay for it. (Combine this with the next tip.)

- Make sure the original shipping materials self-destruct when the product is opened. Don't include a mailing address or any other information about how to return the product.

- Underbid the competitors and then, after the customer is committed, say, "Oops, you really need to buy more stuff to make this work. Did I forget to mention that?"

Did you ever wonder why banks have penalties for early withdrawal on some types of accounts? Do you think their computers use more electricity to process certain types of withdrawals? Or maybe there's an obscure banking law that requires banks to screw the consumer a certain number of times per month to remain accredited. Whatever the reason—and I'm sure it's *very* convincing—other industries will jump on that gravy train in the future.

I imagine my dry cleaner telling me why I have to pay a steep penalty if I ever decide to use another dry cleaner. I'll demand an explanation, and he'll say it's a dry-cleaning regulation. He'll exhibit mock frustration with the system and explain how he's just as much a victim as I am. He'll blame the "home office" and politicians in general. All the other dry cleaners will catch wind of this scheme and start doing the same thing. You'll never be able to switch dry cleaners again.

I pay for an online service that I don't use anymore. The charge shows up on my credit card every month. On a per day basis, it's only about thirty cents. I figure it would take about half an hour to find the phone number for customer service, find my account number, work my way through their audiotex menu options, and cancel the service by phone. It's never worth the time. Every day, by putting that task off, I effectively "buy" thirty minutes of time for myself. I will be paying for the online service as long as my time is worth more than a penny a minute. They have me in their spider-web until retirement. By then I will have paid them about $5,000. I'm the perfect customer.

My favorite spiderweb marketing trick involves selling a complicated and expensive system and then later telling the customer he needs to buy more stuff to make it work. The poor Induhvidual has no choice, because the alternative is to admit defeat and start over with another vendor who will probably pull the same trick. This technique works especially well when combined with a lease contract, because the lease adds its own penalties for changes. The typical lease contract is so complicated it creates spontaneous brain tumors if you read it carefully, so it's fairly foolproof.

The spiderweb marketing we've seen so far is somewhat passive. The customer has to blunder into the service and get stuck before it can work. I expect things to get worse for the consumer.

PREDICTION 44

In the future, companies will make aggressive products that resist any attempts at refunds or cancellation while actively trying to take more of your money.

MARKETS OF THE FUTURE

Today most new products fail because the producer can't locate enough customers. Sometimes that's because the product is a piece of crap; sometimes it's because the company isn't successful at marketing. Those problems will go away in the future, due to the following important trends:

1. More Induhviduals are born every day.

2. We're getting better at identifying them.

3. Induhviduals have money, temporarily.

To illustrate my point, let's say you develop a ridiculous product that no intelligent person would want or need. For example, let's say the product is a "house sweater"—literally, a big, wool, knitted sweater that fits over your entire house with the chimney sticking through the neck opening.

If you tried to sell this product today, you'd sell maybe three of them: One to an eccentric person who thought it would be different, one to a

person who is simply stupid, and a third to someone who ordered it accidentally and was embarrassed to return it. That would be your entire sales
of the house sweater before you ran out of money and closed the company.

There are many more potential buyers out there—people just like the
three who bought it—but there's no economical way to reach them.
Television advertising is too expensive, because advertising rates are based
on the number of people watching regardless of how many of them would
ever want a house sweater. And there's no specialty magazine to advertise
in—no *House Sweater Quarterly*. There are no house sweater interest
groups meeting weekly. It seems hopeless from a marketing standpoint—
at least today.

In the future, these problems will be solved. Computer and Internet
technology will be able to track everyone's bizarre interests and mental
defects. Our house sweater company will be able to buy a customer list of
all the eccentric, stupid, and timid people who own houses and have extra
cash. They'll be able to market directly to the people who are most likely
to buy the product, and that can be very cost-effective.

PREDICTION 45

In the future, it will be easy to find customers who are gullible
enough to buy any product, no matter how worthless and stupid
it is.

Computers on the Internet will cleverly monitor the transactions of
every human on Earth and combine this data with information from credit
card companies, stores, and other public records until there is a complete
profile of just how gullible you are and in what ways you are most easily
duped. We're all gullible about something or other. Currently, we can conceal our gullibilities most of the time. In the future, we won't be able to
keep it a secret. That information will be available to anyone who wants it.

There won't be any customer list of people who want house sweaters, of
course, since the product didn't exist before, but you can draw inferences

from the other behaviors of consumers. For example, the people who buy abdominal exercise machines to lose weight are potential customers for the house sweater, but those names are going to cost you more, since everyone will want a shot at that group.

And more good news for House Sweater, Inc.: The sheer size of the world population guarantees a virtually endless supply of new eccentric, stupid, and timid customer prospects. In fact, there will be so many new prospects that the company will never be burdened with the need to satisfy current customers. It will be cheaper to find new customers and leave them unsatisfied, too. And if you combine this with the spiderweb marketing technique, you can get people to not only keep their house sweaters, but to sign up to receive a ball of yarn every month too for an additional $29.95 apiece.

Once you've bought your list of eccentric, stupid, timid people (let's call them the EST market segment), you can begin to craft your marketing plan.

With this sort of product, you might want to convince people to buy it before telling them what it is. It sounds hard, but insurance companies do this all the time. If you've ever purchased insurance, you know that you can't get an insurance company to tell you what your policy covers until *after* you buy the insurance. Later, after your check clears (because they can't trust you), the insurance company will send you an incomprehensible document. The document will describe what you just bought in a way that is calculated to make you feel stupid and powerless. Eventually, you realize that your best strategy is to mail the insurance company whatever money they ask for and hope for the best.

You can also use this strategy for the house sweater.

TEN

GOOD AND BAD JOBS
OF THE FUTURE

Young people often ask me how they should prepare for the job markets of the future. Obviously, they're trying to steal all of my career secrets so they can take my job and leave me homeless and broke. I generally try to steer young people toward a life of crime in the inner cities, because I never go to the inner cities and I figure that's as good a place as any for crime.

If a young person is hesitant to take my advice, I can usually make my case by pointing out the many disadvantages of the alternatives. I'll do that in this chapter, thereby reducing the need for me to speak directly with young people who are future criminals.

The first thing that young people need to realize is that the concepts of "career" and "job security" are a bit dated.

In the future, most people's jobs will involve scrambling around like frightened chipmunks trying to find the next paycheck in an endless string of unrelated short-term jobs. But since "Frightened Chipmunk" doesn't look very impressive on a business card, people will call themselves entrepreneurs, consultants, and independent contractors.

It will get harder and harder to generate good small talk at parties. Someone will ask you what you do for a living, and you'll have to give a vague answer like, "I work in Cleveland," and hope the interrogation ends. As a rule, if it takes more than two words to describe what you do for a living, it's not a "career" in the classic sense of the word. Doctor is a career. Lawyer is a career. You do not have a career if you describe it as, "I'm working on a meeting to see someone about a project that involves a potential consulting assignment."

If you were foolish enough go to college and major in one of the soft arts, such as journalism, English literature or music, you might have a bit of a shock coming. At best, those majors are excellent preparation for jobs that involve removing wine corks and condoms from the swimming pools of people who studied computer science. And even that is seasonal work.

I'm probably overgeneralizing. There are plenty of other jobs you can get if you have a degree in the squishy subjects, as long as you're not burdened by a lot of excess human dignity.

If you are one of the few lucky people who attended a big-name school, things will be completely different. You'll be highly recruited by large companies and put on the fast track, unless of course you're ugly. The attractive graduates of big-name schools earn obscene salaries, buy expensive stuff, and die in freak accidents. The ugly ones enter academia. Either way it's tragic.

Another career trap you want to avoid is becoming an "exempt" employee, sometimes also referred to as "salaried" or, more colloquially, "gullible."

Exempt employees are paid the same no matter how many hours they work. Companies can increase their earnings by making employees work additional hours for free under the threat of downsizing. This is what we call a bad situation for employees. Ideally, you want the kind of job where your employer has very little temptation to work you until every last bit of life has been drained out of your flabby, decaying body.

Some clever employers will try to disguise their no-overtime-pay scam by dressing it up as something glamorous. When I was hired at Pacific Bell in 1986, they told me I was a "manager." It even said so on my business card. I kept thinking that the people who reported to me must be hiding, because I never met any of them. The trick, as I later learned, is that managers weren't eligible for overtime pay. Eventually, the only thing I managed was—and this took some effort—to resist strangling the Induhviduals who came up with this plan.

I complained bitterly about this situation until my boss agreed to change my title from "manager" to "supreme commander of cubicle 4S700R." I still didn't get paid for overtime, but at least I had the respect of my peers. Well, I would have had their respect, if not for the quality of my work and my insistence that they salute.

There was a time, long ago, when you could park your lazy butt in a large benevolent company and reasonably expect to retire from it in thirty years as a bitter, broken shell of your former self, living out your miserable life on a subsistence retirement income. But things won't be so easy in the future. Now every employee can expect to change jobs up to 7,000 times (I'm guessing on the actual figure). In such an environment, it's a good idea to have a well-planned educational foundation. In particular, I recommend avoiding any ethics classes.

PREDICTION 46

In the future, the most important career skill will be a lack of ethics.

If you acquire too many ethics in college, it will be a severe drain on your earnings potential. The most important corporate skill in the future will be the ability to make sure your co-workers get downsized before you do. Some people might try to optimize their chances of surviving a downsizing by working hard, but as the name implies, that would be both "hard" and "work."

You can predict an impending wave of downsizing by looking for signals in the environment. Those signals might include a company merger, a bad earnings report, a new CEO nicknamed "chainsaw," or really just about any old thing. It doesn't take much to trigger a wave of downsizing these days—a paper jam in the photocopier or somebody forgets to bring donuts and poof, there goes another thousand co-workers.

If you notice any of the signals of downsizing, that is when all of the teamwork of the past pays off. When you're a team, you work closely with one another. And when you work closely with other people, you learn all of their heinous faults. This would be a good time to let everyone else know about them.

Another good skill to pick up in college is mime. If you join a big company, you'll spend a surprising number of hours totally motionless, and you might as well turn it into something artistic. Try pretending your cubicle has an invisible door or ceiling and you're a powerless employee trapped inside. It's a stretch, but you can do it. You can entertain yourself for hours this way. But make sure you don't try to entertain other people, because I've noticed a real stigma against cubicle mimes.

Now that I've thoroughly explored the educational needs of the future, let me turn my attention to some specific jobs you will want to either carefully consider or avoid in the future.

MOTHERS, DON'T LET YOUR CHILDREN GROW UP TO BE VENDORS

The typical employee of the typical company is a bitter and powerless person who longs for any opportunity to spread the pain. There are few opportunities to do that at the bottom of the corporate hierarchy, so employees naturally look to the one class of people who are paid to take their abuse: vendors.

Vendors are people who make a living by enduring an endless barrage of rude and degrading treatment at the hands of their customers. The vendor who endures the most abuse is considered "flexible" and gets the sale. It's that simple.

Some vendors will go out of their way to invent their own abuse in order to win the abuse contest. They'll offer to loan you products they know you'll lose or ignore. They'll send you endless copies of product information no matter how many times you lose it. They'll offer to drive across town to answer a question that could be answered on the phone. If they're motivated enough, you can sometimes get them to poke themselves with sharp pencils just for fun.

Vendors try to be "part of the team," and they are usually the best teammates you could possibly have, because you can abuse them and they won't screw you during the next downsizing. You can cancel meetings with them, insult their products, accuse them of lying, and generally treat them like the stuff that's hard to get out of the cracks in your sneakers.

Although the job conditions are dismal, vendors can make a lot of money. If they are clever enough to cultivate relationships with (i.e., bribe) senior management, they will be in a position to exact revenge on the lower-level employees who tormented them. If you think you have the type of personality to be a successful vendor, you might want to explore career options in related fields first:

Related Occupations

- Hit man.

- Prostitute.

- Sadomasochist.

- Movie producer.

PROCUREMENT

The job of procurement isn't as sexy as it sounds. It mostly involves preventing people from getting stuff they need to do their jobs. The primary qualifications for a career in procurement include this sort of thing:

- Long hairy arms.

- Low forehead.

- Inability to grasp the big picture.

Most dinosaurs worked in procurement before they went into hiding. Many of them starved to death while waiting for a purchase order for edible vegetation. Others evolved into birds, primarily in the penguin family. Those who survived have carried on the tradition.

TEMP

For the young people who are preparing for their futures by watching television, there is an exciting field you should consider. It's called being a "temp," which is short for "I'm *temp*ted to have a real job, but not enthusiastic about the concept."

Companies hire temp workers for much the same reasons that NASA used chimps in its early rocket testing. It's a little known fact, but the people at NASA hate chimps. The whole "race to the moon" thing was just an excuse to get rid of chimps by sending them into space attached to huge, combustible devices. The media covered the first few chimp flights, but then turned their attention to the flights piloted by the humans that NASA hated. (The term "astronaut" is Latin for "let's send this Induhvidual into space.") Meanwhile, NASA quietly launched millions of chimps into low

Earth orbits. The Earth is now surrounded by chimps in rockets. That's why your television sometimes has bad reception.

Companies hire temps for jobs that are too hideous to give to someone they might grow fond of. There are no shortages of these types of jobs. Every day, millions of temps perform important duties such as sitting at desks and staring straight ahead. If you are a child of television, as I was, you are already qualified for this job.

The only downside as far as I can tell is that temps do not get as much respect as the regular employees. And the regular employees don't get any. As a temp, nobody will ask your name or offer to introduce you to the rest of the office. People will walk up to you and abruptly bark orders that are full of arcane acronyms. You will have no idea what they are talking about, but that's okay. No matter what you do, it won't affect your career as a temp. In fact, if you do something that causes a gigantic explosion or mass hysteria, at least it breaks up your day.

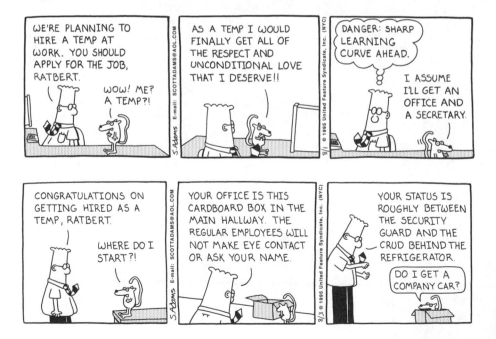

ACCOUNTING, AUDITING, AND DENTISTRY

Accounting, auditing, and dentistry are all excellent career choices for people who don't like other people but aren't coordinated enough to beat those other people up.

If you can't decide which of the three choices is best for you, use this handy test: Ask yourself whether you prefer to hear people scream in pain (choose dentistry), scream in frustration (choose accounting), or scream in a prison shower (choose auditing).

The accounting profession is an excellent way to get a lot of time by yourself. At a party, try saying, "I'm an accountant. Today was an interesting day." Notice how quickly you're standing alone.

Sometimes accountants can get more respect by saying they work in the finance department. Finance is a sexier word than accounting, but the work tends to be similar, as in this example:

Auditors get more respect and more bribes than accountants. That's because auditors are relatively more dangerous. Auditors are generally plucked from the ranks of accountants who had very bad childhood experiences. Those accountants who don't go on to become serial killers have a good chance of becoming successful auditors.

Dentists are the people who filled out their career aptitude tests in high school and checked the box that says, "Would you enjoy reaching into

helpless people's mouths with power tools and causing excruciating pain?"
The people who said yes to that question either become prison interroga-
tors in Third World countries or dentists. I recommend either one of those
careers, because you always have someone else to take your frustrations
out on.

VENTURE CAPITALIST

The very best job I can think of is venture capitalist. Not only does it
sound great at parties, but you're expected to fail 90 percent of the time. I
mean no disrespect to venture capitalists when I say this, but a hamster
with Alzheimer's could make those kinds of numbers. It's good work if you
can get it.

For those of you who are unfamiliar with the venture capital occupation, it mostly involves taking rich people's money and giving it to small
businesses that soon become bankrupt. Once in a while, one of those small
companies becomes huge, and the venture capitalists get rich and buy
four-wheel-drive vehicles for no particular reason. I'm leaving out some
details that involve eating, drinking, and laughing at morons behind their
backs, but I think you get the gist of it.

RECORDS RETENTION

The corporate world is full of jobs that you will never hear about except by reading informative books like this one. Some of these jobs are as close to Nirvana as work can be. My favorite nearly-heaven job is something called records retention.

Most companies generate tons of documents that nobody needs to read yet seem too important to throw away. Employees don't have room to keep all the documents at their desks. The solution is something called records retention. In theory, employees send documents to a person who stores those documents in a huge warehouse, available for retrieval when necessary.

It's possible that this sometimes happens exactly as planned, but I know that if I had that job, I would move a Dumpster into the office with a sign that said, PLACE DOCUMENTS FOR STORAGE INSIDE. Then I'd never go to work again. The ugly truth is that almost nobody goes looking for a document that has been sent to the warehouse. If someone does, you can say it was lost or blame it on the temp whose name you can't remember. Most jobs in corporate life have no value to the economy, but there are scant few that so aggressively ignore any attempt at even appearing useful.

GET PAID TO CRITICIZE OTHERS

If there is one thing you should always seek in a job, it's the opportunity to criticize people who are more skilled than you are. This kind of work is both satisfying and easy.

Good jobs in this vein include newspaper and magazine columnist. If you're a young person who is accustomed to being selected last for teams, these are excellent jobs for you.

As you read this sentence, somewhere there is a columnist writing an article about how much this book sucks. As I type this sentence using the dominant word processing software on the planet Earth, a technology columnist is giving a speech about how bad it is. As the secretary of defense is poring through top-secret intelligence reports to figure out how to keep the planet safe, a writer is researching an important story about how the secretary pays his maid.

I think you can see who has the easier job in these examples.

If you want to be at the top of the criticism food chain, become a publisher or an editor. In those jobs, you will be in a position to criticize not only the people who do real work, but also the people who criticize those people. It simply doesn't get any better than that.

ELEVEN

SOCIAL STUFF

POVERTY

I don't know why everyone says poverty can't be eliminated. The solution is obvious to me. All it takes is what the bankers call the "miracle of compound interest."

This requires a long-term approach to the problem, but it's fairly fool-proof if you're patient. All you do is give each poor person one dollar. There are only about 5 billion poor people, so this is quite affordable as a percentage of the worldwide GNP. That dollar is deposited in a special bank account for each of the poor people with the idea that it stays there for generations collecting interest. The number of poor people doubles every twenty years, but the value of money doubles every ten years, assuming it is well invested, so the gap will close.

In 4,000 years, the descendants of the poor people will be allowed to go to the bank and ask for their money. The bank will inform them that the dollar was taken in fees 4,000 years ago, and the balance of all their accounts is zero. At this point, the poor people will kill the bankers and steal all the money in the banks, thus ending poverty completely.

I'm surprised nobody has suggested it before.

PREDICTION 47

In the future, poverty will be eliminated, along with the people who are hoarding all the money.

THE AGE OF CONSENT

A hundred years ago, the legal age of consent for a woman was ten years old. Now it's eighteen. When I was a teenager in New York State, the legal age for drinking was eighteen. Now it's twenty-one.

The legal ages are creeping up, because it's obvious that the people below those ages are complete morons and can't handle sex and liquor. But what about the people over the legal ages? How bright are they?

True Story (Really. I was there.)

A secretary for a large bank was engaged to be married. She was nineteen and completely uninformed about the various methods of birth control. Her co-workers sat her down and explained the rhythm method, because that was the only method allowed by her religion. They described how she should count the days from her last period to determine when she was most likely to be fertile.

She listened intently and asked only one question, "Do you only count business days?"

Every time the legal age of something gets moved higher, we discover that the people just above the legal age are no smarter than the people just below it. The obvious solution is to keep increasing the age limits until we find the age where people become smart and responsible.

PREDICTION 48

In the future, the age of consent for sex and liquor
will be raised to 120.

This will not have any impact on the amount of actual sex and drinking in the world, but at least we'll know our lawmakers weren't sitting idly by while the world went to hell.

CRIME

PREDICTION 49

In the future, new technology will allow police to solve 100 percent
of all crimes. The bad news is that we'll realize 100 percent of the
population are criminals, including the police.

You might be an undetected criminal already. Review this list to determine whether you're getting away with something:

Have You Committed Any of These Crimes?

- Speeding in your car?

- Using office supplies for personal business?

- Making personal phone calls from the phone at work?

- Violating copyright law?

- "Borrowing" a *Dilbert* book from a dim-witted co-worker?

- Cheating on your taxes?

- Taking drugs?

- Operating a motor vehicle while legally drunk?

- Drinking liquor as a minor?

- Having sex with a seventeen-year-old?

- Threatening to "kill someone"?

- Slapping someone?

- Using a scanner to overhear your neighbor's phone conversations?

- Recording a conversation without someone's permission?

- Sending personal e-mail messages from work?

- Exaggerating expenses on an expense report?

- Lying to a highway patrolman?

- Littering?

- Making lewd comments at work?

- Fishing without a license?

You might argue that, although you have done some of those things in the past, you aren't doing any of them now. I'm sure that's true, unless you stole this book and you're running from the police while you read it. But most convicted criminals aren't committing crimes AT THIS VERY MOMENT either. There are two big differences between the average criminal and you:

1. The average criminal got caught.

2. The average criminal's crimes are "bigger."

In the future, the crimes you commit won't seem "little," because you'll get caught every single time. You'll get a ticket EVERY TIME you exceed the speed limit. The fines will exceed your income, and you'll become a scofflaw. There will be a warrant for your arrest. You'll lose your license and your car insurance, but you'll drive anyway. Then you'll get caught driving without a license or insurance. Eventually, you'll be sent to prison for life or possibly executed. (The courts are getting tougher on repeat offenders.)

If you don't believe everyone is breaking the law, look at your politicians. Virtually all major politicians seem to get caught doing something illegal. There are four explanations for this observation:

Possible Reasons Why All Politicians Seem to Be Crooks

1. Crooks are the only ones who run for office.

2. Politics turns people into criminals.

3. All politicians are being framed.

4. Every person on Earth is a crook, but the only people we check out carefully are politicians.

There's no reason to believe that crooks are the only people who run for office. And I can't believe public service turns honest people into criminals. And I can't believe that all honest politicians can be framed so easily without the people who do the framing ever getting caught themselves. The most logical explanation for the politician/crook phenomenon is that all people are criminals and only the politicians are watched closely enough to get caught.

We like to think the world is composed of honest people on one side and crooks on the other, but all the evidence points to the theory that everyone is a crook. Some people are dumb enough to get caught and some aren't. Consider this true story:

True Story

A co-worker once told me he had a theory about why there were shortages of water in some parts of the world. His theory was that people are drinking it all.

I'll bet he's in jail now. He obviously isn't bright enough to avoid detection for whatever crimes he committed. I have to assume he's sitting in a cell somewhere guzzling water out of the prison sink and yelling, "THEY'LL PAY! THEY'LL ALL PAY!"

Eventually, everyone will be in jail except Marilyn vos Savant, the world's smartest human. She's the only person on Earth who will be smart enough to get away with everything. She'll complain constantly about the taxes she pays to keep the whole planet incarcerated, but on some level she will realize it's her own responsibility, because she's in charge of the planet.

The incarceration of the entire planet will come about due to a chain of events beginning with an increase in terrorism. Here's how it will play out.

At the moment, you still need to be a fairly well-informed terrorist in order to do any serious damage. But what happens when any disgruntled Induhvidual can build a weapon of mass destruction by ordering the parts through magazines? When we reach that point—and you know we will—anyone in a bad mood will be a threat to world security.

In the future, after a few cities are annihilated by miffed figure skaters who think the judges were biased, there will be a spirited debate about whether people should give up their privacy in return for greater security. Both sides will make excellent arguments, but no one will be persuaded.

After a few more metropolitan areas are obliterated, the argument will eventually be won by the people who favor safety over privacy. By that time, our technology will have reached a point where all crimes can be solved as long as we're willing to give up privacy.

There are several evolving technologies that will make it possible to detect nearly 100 percent of all crimes. I'll describe a few. These predictions are based on technology that already exists at some stage of development.

Artificial Noses

There's already a technology that can detect almost anything with an odor and match it against a known smell. Initially, it will be used to sniff for bombs at airports.

A bloodhound can detect a person's scent and follow it hours after the crime, distinguishing it from all other scents. The artificial nose machines could someday be that accurate and portable. Police could grab an air sample from the crime scene and use it to track suspects hours after the crime. Or they could use the technology to "sniff" suspects out of a lineup.

Repeat offenders would have their scents on file—like fingerprints—so computers could find an instant match to the scent at the crime scene. Courts would eventually accept "sniff evidence" like they accept fingerprints and DNA evidence.

DNA Matches

It's almost impossible to enter a room and commit a crime without leaving microscopic pieces of your hair, skin, blood, or saliva. Under our current system, this only helps police after they have a suspect to test. But in the future, if people give up personal privacy for better protection, every citizen will have their DNA pattern, scent, and fingerprints on file with the police.

Investigators will be able to vacuum a crime scene, run it through the DNA analyzer, and get the name and address of every person who has been there lately.

Ubiquitous Video

Many crimes are already being captured on surveillance videos and personal video cameras. There are only two reasons we don't put cameras everywhere: cost and privacy.

Both of those obstacles will go away. The cost of cameras is dropping every day, and our willingness to pay for crime prevention is increasing. Cost will not be an issue.

People will be willing to give up some privacy for increased security. One town in California already has video cameras at virtually all public locations. People got used to it.

I predict we'll have cameras at all *private* locations as well, including your car and all rooms of your house. The cameras will run all the time and record the images in an encrypted form that only law enforcement officers can decipher—but only with a court order. That's similar to the way law enforcement now gains access to any of your personal records or phone conversations (except for the encryption part). You won't like it, but you'll get used to it.

When all criminals get caught, jail overcrowding will become the big issue. But that's Marilyn vos Savant's problem, not ours. We'll be in jail. I just hope she doesn't favor the death penalty, because that will be the most cost-effective solution and I know she can do the math.

NEWS IN THE FUTURE

When the Unabomber was captured, I mentioned something about it to a friend. She stared blankly at me. It was the biggest news of the year, and she had never heard of the Unabomber. Wilting under my barrage of intense questioning, she confessed that a few years ago she decided to make a conscious effort to avoid all news sources. She believes the news is depressing and has no bearing on her life. I was shocked and dismayed, especially when I realized she's right. I've noticed several other friends who are also pursuing an aggressive strategy of ignoring all news. When I say aggressive, I mean they make a conscious effort to avoid even *accidental* exposure to news.

What caused this trend?

Somehow, without anybody really noticing, the news changed from events that affect us—such as major wars and stock market crashes—to stuff that doesn't affect most of us at all, like athletes slaying their wives.

Governments have figured out how to control the big bone-headed catastrophes that made news in the past. These days, you never hear about a cow kicking over a lantern causing a major metropolitan area to be engulfed in flames. Now, thanks to government regulations, all the cows use flashlights and nobody gets hurt.

Rich guys used to be able to manipulate the stock market and make huge profits at the expense of smaller investors. It was big news when the small investors discovered they'd been screwed. Now there are many safeguards against the small investor ever finding out how much he's getting screwed. That means the financial news is limited to interviews with bald guys who try to guess why the market moved ten points today. It's not really "news" in the sense that it has any relevance.

War isn't as newsworthy as it used to be either. All the big countries with impressive weapons can't figure out a good reason to point them at each other. This makes it very difficult for the generals to design realistic war games:

War Games Planning

General: Let's assume that Holland attacks NATO . . .

Captain: I think Holland is part of NATO.

General: It is? Damn. Who's *not* on our side yet?

Captain: Umm . . . Switzerland?

General: Great. We'll kick their little lederhosen butts!

Social problems are reported as statistics that rise and fall for no apparent reason. The only fun part is watching politicians trying to distribute blame without accidentally using the phrase, "I sure hope you voters *are* as dumb as you look!"

Economic news is too abstract for the average viewer. It's hard to be excited about news when you can't even tell if it's good news or bad news. The value of the yen is up? Uh-oh, now what do I do?

The occasional serial killer story is interesting, but the likelihood of the serial killer snuffing me personally is so small that that it's hard to get excited about it. Serial killing is a very bad thing, but logically, nine people killed by a serial killer isn't as bad as ten people who are each killed by a separate killer. Serial-killer stories are the most impressive news we have, and they only sound relevant when they're taken out of context. That's the best evidence that news isn't important anymore.

The other clue that all the important stories are gone is the number of news reports about other news reports. This morning I saw a news story about how a tabloid obtained photos of a crime scene. News about the news gatherers is more interesting than whatever they're gathering news about. Could anything be *less* relevant than news about how someone gathered the news about a story that wasn't relevant in the first place?

PREDICTION 50

In the future, more people will actively ignore the news
because it is irrelevant.

I predict that news outlets will try to compensate for the loss of relevant news by focusing on stories that are more shocking and depressing than ever. At least that way they'll get your attention and sell advertising even if the stories aren't "news" in the traditional sense.

This will limit the reporting to a few stories per year about famous people who are killing other famous people. And if there are not enough of those stories to sell advertising slots, the media will do the only responsible thing—they will start to kill famous people themselves. Eventually, the news people will get caught and go to jail, and that will be the end of traditional news outlets.

PREDICTION 51

In the future, the media will kill famous people to generate news that people will care about.

The end of traditional news outlets will not limit people's access to information. Thanks to the ubiquity of video cameras and the Internet, every citizen will be a reporter. If something happens in your neighborhood, you'll tape it, stick it on the Internet with your own commentary, and make it available to the world. Sports commentary and statistics will be generated by fans who enjoy doing it for free. The weather reports will be computer-generated and constantly available by computer, pager, voice mail, and dozens of other sources. All news gathering will be disaggregated.

PREDICTION 52

In the future, everyone will be a news reporter.

People will have access to software that constantly combs the Internet for "small" news that is relevant to them. The software will learn to filter out reports from Induhviduals who constantly post incorrect information. You will still get misleading reports quite often, but that's no different from today.

Some new safeguards will emerge to check the credibility of Induhviduals who post news to the Net. For example, your software will be able to do a sort of "credibility credit check" on any person who posts information to the Internet. It will compare this information to other reports on the same event and automatically highlight any discrepancies. This won't be foolproof, but nothing is.

This new model depends on people being willing to take the time to put information on the Net without the benefit of payment. Why will people do that? They will do it because that's our most basic human nature:

> People like to talk more than they like to listen.

That's why our mouths are much bigger than the combined sizes of our ear holes. (I realize that statement makes no sense, yet it's strangely compelling.)

It is not only unnecessary to pay people to tell you what they know, it's almost impossible to stop them from doing it.

I print my e-mail address in my *Dilbert* comic strip. I get 350 messages a day. Many of them are filled with stories, anecdotes, jokes, reports on *Dilbert* copyright violators, comments, opinions, and a wealth of other useful information. All that the writers ask in return is a reasonable likelihood that I will read the message. (I do my best.)

Look at the explosion of "personal home pages" on the Internet. People spend untold hours populating their personal web pages with information about their hobbies, opinions, favorite music, and loads of other information that nobody asked for.

Bottom line: We are a species that needs no incentive to give away information. The Internet and video technology will make it easy to share what we know with the world. And boy will we share.

PREDICTION 53

In the future, the thing we'll miss most about the traditional "news media" will be the professional reporters asking penetrating questions.

Here are some of the questions I will miss the most.

Penetrating News Media Questions

- "General, can you tell us where you plan the next secret bombing?"
- "Senator, do you really expect to win this election?"
- "Do you think your economic plan will help the country?"
- "Do you feel that you did anything unethical?"
- "Did you really have sex with a penguin?"

PARENT LICENSES

Most Induhviduals end up having children. That's a bit like putting a poodle in the cockpit of the space shuttle and saying, "Let's see what happens."

I have to think that raising a human being is one of the most difficult things in the world to do right. But it's one of the few things that people routinely do with no training except for asking the advice of other untrained Induhviduals. This is not a good recipe for success.

You need a license to drive a car. You need a license to catch fish. You need a license to own a dog. But you don't need a license to create a human being. Even children can create other children. There is no minimum-qualification requirement for becoming a parent. If you don't think that's a problem, read this e-mail message I received recently.

Subject: Copy Machine
From: (name withheld)
To: scottadams@aol.com

True Story!
Recently our copier broke down. The repair person came and took the copier apart and was amazed at the extensive paper jam. An Induhvidual walked in and admitted that he had jammed the machine trying to make two-sided copies. The repair person then explained to the Induhvidual very, very slowly that the machine does not have an automatic paper feed; those slits were for ventilation.

It would not surprise me if the paper-jamming Induhvidual went home that night and jammed a pint of baby formula in his baby's ears.

Eventually, we'll figure out that untrained Induhvidual parents are the single biggest cause of all human problems. The government will address it in the usual way.

PREDICTION 54

In the future, parents will have to pass a brief written parent test
in order to get tax credits for dependents.

It won't be a hard test—no more difficult than your driver's test—but I think it will help. Most people know they aren't supposed to pass a school bus if its lights are blinking, but many Induhviduals don't know they can turn their kids into felons, auditors, and rhythmic swimmers just by saying the wrong things. This is a very fixable problem.

EUTHANASIA

People disagree on the question of whether it should be legal for a person to commit suicide, but people are in favor of getting tough on crime, including more use of the death penalty. Am I the only one who sees an obvious solution here?

Let's make it illegal to threaten yourself and let's make it punishable by death. If you threaten to kill yourself, the state kills you. That way everyone wins.

PREDICTION 55

In the future, it will be illegal to threaten yourself, and
the penalty for doing so will be death.

Then there's the question of whether doctors should be allowed to assist people in dying. It's easy to predict where this debate will go. For doctors, killing people is relatively easy money compared to keeping them alive. Even if the doctor accidentally mixes the wrong combination of lethal drugs and the patient lives, there's always the option of beating the patient with the IV stand—i.e., "alternative medicine."

Doctors have very powerful lobbying groups. The law will change to make assisted suicide legal (for the doctors, not the killee), thus providing an excellent source of income for the medical profession. There will be a spirited ethical debate among doctors, but I think the outcome is predictable.

Doctors already perform many unnecessary surgeries because the money is good. Does anyone really think they wouldn't be willing to kill you if the price was right? The savings in malpractice insurance alone would be worth it, assuming none of the dead people sue for "accidental life."

The market price for assisted suicide is artificially low right now, because Dr. Kevorkian is driving around in an old van doing them for free. As soon as Kevorkian retires, the market will determine a fair price for assisted suicide. Doctors will realize it's easy work compared to appendectomies—and best of all they won't even have to wash their hands first!

PREDICTION 56

In the future, assisted suicide will be a medical specialty practiced by doctors who don't like people.

I think assisted suicide will become a medical specialty. It won't take nearly as much medical training as other specialties. Ten minutes of training should do it.

Patient: My throat is itchy.

Doctor: Hmm, I recommend assisted suicide.

Patient: Suicide?! What if it's just a cold?

Doctor: I wouldn't want to take that chance.

PRIVACY

Last night I was sitting on my couch with a row of pretzels lined up in the crease of my sweatshirt. I carefully selected each pretzel from the lineup based on its aesthetic appeal and salt ratio. I crunched the chosen one slowly and replaced it with another to repeat the search for a best pretzel.

Meanwhile, a national weather report on television was informing me that there were normal temperatures in places I will never visit. At that moment, I realized that I had accidentally discovered a means of keeping my personal life completely private:

I was dangerously boring.

Let's say that someday technology will allow anybody to find out every possible thing about my life. I can compensate by being so uninteresting that nobody could survive the process of snooping on me without lapsing into a coma. Judging from my friends, I don't think I'm the only person who has discovered this sophisticated privacy technique.

PREDICTION 57

In the future, there will be no compelling reason
to invade anyone's privacy.

Celebrities already have total privacy. Everything you read about celebrities is invented by disgruntled nannies and unscrupulous media people. Their true personal lives are a mystery and will stay that way. Personally, I'm grateful that the news about celebrities is fabricated by the media. I don't want to read a story about Barbra Streisand that says she's a very nice person most of the time, but sometimes she gets annoyed when people do bad work. That would describe most of the people I know. I want to hear that Barbra pistol-whipped the pizza delivery boy because he forgot "extra garlic." Now THAT'S entertainment.

Noncelebrities will also have total privacy in the future. The technology for invading your privacy will improve, but the reasons to do so will completely go away. There are three main reasons that people violate your privacy now:

Reasons for Invading Your Privacy

1. To gather marketing data.

2. To commit crimes against you.

3. To get cheap thrills.

Marketing and advertising techniques get better every year. Eventually, companies won't need to snoop into your consumer preferences. As I described in my chapter on marketing, they'll be able to force you to buy whatever they're selling. Companies only ask one question: Does this person still have money left? Privacy will not be an issue.

Criminals invade your privacy to get your secret banking codes so they can steal your money. Sophisticated systems will be developed to thwart them. You will someday have to submit a urine sample at your ATM and wait for the results of an instant DNA analysis before you can get cash. You won't like it at first, but you'll get used to it. In fact, it might have some hidden benefits.

PREDICTION 58

In the future, you'll hear the phrase, "I'll be right back.
I gotta take a wicked withdrawal."

Sometimes people invade other people's privacy to get cheap thrills, but imagine a future where it's easy to snoop on anyone doing anything anyplace. It would quickly lose its thrill. We know this by examining other cultures.

In my many travels across my living room to the couch to watch *National Geographic* specials, I have noticed that women in some regions of the world go topless all day long. This does not excite the local men, because they are used to it. But if you dropped a nineteen-year-old male from another culture into the middle of that situation, he would quickly get a humiliating tribal nickname such as "one who constantly points the way forward." Over time he would get used to all the nudity and start fantasizing about women who wear thick jackets. I know this is true, because halfway through the *National Geographic* specials, I'm doing the same thing and I'm perfectly normal.

PET SERVICES

In the future, people will spend much more money on their pets and relatively less money on other people. That's because people will realize, as I have, that humans are no more interesting than most house pets, and at least an animal will let you pet it without suing you.

People, as I've explained so eloquently, are horny, stupid, and selfish. Pets are only stupid and selfish, assuming you have them fixed so they can't get horny. Therefore, mathematically speaking, pets are one-third superior to most of the people I know. And frankly, on average they're smarter than many of the Induhviduals I know, especially if you include dolphins in the calculation.

I realize this is an "apples-to-oranges" comparison, because you could have your friends fixed, too. Then they'd be almost as good as pets. But if your friends are like mine, they'll fight you every step of the way and not shut up about it until they're in the car on the way home.

The biggest problem with pet ownership is all of the regular scheduled maintenance. I have a big pile of postcards from my veterinarian reminding me of all the maintenance my cat needs—things you wouldn't know you needed unless someone told you:

- Urinary tract limpholeema.

- Feline diabolical emphlatemi shots.

- Tail stiffener serum.

- Braces.

I'm starting to think my vet is inventing things just to take my money. But I love my cats too much to take a chance, so Freddie goes in tomorrow for something called a petownerwalletectomy, which I understand will set me back a few grand.

This situation opens up a huge market for the future, a market that clever entrepreneurs are sure to fill: low-cost, efficient pet maintenance. Let's call it Jiffy-Pet™.

PREDICTION 59

In the future, there will be drive-through pet-care facilities.

The way a Jiffy-Pet would work is similar to the way specialty oil-changing services work. You'd tie your cat to the hood of your car like a hood ornament and drive into the Jiffy-Cat service bay. Once inside, a uniformed person who speaks too loudly would come out with a clipboard and explain what specials they are running that day.

Jiffy-Cat person:	We've got a special on Catlube 6000.
Customer:	What's that?
Jiffy-Cat person:	Ooh, you need that if you want your cat to last another 10,000 miles.

Customer:	What's it do?
Jiffy-Cat person:	Okay, I see where you're coming from. Maybe you should just initial this box that says you don't love your cat.
Customer:	NOOOO! I LOVE my cat! Please give me some Catlube 6000!
Jiffy-Cat person:	Very good. Should I check her fluid levels?

Financially, this will be very similar to what you spend now at your veterinarian, but it will be more efficient. And you'll probably get a free car wash with every visit. (It will be a good idea to take the cat off the hood first.)

FOOD IN THE FUTURE

Take this quiz to find out if you are destined to become a crabby, dried-up old bag of twigs who dies young.

The thing I care most about is:

1. My body—the gift from God that allows my soul to strive for its highest potential during this brief mortal existence.
2. My automobile.

Generally speaking, people provide better maintenance for their cars than for their own bodies. Think about it. I don't know anyone who ever said, "My car needs oil, but I'm in a hurry so I'll just squirt some toothpaste in there and see if the oil warning light turns off." You wouldn't do that, because it would be bad for the car. Yet I know many people who would say, "I'm hungry. I think I'll have some bacon."

I know what you're thinking. You're thinking I'm one of those wise-ass

California vegetarians who is going to tell you that eating a few strips of bacon is bad for your health. I'm not. I say it's a free country and you should be able to kill yourself at any rate you choose, as long as your cold dead body is not blocking my driveway. I'm only addressing the question of how people pick priorities. Clearly, our automobiles are a higher priority than our bodies, because we take better care of them. But it's not entirely our fault. I blame the food industry.

The oil industry does it right. They make it easy to give our cars the right kind of oil. They refined the crude oil and added just the right combination of chemicals to make it the best oil it could be. It even has little detergents in there for people who are too lazy to clean the inside of their engines after every trip. Engine oil is a well-conceived product.

Why can't the food companies be like the oil companies? If I want to get the exact right combination of food nutrients, I have to bring a supercomputer and a team of scientists to the grocery store with me. And you know that wouldn't work if you've ever taken a team of scientists to the grocery store. They head straight for the Boboli pizza crusts and start tossing them around. Then one of the stocking clerks yells, "THOSE ARE NOT FRISBEES!" The scientists get kicked out of the store and you're stuck with this huge supercomputer and nobody to help run it.

You could ask one of the bag girls to help you run the supercomputer. They might even agree. But I wouldn't get my hopes up, because they aren't even sincere when they ask if you'd like help getting your groceries to the car. In fact, it sounds a little sarcastic when they say it to me. That's why I usually roll up my sleeves, strike a pose, and yell, "Look at those guns! Does it look like I need HELP?"

So I'm on my own when it comes to nutrition. I have a vague idea what foods are "good for me," but how do I know how much of each thing to eat? Clearly, it's important to get the right mix on a regular basis.

Today I ate twelve Snickers bars (the little ones), half a bag of potato chips, a banana, and a bunch of Spanish peanuts. I watered it all down with a cup of coffee and three diet Cokes. Later, I had two bites of a canned pineapple so I wouldn't get scurvy. And the pathetic part of this (if

I can single out one thing) is, "I ACTUALLY CARE ABOUT WHAT I EAT!"

I read a diet book called *The Zone*. Actually, I skimmed it, which is like reading except without the comprehension. Now I consider myself on *The Zone* diet, in the sense that I tend to eat whatever is in the zone of my kitchen when I'm hungry. So far I've lost ten pounds, but mostly muscle. (I'm hoping someone will find my lost muscles and return them to me, because I don't think I can ask for help carrying my grocery bags at this point.)

It's just too hard to eat right. Imagine if the oil companies acted like grocery stores. They'd give you a barrel of crude oil and several bottles of chemicals and tell you to mix it all up yourself. They wouldn't tell you how much of each chemical to use. Instead, they'd give you a government pamphlet with a pyramid showing oil at the bottom and detergent at the top. You'd be on your own to work out the specifics.

PREDICTION 60

In the future, you will not need a supercomputer and a team of scientists in order to get good nutrition.

Someday, you will be able to buy a burrito-like meal that is engineered as scientifically as a can of motor oil. This burrito-like thing will have just the right combination of food to give you 100 percent of what your body needs. It won't require much invention, just combinations of existing foods and some clever packaging.

Imagine the impact on health if people had a convenient way to eat healthy food. If better eating habits could cut health costs by 10 percent— and that's a modest goal—the impact on the economy would be gigantic. Assuming it's cheap (healthy foods tend to be inexpensive), it could be the most economical way to deal with poverty without raising taxes.

If someone doesn't build this burrito thing (or maybe it's a souplike thing), then I'll build it myself. Someone is going to make a trillion dollars selling low-cost, nutritious meals to Induhviduals, and it might as well be me.

First, I'm going down to my kitchen zone and eat a big bag of potato chips for dinner. I wish I were kidding.

TWELVE

ENDANGERED SPECIES

I have whale guilt. I don't mean I feel guilty that the whales are an endangered species, I mean I feel guilty that I don't care as much as I should.

Whales don't have much impact on my life. Whenever I'm removing a staple from a document, I do not say to myself, "This would go much easier if I had a whale." A staple remover works just fine. In a pinch, a fingernail will do.

When I'm lonely, I never say, "If only I had a whale to keep me company." I have television to fill that void. A whale would just ruin my carpet.

I might feel different if I'd ever seen a whale in person. I tried to see a whale once. In San Francisco, there's a boat that takes tourists out to spot whales. I went on the tour, but the closest I got was when someone on the other side of the boat yelled, "I SAW A TAIL." I raced over just in time to hear, "It's gone now."

This process repeated itself many times until I started getting into the spirit myself. I'd yell, "THERE'S ONE! AND IT'S WITH A BABY!" The other tourists would stampede to my side just in time to hear me say, "It was unbelievably cute. But they're gone now. It changed my life. Give me all of your addresses and I'll send you pictures."

It took a while for them to catch on. I think I lost my credibility when I yelled, "IT'S A GREAT WHITE! AND IT HAS THE CAPTAIN IN ITS MOUTH! AAAAHHHHHH!"

Now I'm banned for life from the whale-watching tours. But I'm not worried about seeing additional whales. I predict that in the future the problem will be too many whales, not too few, thanks to genetic engineering.

PREDICTION 61

In the future, there will be so many new kinds of whales, we'll all be sick of looking at them.

I think the scientists will be able to whip up any kind of whale we want in the lab and then release it in the bay, sewer, or anyplace else we think would look better with a few whales. And you won't have to make do with the boring gray and humpback whales we have now. We'll have polka-dot whales, two-headed whales, talking whales, whalephants, flying whales, you name it. I'm not saying this will be a good thing, but it will give us a whole new attitude about how many species are too many.

THIRTEEN

SOME THINGS WON'T IMPROVE

Most things will improve in the future, but some things won't, because the designers who make those things prefer to keep them in their current sadistic form.

PREDICTION 62

Two things that will never improve in the future are airlines and bicycle seats.

AIRLINES

In the future, airline travel will be just as uncomfortable as it is today. Airline comfort hasn't improved in my lifetime. There's no reason to think it will get better in the future. I was baffled by this lack of progress until I finally figured out why: Those jets last thirty years.

Jets cost millions of dollars, so you have to keep them until they plow into the side of a mountain. Airlines can't afford to throw out the old jets and buy new ones. Nor can they realistically have a fleet that is partly old uncomfortable planes and partly new comfortable planes. That would make people complain every time they flew in the old planes. So the obvious solution is to make new planes as uncomfortable as the old ones. That way nobody knows what they are missing. The newer jets have better fuel efficiency and safety features, but comfort-wise, they are the same as the old ones.

The thing that bothers me the most about the flying experience is checking in. I want someone to tell me what all the typing is about.

BICYCLE SEATS

Bicycle seats will never improve. The bicycle industry has apparently decided that the perfect design for a bicycle seat is a hard plastic object carefully engineered to avoid contact with the two padded portions of your buttocks.

It is very difficult for me to understand why my office chair can be designed to accommodate my entire bottom, but a bicycle seat cannot. Do the inventors of bicycle seats think their customers have magic buttocks that change shape when they exercise? I have no clue. But whatever the reason, it's not likely that bicycle seats will improve in the future.

FOURTEEN

A NEW VIEW OF THE FUTURE

Despite the fact that the future will be filled with an ever-growing number of idiots, I remain optimistic. This chapter will explain why I feel immune from their influence and why you might, too.

My explanation starts with a serious prediction that will make you shake your head, roll your eyes, and wonder what's gotten into me.

PREDICTION 63

The theory of evolution will be scientifically debunked in your lifetime.

The remainder of this book will be more bizarre and thought-provoking than whatever you expected. I'm turning the humor mode off for this chapter (except for the comics), because what you're going to read is so strange that you would be waiting for the punch line instead of following the point.

My prediction about evolution being debunked is part of a larger prediction. I believe that the next 100 years will bring about new ways of looking at existing things, as opposed to finding new things to look at. It will be about perception and not vision.

PREDICTION 64

The next 100 years will be a search for better perception
instead of better vision.

Most of human history has been an obsession to improve our visual understanding of our Universe. Almost everything we know is based on looking at things. We do experiments and we look at the results. We build microscopes to look at small things. We build telescopes to look at distant things. We build vehicles to take us where we can look at new territory. One of our most fundamental beliefs is that the things we see with our eyes are a good approximation of reality.

We use our other senses, too, but mostly we look at things and draw conclusions. That has worked well for most of human existence. But there have been some big-time blunders caused by looking at the world and using our brains to draw conclusions.

The most well-documented blunder caused by our vision was the historical belief that the Sun revolved around the Earth. It sure looks that way. Until an alternate theory was suggested, no other possibility was obvious. Here were the two biggest and most important objects in our field of vision—the Earth and the Sun—and virtually every person who looked at them got a totally backward perception of their movements.

People thought the Earth was flat because that's the only model that fit the way things looked. People didn't change their minds until someone took a boat and sailed out for a better look.

You might be tempted to say that these are isolated instances involving primitive times in our history, so it's not relevant to the future. But these isolated instances involved the biggest objects in our reality. These were not trivial misunderstandings. Our eyesight was inadequate for the task. It took some experimentation and a lot more looking to find the truth.

What if there are other optical illusions about our existence that are just as major as the illusion of the Sun revolving around the Earth? If so, how big are the opportunities that would emerge from a clearer perception?

What are the odds that you live in exactly the window of human existence when all of the major optical illusions have been discovered? Wouldn't that be an amazing coincidence, since every previous generation of humans has believed they were born in that window of time? They were all wrong, but they all thought they were right, just like we do now.

This is a hugely important question, because if your view of reality is flawed, then your strategies for succeeding are also probably flawed. If you change your assumptions, you have to change your plan.

For the rest of this chapter, I'm going to give you some mental exercises and scientific tidbits that might change your view of how much you understand about your reality. In so doing, I'll give you an alternate view of reality, one in which evolution makes no sense.

Don't worry, I won't be addressing the religious interpretations. There's nothing here that contradicts your religious beliefs, no matter what they are. I'll be talking about the limitations of eyesight as a source of knowledge, nothing more. I don't think the reality I'm going to describe here is the "right" one or the "only" one that could be described, but I think it's as logical as what I'll call the "normal" view.

It has been my experience that when I craft my strategies for success around this alternate reality, I get better results than when I assume reality conforms to the normal view. I realize that my personal experiences are not persuasive from a statistical perspective, but statistics mean nothing in my alternate view of reality (you'll see why). So neither perspective can be used to verify the other.

Are you getting curious yet or just confused?

I'm sure that some—if not all—of what I tell you next is scientifically inaccurate and maybe even illogical. It won't make any difference for my purpose. I'm just trying to help you imagine how your reality COULD be completely different from what you perceive and still LOOK exactly the way it looks. That alone will give you some freedom to try other approaches to success. Sometimes the first step to finding a better approach is to recognize the limitations of the current approach. That's as far as I can take you.

I'm not intentionally making up any facts in this chapter, but I'm not bright enough to get all of the scientific stuff exactly right either. Nor am I sufficiently interested in accuracy to spend a lot of time researching it. But if any of the points I make ring true, it will help you imagine a different world. That's all I'm aiming for. Read it with as many grains of salt as you need to be comfortable.

If you feel inspired to do so, I encourage you to research the scientific tidbits, think about the logic of it all, and tell me how uninformed and stupid I am. If that process makes you think about anything differently, this chapter did its job, regardless of where you come out.

In your normal view of reality, there are several things that seem unquestionably true. When I say "seem true," I mean that they look to be true from a visual perspective and you can't imagine any alternative. Here are some things I think you assume about reality.

Assumptions About Reality

1. Time goes forward.

2. Objects move.

3. Gravity exists.

4. A "cause" can only have an "effect" on something it physically contacts, directly or indirectly.

Obviously, if any one of those assumptions is wrong, your entire view of reality is totally, fundamentally, completely wrong. And so are your strategies for success. I'm going to cast some doubt on each of those assumptions, as unlikely as that might seem.

I can trace the beginnings of my own doubts about reality to a childhood friend named John. His family vacationed in my little town in upstate New York every summer. As a preteen, I spent hours with John and various members of his clan playing poker, Monopoly, and other games that required more luck than brains.

I never won.

John and his entire family boasted openly about their Irish luck. I can vouch for the fact that it seemed to defy statistical odds. To them, luck wasn't an abstract concept; it was palpable. They expected it and they got it with absurd regularity. If you spent much time with them, you got the impression that somehow they could make luck happen and they knew it.

One day his family and mine both visited a church charity event featuring booths with ring tosses, pop-gun shooting, and similar games of "skill." The games were designed to be unwinnable except by luck. My family dutifully complied, emptying our pockets in record time and having no prizes to show for it. But John's family had a different experience. I still have the image burned in my memory of John's mother making a special trip back to the car with an armload of impossible-to-win prizes. It was like a scene from a bad comedy. They weren't just winning, they were winning the things you aren't supposed to win no matter how lucky you are: cameras, telescopes, large stuffed animals. It was obscene. I believe they only stopped playing the games out of a sense of guilt.

The last time I saw John and his family was right after they found out they had won the grand prize in the Irish Sweepstakes—$120,000. This was the Sixties, so it was a much bigger pile of money than it seems today, and I believe it was the biggest prize of its kind in the world.

I realize that someone has to win the top prize, and I realize that statistics allow for clustering of unlikely events, but it was their expectation of luck that made me question my understanding of how the Universe was wired. It opened my mind to the possibility that luck can be managed.

You probably don't know anyone like John and his family. I've never met any group like them before or since. But you probably know someone who expects to have *bad* luck and seems to consistently experience it. Think about that person right now and use that thought as a doorway to the rest of this chapter. You're about to take an interesting trip.

THE DOUBLE SLIT EXPERIMENT

I read about the double slit experiment in *Newsweek*. It's a well-known experiment among the physics crowd, and it's repeatable. I'll try to explain it in simple terms. You'll still have to read this section several times before you convince yourself you've read it correctly.

Here's how it works. You take a light source and shine it through a barrier that has two slits. Then you examine the light pattern on the surface behind the barrier. You would expect to see two bars of light corresponding to the slits, but you don't. You see multiple bars, like a venetian blind pattern.

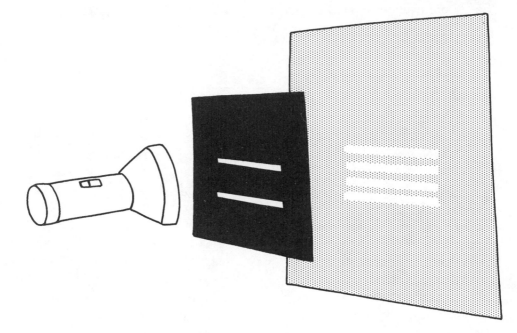

This nonobvious result interested the scientists who devised the experiment, so they hooked up some equipment that would record information about the light passing through the slits. When they recorded information about the light, they didn't get a venetian blind pattern anymore. They saw a blotch pattern instead.

You're probably thinking that the way they measured the light must have changed it. The scientists thought of that, too. So they did the experiment two ways, each time measuring the light the same way, but in one case the measured information was automatically erased after being measured.

When the information was automatically erased, the light pattern was a venetian blind, but when the information was *not* erased, the light pattern was a blotch.

The Scientists' Conclusion:

Information in the present can change the past.

Read that sentence again. I'll wait.

Let me say it another way, because I know it's hard to grasp. When the scientists had access to the recorded information about the light in the present, the light pattern in the past was a blotch, but when the scientists did *not* have access to the information in the present, the pattern in the past was a venetian blind.

It might seem impossible for you to conceive that time doesn't always march in one direction, bringing with it a perfectly ordered sequence of causes and effects, but it's not hard for me to imagine it, because I'm dyslexic.

When I hear a phone number spoken quickly, I hear all the numbers, but don't have any impression in what order they were spoken. It's as if they came in all at once. I have no problem imagining a reality where everything happens at once and some aspect of our perceptions straightens it all into an artificial sense of order. To me, disorder in the direction of time seems normal, at least some of the time.

Obviously, the brain is capable of perceiving time in an incorrect order. In fact, it happens all the time, even to nondyslexic people, but we don't acknowledge it.

In laboratory tests, it has been shown that sometimes the portion of the brain responsible for making a decision doesn't even activate until slightly after the action has been made. If I poke you in the butt with a pin, you jump before your conscious mind realizes what happened. But your immediate memory will be that you felt a poke and then moved. In this example, you would have perceived time backward, because what really happened is that you jumped from reflex and only afterward realized why.

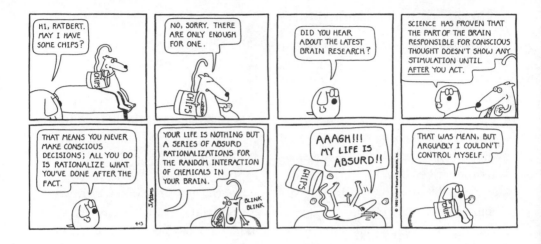

If brains can perceive time in any order, it raises the question of whether time is an independent thing or just a perception. Your perception of color might be a good analogy. Objects seem to have color, but, in fact, it's just a perception caused by the reflection of light. The color is a perception created by your mind. It is not a quality of the object.

Could time be in your mind and not in the environment? Time, like color, is something you can't put in a bottle. You can't get a handful of color or a handful of time. Most physicists have dispensed with the word altogether, preferring the phrase space-time, because it allows them to create a definition that's more useful for the physical world. I'm not sure what space-time means to physicists, but I'm sure it's different from my perception of the passage of time.

OBJECTS MOVE

Most people would agree that reality is full of objects that move around. Planets move, people move, molecules move. Everything is moving all the time.

What if all the motion we observe is an optical illusion? Let me paint a picture where you can imagine how nothing that appears to be moving actually moves, yet still looks like it does.

In cartoons, Bugs Bunny appears to be moving, but it's an illusion caused by lots of still frames being shown in sequence. Some physicists theorize that reality is like the frames of an animated movie, with infinite universes existing at once.

What if every possible universe existed simultaneously, each one only slightly different than its neighbor, like the frames of an animated movie? None of the universes in this model have movement. All the people and objects are frozen in one position. The only thing that moves in this reality is your perception (some might call it a soul), inhabiting one "you" after another in an endless string of nonmoving universes. Your perception would be that you were in one universe, but everything in it was moving. In fact, the only thing moving would be your line of perception from one "you" to another in each adjacent universe. And because each frozen universe is slightly different, your perception is that the things in it are moving.

Have you ever pulled up to a stoplight next to a city bus? If you see the bus gradually moving out of the corner of your eye, you sometimes think incorrectly that your car is rolling in the opposite direction—because your field of reference is changing. You press your brakes frantically to stop it. In this case, your perception of motion is completely opposite from reality. The bus is moving, not you. Reality could be that way, too, and it would look just the way it looks to you now.

The view of reality I'm describing can't be proven, but it can't be disproved either. The same holds true for your current view of reality. It cannot be proven or disproved. Maybe there are lots of other models that would result in our current perception yet are quite different from what we assume.

GRAVITY EXISTS

It's hard to doubt that gravity exists. Every single thing you see appears to be affected by it. Gravity appears to be a force that reaches across space and somehow connects two objects, making them attracted to each other. That's what it looks like.

But scientists can't find gravity. They can only measure its effect. You can't fill a cup with gravity or block its effect with some sort of shield or find its molecules under a microscope. So where is it?

The best explanation that Einstein could come up with about gravity is that it was like a bowling ball on a bed—a heavy object bending the fabric of space. That explanation is virtually useless for a visual understanding. Physicists talk about gravity in terms of multiple dimensions, but we're not capable of seeing in more than three dimensions. It's safe to say that whatever we perceive about gravity—our simple model of objects being attracted—is an optical illusion.

To understand how gravity can look and act the way it does and be an optical illusion, let me describe a hypothetical universe. In this universe, there are only two objects: you and a huge planet-sized ball.

There is no gravity in this hypothetical reality in the classic sense of objects being attracted to each other. There is only one rule: Every piece of matter in this universe is constantly expanding, doubling in size every second.

You wouldn't notice the doubling, because both you and the huge ball would remain in the same proportion to each other. There would be no other reference points. And you wouldn't feel your own matter doubling any more than you feel the activity of the atoms in your body now.

In your current universe, you don't feel your skin cells dying, and you don't feel yourself being propelled at high velocity around the Sun or spinning with the Earth's rotation. So it shouldn't be hard to imagine how you could be doubling in size every second without being aware of it in the hypothetical universe.

The only effect you would feel from this doubling in size is the illusion of gravity. The ball's growth would cause a constant pushing against you. If you tried to "jump" away from the growing ball, you would create some space temporarily, but the ball's growth would catch up with you and close the distance quickly. To you, it would feel as though you were attracted to the huge ball and whenever you jumped "up," you would be sucked back down to it. There would be no gravity, but it would look and feel exactly like gravity.

Visually, it would seem that the huge ball had more "gravitational pull" than you do, because you seem to be attracted to it and not the other way around. This corresponds to our classic view of gravity—that huge objects have more of it.

Imagine a marble and a bowling ball. Now imagine they both instantly double in size. The marble still looks pretty much like a marble, but the bowling ball appears huge. When a large object doubles in size, it seems to have a disproportionately significant impact compared to a smaller object. So if gravity is an optical illusion, large objects would appear to create more of the illusion than smaller objects. That's consistent with what we see.

Now let's move from the hypothetical universe to our current universe filled with planets and other matter. You'd have to add another rule in order for the expanding matter theory to replace gravity in the current universe. You'd have to have a universe where all the major planets are moving away from each other quickly, otherwise they'd grow until they all bumped together.

In fact, the current universe does appear to be expanding, so that's no obstacle to the expanding matter theory. I can't think of anything in the "real" universe that would contradict the notion of gravity being an illusion caused by expanding matter. I'm not suggesting the theory is correct, only that it's a good mental exercise for seeing how things could be very different than you imagine them and still look the same.

The expanding matter theory came to me at 3:00 A.M. one day. I woke suddenly and sat straight up in bed with the idea fully formed in my head. I don't remember if it was inspired by a dream. At first, I thought it was either brilliant or totally stupid. I still don't know which it is. I first floated the idea in my *Dilbert Newsletter*, knowing that a million people would read it and some of them would surely write to tell me how stupid the idea was. I wrote it up as a whimsical theory from my cat Freddie, thus putting the blame on him. To my surprise, I received no reasonable criticisms of the theory. Instead, I heard a story about one physicist who had seriously pursued the same theory years ago, with no luck whatsoever, since there is no way to prove it experimentally.

I also heard that the theory was the subject of at least one science fiction book, although I'm not sure which one. So it's not a new idea. It's just an interesting one.

CAUSE AND EFFECT

You can't question the law of cause and effect, can you? When two things come in contact, they have an effect on each other. Logically, it's also true that if two things don't come in contact, they don't have any impact on each other.

The trouble is, how can you tell what things are really affecting other things and what are just optical illusions? Gravity seems to affect things at a distance. So do magnets. Yet there's no evidence that they touch.

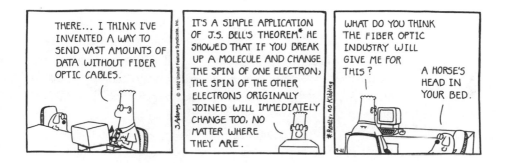

A physicist named John Stuart Bell performed a very strange experiment that was suggested by one of Einstein's theories. I'll simplify the explanation, probably getting the details wrong in the process, but you'll get the general idea.

You take a molecule and break it in half. If you change the rotation of the electrons on one of the halves, the electrons on the other half change at the same time. It doesn't matter how far apart the two halves are when you do it.

Whatever is happening in Bell's experiment defies our ability to understand it visually. Are the two halves of the molecule connected by some invisible force? Or is it an optical illusion and the two halves are never really separated? Or could one cause have two effects? We can't picture any of these explanations being correct.

Now consider the experiments that have been done to detect ESP. If you're a natural skeptic like me, you probably think there could be nothing flying through the air undetected that would allow ESP to work. Yet we read of experiments where some people seem to consistently beat the laws of averages in controlled ESP tests. Still, it seems impossible that ESP could be genuine. I am thoroughly unconvinced by media reports of *anything* unusual—much less ESP—because the media is so easily misled. This is the sort of thing I would have to experience firsthand in order to believe. And I have.

Years ago when I was taking a class to learn hypnosis, I met a woman who claimed to have psychic powers. I was highly amused by this concept and asked if I could hypnotize her so she could test her so-called powers in a trance. I'd heard reports that psychics are more accurate under hypnosis, so it was a good way to test my skills and also debunk the psychic for my amusement.

It didn't work out the way I planned.

I asked her to bring her deck of tarot cards. She did. We were in my home with no other people in a setting that I could totally control. I sat across the room from her and started the hypnosis. She slipped into a deep trance almost instantly. (There is anecdotal evidence that psychics are easily hypnotized. She certainly was.)

Then I shuffled her tarot cards and picked one. I asked her to describe what card I had in my hand. She described in detail the wrong card. My skepticism seemed justified. I picked another card and repeated the process, not telling her about her failure on the first. Again, she described the wrong card. But oddly enough, the wrong card she described was the first card I had picked. It was a coincidence, but still wrong. In all, I picked five cards, and she missed all five. Amazingly, the five cards she described were the five I picked, just out of order. I had been careful to keep them all close to my chest to remove any possibility that she was somehow peeking. And we were alone in my house, so no accomplices were involved.

I asked her why she guessed the cards out of order, and she explained that she can't distinguish between the near past and the near future. They are not relevant concepts to her. In her reality, the past and the present exist at the same time.

While still in a trance, and not in response to any question from me, she told me she saw a break in my aura. She traced her own body to show me where the break was in mine. Her hand stopped under one armpit. I was stunned.

I had a bad rash under that arm that I was having lots of trouble treating. It wasn't bad enough to cause itching or anything that would have tipped her off. We had no friends in common to feed her this information. Her information seemed to come out of nowhere. How lucky would you have to be to guess someone has a problem with one armpit?

Then, again without asking, she told me I was afraid of water. In fact, water is my *only* irrational fear. I have a healthy respect for many forms of danger, but only one truly irrational fear. And I've never known why.

Then she said, "And the reason is . . . "

At that point I was VERY interested, because I didn't know any reason I should fear water. Her credibility with me was growing by the moment. Suddenly, a picture formed in my head. It was a clear memory of an early childhood moment on a bridge with my parents. I was a toddler, and my father lifted me above the side railing so I could see a barge passing below. I remembered being filled with stark, blinding fear that somehow my father would lose his grip and I would fall into the water below the bridge.

The moment the image filled my head, my psychic friend said, "I see a bridge."

As you can imagine, much of my skepticism disappeared at that point. She made many other predictions that night and in later conversations, most of them eerily accurate.

I don't expect you to believe the story about the psychic, although it's true. After all, I'm the media to you, and you should apply all due scrutiny when you hear a story like that one. But there might be an analogous situation in your own experience.

If you're a religious person, you believe that your body can be influenced by something nonphysical, specifically the soul. That would mean there is some connection between physical and nonphysical things, otherwise one could not influence the other.

Regardless of your personal experience or religious preferences, there's one thing we can agree on: Things in the Universe are connected in ways that we don't understand. It's certainly true with gravity, and it's true with the molecules in Bell's experiment. It seems plausible that if the Universe has connections that we can't see, then there are probably useful strategies for influencing the environment that we are not taking advantage of. I don't know if my psychic friend was taking advantage of some of these unseen connections or if souls do, but I no longer doubt it is possible.

CHAOS THEORY

What if our thoughts could influence the environment? It sounds ludicrously New Age–like to even consider the possibility, but when you think about the double slit experiment and how knowledge seems to influence the past, you begin to wonder how separate the mind and reality really are.

Even if you can't understand the invisible connections in our reality, maybe you can still use those connections. I can raise my arm simply by wanting it to happen, even though I have no idea how the thought is transformed into apparent motion.

What if your thoughts can influence things at a distance—but only in the tiniest ways—on the order of electrons, light particles, or even smaller? Could those tiny influences make any significant difference in your life?

According to chaos theory, the answer is yes.

Here again, I'm plunging into scientific waters way over my head, but I'll give you enough information so you'll get the basic idea. In chaos theory, you can show that the tiniest error in assumptions will cause any "complex iterative model" to give completely useless predictions.

An example of a complex iterative model would be a computer program for predicting the weather of the Earth. It's iterative in the sense that it calculates what each moment would be like and then uses that as a basis for calculating the next moment. Any tiny error in the first iteration would become compounded in the next, growing ever larger until the predictive ability of the program is useless.

Here's the classic explanation of chaos theory, which I'll borrow because it works so well: Suppose you had a weather model (a computer program) that could account for all the effects of wind, pressure, temperature, terrain, moisture, and sun. And suppose you fed the program with perfect information—except that you forgot to account for the impact of one butterfly beating its wings somewhere on Earth.

Chaos theory shows that your weather program would be effective at forecasting the weather tomorrow, because the butterfly effect is trivial on the first day. But over time, the omission of the butterfly causes each successive day's assumptions to be increasingly off. Eventually, the program will be completely useless. The nonobvious part of all this is how quickly and how hugely the tiny change can magnify itself. It defies visual logic.

Your life is a complex iterative model. Everything that happens today forms the basis for what can happen tomorrow. Infinitesimally small changes in your day today can magnify into huge changes over time. Every person who wins a lottery does so by the tiniest margin. The important people you meet could just as easily have been elsewhere that day. The virus you get, the memory you keep or lose, the inspiration you have—they all depend on the tiniest of electronic and chemical reactions.

We know that thoughts cause an electrical change in the environment outside your head. Scientists can put sensors on your scalp and detect slight changes in electrical impulses that correspond to your thoughts. Could this tiny change in electricity—barely detectable by sensors on your head—cause larger changes than our vision and common sense would allow us to believe?

If your thoughts can influence the environment—and there's circumstantial evidence that it can happen—can it happen in a planned way? Or is it all just random?

Suppose there really are an infinite number of motionless universes as I described earlier, and only your perception moves from one to the next. Can you steer your perceptions toward realities that are more to your liking?

AFFIRMATIONS

If it's possible to control your environment through your thoughts or steer your perceptions (or soul if you prefer) through other universes, I'll bet the secret to doing that is a process called "affirmations."

I first heard of this technique from a friend who had read a book on the topic. I don't recall the name of the book, so I apologize to the author for not mentioning it. My information came to me secondhand. I only mention it here because it formed my personal experience.

The process as it was described to me involved visualizing what you want and writing it down fifteen times in a row, once a day, until you obtain the thing you visualized.

The suggested form would be something like this:

"I, Scott Adams, will win a Pulitzer Prize."

The thing that caught my attention is that the process doesn't require any faith or positive thinking to work. Even more interesting was the suggestion that this technique would influence your environment directly and not just make you more focused on your goal. It was alleged that you would experience what seemed to be amazing coincidences when using the technique. These coincidences would be things seemingly beyond your control and totally independent of your efforts (at least from a visual view of reality).

The book also suggested picking a goal that you knew wouldn't happen by your extra effort alone. The author said you would never know if the affirmations worked unless you chose a highly unlikely goal.

So I tried affirmations. I figured it didn't cost anything so I had nothing to lose. My friend said it worked for her, coincidences and all, so I had a testimonial that sounded credible. It wasn't proof, but it was better than no testimonial at all. I picked what I thought was a very unlikely goal and went at it.

Within a week, coincidences started to happen to me, too. Amazing coincidences. Strings of them. I won't mention the specific goal I was working on, as it was a private matter, but within a few months the goal was accomplished exactly as I had written it.

I wasn't convinced the affirmations helped. Coincidences do happen on their own. And after all, maybe I had made some of my own luck. I considered the test inconclusive.

So I picked another goal—to get rich in the stock market. I wrote my affirmation down every day and waited for an inspiration. One day it happened. At about 4:00 A.M., my eyes snapped open, I awoke from a sound sleep, sat bolt upright in bed, and discovered the words "buy Chrysler" repeating in my head. (This kind of thing happens to me occasionally—the part about waking suddenly with a strange thought.)

At the time, this seemed like a very dumb thing to have in my head. It was during Chrysler's most bleak period. The company had only survived because of government loans. The stock was in a deep hole. (I forget the exact year, but if you've learned anything from this book, it's that I don't do research to get facts straight.)

Thinking that "buy Chrysler" was my inspiration, unlikely as it seemed, I quickly called a discount brokerage service to set up an account and buy some Chrysler stock. (Obviously, I didn't need a full-service broker, because I was getting all the advice I needed from the voices in my head.)

It took about two weeks to get the brokerage account established because of mail delays. During those two weeks, Chrysler stock climbed substantially. I figured I missed the window for buying it and cursed myself for not having a brokerage account set up in advance. Then a funny thing happened. Chrysler's stock kept growing. The company paid off its government loans earlier than anyone expected and went on a rampage. That year, Chrysler was arguably the best stock you could have owned.

I don't know how many stocks there are in the world, but it seemed awfully odd that during the time I was doing affirmations I woke up somehow knowing one of the best ones to buy. I wished I had followed my own advice.

So I tried again, this time promising myself I would follow my own inspiration no matter how flimsy and stupid it seemed. I wrote the affirmations and waited. Then one day I woke up somehow knowing that this was "the day." I picked up the newspaper and opened it knowing I was going to find my stock to buy. And there it was—a large announcement that a company called ASK was going public. I didn't know what their product was, except that it involved software. And I didn't care. This was my stock. I dialed my broker and bought $1,000 worth, which was the majority of my net worth at the time.

The stock climbed 10 percent almost immediately. Realizing that I was a brilliant investor, and wishing to lock in my gains, I sold after holding the stock only a few days. I pocketed a clean fifty bucks after taxes and commissions. I felt like a Rockefeller. Clearly, this affirmation technique worked.

Then a funny thing happened. ASK stock kept climbing. The media discovered it and wrote glowing assessments of its potential. It went on a rampage. That year, ASK was one of the best stocks you could have owned.

I don't know how many stocks there are in the world, but the odds of one idiot picking Chrysler and then ASK during that period were exceedingly small, especially if you take into account my sophisticated stock-picking methods.

I decided to unleash my affirmations on another goal that I had long since abandoned. I wanted to get my MBA from the University of California at Berkeley. They had the best evening MBA program within driving distance, and I needed that degree to become the business tycoon I always wanted to be.

The trouble was, I had already taken the GMAT exam several years before—it's a requirement for most MBA programs—and I earned a meager seventy-seventh percentile score. That wasn't good enough for Berkeley. It wasn't even close. I knew I had to be above the ninetieth percentile to have a chance.

I picked the ninety-fourth percentile as my specific outlandish target. My friend who told me about affirmations said I should be as specific as possible. I visualized the ninety-four exactly as it would appear on the results form, which was easy, because I'd seen the results form after my first GMAT.

I bought GMAT study books and took GMAT practice exams in the books for weeks before the actual test, each time scoring at about the seventy-seventh percentile. The experts say you can't improve your score dramatically by practicing, and I was proving them right. Hitting the ninety-fourth percentile was certainly going to be a stretch.

The day of the GMAT came. It felt just like the practice tests, no harder and no easier. Afterward, I kept up the visualization and the affirmations as I waited for the results in the mail.

I remember the moment I took the results envelope out of my mailbox. My heart was pounding. My future was in that envelope. I opened it and focused my eyes on the box that I had visualized a thousand times before. It was a ninety-four.

I looked again, certain I had misread it. It was still a ninety-four. I took it inside and looked again. Still ninety-four.

That evening, I sat in a chair with the GMAT results next to me, alternately staring at the wall and then staring at the ninety-four. I kept expecting it to change. It didn't. And that night I knew that nothing would ever be the same for me. Everything I thought I knew about how the Universe was wired was wrong.

I used the affirmations again many times, each time with unlikely success. So much so that by 1988, when I decided I wanted to become a famous syndicated cartoonist, it actually felt like a modest goal.

The odds of becoming a successful syndicated cartoonist are about 10,000 to 1. I knew the odds, but I figured they didn't apply to me. When I submitted my samples by mail to the major cartoon syndicates, I had a feeling of being exactly where I needed to be and doing exactly what I needed to do. I never once doubted it would work out the way it has.

Reporters often ask me if I am amazed at the success of the *Dilbert* comic strip. I definitely would be amazed, if not for my bizarre experiences with affirmations. As it was, I expected it.

I wasn't satisfied that *Dilbert* allowed me to make a comfortable living. I turned my affirmations toward making it the most successful comic on the planet. I figured that was another 10,000 to 1 shot. But as before, I figured the odds didn't apply to me.

It's hard to define what is "most successful" with comics. Everyone has their favorite. You can't really rank art or humor objectively. I took a pragmatic approach and decided the best measure was the number of *Dilbert* books sold. My reasoning was that people have to make a genuine choice with their own money when they buy a book, whereas you have no real influence over what runs in the newspaper. And as far as the "quality" of the strip, I decided the market could sort that out in book sales. If people liked the quality, they'd buy the book.

In June of 1996, *The Dilbert Principle* hit the number-one spot on the hardcover nonfiction list of the *New York Times*. It stayed in the top three all summer. In November, it was joined by *Dogbert's Top Secret Management Handbook*, giving me the number-one and number-two positions simultaneously for one week. For that brief period of time, *Dilbert* was the "most successful" comic on the planet, according to the limited definition I had set for it.

I don't know if there is one universe or many. If there are many, I don't know for certain that you can choose your path. And if you can choose your path, I don't know that affirmations are necessarily the way to do it. But I do know this: When I act as though affirmations can steer me, I consistently get good results.

I know that I have a better outlook on life when I think of reality in terms of infinite universes. When I think back to my GMAT results, I believe the contents of the envelope were variable until the moment I perceived what was inside. (For physics buffs, read about the Schrödinger's cat experiment to see how reality might actually exist in more than one state.)

In a world with infinite universes, there are infinite chances to get what you want, as well as infinite chances not to. If affirmations help you steer, maybe your odds are a matter of your control.

Several years ago, after having considerable success with affirmations, I developed a large lump on my neck. When the X rays came back, the cancer expert told me it was "probably" cancer. If it wasn't, he couldn't think of anything else it could be. But sometimes these lumps turn out to be, in his words, "just one of those things that go away." To me, the envelope wasn't open yet. Not until the biopsy.

I had a week to think about it. It's the kind of week you don't forget. I knew that the needle would enter the lump and draw out a sample of its contents. If the sample was red (blood), it was cancer. If it was clear, it was just "one of those things." I decided it would be clear. The doctor was surprised when it came out clear. I wasn't.

I have heard that patients who are prayed for recover better than those who are not. The patients themselves are not aware which group is being prayed for and which is not. The tests are small and inconclusive, but when viewed in the context of this chapter, they make you scratch your head. Depending on your religious views, you could replace everything I've said about affirmations with prayer and it starts looking very similar. And in the discussion of multiple universes, you could replace "point of view" with "soul" and lose nothing in the discussion.

At the time of this writing, I got a new car. I've been obsessing over how long it would be before it got its first dent. The thought was constantly on my mind as I drove it. I imagined every other car to be a potential missile heading my way. It bothered me that I couldn't relax and enjoy this lovely vehicle. A nice gentleman put me out of my misery by plowing into the car while I was parked at the gas station for its first refill. Did I somehow cause this to happen?

My last three cars have gotten bruised in the first month I owned them and then never again. In each case, the cars were parked when it happened. When I worried about the cars getting hit, they got hit. When I didn't worry, they didn't get hit. Every day it gets harder for me to believe my thoughts are separate from my reality.

Other people have read media reports of my use of affirmations and tried it themselves. Many of them have told me it worked for them, too. I have no proof that it works for me and even less evidence that it worked for them, but I do know it doesn't cost you anything to try.

I started the chapter by predicting that evolution would be debunked in your lifetime. I think physicists will raise enough questions about the nature of the Universe that evolution will require a second look. For example, if time doesn't move forward, or if there is no cause and effect, evolution makes no sense as a concept. I don't know the specifics of how evolution will lose its appeal, but I feel it coming.

I doubt the physicists will find a universe that has much in common with one described by a cartoonist, but I think it's a safe bet that our new understanding will be remarkably different from our current one. And in that new understanding of the Universe, all rules are off.

This makes me optimistic.

It would be easy to feel helpless in a vision-based universe where you're surrounded by idiots. Their sheer numbers would guarantee that you can't escape their impact no matter how clever you are or how hard you work. But I predict that will change.

PREDICTION 65

In the future, science will gradually free us from the optical illusions
that restrict our view of reality.

We may not have the capacity to fully understand "true" reality—if
indeed there is one—but we can shed the popular view of reality, the one
that keeps us in a prison of statistical likelihood. When we open ourselves
to new possibilities, it allows us to try new strategies.

Figuratively speaking, the year 2000 could very well be the "end of the
world" in terms of our outdated vision-based understanding of it. I think it
will be the beginning of something better— a world where our intentions
define reality in a more direct way than we ever imagined possible.

Personally, I can't wait.

MORE WEIRD STUFF

Lots of folks wrote to ask where they could read more about the double-slit experiment and other interesting quantum physics oddities. I recommend a book that was recommended to me by a reader: *Schrödinger's Kittens and the Search for Reality,* by John Gribbin, Ph.D. It's about quantum physics, time, space, and the nature of reality. It's written for non-scientists. It's great.

If you're a skeptic, check out *The Conscious Universe,* by Dean Radin, Ph.D. Compare it to what you're reading in your *Skeptical Inquirer* magazines and make up your own mind.

GRAVITY REBUTTALS

I got many e-mail messages about my gravity theory in Chapter 14. Many people accepted my implied challenge and wrote to offer their reasons why expanding matter could not be the cause of gravity. I didn't have a chance to answer them all by e-mail, so I'll do it here.

First, remember that I don't claim that the expanding-matter theory is an accurate explanation of gravity. My point was that it's difficult to refute the theory with visual evidence and everyday logic. I accept no burden of proving my theory since it was only used to make a point about perceptions. Still, silly as the theory is, it's remarkably robust. That's what makes it a good thought exercise.

The people who offered arguments against the theory generally fell into two types. One group offered highly complicated mathematical explanations that I didn't understand, based on highly sensitive scientific observations that I can't verify. But as far as I could tell (which isn't far in this case), those arguments served only to show that the expanding-matter theory doesn't explain everything. That's different from proving it wrong.

The second group of dissenters were truer to the thought experiment and tried to use their own observations and logic to disprove the expanding-matter theory. Despite their cockiness, most of them fell short. I'll summarize their arguments and tell you where the holes are. I'm being argumentative for fun, so I'll present my opinions with more force than they deserve.

Argument 1: The current theory of gravity fits the data better.

What current theory of gravity? We can measure and predict the effects of gravity very accurately, but when it comes to a theory, it's still an open debate. Is gravity an illusion caused by the bending of space, or is it the transfer of gravitons, or is the truth somewhere in the amazingly complex theories involving superstrings or ten-dimensional space? It depends which physicists you ask.

The expanding-matter theory has holes, but so do most theories until they are refined. Who knows how many holes could be plugged if the expanding-matter theory were refined? You can't eliminate a brand-new theory on the basis that other theories have fewer holes. Every theory about gravity has problems.

Argument 2: How do you explain orbits and tides with expanding matter?

I don't have to. One theory doesn't have to explain every attraction of objects in the universe. Magnets are attracted to steel without using gravity. A vacuum cleaner can attract dirt without gravity. Orbits and tides might be the product of complex interactions of forces that are either undiscovered or hard to sort out. Yes, this is a weasel argument, nevertheless it's valid.

Argument 3: How do you explain black holes? These are collapsed stars that are so dense that gravity won't let light escape. How can expanding matter explain that observation?

Maybe black holes are the only places in the universe where nothing is expanding. From an observer's viewpoint, anything that got near a black hole would appear to shrink to nothing. Light would appear to be trapped in the black hole when in fact it was just too small to interact with the enlarged universe or be seen by an enlarged observer.

Everything we know about black holes is based on theories and interpretation of faint clues. No one has seen a black hole directly. So no one really knows what's happening there. (My argument here had so much weaseldom that I think I just grew a snout.)

Argument 4: If matter is expanding, then when you dropped two balls, they would grow to touch each other before hitting the ground. But they don't.

They wouldn't grow fast enough to be noticeably closer before the earth expanded up to meet them. But if you fired two balls across space on parallel paths, they would indeed eventually touch. But that's true of all theories of gravity. Any two objects would exhibit their own gravity and eventually come together.

Argument 5: Why do dense objects have more gravity? The expanding matter theory would predict that the *size* of an object determines gravity, not density.

Dense objects might expand faster than less dense objects that start out at the same size. That would satisfy the observations that dense objects have more gravity. The problem with my explanation is that no one has observed dense objects getting bigger relative to the things around them.

But would we notice if they were?

We don't notice the gravitation difference between a cue ball and a

Ping-Pong ball, despite their different densities. That's because the gravity of each of them is so small. If the differences in their growth rates are similarly small, the cue ball could be expanding faster than the Ping-Pong ball and not be noticed in our lifetime.

Objects need to be planet-sized before density makes a noticeable difference in gravity, under any theory. Has anyone measured the sizes of planets with different densities to make sure they haven't changed in relation to each other? If so, how accurate would those measurements have to be? Remember that the perceived size of an object is determined partly by its speed relative to the observer. (Einstein said so.) So if we start measuring planets in relation to each other, it's no easy task, since they all orbit and spin at different speeds.

Argument 6: If you were in a house and all matter expanded, wouldn't the walls close in and squish you?

No, because the floor would get wider too, pushing the walls away from you.

Argument 7: If you put two objects in a tub of water, they will eventually be drawn together by their tiny gravitational forces. Expanding matter can't explain that.

It doesn't have to. Why must gravity be the only attracting force? How about magnetic attraction?

Believe it or not, those were the best arguments I got. I'm sure there are lots of good reasons why the expanding matter theory of gravity is wrong, but it's surprisingly resilient to casual attacks. And it's fun to think about.

REVENGE OF THE SKEPTICS

After the hardcover of *The Dilbert Future* came out, I was flamed by many skeptics who ridiculed me for the story in Chapter 14 about my encounter with a self-described psychic. Judging from my mail, "skeptic" is the Greek word for "obnoxious people with poor reading comprehension." The e-mail messages from skeptics were eerily similar to each other, in an almost cult-like way. They wrote to tell me I was obviously fooled by a skilled magician. Furthermore, I was promoting ignorance of science by telling that sort of story to the gullible masses.

For the benefit of any skeptics reading this now, let me explain a concept called "context." Had the story been in a chapter entirely about unproved psychic phenomena, it would be perfectly appropriate for readers to make assumptions about my gullibility and irresponsible authoring. However, the context of Chapter 14 was entirely about how easily people are fooled by what they see and experience. In that context, it's not so important whether the reality behind my story involved an excellent magician, an unexplained phenomenon, or just incredible luck. My story was about the many different experiences that led me to question my ability to accurately perceive reality. It was a chapter about raising questions, not about providing answers.

For the skeptics who scoffed at how easily I was fooled by a simple magician's trick, let me provide some more details of that encounter so you can tell me how it was done. Most skeptics assumed the tarot cards were marked on the backs. I don't know if psychics often carry marked tarot cards—since they wouldn't need marked cards to do a simple card reading—but that's certainly a possibility. I thought of that at the time. That's why I made sure she couldn't see the fronts *or backs* at any time during the test. I checked the faces to make sure they were all unique cards and then I shuffled thoroughly. She never touched the cards again after she gave them to me. During the test her eyes were closed and she was ten feet away, facing at right angles to me. Even if she opened her eyes, she would still have had to see out of the side of her head, across the room, and through a solid object to see the cards.

Magic is a hobby of mine. I know how most classic magic tricks are done and I can usually recognize patterns of misdirection in new tricks. That knowledge couldn't protect me from getting suckered by a skilled magician, but my odds of being fooled were lower than that of a person who doesn't study magic as a hobby. I mention it only so you can rule out the clumsiest forms of trickery and assume that if it was a trick, at least it was a good one. I hope you'll give me that much credit.

The so-called psychic didn't know in advance that I was going to ask her to guess cards. She brought the tarot deck because we had discussed doing an ordinary reading. I didn't decide to do the guessing test until after she got to my place. It was my home, where I lived alone. She had never been there before. No one but the two of us were there during the test. If accomplices were at work, they were very clever.

Given all that, is it possible that I was fooled by a magic trick? Yes, of course. (But I'll pay $1,000 to the first person who can duplicate that trick with me and show me how it was done.) It's also possible it was luck. Or that I was hypnotized. Or that I have a faulty memory. Or, from your perspective, I might be making the whole thing up. I wouldn't put "psychic phenomenon" ahead of any of those other possibilities. No matter which explanation is true, it's consistent with my main point in Chapter 14, that people are easily fooled by their perceptions.

Viewed out of context, the psychic story is only an interesting anecdote with no conclusion. But combined with lots of other gigantically unlikely events in my life, it provided the context for me to be open-minded about how things work. As part of the explanation of why I do the things I do, the story is useful. As evidence of the existence of psychic phenomena, it has no value whatsoever. On that point, I agree with the skeptics. I tried to say that in the chapter. Apparently that wasn't clear to everyone.

MORE ON SKEPTICS (PUN INTENDED)

The most shocking thing about the skeptics who flamed me is how dogmatic and illogical they were. My sample was small, but it was enough to scare me. I always thought skeptics were the elite keepers of common sense, protecting us all from our own gullibility and irrational desires. To my surprise, most of the skeptics I heard from turned out to be true believers in their own analytical infallibility. Here are some of the beliefs

the skeptics all repeated like mantras. I include my reaction to each of them in case any skeptics are reading this and wondering what my problem is.

Skeptics say, "Extraordinary claims demand extraordinary proof."

Okay, but who gets to decide which claims are extraordinary? And who gets to decide when the proof is extraordinary enough? And if something seems to work—like electricity, for example—is it okay if I use it without giving anyone some extraordinary proof? And would it be sufficient that someone I don't know provided some extraordinary proof to other people I don't know? Or must I personally give extraordinary proof of everything I find useful to every skeptic who demands it on an induhvidual basis?

"Extraordinary" proof? What kind of scientific standard is that?

Skeptics say, "Magicians can replicate anything a psychic claims to do."

Magicians can also replicate anything a scientist can do. And anything a skeptic can do. What exactly does that prove?

I think skeptics have delusions of adequacy because they always prevail when they debunk palm readers, spiritualists, and UFO abductees. If you test a thousand frauds and always get the result you expect, pretty soon you think

you have a monopoly on intelligence. That's what inspired the cartoons on the previous page.

Skeptics say, "Until scientific tests are independently replicated, no conclusion can be made about the thing being tested."

That's great, except I will live my entire life without ever personally testing anything with scientific rigor. All I will ever use are unreliable media reports about other people who tested things. Unreliable information is the only kind I've ever had and the only kind I ever will have. If my neighbor tells me that he has a magic rock that cures baldness and it worked for all his friends, I'll be over there in a flash to rub it on my head. That's not irrational. That's living in the real world. Where do the skeptics live? The scientific method is spectacularly successful. I have nothing against it. It just doesn't apply to every aspect of my ordinary life.

Skeptics say, "The simplest explanation is usually correct." (Also known as Occam's razor.)

In my own experience, I find that the simplest solution is usually the one given by the guy who has the least knowledge. In the real world, complexity is the norm. William of Occam—to whom the observation is credited—lived a long time ago. Things must have been simpler then.

Occam's razor still works pretty well in some areas, like human behavior. If you stumble upon a bloody crime scene and the only person alive is

a disgruntled postal worker with an Uzi, then indeed, the simplest explanation is probably correct.

But if you're talking about digital computing, human consciousness, or quantum physics, the simplest explanation is rarely correct. To demonstrate this point, I will describe my simple solution to a problem that most physicists think is complicated: the Unified Field Theory. It stumped Einstein. And so far it has stumped all the other physicists. But that's because they were looking for complicated solutions. Maybe the skeptics didn't tell the physicists about Occam's razor.

The Unified Field Theory tries to explain how the seemingly diverse forces of gravity and magnetism and the strong and weak nuclear forces are all connected. I will explain my simple theory below. This will support my point that the simplest explanation is usually the stupidest.

MY UNIFIED FIELD THEORY

What follows is incredibly geeky. If you don't like that sort of thing, this would be a good point to put down the book, call it done, and bask in the wisdom and humor you've obtained so far. But if you enjoy turning your brain inside out, this next section might be fun.

Quantum physics tells us that particles don't exist in an absolute location in space. Every particle has only a probability of existing in a specific place. There is a tiny but definite possibility that a particle you expect to be in one place is actually across the universe somewhere. It's hard to conceive, but it's generally accepted in physics. I took that simple fact, added a layer of complete cluelessness, slathered on some misunderstandings, and created my Unified Field Theory. If you read it quickly, without thinking too hard, it actually makes sense.

My theory says that every particle in the universe is constantly popping in and out of existence. I don't know where they go when they disappear, maybe another universe. That part doesn't matter. Now let's say that each time a particle pops back into existence in our universe, its new location is determined by a statistical distribution curve, with the two opposite ends of the curve representing these two influences, according to me:

1. Momentum

2. Like attracts like

Momentum means that when a particle pops back into existence, it will have some likelihood of being on the same path it was traveling before it popped out of existence, creating the illusion of movement. Other times it will reappear in about the same location it was before. The more skewed the probability curve is for that particle, the greater the illusion of speed.

The second influence—"like attracts like"—is the statistical tendency for similar things to be in the same place. The more similar two things are, the greater the likelihood that the next time they both pop into existence they will be nearer. There's no reason why this should be true, but when you talk about the most fundamental forces of the universe, everyone agrees there isn't a "reason." It's simply the rules. Get over it.

If I refine my definition of what makes one particle "like" another to include location in space, then that's all you need to explain gravity. The closer a meteor gets to a planet, the more the particles of the meteor and the particles of the planet are alike. So each time the meteor's particles and the planet's particles pop into existence, they are closer to each other. Hence, gravity. And the denser the planet, the greater the statistical likelihood. It all fits rather nicely.

Now visualize all the stars and planets in the universe as clusters of probability. In statistics, clustering is normal. If every particle only has a probability of being where it is—according to quantum theory—then it follows that planets are locations where probabilities have clustered. There need not be a reason for these probabilities any more than there is a reason you get "heads" about 50 percent of the time when you flip a coin.

On to magnets. Here is an extreme example of "like attracts like." A magnet is more like another magnet than a magnet is like anything else. So the illusion of attraction is strong between two magnets. Every time the particles in a magnet pop into existence, they tend to be closer to any nearby magnet.

A magnet is somewhat like steel at the particle level, but less organized. So steel is also attracted to a magnet, but not as strongly as two magnets are attracted to each other. That seems consistent with my theory.

If you run a magnet across steel and temporarily organize the steel's particles, it becomes like a magnet itself and then steel can attract other steel. That's consistent, too.

Now consider wood. Its particles are very different from those of a magnet or metal, so it displays very little attraction to either one, barely enough to measure with the most sensitive tests.

But why do magnets repel each other if you turn one around? I need to refine the definition of what it means for one particle to be "like" another particle. Let's say that a key aspect of what makes one particle similar to another is the direction the particles are facing. That difference might seem trivial in the big world, but when it comes to physics, things like direction, location, and momentum are critical. By analogy, consider a one-way mirror. One side reflects light. The other lets it pass. In the case of the mirror, the direction it faces defines it. It becomes its own opposite when turned backward. So it's not such a stretch to say the direction that a particle faces defines its basic nature as well.

Under my theory, all momentum can be tracked back to the moment of the Big Bang. The only counter-influence—the thing that keeps everything from moving in a straight line—is the second influence of "like attracts like." That balancing force is the statistical impulse of matter to re-create its original condition of togetherness at the moment of the Big Bang. In essence, the universe is like a coin that has come up heads a gazillion times in a row. Eventually, the universe will trend back to its norm and every particle in existence will pop into existence to occupy exactly the same point in space. That's gonna hurt.

My Unified Field Theory hasn't yet explained the strong and weak nuclear forces. That's because I'm not sure what those are. The simplest way to deal with them is the way scientists deal with lots of things—to define them as trivial and move on.

I think you'll agree that my theory is the simplest Unified Field Theory around. According to Occam and the skeptics, my simplicity is a good indication that I'm right. It's not an indication that I'm an uninformed nut-job. According to the skeptics, the physicists at Princeton who are filling notebooks with equations are way off-base. Someone should tell them.

APPENDIX A

AFFIRMATIONS TECHNIQUE

This technique is essentially stolen from a book and an author that I would credit if I knew how. I wouldn't normally do this, except my personal story has a huge gap without it.

If anyone can point me toward original work in this area, I will try to make that information available and give credit where it is due.

How to Do Affirmations

1. Have a specific goal, one that you can visualize.

2. Write it down fifteen times in a row, once a day, using the form:

"I, SCOTT ADAMS, WILL GET/DO/ACCOMPLISH WHATEVER."

3. There's no set time to expect results, but if I did it for six months without any movement toward the objective, I'd assume it doesn't work and I'd stop.

4. I don't think it matters how many times you write it, if you have multiple goals, if you forget to write it for a week, or if you type it instead of writing it. I don't have any reason to believe the method is so fragile that those things matter.

5. I don't think you need faith in the affirmations in order for the process to work, any more than you need faith to steer your car.

I'm fairly certain you would get the same results if you wrote the affirmations while thinking the whole thing is a load of crap. Be as skeptical as you like.

Affirmation Pitfalls

The only affirmation mistake I've seen is a lack of clarity in the goal. One person told me he was writing the following affirmation every day and having no success:

"I, JOE BLOW, WANT TO BE A FAMOUS JAZZ MUSICIAN."

I told him that, in fact, his affirmation had already worked exactly as he wrote it—he "wanted" to be a famous jazz musician. The better form would have been:

"I, JOE BLOW, *WILL BE* A FAMOUS JAZZ MUSICIAN."

The second problem is that his name wasn't Joe Blow, just in case you wondered.

I would also caution against affirmations that have specific deadlines, such as "I will get promoted by the end of this month." There are lots of ways to get to your goal, so leave some wiggle room.

And I don't recommend affirmations on things that can only happen one way—such as winning the lottery. That's asking a lot of your ability to steer. Better to set goals that have many ways of being realized. In the case of the lottery, your real goal was probably wealth. There are lots of ways to get wealthy. Don't constrain yourself.

Affirmations Update

After the hardcover edition of this book came out, I got more e-mail on the topic of affirmations than anything else. Lots of people wrote to say they tried the technique and got amazing results. A few people said they tried it for a while and nothing happened. Others wrote to remind me that

I'm insane. I don't put too much stock in anecdotal reports about affirmations, much less opinions about my mental health, but I thought you'd be interested in knowing how people reacted.

I also got a number of clarifying questions about affirmations. Everything I've already said on the topic falls into the category of guesswork and "why not." So I see no reason to limit my valuable advice just because I don't know anything. Here are the most common questions about affirmations and my best guesses for answers.

Do I need to keep the paper that I write the affirmations on?

If affirmations work, I'm fairly certain it has nothing to do with the paper or how long you keep it. The purpose of the writing is to focus your concentration.

Can something bad happen as a result of affirmations? Suppose I use affirmations to achieve wealth and then someone I love dies and I collect the insurance?

That's a good reason not to tell your relatives that you're using affirmations. I can only tell you that I haven't had the problem of unintended consequences myself. However, none of my relatives are heavily insured.

Can I type the affirmations or do I have to write them by hand?

It's probably okay to type them. It's probably not okay to cut and paste the one sentence fifteen times, or to write a program that types them for you. But your guess is as good as mine.

What if someone else does an affirmation that is in direct conflict with my affirmation?

I don't have a good answer for this, but I suspect it's the least of your worries. If there are infinite universes, maybe both of you get what you want. If not, maybe you should try writing your affirmation down sixteen times a day and hope the other person is only doing fifteen. If you're still worried about it, modify your affirmation so it isn't in conflict with anyone else. There's plenty of money, happiness, health, and love to go around.

Can I do affirmations that involve improving the lives of other people?

It depends how affirmations work, assuming they work at all. Some people think affirmations only work to improve the performance of the person doing the affirmations, creating the illusion that the environment is conforming to the person's will. That's a plausible theory, maybe even the best theory. My own experience, and that of others who wrote to me, suggests that the effects might extend to other people.

Did you ever find the name of the affirmations book you mentioned in the chapter?

Lots of people sent me the names of books that deal with affirmations. I don't know if any of them were the book that influenced me. Below are the books that were mentioned to me most often. I haven't read any of them, so I pass them along without opinion.

The two "classics" on the subject are *Creative Visualization,* by Shakti Gawain, and *Think and Grow Rich,* by Napoleon Hill.

I Deserve Love, by Sondra Ray. Subtitle: *How Affirmations Can Guide You to Personal Fulfillment.*

Julia Cameron's recent books, *The Artist's Way* (with Mark Bryan) and *The Vein of Gold,* have sections on the affirmations process.

DISCLAIMERS OF ORIGINALITY

I don't read many books. There are a lot of ideas floating around that I haven't been exposed to. Many of you will see ideas in this book that you'll be sure I stole from another author (beyond the ones I mentioned). It happens with my cartoon strip all the time. People write and say things like, "It's obvious from today's strip that you're reading J. P. Ferstershweizen's book *The Algonquin Paradigm*." To which I say, "Huh?"

Sometimes there are things I write or draw that are lifted from other authors, but it's usually subconscious. All authors do that. If I know I'm being influenced by an idea, I can generally change it enough to disguise it. My genuine thefts tend to go undetected. At my level of visibility, it would be dumb to plagiarize intentionally. In the vast majority of the cases where you see a distinct similarity between my work and someone else's, it's a coincidence involving an idea that wasn't all that creative to begin with.

I've witnessed at least a dozen people invent the phrase "roadkill on the information superhighway." They were all being "original" in the sense that they hadn't heard it someplace before. But it's an obvious idea.

I once thought I invented the idea of combining a Laundromat with a bar so single people could meet while doing laundry. I've met lots of people who think they invented that idea, too. And since the day I "invented" the idea, I've seen a number of news stories about entrepreneurs who have actually built such a business. In retrospect, it was an obvious idea. But sometimes it's not obvious which ideas will be obvious to someone else.

One day I drew a *Dilbert* cartoon about an opera singer who was an impostor. I referred to him as the "Placebo Domingo." I was very proud of that pun. That same afternoon, I opened my local newspaper and saw the exact same pun in another cartoon. Mine hadn't even been inked yet. If my cartoon had been published, the other cartoonist would have been suspicious that I lifted it from him. I threw mine away and drew another.

While I was writing my section in this book about video surveillance cameras being everywhere, I took a break and turned on *Oprah*. It was a show about how there are hidden surveillance cameras everywhere. I've never written on that topic, and I've never seen a show about it. They both happened in the same one-hour period of my life.

These are strange coincidences, but they happen more often than you would think possible. It is unlikely that even one idea in this book is "original" in the sense that nobody ever had a similar thought.

There are a few analogies in the last chapter of this book that I've seen in other works; e.g., the description of color as a perception and the discussion of the Earth rotating around the Sun. There might be others. I borrow them because they are useful and reasonably obvious. And they aren't central to what I'm saying.

If you have any comments on this, send me an e-mail message at scottadams@aol.com.

THE JOY OF WORK

THE
JOY OF
WORK

Dilbert's Guide to Finding
Happiness at the Expense
of Your Co-workers

SCOTT ADAMS

A HarperBusiness Book
from HarperPerennial

A hardcover edition of this book was published in 1998 by HarperBusiness, a division of HarperCollins Publishers, Inc.

Designed by Nancy Singer Olaguera

First HarperPerennial edition published 1999.

The Library of Congress has catalogued the hardcover edition as follows:
Adams, Scott, 1957–
    The joy of work : Dilbert's guide to finding happiness at the expense of your co-workers / Scott Adams. — 1st ed.
      p. cm.
    ISBN 0-88730-871-6
    1. Humor in the workplace—United States.   2. Corporate culture—United States.   3. Industrial management—Social aspects—United States.   I. Title.
    HF5549.5.H85A32   1998
    650.1—DC21   98-27083

ISBN 0-88730-895-3 (pbk.)

99 00 01 02 03 ❖/RRD 10 9 8 7 6

*This book is dedicated to the wonderful people
who have helped populate the Dilbert comic
and Dilbert books with their suggestions, anecdotes,
and observations. And Pam too.*

Contents

1 THE JOY OF WORK   1

    Happiness Creates Money   3

    Happy People Get Better Jobs   9

    Being Funny Makes You Look Smart   11

    Giving Yourself a Stealth Raise   12

2 MANAGING YOUR BOSS   13

    Boss Types   13

    Boss-Managing Strategies   17

    Avoiding Being Measured   39

3 REVERSE TELECOMMUTING   47

    Internet Connections   47

    Cubicle Sex Rumors   48

    Cubicle Yoga   49

    More Sleeping Tips   50

    Multishirking   53

    Pretending to Work   53

    Inventions Needed   55

4 LAUGHTER AT THE EXPENSE OF OTHERS   59

Yanking the Chains of Your Co-Workers   62

Starting False Rumors for Fun   64

Problems Are Entertainment in Disguise   68

Infecting Your Co-Workers   70

Wastebasket Fun   71

Complaining to the Ombudsman   74

The Joy of Bad Ideas   76

Pretending to Be Psychic   78

Being a Technology Prima Donna   82

The Joy of Creating Lovely Documents   90

The Joy of Sarcasm   92

5 OFFICE PRANKS   97

6 SURVIVING MEETINGS   141

Personal Digital Assistants   142

Robot Visualization   142

Embarrassing the Presenter   143

7 MANAGING YOUR CO-WORKERS   147

Cubicle Flatulence   147

Bossing Co-Workers Around   148

Be in Charge of the Office Move   149

Dealing with Irrational Co-Workers   150

8 BRINGING HUMOR AND CREATIVITY TO YOUR JOB   157

   Where Creativity Comes From   158

   Manage Creativity, Not Time   159

   Creating Humor   197

9 HANDLING CRITICISM   239

   The Trouble with Norman   252

10 THE DOWNSIDE OF SUCCESS   261

FINAL POSTSCRIPT   265

1

The Joy of Work

*I cried because I did not have an office with a door,
until I met a man who had no cubicle.*

—DILBERT

Maybe you've heard of something called the "open plan" office design. It's getting a lot of attention lately. Under the open plan, employees have no offices or cubicles, just desks in a large open area. Storage areas are virtually eliminated. This is not a good trend.

After your boss has taken away your door, your walls, and your storage areas, there aren't many options left for the next revolution in office design. One of the following things is likely to go next:

▶ The floor

▶ The ceiling

▶ Your happiness

I think the floor will stay, but only because your company would have to dig a huge hole all the way to the other side of the earth to get rid of it. As you can imagine, a huge hole through the earth would represent a serious threat to office productivity. Depending on your global location, the other side of the world might have hordes of refugees who would run through the hole, take one look at your office, scream in horror, and run back home. It's hard enough to concentrate while your co-workers are yammering, but if you add hordes of screaming refugees coming out of a hole, things would only get worse. And don't get me started about the problems with molten lava, or the fact that if you puncture the earth, all the gravity would escape.

Your company won't remove your ceiling. You need the ceiling to keep the people who are on higher floors from falling on your head. The only exception is the people on the top floor of your building, i.e., the ones who ordered your cubicle to be taken away. They'll keep their ceilings too, because all of the discomforts that make regular employees *more* productive are exactly the kinds of things that make senior executives *less* productive. No one knows why.

I think the next wave of office design will focus on eliminating the only remaining obstacle to office productivity: your happiness. Happiness isn't a physical thing, like walls and doors. But it's closely related. Managers know that if they can eliminate all traces of happiness, the employees won't be so picky about their physical surroundings. Once you're hopelessly unhappy, you won't bother to complain if your boss rolls you up in a tight ball and crams you into a cardboard box.

As soon as I noticed this disturbing threat to workplace happiness, I did some investigative work and discovered it wasn't confined to the issue of office design. Companies were making a direct frontal assault on employee happiness in every possible way! I knew there was only one thing that could stop the horror.

It was time for another Dilbert book.

It might sound corny, but I felt an obligation to society. People told me it was time for me to "give something back to the community." This scared me until I realized that no one knows I furnished my house with street signs and park benches. So I interpreted the "give back to the community" message as a plea for me to write this book and then charge the community to read it.

In the first part of this book I will tell you how to find happiness at the expense of your co-workers, managers, customers, and—best of all—those lazy stockholders. The second part of the book teaches you my top-secret methods for mining humor out of ordinary situations, thus making it easier to mock the people around you. The third part of the book is made entirely of invisible pages. If the book seems heavier than it looks, that's why.

▶ HAPPINESS CREATES MONEY

In recent years, large companies revived an economic theory that had been out of fashion for hundreds of years. It goes something like this:

Economic Theory of the Nineties

Anything that makes employees unhappy makes the
stock price go up.

Economics is a murky field, so when you find something that's easy to understand, you tend to latch on to it. You couldn't fault managers for reaching the conclusion that employee happiness and stock prices are inversely related. The evidence was impossible to ignore.

Things That Make Employees Unhappy	Result
Downsizing	Stock goes up
Reduced benefits	Stock goes up
Unpaid overtime	Stock goes up
Doubling the workload	Stock goes up

The old saying about capitalism was, "A rising tide lifts all boats." If you own a boat, that's an inspirational thought. But if you work in a cubicle, rising water means one of your brilliant co-workers tried to flush the company newsletter down the toilet. Obviously, one theory does not fit all people. The economic theory that is good for stockholders is not necessarily the exact same one that is good for employees. You need your own economic theory—one that puts value on the things that matter most to you: happiness and money.

I'm highly qualified to create this new theory of economics for employees because I'm more than just a comic strip writer. *I was an actual economics major in college.* I didn't master every little nuance about economics, but I did get a good grasp of the major concepts, which I will summarize here so you don't need to become educated:

EVERYTHING I LEARNED FROM ECONOMICS CLASSES

▶ Something about supply and demand

▶ Boredom can't kill you, but you might wish it could

Those economic insights won't solve all of your problems right away, but it's a strong foundation upon which we can build.

Let's start by examining our economic assumptions. The strong economy of recent years has turned the old assumptions upside down. In the past, it was always true that if you had money—even a little bit—you could buy a lot more happiness.

Two hundred years ago, for example, a few extra dollars meant the difference between sleeping cozily indoors versus shivering under a pile of leaves until you were eaten by coyotes. Thanks to a robust economy, not to mention confusing new IRA options, life has vastly improved, coyote-wise. Money is no longer the difference between life and death for most white-collar workers. If you have a reasonable job, money can't buy nearly as much happiness as it used to. The economists would express it this way:

$$\text{happiness of driving[Porsche – Hyundai]} <$$

$$\text{happiness[(not eaten by coyote) – (eaten by coyote)]}$$

Historically, your happiness was so closely related to money that you and your employer had compatible goals. Your company wanted to make money, and you were glad to help, because it improved your odds of prying some of it out of their greedy, clenched fists. That symbiotic situation persisted for decades, until the nineties, when managers realized it was more profitable to screw their employees than to sell more products. Businesses used the "screw the employees" economic strategy to rack up incredible profits. Employees were left without a viable economic strategy of their own. Until now.

I have developed a new theory of economics for employees. According to my theory, employees should stop trying to make money directly (by doing good work) and concentrate on making themselves happy (using the powerful methods in this book). The money will follow. I'll explain how.

New Economic Theory for Employees

Happiness Creates Money

Technically, a theory is not a theory until someone tries to explain why it works. I believe there are several reasons why happy people make more money. The first reason has to do with risk.

RISK

In business, whenever you take higher risks, you improve your chances of getting rich, unless you choose a dead-end career, like skunk juggler, or prison guard, or journalist. In those cases, extra risk won't help one bit. But, in general, risk-takers make more money.

If you get your happiness from enough different sources, you aren't bothered too much if one risk goes bad. For the happy person, it's no big deal to take career chances that could result in humiliation, embarrassment, and job loss. Those things are all temporary in nature and won't have much impact on the person who has a well-diversified portfolio of happiness.

Under bad economic conditions, my theory that happiness creates money doesn't hold. The risks are too high. At the first sign of unauthorized mirth, you'll be downsized. From a manager's perspective, it's always easiest to fire the employee who isn't already an emotional basket case. Being happy during bad economic times is like painting a target on your back. If you're smart, you'll avoid any outward displays of happiness when the economy is bad.

Luckily, we aren't in bad economic times. In a booming economy you can take some extra happiness-related risks at work. Your boss won't want to fire you because he'll have to pay more money for your replacement—if he can even find one. And the replacement might be an even bigger troublemaker than you are. The balance of power has changed. Now it's even safe to make insulting jokes at the expense of your boss. You'll be amazed at how much whimsical insolence your boss is willing to tolerate. Take full advantage of this situation while it lasts.

In the unlikely event that you do get fired, you'll probably end up happy that it happened. There isn't much of a stigma to getting fired anymore, because so many people have been downsized through no fault of their own. In a few short years, getting fired has gone from a horrific experience to, arguably, an excellent way to enjoy some time off and then advance your career. If you're working in a company that gives money to people when they're fired, that's the best of all worlds. Take the money and find yourself a higher-paying job at a company that has a sense of humor.

► HAPPY PEOPLE GET BETTER JOBS

When the economy is slow, all the best jobs are taken by people with great hair. The rest of us are forced to scramble for the crumbs. But in the current robust economy, there aren't enough pretty-haired people to fill the best jobs. In good economic times, happiness—specifically a good sense of humor—can give you an edge. Humor is a tie-breaker for people whose hair has limited career potential. A good sense of humor will allow you to rise above the humorless masses and get the high-paying job you know you don't deserve.

Don't worry so much about your actual qualifications for a higher-paying job. The next employer who interviews you isn't likely to be any better at spotting your defects than your last employer was. Most managers are exceedingly bad at making hiring decisions. If you gave Charles Manson a shave and combed his bangs over the swastika on his forehead, he could get hired as the CEO of Apple Computers tomorrow. This might sound like an exaggeration, but remember: The one thing that all workplace violence has in common is that the person doing the violence got hired by a manager who didn't see the early warning signs. You have to wonder how those job interviews went:

Manager: Your résumé says your hobbies include setting fire to helpless woodland creatures. Tell me about that.

Applicant: Stop badgering me. I'm warning you.

Manager: Did you have a salary range in mind?

Applicant: There's a salary?

Managers know full well that they can't tell the difference between one job candidate and the next. All things being equal, hairwise, a hiring manager will choose the job candidate who is the most entertaining. Later in this book I'll teach you my secret formula for creating humor. That's all the training you'll need to impress your next job interviewer and land a cool job that you previously thought was out of reach, e.g.,

► Space shuttle pilot

► Designer of nuclear-tipped warheads

► Heart-transplant surgeon

Don't worry that you're not qualified for those positions. No one is qualified for any job on the first day. And most jobs are not as complicated as you would think. For example, it *sounds* like it would be hard to drive the space shuttle. But do you think NASA would spend a bizillion dollars building a spacecraft and then make the mistake of giving it a stick shift? The shuttle probably flies itself. It goes up, it flies in circles, it lands. They're not asking anyone to navigate through an asteroid field and bomb a Death Star. The pilots probably spend the entire time in the cockpit making rocket noises with their lips and trying to resist the temptation to touch buttons. I'll bet the shuttle pilots could trade places with the experimental gerbils in the back and you'd get the same mission results.

It sounds like it would be hard to design nuclear-tipped warheads. It probably would be hard if you cared whether your warheads actually explode. But if you think about it, the only time anyone will find out if you did a good job is when the air is filled with incoming nukes from the other side. I doubt you'll be worried about your next raise. And if that day never comes, no one will be the wiser that the detonation mechanisms for your nuclear warheads are actually the insides of old clock radios.

As for heart-transplant surgery, no one will know you didn't study medicine if you stick to highly experimental methods that are expected to fail anyway. While other surgeons are putting human hearts in human patients, you could be the doctor experimenting with the controversial procedure of putting artichoke hearts in pigs. No one will expect a high success rate there, and when the patient dies, you've got most of the fixings for a luau.

▶ BEING FUNNY MAKES YOU LOOK SMART

It's an established fact that a good sense of humor is highly correlated with genius. I say this partly because I'm in the midst of writing a humor book and partly because when you say "it's an established fact" no one ever checks to see if it really is. Whether it's true or not makes no difference. All that matters is that people *think* humor is correlated with genius. Therefore, the more humor you bring to work, the smarter you look. In the business world, a false image of intelligence is a valuable asset for your career. In fact, fake intelligence is even more useful than real intelligence. People who are genuinely smart get peevish during meetings because they have the misfortune to understand what's going on. But if you're only *pretending* to be smart, the pay is the same as if you *actually* are smart, and almost nothing can ruin your day.

Humor is the easiest and safest way to pretend you are smart. If you try to demonstrate your brilliance by, for example, shouting the solutions to complex math problems, people will think you're a dork.

But if you crack jokes all day, you'll look like a brilliant employee who is simply too modest to perform any conspicuous acts of competence on the job. As a funny employee, you'll be able to bungle one project after another without drawing suspicion that the problem is you.

▶ GIVING YOURSELF A STEALTH RAISE

The only reason your company pays you is because you'd rather be doing something else. The entire economic system depends on the fact that people are willing to do unpleasant things in return for money. The more hideous the task, the more money you get. Take brain surgery, for example. That job pays very well, but you have to touch people's brains all day. I don't know about you, but I'm sufficiently frightened by what comes out of people's mouths; I sure don't want to get my fingers any closer to the source. And although I haven't tried it, I'm certain I wouldn't enjoy any activity that involves handsaws and human skulls. To me, that's unpleasant.

In a sense, there's a rough equivalence between money and unpleasantness. If you accept more unpleasantness, you can make more money. Likewise, you can often decrease the unpleasantness in your life by spending money to make it go away.

(more money) = (less unpleasantness)

If you can decrease the unpleasantness that you experience at work, without taking a cut in pay, it's almost the same as giving yourself a raise. It's like a stealth raise, because your boss might not even notice. The best way to reduce your total daily exposure to unpleasantness is to crowd it out with liberal doses of happiness. This book will give you lots of strategies for adding happiness to your workday, leaving fewer hours for listening to your boss, or sawing skulls, or whatever it is that you do.

2

Managing Your Boss

Nothing is more critical to your happiness than learning to manage your boss. The alternative can be a disaster. If your boss tries to turn the tables and manage you, the next thing you know, you'll be doing moronic tasks in return for money.

In this chapter you will learn a number of boss-managing strategies that have been proven in the field. Your choice of strategy will depend on what type of boss you have. Use this grid to identify your boss.

▶ BOSS TYPES

	Harmless	Evil
Capable	C-H	C-E
Incompetent	I-H	I-E

If your boss falls into the Incompetent-Evil (I-E) quadrant, select the strategies that help you stay away from him. As a rule, it's a good idea to stay away from anything in life that has "evil" built right into the description. But it's especially true where a boss is involved. When evil is combined with incompetence, it becomes more unpredictable. Your only defense is distance. Pick the strategy that puts you far out of harm's way, as this gentleman did by leaving the company.

From: [name withheld]
To: scottadams@aol.com

Each day my ex-co-workers and I picked a new word of the day. On the day I resigned, the word was "acephalous." Acephalous means "headless or lacking a clearly defined head" or "having no leader."

Later that day I was asked by the president why I had decided to leave the company. I explained to him that we had differing management styles and that, "I cannot bring myself to agree with your acephalous management practices."

He replied, "That's because you don't have the experience I do in these matters." I agreed.

In the unlikely event that your boss is in the rare category of Capable-Harmless (C-H), try to upward-delegate as much of your work as possible. You want your company to be in the hands of capable people. That way your employer can make enough money to pay people like you for doing things like reading this book.

From: [name withheld]
To: scottadams@aol.com

After experimenting with many methods, I have found that the best method of managing my boss is to keep a fresh supply of sweets in the candy jar on my desk. First, this ploy guarantees that he'll drop by my office a minimum of three times a day—and these visits make great opportunities to practice my "upward delegation" skills. Second, it ensures that my boss is on a permanent sugar high—which typically makes it easier to get positive responses from him on many crucial issues like budget approvals, extra time off, etc.

If your boss is an Incompetent-Harmless (I-H) type, you might want to keep him nearby just for the entertainment value. Several of the strategies below will help you get the most out an I-H boss.

From: [name withheld]
To: scottadams@aol.com

I work in a cube farm with about 30 feet between the rows, which is exactly the required distance for a game of "Boss Pong." To start the game you wait until the "ball" (clueless management drone) walks through, then call him over.

Now it's the opposite side's turn to divert him over to their side, otherwise we score a point.

The "ball" usually tires of the game after several volleys and won't play for a few days. With practice you will be able to play games with multiple "balls." We have had as many as four in play with seven volleys.

If your boss is a Capable-Evil (C-E) type, use the strategies that encourage him to focus on your co-workers. Hiding won't help you manage a C-E boss. He's too smart for that. Your only hope is to redirect his evil intentions where they won't hurt you. This is essentially the same strategy you use if you are being chased by a monster, i.e., throwing someone else in the path so you can get away. Here's how one employee trained his boss to focus elsewhere.

From: [name withheld]
To: scottadams@aol.com

To minimize all contacts with my boss I pretend to be even more boring than I really am. When he stops by, I'll talk about weather or science fiction stories I've read. If he asks how I'm doing, I'll start talking about a little flu I had two weeks ago, or some other nonsense, and it all ends very quickly. I've managed to manage my boss out of my life while still getting paid.

▶ BOSS-MANAGING STRATEGIES
STRATEGY 1: INDUCE TENSION

Always be prepared to unload a batch of gnarled, rotting "issues" on your boss anytime he gets within a hundred yards. Before he opens his mouth, say, "I was just looking for you!" and then proceed to describe a business problem that is as unsolvable as it is demoralizing. Here are some examples of the types of issues to unload on your boss:

Issues for Your Boss

"The Federal Trade Commission just asked for all our documents. Don't worry, we've covered the furniture with gasoline and we're waiting for your signal."

"The bad news is that there's a deadly bacteria in our air-conditioning system. The good news is that we think the asbestos in the ceiling will kill it."

"There was a mix-up in the graphics department. The logo on your new product seems to be a dead goat. At the national press conference today, try to cover it with your thumb."

If your boss has any sort of central nervous system at all, his body will suddenly stiffen and his blood pressure will rise until his eyeballs look like a freeway map. He might spontaneously grow a hunch on his back right there in front of you. Offer no proposed solutions to the "issues." Look to your boss for the answer. Act miffed if he draws a blank. The miffed expression helps convey the message that you're disappointed in his leadership. Your goal is to make every interaction a life-draining, painful experience (for him), but not in a way that could get you fired. After all, it's your job to raise issues. There's nothing wrong with that.

In time, your boss will experience something like a mild panic attack whenever he thinks of you. This will reduce his desire to give you new assignments, while at the same time making you seem like someone who cares about the big picture. Consistency is the key to this strategy. If you keep it up, eventually your boss will lose any interest in knowing what you do all day. That frees up lots of time for your important hobbies, such as napping and snacking.

STRATEGY 2: YOUR BOSS'S BOSS

If possible, try to carpool with your boss's boss. Move to a new town if you have to. It's worth it. Mention your carpooling situation to your boss often, while referring to your boss's boss by an affectionate nickname that you make up, such as Spanky or Thumper. If your boss asks you to do something you don't want to do, agree to do it, then shake your head and mumble, "Spanky will get a good laugh over this."

Alternately, join the same church as your boss's boss, even if it means switching religions. (You can always switch back after you retire, usually with no penalty in the afterlife.) While your boss might try to stop you from carpooling—by switching your work hours, for example—he wouldn't dare try to talk you out of your religion. Especially if it's the same religion as his boss's.

Whatever your method, don't get to your boss's boss during work hours. That's insubordination any way you slice it.

STRATEGY 3: WITHHOLD INFORMATION

It's safe to give your boss "issues," but never give your boss any other information about a project. If you give him actual information, he'll try to make a decision. If that doesn't worry you, consider that your boss allows you to keep your job, and you're reading a book about how to screw him. Obviously your boss's judgment isn't good. To compound matters, decisions made by your boss usually result in more work for you.

If your boss insists on status reports, use the power of "big words" to obscure any meaningful content. Here's a status report that you can use for just about any situation:

> The project initiatives are performing according to the variable methodology described at our strategic directional pre-consensus framework.

Another approach is to pretend you are even more frustrated than your boss with the fact that the information isn't available. This e-mail explains it best.

From: [name withheld]
To: scottadams@aol.com

Whenever a question is posed to me in a meeting, I carefully weigh whether or not the person asking will understand the full implications of an honest answer. When I decide that the real answer would not be the most appropriate response for this person, I simply bang my fist on the table and declare, "That's what I want to know!" This has been especially effective in meetings when the pressure is on me to provide information that is not at hand.

By varying the inflection in your voice and really emphasizing different words, this phrase can serve you well:

1 — **THAT's** what I want to know!

2 — That's what *I* want to know!

If you are forced to give regular status reports during staff meetings, make sure your report is laden with excruciating detail about trivial elements of your job. Be passionate about these details, so your boss is dissuaded from interrupting you. Eventually your boss will learn to schedule shorter meetings so there isn't time for people like you to give status reports.

An effective way to withhold information is to deluge your boss with so much information that the real messages get lost or ignored. You can train your boss to never read an e-mail message from you again. Once you've established that reflex in your boss, you have complete deniability if accused later of not keeping him informed. Just look him straight in the eye, act exasperated, and say, "I sent you four e-mail messages on that topic. Aren't you reading them?"

The degree of information you withhold should be directly proportional to the level of management you're trying to manage.

The higher up the chain, the more damage they can do with less information. A good rule of thumb is that information should be completely scrubbed of all content if it will be viewed by a manager who is two levels or more above you.

STRATEGY 4: PROXIMITY AVOIDANCE

There is a direct correlation between your boss's proximity and your happiness. I will express the relationship here in movie terms.

Boss's Proximity	Your Mood
In your cubicle	. . . like Sigourney Weaver in *Alien*.
In his own office	. . . like E.T. hiding in a closet.

Boss's Proximity	Your Mood
Another building	. . . like Dorothy after the flying monkeys leave.
Out of town	. . . like Richard Dreyfus in *Jaws,* when the water is too quiet.
Iraqi prison	. . . like Jimmy Stewart in *It's a Wonderful Life.*

One approach to the proximity problem is to stop going to the office and see how long it takes anyone to notice. But this is only a short-term solution, because if it works, your co-workers will stay home too. Soon your company will fail. At that point your boss might notice that his checks stop coming. That's when your little plot will unravel. A more clever approach is to go to work every day but find ways to get your boss out of the office, preferably to a despotic nation that considers itself at war with yours.

Scan trade journals for advertisements about faraway conferences. Pick conferences that have important-sounding words in the name, like Global, or Tech, or Symposium. Then plead with your boss to let *you* attend. This is a trick, because you have no intention of attending. Most bosses will take the bait and tell you that conferences of that sort are intended for higher-level managers. Why else would it have "Global" in the name? Curse softly and shuffle away. Repeat.

STRATEGY 5: DECOYS

Your boss has a deep psychological need to feel that he has "helped." Unfortunately, the quantity of "help" that your boss provides will have no correlation to his abilities or your needs.

Every employee who interacts with the boss will get a little dollop of "help" no matter how much is needed. That's why you need decoys.

Before making any proposal to your boss, insert some decoy steps. The decoys are elements of your plan that you don't actually intend to do. Make sure the decoys are the most obvious parts of the plan—ones that cannot be missed. Your first slide might read this way:

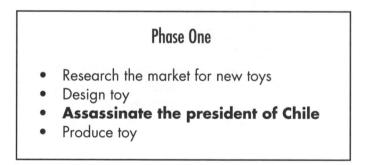

Phase One

- Research the market for new toys
- Design toy
- **Assassinate the president of Chile**
- Produce toy

Your boss will notice that the third bullet "doesn't fit." He'll demand that you get rid of that step. Put up some resistance (just for show) and then reluctantly agree. Ask for more money in your budget to make that change. This will satisfy your boss's need to "help." Later, confide in your boss that although you doubted him at the time, it turned out to be a good decision to cancel the hit.

STRATEGY 6: DO BAD WORK IN IMPORTANT-SOUNDING FIELDS

Don't make the mistake of working extra hard in hopes of getting the biggest raise in your department. The difference between performing at "exceeds expectations" levels versus "meets expectations" is likely to be about 2 percent per year. Mathematically speaking, in the long run you're much better off doing a lousy job at something that looks good on a résumé as opposed to doing a superb job at something that sounds dull. If your boss assigns you to something that won't help your résumé, just ignore him and dive into a job that looks good on paper, no matter how unqualified you are. Your boss won't like it one bit, but remind him to be nice because someday he might be working for you, and he'd better not burn any bridges.

You're probably not planning to stay with your current company forever, so it doesn't really matter how often you blow things. If you don't quit after a few years, you'll be downsized in the next corporate merger anyway. So building a track record of success is a silly strategy for your career.

When you interview at the new company, they won't ask your current employer for a reference, because that would reveal your disloyalty to them and get you in trouble. The only thing the new company can find out is your job "experience," not your competence. Experience is reflected in the job titles you held, without regard to your massive disloyalty, sloth, and fiduciary misconduct. If you've spent five years designing advanced aircraft engines, it doesn't matter that you only designed one engine and it leveled a nearby logging town. That information doesn't travel with you. Only the good news does: You designed advanced aircraft engines.

STRATEGY 7: SIC YOUR BOSS ON CO-WORKERS

Talk to your boss about how poorly things are going on a project in which you are not involved in any way. Make stuff up, then cover yourself by saying it's "only what you heard." Get your boss all lathered up, aim him in the right direction, and get out of the way. It might take days for him to find out that everything you said is a lie. But that won't stop him from finding problems with that project once he starts rooting around over there. When he reports back that the problems you mentioned weren't true, say it was all a misunderstanding, then repeat with a rumor about a different project.

STRATEGY 8: MEETING TRAPS

Any time you are in a meeting with anyone, for any topic whatsoever, suggest to the attendees that they should set up some time to talk to your boss about subjects that do not involve you. Find out what the meeting attendees need and then inform them that your boss is a renowned expert in that area, although it might not be obvious from his job title. In all likelihood your boss will agree to meet with these people out of confusion and timidity. With luck, he'll end up on their working committee, thus being too busy to interfere with your daily enjoyment.

STRATEGY 9: BE LOW-MAINTENANCE

One unintended benefit from all the downsizing of the nineties is that there are fewer managers per employee. To make the best of this situation, try to find a job in a department that has several high-maintenance, troublesome employees. You know the type— for some reason the world is always crumbling around them. They are surrounded by crises that need immediate resolution. They park in your boss's doorway every hour and try to remove the oxygen. If you have some of those people in your department, your strategy should be to become the most easily managed, low-maintenance employee your boss has. Create that illusion by going to your boss with easy-to-solve problems, along with your recommendations. Example:

> **You:** Our competitors launched a new product. I recommend that we wait and see what happens.
>
> **Boss:** Good. Do that.
>
> **You:** I'm all over it.

Then don't talk to your boss again for a month, creating the impression that everything is under control. You will gain a reputation as the one employee who needs no management assistance, allowing you to perform your unsupervised shirking at any pace you see fit.

STRATEGY 10: BOSS DELETION

For some voice-mail systems, you push the 3 key on your phone to delete a message. The same thing works for deleting live phone conversations with your boss. Next time your boss calls, press the 3 key. Your boss will hear an annoying beep and ask you what it was. Say you didn't hear anything, then do it again. Continue pressing the 3 key until your boss is too upset to continue the conversation.

STRATEGY 11: OPINION SUPPRESSION THERAPY

You can teach your boss to suppress his opinions by making sure he embarrasses himself anytime he opens his mouth. During meetings, ask his opinion about the feasibility of things that have already been done.

Example:

You: Do you think NASA will ever land an unmanned vehicle on Mars?

Boss: No way. It's too far.

You: You'd better tell NASA. They think they already did it.

STRATEGY 12: BAD ADVICE

If your boss can't tell the difference between good advice and bad advice, give him only bad advice. This will virtually guarantee that he spends less time with you and more time apologizing to people, fixing things he broke, and figuring out why he doesn't get invited to meetings anymore.

STRATEGY 13: SUBMIT YOURSELF FOR AWARDS

Your company probably has some sort of award program for employees who do outstanding work. Take every opportunity to submit yourself for the award, regardless of how shoddy your actual performance is. Eventually your boss will get pressure from someone higher up the command structure to dole out a few employee awards to improve morale. Your boss has to give the awards to someone, and your co-workers probably aren't any more "outstanding" than you are. But you will be the path of least resistance if you plan it right.

Whenever you spend money on anything, claim you saved a huge amount compared to what you originally estimated it would cost. If you buy a new PC for $1,500, submit yourself for an award for not spending $2,000. If that's not a big enough savings, propose a departmentwide policy that all PC purchases be $1,500. Then claim the savings on every machine that might be purchased in the future.

All your boss needs is a flimsy rationalization in order to take the award to his boss for approval. He won't probe your logic too hard because you're solving his problem too.

Once you have the award, you automatically become the front runner for the next round of raises and promotions. In a few months your boss might not recall what the reward was for, but he will remember that you're a bit more "outstanding" than your co-workers.

STRATEGY 14: TURN YOUR BOSS INTO YOUR MINDLESS ZOMBIE SLAVE

Have you noticed that when you yawn, other people yawn too? Or sometimes you'll be in a meeting, and you'll lean on the table with your hands together by your chin, then you notice that other people will do the same thing subconsciously? That's a subtle form of hypnosis. You can develop that skill to a higher degree with a little practice. What I'm about to describe will sound implausible, but I used this method often during my cubicle career (after taking a course in hypnosis), and it works more often than you'd imagine.

You don't have to put someone in a trance to influence behavior. All you need is a basic hypnosis technique called "pacing and leading." Pacing is when you mimic your boss. If he speaks softly, you speak softly. If he uses visual language—like "I see what you mean"—then you use visual language, like "I saw it coming." If your boss leans on his arm, you lean on your arm. You can even learn to match breathing patterns. The more behaviors you pace, the better it works.

Avoid pacing the big, noticeable things, like the way he dresses or the specific malaprops he uses. That will make you look more like a pathetic suck-up than the puppetmaster you are. Stick to the little, subconscious behaviors. And do it every chance you get.

After you've paced your boss for a while—ten minutes is plenty—you're ready to "lead." Test your control by putting your hands in a certain position and seeing if he follows. If he does, his brain is already under your subtle control. At this point, the things you say will seem more persuasive.

If you say something and then your boss says, "I was just thinking that," you can assume you have total control. You won't be able to order him to assassinate anyone, but he might think your ideas are excellent even if they aren't.

Bonus tip: When your boss is standing in front of a group of people, it's fun to pace him until you have control, then act as though your entire body is suddenly very itchy.

STRATEGY 15: PLANT FALSE MEMORIES

This strategy works best with accomplices. Any time your boss asks you why you're doing something a certain way, tell him you discussed it with him last week and he decided this was the way to go. Look surprised and bewildered that he is rehashing this old decision.

If everyone in the office uses the same trick, your boss will believe he is losing his memory. He won't be willing to see a mental-health professional for fear of finding out the worst. If your boss insists that the problem is on your end, don't argue. Just shake your head and mutter, "Same thing Grandpa used to say."

STRATEGY 16: BAD-NEWS INOCULATIONS

If you have mildly bad news for your boss, inoculate him first. You do that by inventing an unverifiable story that is much worse than the real bad news. For example, if the mildly bad news is that your product development is going to be a week late, you might say, "My sources tell me Microsoft is planning to make the same product that we are. It's their top priority."

Wait a few days for the inoculation to take hold, then tell him the mildly bad news about your schedule. Give that a few days to sink in too. Then tell your boss that you did extensive research (on your own time) and found out that the Microsoft rumor was totally false! The good news is that your product will only be a week late.

BOSS-MANAGING STORIES FROM THE FIELD

Here are some stories from people who developed their own methods of boss management.

From: [name withheld]
To: scottadams@aol.com

My boss required semidaily progress reports, and we all know nothing changes that quickly, especially when you work in a group of 300 software engineers on one project.

I created a computer file of status keywords like: 55% complete, process inspection, communication with engineers, advanced investigation, etc. Then I wrote a program that randomly combined the nonsense status phrases based on an algorithm involving the seconds showing on my PC clock. Once created, the program would automatically send the status report to my boss.

Eventually my boss used me as an example of an engineer who was following the process!

From: [name withheld]
To: scottadams@aol.com

I have found a great way to keep my boss convinced I'm working. I have a $10 fake security camera complete with battery-powered blinking red light (stamped "Security Camera") mounted in my cubicle and pointed at me. All my co-workers and my supervisor are convinced I'm working all the time, as who would slouch off if they're being watched!

It also keeps people from stealing pens and using my phone when I'm not there!

From: [name withheld]
To: scottadams@aol.com

Here's what we did to my boss. He bought this new
Cadillac (which he was able to afford thanks to our blood,
sweat, and tears). Being a sensitive guy, he lorded it over
us because we are nothing. Being sensitive employees,
every time he would park his beloved baby in his super-
important reserved indoor parking spot, we would sneak
down there and pour motor oil on the floor beneath his
engine. Naturally, he freaked out and we could hear him
screaming at the dealership all the way across the office.
He took it back to them to fix it. We let it rest two days
and resumed the pseudo–oil leak. He took it back again,
demanding they fix it or give him a new car. He now
wants to sue them. I told him I know of a great mechanic
who, for the right price, will guarantee he can fix it.

From: [name withheld]
To: scottadams@aol.com

I once had a boss who was the worst micro-manager in the
known universe. He would literally stand behind you and
tell you what keys to press on the keyboard. I repro-
grammed my keyboard so that nothing he told me to do
worked. He finally got the idea and gave up bothering me.

From: [name withheld]
To: scottadams@aol.com

I have a boss who is a hypochondriac. If I don't feel like
dealing with him on a given day, the first time I see him, I
cough and say, "I think I'm coming down with something."
He always leaves me alone for the rest of the day.

From: [name withheld]
To: scottadams@aol.com

I used to have a boss who spent far too much time talking
to people when they were trying to get work done. To
resolve this problem, my co-workers and I devised a rotating assignment called "Boss Duty." If it was your day, you
were obligated to see that the boss was entertained and
not communicating to engineers on the critical path of the
project. On your "duty day," you were expected to
respond within five minutes to e-mail reports of co-workers
who were trapped in their offices with the boss. I believe
that he never caught on to this productivity enhancement
system we installed on his behalf.

From: [name withheld]
To: scottadams@aol.com

One slow day at work in a small store, I was talking to my friend the cashier, and my boss comes up and says, "Why aren't you working?"

I said, "There's nothing to do."

He says, "Pretend you're working."

I said, "YOU pretend I'm working. Then pretend you're taking over for me and I can go home."

From: [name withheld]
To: scottadams@aol.com

I had a boss who wouldn't consider any suggestions made by subordinates. So whenever we had an idea, we told him that it was his boss's idea.

From: [name withheld]
To: scottadams@aol.com

My boss and I were asked to audit a branch office. She wrote the first draft of the audit, which was pretty scathing, and we passed it on to her boss, the VP.

The VP sent it back and asked us to "edit it for tone." So we took the report that was printed single-sided, recopied it double-sided, bound it, and submitted it again. The VP expressed his complete satisfaction with the new, thinner version.

From: [name withheld]
To: scottadams@aol.com

The best method I have found for managing bosses is the tried-and-true Jedi Mind Trick. For example, if your boss asks you, "Have you finished that project yet?" just look your boss straight in the eyes, and with a wave of your hand reply, "These are not the droids that we are looking for, move along."

This proved successful on many occasions during my first job at an investment bank. I became so skilled that I actually trained my fellow employees in the ways of the Force.

From: [name withheld]
To: scottadams@aol.com

When I was a secretary I discovered that the best way to manage my boss (an investment banker) was to borrow the techniques I used as a baby-sitter when I was a teenager. As long as you're firm, unafraid of putting them in their place, and treat them like small children who don't know what's best for them, you can pretty much ensure that things will run the way you want them to.

It also helps if you're the only one who knows their social security number, credit-card numbers, cell phone password, computer password, mother's maiden name, girlfriend's birthday, etc., so that they're forced to depend on you for every aspect of their everyday life. And, of course, when your boss is away on business trips you should rearrange all the files so that you're the only one who knows where anything is.

After a while my boss developed such trust and dependence that he actually called me from an airport to ask if it was the right one, because the plane wasn't there and he hadn't bothered to check his itinerary or even tell the driver which airport to take him to. He'd just gotten into the car like a trusting little lamb and never bothered to look out the window to see where they were going. Naturally he'd taken someone else's car by mistake and had gone to Newark instead of La Guardia. Whoops.

He seemed taken aback when I explained that the best I
could do to remedy the situation was to book him on a
new flight (under a different name, of course, so that the
computer wouldn't nix him) and that actually holding or
rerouting the plane was beyond even MY powers!

Don't worry that your boss will not be able to accomplish his
duties if he is managed by you. In a good economy, where employees switch companies at the drop of a hat, managers have only
one important function:

▶ AVOIDING BEING MEASURED

The biggest threat to workplacc happiness is something called
the Employee Evaluation. Few things in life are more aggravating
than being critically evaluated by the Village Idiot, i.e., your boss.
Every time your boss measures you against your objective, it
drains a little bit of happiness out of your body.

You could try to find a job where your performance is not
measured at all, but those are rare. Your best bet is to get a job
where you are measured for all the wrong things, thus allowing
you to subvert the system for your personal enjoyment.

For example, in my first job out of college, I was a bank teller. My only measurable objectives involved avoiding screw-ups. Being a well-intentioned rookie, I also tried to provide quick and courteous service, even though it wasn't a measured objective. I handled twice as many customers per shift as other tellers. I also had twice the mistakes and was robbed at gunpoint twice as often (two times in six months). It seemed like I was constantly in trouble. My co-workers, some of whom were later charged with embezzlement, appeared to be model employees. They enjoyed stress-free days and generous raises. Clearly, my strategy of "quick and courteous service" was a loser.

The veteran tellers were clever. They realized that the best way to avoid mistakes—and bank robbers—was to serve the fewest customers possible. The smart tellers developed crafty and elaborate strategies for minimizing customer contact while appearing to be working. During the few minutes per day when they actually helped customers, they would keep the nice ones at the window as long as possible. It was common for my co-workers, many of them single, to flirt shamelessly and try to get dates with any customer who deposited a large check. Meanwhile, I would be trying to explain to angry foreigners why it was in their best interest that the bank didn't let them withdraw their own money.

It took me a long time to realize that I wasn't being more efficient than my co-workers, I was being more stupid. The thing that finally tipped me off to their treachery was the realization that I always ended up waiting on one notoriously difficult customer, against all odds, no matter how many windows were open. When that customer was next in line, my window always opened up first. The customer-from-hell ran a small cash-based business nearby. She was a stern older woman from a country that outlawed smiling centuries ago. She would dump a huge bag of rumpled and filthy money from the day's commerce and scowl at me while I counted it. Invariably, my count would disagree with hers. The next hour would entail a spirited search for truth, including her theories that some of the money might have fallen in invisible cracks while it was being counted. When I confronted my co-workers about the odds of that customer always ending up at my window, they confessed that they watched for her in line every day, then stalled their customers until my window opened. My co-workers were weasels, but they were smart weasels. And they knew how to protect their happiness at work.

From: [name withheld]
To: scottadams@aol.com

I work in a technical support group. Our manager decided that the best measure of our performance is the number of calls we take in a day. Since we have three phone lines, our staff has found that using one line to call yourself on another line will give you credit for a call. It's beautiful. The tech support center's stats have been rising steadily, while the number of incoming outside calls has been on an annual downswing.

It might be inspirational to know that this conflict between the measurer and measured has been raging for thousands of years, and the employees always win. In fact, that's why some of the wonders of the ancient world were so oddly shaped.

For example, scholars have long debated why the pyramids are pointy. One theory is that the pharaoh's marketing department designed the pyramids in the shape of their own heads. Another theory is that the marketing department came up with the name "pyramids," and everyone agreed that it sounded like something pointy. So the engineers wisely built the pyramids with pointy tops; that way they wouldn't have to spend their lives explaining why the buildings weren't called squaramids. They avoided a billion conversations that would have gone like this one:

Tourist: I thought you said you were taking me to the pyramids.

Guide: These *are* the pyramids. For the millionth time today, they are *supposed* to be rectangle-shaped. The pharaoh's marketing department printed the brochures and then it was too late . . . oh, just forget it.

Tourist: I want my money back!

Guide: I hate my job. Just get back on the camel.

Tourist: I call no hump.*

---

*In the first draft of this book, some people were confused by the hump reference. It is intended as a clever allusion to the floor hump in the backseat of a car, but in this case referring to the camel where the hump is harder to avoid. It is not, as some suggested, a reference to the tourist's romantic preferences.

To me, it's obvious that marketing wasn't responsible for the shape of the pyramids. In those days, if your only skill was marketing, your contribution to major construction projects was in the capacity of tile grout. It took thousands of years before people who had no useful skills realized they could earn money by wearing nice clothes and designing deceptive brochures.

The real reason that the pyramids are pointy-shaped is that the pharaohs made the mistake of giving their engineers only two measurable objectives: (1) the size of the base and (2) the height. The pharaohs expected the building to be something in the rectangle family, but that was never specified. It didn't take long for the Egyptian engineers to figure out how to play the game. Every day the pharaoh would get a report from the lead engineer that the pyramid was another ten feet higher and ahead of schedule. It was bonus figs all around.

The engineers weren't afraid of getting in trouble. Back then, the average person had about the same life expectancy as a fruit fly in a blender. There was a good chance the engineers would be dead before the pharaoh found out that the upstairs bonus room was three inches square. In the unlikely event that the pharaoh performed a surprise site visit, it was a simple matter to drop a huge rock on his frail body and flatten him. This happened a lot, apparently, because all the drawings of early Egyptian royalty looked like flattened people.

Although life expectancies have improved a great deal since ancient times, the science of management is limping along pretty much the same, except for one important change:

Jobs are harder to measure now.

In the modern economy, millions of people have the kind of jobs where their contributions are impossible to quantify. They're doing squishy stuff like designing, thinking, planning, positioning, networking, communicating, and creating. Your manager can't see any of those things, much less measure them. But measure he must, because that is what distinguishes managers from inorganic matter.

The danger here is that everything your boss knows about you is based on what he can see.

WHAT YOUR BOSS KNOWS ABOUT YOU

▶ What you look like

▶ The number of hours you are in the office

Your outward appearance and your physical location are more important than ever, because that's the only part of your job performance that your boss can see. Your inner talents and the intangible contributions won't have much impact on your career.

You have to satisfy both of your boss's visual requirements—

working long hours and looking good. If you come up short on either of those areas, your boss will be all over you, and you will not be happy. Here's a good example.

From: [name withheld]
To: scottadams@aol.com

This incident happened to a former colleague at a bank. Let's call him "Bob." Bob was assigned an urgent project with very high priority, which involved designing a new product in a very short period. Bob worked 18-hour days for weeks. He treated weekends just like weekdays. He only went home to sleep. The project was completed on time, and Bob's boss, who we'll call "Satan," was congratulated heartily by the bank's executives.

The next week was time for Bob's performance review.

The meeting took five minutes. Satan sat Bob down and said, "Bob, I think you may be a little disappointed with the rating I have given you. Generally speaking, you have been working well; however, there are two problems you have which need to be addressed. First, I have never seen you go a whole day without unbuttoning your shirt and loosening your tie. Second—and this is more important—you have a habit of stretching out at your desk and kicking your shoes off. Frankly, that is offensive. If it weren't for these problems, you would rate a solid 'competent.' As is, you are scruffy, and I'm afraid that means you are 'developing.'"

Bob is now talking with employment agencies.

I can't give you any tips on looking good. I spent most of my career working with engineers. The best clothing suggestion I ever got was from an engineer who always wore ankle-high dress shoes that looked like little boots. His reasoning was that the booties covered his socks completely, so no one knew he always wore the same type of white socks. And since white socks are all interchangeable, he not only looked good, he saved time sorting his laundry. That's all I know about looking good.

But I'm highly qualified to teach you the secret of spending long hours in the office doing almost nothing but pursuing your own happiness. Follow the advice in the coming pages and you can transform your time in the office into a virtual vacation playland.

Reverse Telecommuting

I didn't invent the term Reverse Telecommuting, but I wish I had. It refers to the process of bringing your personal work into the office. It's the perfect place for paying bills, playing games, checking on your stock investments, handling errands, calling friends, and making copies. To the casual observer, those things look just like work. Most of it is made possible by your friend, the Internet.

▶ INTERNET CONNECTIONS

If you don't have an Internet connection in your cubicle yet, you must get one. This is the mother lode of all entertainment. If you don't have a job that has a legitimate excuse for an Internet connection, change jobs immediately. Take a cut in pay if you have to. If you're not spending your day playing on the Internet, you're not getting full value from the stockholders.

47

Many companies monitor how employees use the Internet. Managers can get reports of who has been looking at what. Some companies go further, blocking access to entertainment-oriented Websites. Avoid that sort of company at all costs.

When you interview for your new job, ask if they have unmonitored Internet connections for employees. If the interviewer says yes, pump your arm in the air and yell "Woo-hoo!!" It's good to show enthusiasm during interviews. Then ask if the company offers in-office chair massages. If the interviewer says yes, insist on getting yours now, then strip to the waist. That is the sort of company you want to work for. Don't settle for less.

▶ CUBICLE SEX RUMORS

You don't need gadgets to have fun in your cubicle. I've heard many rumors of employees who had sex in their cubicles during work hours. If you play your cards right, you might be lucky enough to hear some rumors too. You don't have any hope of having actual sex in your cubicle. I've come to believe that no one ever has. But you might hear some good rumors, and that's entertainment too.

Rumors of sex in cubicles are like rumors of people who joined the Mile High Club—the people who claim to have had sex on airplanes in flight. I have flown many times and never seen anyone having sex. If all the people who claim to have gotten lucky during commercial flights are telling the truth, I need to get a new travel agent. All I get on my flights are tiny pretzels. I'm lucky if I can get my carry-on luggage in the overhead bin, much less have vigorous unprotected sex with another passenger. I have real trouble believing anyone else is doing the wild thing up there.

I suppose it's possible that the pilots are having sex up in the cockpit. That would explain all the turbulence on clear days, and the fact that they always sound like Charlie Brown's teachers on the announcements.

> Out of your left-side window you can see . . . MWA MWA MWA . . . Grand Tetons . . . MWA MWA MWA . . . French Lick.

► CUBICLE YOGA

Tell your boss that yoga is part of the company's recommended ergonomic safety program. If you don't know how to do yoga, don't worry. I'll teach you the basics here. Believe it or not, I know more about yoga than I know about economics. There are two types of yoga:

TWO TYPES OF YOGA

1. The kind that hurts like crazy

2. The kind that looks like you're sleeping

I recommend the second type. The tough part about yoga is keeping your head balanced after you fall asleep. The yoga masters have learned to sleep for days without allowing their heads to fall over and snap their tiny necks. Until you develop that level of control, consider wearing a neck brace—the kind used by accident victims. That will keep your head upright so you can sleep comfortably in your chair. Tell everyone you got injured skiing. They'll think you're a sporty risk taker. You'll get some sympathy as well as respect. If you don't feel comfortable with that sort of lie, just wear a turtleneck to cover the neck brace.

If you're worried that your yoga isn't moving you closer to enlightenment, try adding a mantra. A mantra is a word you repeat over and over again until you fall asleep. I recommend the mantra I used every day of work for seventeen years: home . . . home . . . home. . . .

Once you've mastered the art of sleeping while sitting up, combine that skill with the technique described below and you will be on your way to career success.

From: [name withheld]
To: scottadams@aol.com

Four years ago I was hired as a consultant. I was told there was an incredible number of projects waiting to be done. I sat there for three weeks before I figured out that there was no work to do.

I used the Windows recorder on my PC to record moving Windows, picking up applications and closing them. I sat there for hours with my hand on the mouse, just staring at the moving screen. Eventually they hired me as a project manager because I was the only one working!

▶ **MORE SLEEPING TIPS**

Tell everyone in the office that you need to wear dark sunglasses all day to protect your eyes. Not only will you seem ultracool but you'll never have to miss another minute of sleep during the workday. If you're worried that your nonresponsiveness during meetings will give you away, apparently you've never been to a meeting. There's always at least one person who says nothing. That person could be you. The only real risk is that people will think you're a worthless sponge-person and not so much a valuable team player.

To counter that accurate perception, I recommend using the "knowing grin" during your rare waking moments. The knowing grin is a method I developed to make myself seem smarter than I really am. The way it works is you wait until someone says something incomprehensible during a meeting and then you smile slightly, as though you know exactly what it means. Make sure everyone else sees you do it. To the ignorant observers it will seem that you understand something that confuses everyone else at the meeting. Moreover, you understand it at such a deep level that you can see the humor and irony behind it too. You are a complex person who operates on many levels. Not a worthless sponge-person.

The grin sends a signal that you are the quiet, confident type who does not need to prove anything by talking. That is all the misdirection you need in order to sleep through long stretches of any meeting without attracting attention.

If you're asked a question, you can always count on one of your co-workers to cut you off and dazzle the room with an assortment of factual inaccuracies and misunderstandings. It's no different from being awake.

If you don't look good in dark glasses, here are some other techniques that can help you get the rest you deserve without bowing to your employer's irrational insistence on productivity.

From: [name withheld]
To: scottadams@aol.com

The best way to get a nap in at the office was practiced by one of my friends. We have actual offices with doors that shut. He would go into his office after lunch and "spill" his paper-clip holder about six feet from the door. Then he would lie down and go to sleep with his feet against the door and his hand in the pile of paper clips. If anyone knocked, he would quickly rise to his hands and knees and shout, "Come in . . . excuse me . . . I'm picking up a little spill here."

From: [name withheld]
To: scottadams@aol.com

A way to sleep on the job I learned about 35 years ago, and it still works! Place a piece of paper on the floor in the foot space by your desk. Let the arm nearest the paper hang down toward the floor while using the other arm as a pillow for your head at the edge of the desk.

Place your head on your arm and go to sleep. As soon as you hear someone walk into your office, make a slight grunting sound as you extend the hanging arm toward the piece of paper and pick it up. It really does seem as though you were just caught in the act of picking up a piece of paper that had fallen on the floor. I've used it many times, and the fact that I'm unemployed today had nothing to do with its use, honest!

▶ MULTISHIRKING

If you don't have a hands-free headset for your telephone, get one, even if you have to use your own money. Once you're properly equipped, you can make personal phone calls while simultaneously using your computer for personal entertainment. To the passerby, it appears that you are doing two work-related activities at once. But in reality you are doing what one *Dilbert* reader calls multishirking, i.e., doing two nonwork activities at once.

Multishirking is not only fun; it doubles the odds that an observer will think you're doing at least one work-related activity.

▶ PRETENDING TO WORK

There are many times during the workday when you wish you could be paid for doing nothing but wandering around the hallway. You can achieve that dream. All you need are the right tools.

From: [name withheld]
To: scottadams@aol.com

To avoid work, walk around with a flashlight and a clipboard full of papers. Inspect your work area, occasionally stopping, shining the light at the ceiling, then writing gibberish on the clipboard.

Clipboards and flashlights are a good start, but to be more convincing, carry a tape measure and a large funnel. If anyone asks you what you're doing, just shake your head and say, "You don't want to know." You can use this approach successfully by carrying just about any two unrelated items, such as a car battery and a ball of twine, or a paint roller and jar of honey. A person carrying that sort of combination is sending the message, "I have a long and sad story to tell, if only someone had an hour or two to listen."

From: [name withheld]
To: scottadams@aol.com

Here are some of my favorite ways to pretend to work.

▶ Erase and rewrite stuff on your dry erase board.
▶ Reshift the Post-it notes and other crap on your desk a couple of times a day.
▶ If possible, always wait for the boss to go to lunch first, then leave immediately thereafter. That way you can get at least a ninety-minute lunch without the boss knowing exactly how long you've been gone.
▶ Pretend to work by spending roughly twenty minutes typing smart-ass comments to nationally known cartoonists while in full view of everyone.

From: [name withheld]
To: scottadams@aol.com

I work for the highway department. If I want to look like
I'm working, all I do is stand on the edge of the road as
though I'm waiting for a break in traffic so that I can cross
the street. When there are no cars blocking my way, no
one is there to see that I am actually daydreaming.

▶ INVENTIONS NEEDED

The office is already well equipped for entertainment, but
there are several inventions needed before cubicle dwellers can
achieve complete nirvana at work.

CUBISCOPE

I'd like to see someone invent what I call the Cubiscope. It's a
periscope device for the cubicle, with a simple video camera on
the top of a telescoping pole. The user controls the raising, lower-
ing, and direction of the camera from a software control panel on
the PC. The camera would send a picture to a small window on
your screen. This would be invaluable for notifying you of any
approaching bosses or annoying co-workers. You could have
hours of fun while searching for targets to torpedo. Ideally, the
software should show crosshairs so you can lock on and destroy
passersby, at least in a virtual sense. Here's how it could work:
The software could compare the video background scene before
and after your target entered the field. Then it could generate an

image of the torpedoes firing, followed by a virtual explosion on-screen. The software would immediately switch the video image back to view the way it looked a moment before the target entered. It would look like you vaporized your victim. The more satisfying annihilations could be saved to video files for later play-back.

MOTION DETECTOR

Another much needed invention is a cubicle motion detector with an infrared link to your computer. There are at least three applications that I can imagine with this device. If you're playing video games or surfing the Web on company time, sometimes you don't hear people sneak up behind you. That can be bad for your career. With the motion detector, a signal can be sent to your computer at the speed of light. Speed is important here. When anyone approaches, the motion sensor triggers a background program on your PC that instantly minimizes your game window and brings a work-related screen to the front. It would become literally impossible for anyone to sneak up and catch you playing games.

Another use for the motion detector is to scare people who sneak into your cubicle when you aren't there. You could have a program linked to the motion detector that played a loud sound file when anyone came within your boundaries:

> **You have entered Scott Adams's cubicle. Do not leave things on his chair. Do not make long-distance calls on his phone. Do not borrow his computer manuals. Do not chew on his pen cap while leaving a note. Do not put toxic waste in his recycling container. Get out now.**

Thirdly, your motion detector could be part of a stupidity detector, like Dogbert's invention here.

POOR MAN'S CABLE TV

I would like someone to invent a subscription service for cubicle dwellers that lets them use their telephones to receive audio of their favorite TV and radio programs. The subscriber would call a local number, then select the channel by pressing keys on the phone. You could call up your favorite soap opera or talk show, lean back, close your eyes, and enjoy the show. You wouldn't miss much by having no pictures to look at. Regis and Kathie Lee don't change that much from day to day. And remember, the alternative is usually work.

Another application, using a similar service, would be to have a dial-in channel programmed with random business phrases that go on forever. Dial into that channel, switch on the speakerphone, and pretend to be on a conference call. This gives you the moral authority to shoo off anyone who comes within hearing distance.

STEALTH BOOKS

I'd like to see books that are printed on regular paper, the kind that comes out of the copy machine. You could be sitting four feet away from your boss, reading a bodice-ripping romance novel, and still look like the hardest-working employee in the room, especially if you're red and perspiring. Ideally, the "book" would include randomly highlighted phrases, to give it that studied look. It would be packaged with a yellow marker so the reader can appear poised for additional highlighting at any moment. The text could include stage notes that remind the reader to groan or sigh in a work-related way at strategic intervals. For example:

> The pirate swept her off her feet and carried her up the marble stairway to the master bedroom where he **[reader note: exhale sharply and pretend to highlight something]** shook her hand and then left to play point guard in the midnight basketball league.

Another source of leisure reading on company time is public-domain books that are on the Internet, courtesy of Project Gutenberg at *http://promo.net/pg*. Use your Web browser at home to download the text of classic books whose copyrights have expired. Then e-mail the text to yourself at your office, or load it on your laptop. You'll be able to mentally escape the oppression of your office by enjoying the feel-good writing of Dickens.

4

Laughter at the
Expense of Others

The quickest way to increase your happiness at work is through the magic of laughter. You already know that laughter improves your mood, but scientists have discovered that it's good for your health too. I think scientists base that conclusion on studies that indicate no one is ever laughing at the time of death.

Scientists don't specify which sources of laughter are better than others, health-wise, so I recommend laughing at other people—your co-workers in particular—at least until we have more data. If you know any scientists, you can laugh at them too. They won't take it personally because they'll understand you're doing it for medical reasons.

From a purely quantitative standpoint, it makes more sense to laugh at other people than to laugh at yourself. You're only one person, whereas there are new batches of "other people" born every minute, many of whom are hilarious without even trying.

If your co-workers aren't providing you with all the entertainment that you desire, don't be satisfied with that situation. You must learn to nurture the humor potential in your co-workers—like a farmer nurtures a cow, except without touching their nipples.

Farming is a good analogy, and one that I know quite well. I worked on my uncle's dairy farm when I was a kid. I became quite an expert in all things cow-related. All of the lessons that apply to cows can be applied to coworkers. There are many parallels. For example, the definition of a cow is "a big dumb mammal that eats grain and turns it into manure." The definition of a co-worker is "a big dumb mammal that eats doughnuts and turns them into Powerpoint slides." Now, you could argue that a doughnut is different from grain—because sugar and heat are added to make a doughnut—but I think that's splitting hairs.

One of my primary duties on the farm was to round up the cows from the godforsaken swamp that my uncle called the pasture. During the day, the cows would hang out in the pasture, chewing their cud. (Cud is the cow word for gum.) In the early evening, the cows had to be rounded up and taken to the barn for milking. It was my job to get them to the barn. I didn't work alone; I had a cow-worker: a highly trained farm dog named Ringo. The cows respected Ringo. He was a natural leader. When he barked, the cows would instantly line up at the barn door and offer to milk themselves. The cows had far less respect for me. I got an entirely different level of cooperation on the days I worked alone, when, for example, Ringo was driving the truck into town to get supplies.

My solo attempts at cow herding seemed to drive the cows deeper into hiding. They became masters of disguise. Some would submerge themselves in swamp water and breath through tubes. Others ran away to become guests on talk shows, where they got makeovers, then blended into society.

My preferred method of cow herding involved yelling an unintelligible phrase that had been handed down, farmer to farmer, for decades. It goes something like this: KEWBOSSIE!! KEWBOSSIE!! No one really knows what that means, especially the cows, who were busy building underground tunnel cities. My other method was to chase each cow with a menacing stick. Everyone who worked on the farm got to make his or her own menacing stick, using trees grown especially for that purpose. You wanted just the right mix of stiffness, length, and aerodynamic properties. (What might seem to city slickers as a system of planned cruelty to animals was something we called "farming.") One by one, I would seek out each hiding cow and whack it vigorously with my menacing stick, while yelling KEWBOSSIE!! KEWBOSSIE!!

As you might expect, this had no impact whatsoever. So I ended up waiting until Ringo was done buying supplies, cooking dinner, and upgrading the electrical systems in the barn. He'd wander over, bark twice, and look at me like he thought I was a huge pile of Powerpoint slides. It was humiliating, really. And it was perfect preparation for my life in corporate America. Those cows taught me valuable lessons about the joy of yanking other people's chains.

▶ YANKING THE CHAINS OF YOUR CO-WORKERS

One excellent way to entertain yourself at work is to constantly bring up topics that you know will set your co-workers into spastic fits. For example, if you work with someone who is a passionate environmentalist, start your next meeting by pointing out how your project might wipe out a particular species of salamander. Dismiss the problem by saying it doesn't matter because all bugs look the same. Then sit back and watch the fun.

Chain-yanking works best when you take advantage of the stereotypical tendencies of people from different disciplines. For example, people in marketing are trained to put form over substance, so customers don't realize how much they're getting reamed. People who work in technical fields are almost the opposite. They're trained to eliminate the frivolous. That's why it's fun to put marketing people and technical people in the same room and get them torqued up. Here are some fun things to say to those and other professionals:

FUN THINGS TO SAY TO MARKETING PEOPLE

▶ "Why don't we just tell the customers the truth?"

▶ "I noticed that some words are spelled wrong on the new brochures. Is it okay if we correct them with a pen and send them out?"

▶ "I can see your fillings when you talk!"

FUN THINGS TO SAY TO TECHNICAL PEOPLE

▶ "We're only making a few changes. There's no reason to test it again."

▶ "Does everyone agree that Microsoft makes the best software?"

▶ "You don't need *another* technical training class. You went to one last year."

▶ "I need to take your only prototype with me to show to a customer. I won't lose it."

▶ "I don't know what I need, but if you put something

together based on this conversation, I'll let you know if you got it right."

FUN THINGS TO SAY TO ACCOUNTING PEOPLE

▶ "If my actual expenses don't match the budget, isn't that proof that the budget process is a sham?"

▶ "Give me the money now and I'll get the budget approvals later."

▶ "What do you mean you can't give me more money in my budget? Just change the numbers on the spreadsheet."

▶ "I had a budget surplus at the end of the year, but don't worry—I took care of it."

▶ "Is it okay if I spend my depreciation budget on travel?"

FUN THINGS TO SAY TO SALESPEOPLE

▶ "Your advance sales are excellent, but we changed our mind about making that product."

▶ "We should redesign your compensation plan to give you more incentives."

▶ "Why don't you take one of the engineers to meet with your customers?"

▶ STARTING FALSE RUMORS FOR FUN

It's fun to spread false rumors that cause senseless panic in the office. This is a form of employee motivation that isn't discussed much in the popular literature. If you follow my excellent advice, you can make your co-workers run around and cluck like a bunch of chickens who just drank a keg of coffee and rolled around in itching powder. This is every bit as entertaining as it sounds.

It's best to leave some vagueness in your rumors so your gullible co-workers can fill in the holes with whatever scares them the most. That's a trick I learned when I was a Navy SEAL. Actually, technically, I learned the trick as a budget analyst at a big bank. But that is similar to being a Navy SEAL.*

Budget analysts were usually the first to know of any big changes in company plans. We were sworn to secrecy, but that didn't limit our ability to leave frightening clues of impending doom.

How to Frighten Co-Workers:

Me: Bob, I'll need your budget projections by tomorrow. It's urgent.

Bob: Okay.

Me: Ted, same thing. I *must* have your projections by tomorrow.

Ted: Will do.

Milton: I guess you need my budget projections tomorrow too, huh?

Me: Whatever.

---

*Navy SEALs have a rule about never leaving a fallen buddy behind. Budget analysts typically torture their own wounded just to watch them yell. Otherwise, it's similar.

Speaking of South Dakota, the best rumors are the ones that—if true—would make your job approximately as enjoyable as tongue-washing the faces of the presidents on Mount Rushmore, in February, while your supervisor yells, "Don't forget the nostrils!"

Here are some rumors that will get your co-workers' clucking:

RELOCATION RUMORS

Tell your co-workers that you heard the company is relocating to a place where the cost of living is VERY reasonable. You don't know the specifics, but you did hear that a five-bedroom home with an animal-carcass roof can be purchased for under four dollars. You've heard that crime in this new place is virtually nonexistent, largely because criminals prefer to reside in inner cities where they will be slain in drive-by shootings. The worse thing that can happen in the new location is that you get abducted in your sleep and forced to marry a reindeer farmer. That might seem unpleasant if you don't like beard stubble, but you get all the free deer cheese you want.

And don't worry that the weather report is routinely expressed in terms of suicide rates. Employees will be given the option of moving to this place or accepting a generous retirement package. The generous package consists of your personal belongings shoved in a Hefty bag and heaved from the roof onto the heads of litigious pedestrians.

The company realizes that relocation can be stressful. They plan to address the stress problem head-on by holding a mandatory weekend conference called "Don't Be Afraid of Change." Be prepared to do a skit entitled "The Aerobic Benefits of Fear."

NEW BOSS RUMOR

Start a rumor that you're getting a new boss who is twenty-three years old. Tell everyone that she was a nail-care specialist until she was "discovered" by your philandering CEO. Her management experience includes raising dozens of dogs in her apartment until the Humane Society took them away.

She has been quoted as saying, "I've managed cuticles for over seven months. How different could cubicles be? That's just one letter difference."

She has a record of working well with executives, including your married CEO, the principal of her high school, and a guy who always dressed in brown—who she thinks was an important executive because he got permission to use a UPS truck for their dates.

She doesn't have much formal education, but you could say she did attend the school of hard knocks—mostly in the back of the UPS truck.

HANDWRITING ANALYSIS RUMOR

Tell co-workers that you are collecting handwriting samples for the security department but you aren't allowed to say why. If a co-worker insists on knowing why, take him aside and explain that the company has a handwriting expert who can detect deviant sexual preferences by looking at writing samples. According to the expert, deviants have sloppy handwriting and tend to spell words incorrectly. Ask the person to write this sentence as you dictate it: "The picnickers ate broccoli on a toboggan." If your victim asks how to spell any of those words, gasp audibly and scurry away with a frightened look.

BOSS GENDER-CHANGE RUMOR

Tell new employees that your boss had a sex-change operation and is hypersensitive about any use of gender-specific pronouns like "he" or "she." Inform the new employees to use only gender-neutral words like "it" and "they" to avoid making a scene.

TAPED CONVERSATIONS RUMOR

Tell gullible co-workers that sometimes management will wire an employee with hidden microphones to gather incriminating information about other employees. You can tell which employees are wearing a wire because they are the ones who ask a lot of questions. Sometimes they'll act confused just to make you repeat yourself.

▶ PROBLEMS ARE ENTERTAINMENT IN DISGUISE

Perhaps your boss has told you that problems are really opportunities in disguise. It's true, but only if the problems belong to other people. Those problems are indeed opportunities for you to get free entertainment. I think you'll agree there is no laugh that is quite as satisfying as the one you get at the expense of your co-workers.

For example, if a co-worker came to you in distress and said,

"It's an emergency! I need your help to do something that I would have done last week, if only my brain weren't made of pork rinds!" (Your co-worker might word it differently, probably saying "wasn't" instead of "weren't.")

Your response—also known as your "opportunity"—might sound something like, "**HA** HA HA HA HA HA!!!" Or, if you're dyslexic like me, it might sound something like, "HA **HA** HA HA HA HA!!!"

Make sure your co-workers don't detect any traces of empathy as you listen to their problems. Everyone knows that if you have empathy, you probably have the capacity for guilt too. And guilt is all your co-workers need in order to turn you into their personal problem-solving slave. They'll control you by creating an endless series of self-inflicted disasters that only you can fix. I call it the "Jumping off a Ledge" strategy. The metaphor is this: You're walking along the sidewalk when a co-worker jumps off a third-story ledge above you. He screams your name as he plummets. Somehow (because this is a poorly constructed metaphor) you know this isn't a suicide attempt; it's just your idiot co-worker's way of taking a shortcut to his car.

Should you do nothing and watch him fall, thus proving to everyone that you are not a team player? Or do you cushion his fall with your body, thus proving to everyone that jumping on your head is an acceptable shortcut?

Fortunately, those aren't your only options. I recommend a more humorous approach: Act as though you are **trying** to catch the falling body but you're too spastic to get to the right spot on time. This solution has many advantages: You won't get hurt. You won't appear selfish. No one will be quick to try that shortcut again. You'll have a funny story to tell, especially when you act out your spastic part. And best yet—you'll be the first one to get any spare change that's freed up by the impact.

▶ INFECTING YOUR CO-WORKERS

Just because you're sick, that's no reason to stay home. The body is an amazing machine, capable of enduring the most ghastly germs and bacteria until they can be safely transferred to your co-workers. If you can move at all, you might as well go to work and enjoy one of the few legal ways you can intentionally cause bodily harm to other people.

Disease can be spread in many ways, including insect bites, unwashed hands, mad cows, ISO 9000, unsafe sex, Israeli assassination teams, and shared whistles. Most of those methods I can't recommend. For example, I don't know anyone who would want to spread disease by biting insects. Your best bet is a combination of unwashed hands and projectile coughing.

The cough has one big advantage over the sneeze. People don't say "God bless you" when you cough. That's important because you really don't want to attract God's attention in this situation. I realize he's omnipotent and omniscient and all that, so technically he could watch *everything* if he wanted to. But if I were a supreme being I would spend very little time looking at sick people. I'd have hobbies, such as hunting.

Having an illness at work is like having a super power but without the burden of being raised by kindly farmers who ruin your fun by giving you a bunch of ethics. When you're germ-laden, you're like the evil criminals who escaped jail on Krypton just before the planet exploded. People fear you when you're sick. Try wearing a cape and tall boots to accentuate the effect. Then yell "Bow before me!" before you cough on a co-worker.

▶ WASTEBASKET FUN

If you work in a cubicle, you probably have only one tiny trash receptacle. Or if your company cares about the environment, it's called a recycling container. In either case, it gets hauled to the landfill in huge trucks and emptied onto the heads of seagulls.

The problem is that you have several tons of unwieldy trash coming into your cubicle each day. You've got old binders, junk mail, cardboard, vendor giveaways, newspapers, lunch scraps, you name it. Your garbage far exceeds your receptacle's capacity. To further complicate things, your company probably has rules about what kind of trash is "acceptable" for your trash receptacle. This is where the challenge comes in.

Let's say, just for the sake of example, that you have a six-gallon jug of anthrax virus that you don't need anymore. What do you do with it? There's probably some corporate guideline about this sort of thing, but it would take all day to track down someone with an answer. And you know the answer would be one you don't want to hear:

Anthrax Policy

All anthrax virus must be wrapped in a radioactive asbestos blanket and buried in a limestone quarry for ten thousand years. Have all forms notarized. Keep a tickler file.

You will weigh the limestone-quarry option carefully and compare it to the alternative: putting the anthrax jug in someone else's cubicle before you go home at night. That person will probably do the same thing to someone else the next day. Eventually the jug will find someone who is uncaring enough to dump it in the water fountain on another floor. That's the best you can hope for; the anthrax is gone and your conscience is clear.

The process is the same for nonliquid refuse, such as banana peels and dead animals. As long as there are lazy people who go home sooner than you do, there is no limit to your opportunities for creative trash disposal.

Some companies supply attractive recycling bins for each cubicle. At Pacific Bell, one of my co-workers decided that the recycling bin was an excellent place to keep his most important documents during the day. This method worked very well until one night when he forgot to take the important documents out of the recycling bin and put them in his drawer before he left for the night. Somewhere in Michigan a little girl is blowing her nose with his important documents. This is the sort of mistake that my co-worker found difficult to blame on someone else, but that did not stop him from trying. He called the building maintenance manager and chewed him out for stupidly recycling the documents that were in the recycling bin.

This story suggests a good prank to play on new hires. Tell them the bins labeled "recycling" are intended for the important documents that you use over and over again (hence the name "recycling"). Get accomplices to put their important documents in their recycling bins during the day too, so the pattern is well established for the rookie. If the new employee gets suspicious of what "recycling" really means, tell him it's a word that comes from Quality training. Offer to sign him up for a class if he wants to get more details. The new employee will quickly fall in line for fear of being trained. When your victim finds out his important documents have disappeared, suggest that he take it up with the building maintenance manager.

▶ COMPLAINING TO THE OMBUDSMAN

For those of you who do not work at large companies, let me explain what an ombudsman is. As the name implies, an ombudsman is what you get when you combine words from the diverse fields of meditation, beer, and something called "sman." An ombudsman's job is to listen to the complaints of employees on any ethical matter, then recommend solutions that help the employee move from a feeling of discomfort to a feeling of utter despair.

Example:

Employee: My boss is a sadistic, demented, Satan worshiper. He's using his position of power to create an army of devil-slaves.

Ombudsman: Have you tried talking to your boss about your feelings?

Employee: Yes, once, but he threw goat blood on me, drugged me, then tied me to his credenza for some sort of ceremony that I don't fully remember.

Ombudsman: I'll send him a letter to tell him our policy about that sort of thing.

Employee: But then he'll know I complained and he'll kill me.

Ombudsman: Well, if you prefer, I'll just do nothing.

Employee: That's what you said last time I came here. Do you ever do anything?

Ombudsman: I tried that once. It didn't work out.

That's what the normal ombudsman experience is like. But you can have fun with your ombudsman by inventing imaginary ethical dilemmas. Here are some good questions for your ombudsman.

QUESTIONS FOR THE OMBUDSMAN

▶ Every one of my co-workers is mentally undressing me. It makes me feel like a . . . what the . . . what are YOU looking at??!!

▶ One of our vendors gave me a sports utility vehicle. But it's not the color I wanted. Is it okay if I kidnap his dog?

▶ When I phone in a bomb threat to the office, is it wrong to use my company calling card?

▶ I discovered that my boss has been embezzling from the company. Should I stop dating him?

▶ My travel allowance for food is $30 per day. Can I spend some of it on drugs if I eat them?

▶ THE JOY OF BAD IDEAS

Thinking is easier than working. And the best kind of thinking is the kind where you don't have to write anything down, i.e., "meeting thinking." When you think up an idea during a meeting, all you have to do is blurt it out. You won't have to involve any parts of your body except your mouth and maybe your brain stem.

The quality of your ideas is irrelevant. You can get away with spewing bad ideas all day because no one can tell the difference between a great idea and a bad idea. For example, imagine if Picasso had to explain his ideas to some sort of art committee before starting each new painting.

Picasso: I'm thinking of going in a whole new direction.

Committee: That's terrific. It sounds very artistic. Tell us more.

Picasso: I think my portraits should have the eyes on the same side of the head sometimes.

Committee: Uh-huh.

Picasso: And the drawings should look like scribbles. It's hard to explain, but trust me, it will look great!

Committee: Couldn't you draw dinosaurs instead? They're very popular.

Picasso: No, trust me, I have something here.

Committee: Or how about fruit? Now *that's* art. Or dinosaurs eating fruit! Or how about one of the dinosaurs slips on a banana peel and says, "I've fallen and I can't get up."

With that, the committee members high-five one another and vote on the dinosaur painting. Picasso takes out his Swiss Army knife and tries to cut off his ear, stopping only when he is reminded that Van Gogh was the one who did that.

The most entertaining ideas are the kind that make your co-workers do unnecessary work. Try to limit your ideas to ones that sound logical on some level but are clearly failures waiting to happen.

LOGICAL-SOUNDING IDEAS

▶ Include the legal department in your next brainstorming session.

▶ Ask the marketing department if they'll give you some of their budget.

▶ Invade Russia in the winter.

If your ideas have any trace of logic, your co-workers will be unable to defend themselves to your boss. You'll enjoy the immediate satisfaction of watching them squirm, followed by the long-term satisfaction of watching them flail helplessly as they slide toward doom.

▶ **PRETENDING TO BE PSYCHIC**

When you move to a new job, even if it's within the same company, use the opportunity to reinvent yourself. As far as your new co-workers know, you're not lazy, unscrupulous, and selfish. It could take them days to figure that out. In the meantime, you can pretend to have many admirable attributes and no one will be the wiser. I recommend pretending to be a psychic.

It's easy to be a psychic. Start with easy things. When you meet a new guy, glance at his company ID badge and say, "You look like a Dave. Am I right?" Eighty percent of the people you try this on will realize you're looking at the ID and laugh at your lame joke, thus thinking you are highly intelligent because you use humor. The other 20 percent will offer to shave their heads and give you all of their worldly possessions. Remember, we're talking about a general population where a third of the people are planning their lives around the zodiac. It won't take many demonstrations of supernatural talent before you're running your own cult.

Here's another psychic trick I learned. I can correctly call a coin flip 100 percent of the time, as long as I'm the one flipping the coin. I had to learn this trick because I lose all coin flips unless I cheat. People are dumb enough to let me be the coin flipper only about half of the time, so statistically it all works out.

Here's how to rig a coin flip. Always use a new United States quarter. Don't use any other coin. A new quarter feels distinctly smooth on the George Washington side and distinctly ridgy on the eagle side. See for yourself. Put a new quarter in your palm and run your second-smallest finger from the same hand across its surface. With a little practice you can tell the smooth side from the ridgy side almost every time without looking. Now, all you need is a minor diversion during the coin toss so you have time to check the coin in your hand with your finger before slapping it down.

Flip the coin high in the air, then reach out and snatch it on the way down, about head level. Bring your other arm up so you can slap the coin on your arm. Look the other person in the eye and say, "The coin is . . ." This slight delay gives you enough time to run your finger across the surface of the quarter. Slap the coin on your wrist and keep it covered. The side opposite the one you felt will now be showing when you remove your hand.

(Note: If there are any old girlfriends of mine reading this, I think we can look back now and laugh.)

I've also developed a system for reading minds. It's a way to tell if people are lying about their guilt. The method is about 90 percent accurate. All you do is unexpectedly ask the most direct question you can, then listen for which of two possible approaches the person uses to respond. For example, you might say, "Did you kill your neighbor?"

Innocent people answer that sort of question by saying, "No, I didn't!" or "Are you &%#$ crazy?" or "I can't believe you're even asking me that."

Guilty people say, "Whatever gave you that idea?" or "There's no evidence of that!" or "Why would you even ask such a thing?" or "Did someone say I did?"

The main difference is that the guilty people are attacking the evidence, not denying the event. Innocent people will deny the event and get mad at the person who asked the question. If you get a mixture of responses, give more weight to what the person says first. You will be astounded at how well this method works.

For practice, you can play this game at home when you watch any news-oriented show in which people are being asked about their guilt. When Mike Wallace shoves the microphone in front of some widow-cheating scumbag, just listen to the choice of words the scumbag uses to defend himself:

Mike Wallace: Did you cheat those senior citizens?

Scumbag: There's no reliable evidence of that!

After some practice with the television, when you think you have the hang of it, try an ambush interview on your boss.

You: Is the project I'm working on doomed by upcoming budget cuts?

Boss: Whatever gave you that idea?

Once you've established your powers of mind reading, enhance your psychic credentials by making predictions that are spookily accurate. This is easier than you might think. Here are some predictions that will fit any business situation with 90 percent accuracy:

FOOLPROOF BUSINESS PREDICTIONS

▶ The department will be reorganized within six months, for no compelling reason.

▶ The biggest weasel in the department will be promoted soon.

▶ The project will be delayed by huge unforeseen obstacles.

▶ The computer network will experience many outages.

▶ The new employee who had so much promise will turn out to be ineffective.

▶ The project will cost more than anyone expected.

You can also take advantage of stereotypes to make it appear as though you can read minds. The trick is to avoid the most obvious guesses and go for the ones that are at one remove. For example, let's say you meet a co-worker and notice he is wearing cowboy boots under his suit. The obvious insight would be, "Brent, I'll bet you like country music." But no one will think you're psychic with that sort of obvious guess. Instead, say, "Brent, I've got a hunch that you like dogs."

The dog prediction will be correct because all people who wear cowboy boots also like dogs. Boot-wearing men generally think that cats are girlie pets.

Now let's say you meet a co-worker who has a gigantic butt. You could go for the obvious and say, "I predict that you like to eat ice cream." But that's not very psychic. And it might be construed as an insult, thus thwarting your attempt to build goodwill. A better strategy would be to say, "Randy, I'm just guessing, but I think you really enjoy renting movies and watching them at home."

This will be exactly correct, because all people with large butts enjoy renting videos and watching them at home. By moving your stereotype one step away from the obvious, you avoid insult while retaining all of your accuracy.

▶ BEING A TECHNOLOGY PRIMA DONNA

There's never been a better time in history to be a Technology Prima Donna. Good employees are hard to find, but good employees who understand technology are even rarer. If you have any technical skill at all—or you can fake it—take full advantage of the raw power and happiness that comes with being a Technology Prima Donna.

If I were a famous psychologist—and thus free to make up stuff and still be credible—I would propose two possible explanations for why Technology Prima Donnas get away with their behavior. The most obvious is that everyone believes Technology Prima Donnas are capable of going on a killing spree, so it's a good idea to give them what they want. But there's another theory that is equally plausible: Most people foolishly believe "You get what you pay for."

The Technology Prima Donna makes you "pay" a higher psychological price for knowing him or her. Therefore you rationalize that there must be some value to justify the high price. (I would be an excellent fake psychologist.) If the Technology Prima Donna in your department doesn't get fired right away, you start to think the person must have some substantial hidden talents that make the abuse worthwhile. Within a month, you're telling other people what a genius this sociopath is. The Technology Prima Donna's reputation spreads. Soon it becomes impossible to fire the Technology Prima Donna because everyone will think the business depends on this one person.

Common sense might tell you that people who act like Technology Prima Donnas would be killed by angry mobs while the police turn a blind eye. But it doesn't work that way. Technology Prima Donnas are treated as stars and given extra money and larger cubicles. Sometimes even offices! As a worker, your choice is to suffer the indignities of interacting with Technology Prima Donnas or to become one yourself. I suggest becoming one. All you really lose is friends, and you can get more of those on the Internet.*

Most departments can survive having only one or two

---

*The Internet is the best place to find friends, because you can pretend to be someone else. Your Internet friends will also be pretending to be other people, so in essence you will be creating fake people who will be friends with each other, but that's close enough. At least no one will ask to borrow your stuff.

Technology Prima Donnas, so make sure you're one of them. It won't be hard to fool your boss into thinking you're a Technology Prima Donna if you follow these guidelines:

HAVE A BAD PERSONALITY

No one will believe you're a Technology Prima Donna unless you have a personality so unpleasant that your dog stuffs Gravy Train in his ears whenever you're near. Make it clear to those who would impose on you that there is a price to pay to be in your presence, and that price is exposure to your personality.

The Technology Prima Donna's Golden Rule

Anyone who asks a question is a moron.
The people who don't ask questions are morons too.

As a Technology Prima Donna, you have the right to look down on the ignorant masses who don't have your technical brilliance. But it's not sufficient to merely think contemptuous thoughts about others. You must let them know what you are thinking, through words and actions.

User: I have a technical problem.

Prima Donna: That figures.

User:	I can't print, for some reason.
Prima Donna	I think I know the reason, but I'd have to x-ray your head to be sure.
User:	I think it's a software conflict.
Prima Donna:	Pffft (said with spittle).

NEVER RESPOND TO QUESTIONS

The only downside to being a Technology Prima Donna is that your co-workers will continually ask you questions. If you give simple and helpful answers, that will only encourage more questions. And if you admit you don't know the answers, that will blow your cover as a Technology Prima Donna. Your best bet is to avoid giving any answer at all. There are two good ways to do that. The first way is to simply ignore the people who ask the questions, as if they don't exist. Most people will repeat the question, louder each time, until finally giving up. As the defeated person turns to leave in anger, say, "It depends." That makes it seem as though you weren't ignoring the person, you were only thinking hard about the question. Most people will give up at this point, realizing that a conversation with you could take months. That's just enough effort on your part to protect you against accusations of unhelpfulness.

The second way to avoid giving answers is to tell people to reboot their system, no matter what the problem is. That rarely works, but it buys you time to escape. Look at your pager and mutter "Uh-oh," then walk briskly to your nearest hideout. In all likelihood, the user's problem will be solved before you can be located.

DRESS LIKE A BLIND HOBO

Your dedication to looking unattractive is the most reliable indicator that you have godlike technical skills. The Technology Prima Donna's wardrobe should look like it were stolen from a blind hobo, who, despite being visually challenged, put up a mighty struggle as he was being stripped.

Say yes to facial hair, but only the scraggly kind. If you're capable of growing a thick, attractive beard, you'll have to pluck out some in-between hairs to get the look you need. If you're female, you'll have to harvest some hair from elsewhere (don't make me say it) and glue it to your chin.

The hair on top of your head, if you have any, should be a mirror image of your chin. If you match your eyebrows to your mustache, you have a good chance of looking the same if turned upside down. That can come in handy. For example, if you drop a pen, and you're bending down to pick it up just as someone comes up behind you, you can look from between your legs and freak him out.

YELL WITHOUT PROVOCATION

As a Technology Prima Donna, you don't need a reason to yell. Nor does it matter if you're yelling at anyone in particular. Your anger at the slightest imperfection in others is a sure sign that you have high standards. (Double standards, but high nonetheless.) There are two types of yelling, both worth doing. The first kind is the "crazy street person" yell that is not directed at anyone nearby. It should be loud enough that people throughout your department can enjoy it, and obscene enough to show how passionate you are about your work. Let one fly periodically whether you're angry or not.

The second kind of yelling is the "I might hit you" yell that is so effective in meetings. Normal employees would be fired for verbally abusing a co-worker or vendor, but you are not normal. As a Technology Prima Donna, you have every right to rise out of your chair, scrunch your face up in a pained expression, and insult anyone who has disappointed you. Vendors are the easiest targets, because they won't fight back. But you can attack co-workers too, as long as you include in your rant something about "the benefit of the stockholders." It's the stockholder reference that distinguishes the Technology Prima Donna from ordinary suspected serial killers.

BE MYSTERIOUS AND ECCENTRIC

Leave ambiguous clues about your wild and dangerous lifestyle. Put motorcycle keys on your desk where people will see them, even if you don't own a motorcycle. Dress entirely in leather at least one day per month. If another motorcycle enthusiast asks what kind of bike you ride, ask him to first tell you what he rides. When he does, just mutter, "Lawnmower." Then walk away.

Drape an empty gun holster over your guest chair. If anyone asks where the gun is, say, "Depends. Whose side are you on?" That will give you a reputation as a mysterious and dangerous player.

All Technology Prima Donnas have eccentric hobbies, like ostrich wrestling, or dung sculpture, or playing bridge. Invent an odd hobby for yourself and leave early one day a week to pursue it. Odd hobbies are a sign of brilliance, so it further reinforces your mystique.

DON'T RETURN PHONE CALLS

Technology Prima Donnas are much too busy to return phone calls. If you make the mistake of returning a call, you will seem accessible and underworked. Those are the wrong signals to send. Soon, more people will call you and try to make you work. Returning phone calls is a no-win situation. If you must return a call, do it when you know the person is not there, and leave a message without your return phone number, in case the person has already lost it.

A good way to avoid phone conversations is to have your voice-mail greeting tell callers they can only reach you by paging you. It's more credible to claim you didn't get a page than a voice-mail. You might need that extra level of deniability in case you get cornered in the cafeteria by the victim of your ignorement.

MUMBLE UNINTELLIGIBLY DURING MEETINGS

There are two types of communication that sound exactly the same to your co-workers: (1) nonsense, and (2) highly intelligent stuff. No one will suspect you of speaking nonsense if you remember to look down your nose at people when you talk. Your co-workers will sit quietly and listen, feeling increasingly stupid for not understanding a word you say. To increase the discomfort of your co-workers, mumble. They'll not only feel dense, they'll also feel as though they're going deaf. If anyone insists that you speak up, yell. Try to avoid any volume in between the extremes.

DRAW ABSURDLY COMPLICATED DIAGRAMS ON WHITEBOARDS

Diagrams are the physical equivalent of mumbling. If you are forced to write anything down, make sure it's on a whiteboard where it cannot easily be saved or duplicated. And make sure it's absurdly complicated. Your diagrams should be bristling with lines and boxes and acronyms, the type of markings you might find on an advanced alien spacecraft. Don't restrict yourself to the normal human alphabet. Invent new letters and sprinkle them in the mix. If anyone questions it, explain that some ideas are too big for the alphabet. At night, sneak into the office where you wrote on the whiteboard and erase everything. The janitor will take the rap.

COMPLAIN

You're not a Technology Prima Donna unless you're complaining about something. It will take some practice, but you can train yourself to hate everything in your immediate environment, plus all of the things you've read about in magazines. If a co-worker mentions a new technology, launch into a lengthy harangue about its inherent limitations and lack of backward compatibility. One of the marks of a genuine Technology Prima Donna, ironically, is an obsessive preference for old technology. Any mention of replacing your existing systems with new systems should be met with the sort of scorn normally reserved for war criminals and Congress.

INTERVIEWING FOR FUN

In many fields, especially in technology areas, there are more jobs than there are qualified candidates. If you're a qualified candidate with highly sought-after skills, take advantage of the opportunity to go on interviews just for fun. It's your chance to act like a minor celebrity. There are few things more enjoyable than sitting in a comfortable chair, wearing your nicest clothes, eating doughnuts, and listening to some stranger tell you how talented and valuable you are.

Once you're full of pastries and beverages, start making impossible demands of your prospective employer. Ask if the company will provide twenty-four-hour bodyguards for you. Refuse to explain why you think you need one. Ask for a company car. If you get the car, ask if the interviewer would agree to be your driver. Make ridiculous salary demands based on comparisons to other industries.

"Travolta gets twenty million per movie. I'm thinking of something in that range."

Eventually your prospective employer will realize it's hopeless and end the interview. But not before giving you some free stuff, like a cool jackknife with his company's name on it, or possibly a desk clock. These make excellent gifts for co-workers. Ask to have them gift-wrapped.

▶ THE JOY OF CREATING LOVELY DOCUMENTS

If you work in a cubicle, it's hard to get any satisfaction from your accomplishments. Generally speaking, your work gets combined with the work of other people until your contribution is diluted or deleted. And because your contribution to the company often has no physical dimensions, you rarely get a chance to step back and admire the beauty of your work. That's where the joy of creating lovely documents comes into play.

If your job requires you to create documents or presentations, this can be a source of great job satisfaction. Early in your career you might have been under the impression that documents are just a means to an end. Eventually you figure out that the "ends" are enjoyed by the stockholders, not you. You must find a way to get joy from the means, because that's the only part of the process you'll experience. Solution: Create lovely documents.

You can spend your entire day creating a Powerpoint presentation that has no significance to the world, yet it brings you great personal satisfaction. I used to enjoy printing out my Powerpoint slides and just staring at them, reveling at the beauty of the layout and the clarity of the words. No one else got any joy out of my Powerpoint slides. Often they weren't even used because the meetings got canceled. But communicating information wasn't the point. It was all about beauty. Powerpoint slides are like children, in the sense that no matter how ugly they are, you'll think they are beautiful if they belong to you.

The best part of making lovely documents is that not only does it *look* like work, it *is* work! It's just as fun—and just as unproductive—as avoiding work, but it carries no risk. If your boss sees you spending the entire morning pasting clip art of animals and clouds into your worthless-but-beautiful Powerpoint slides, you might even get some sort of employee award.

► ## THE JOY OF SARCASM

Sarcasm can get you fired if your boss realizes you aren't being a team player. But that risk is low. Your sarcasm will go safely undetected if you simply use your boss's own words. This is obviously the easiest form of sarcasm to master, since it requires no creativity. It doesn't even have to make sense.

The difference between sarcasm and sucking up is a subtle one. In both cases you're thinking to yourself, "I am a lying weasel." Only your facial expressions are different. Suck-ups tend to look like cult members, with those big dopey eyes that say, "Thank you for taking all of my assets." Sarcasm requires the practitioner to appear earnest but not brainwashed. This can be achieved with a variation of the poker face that I call the "pucker face."

The look of earnestness is controlled primarily by two parts of your face: Your lips and the little wrinkly space between your eyebrows. (Note: If you're one of those people who have one long eyebrow, shave a hole in the middle so your wrinkly part will show.)

Never laugh when you're being sarcastic. It will ruin the effect. If you feel the uncontrollable need to giggle, wait until your boss says something hilarious, such as, "Is this only Wednesday? It feels like Friday already!" Then you can throw back your head, open your mouth like you're about to swallow a live porpoise, and laugh like a naked teenager in a field full of pussy willows. Sincerity like that will make your sarcasm all the more convincing.

When you're being sarcastic, remember to smile, but not a normal smile. The lips should be distended slightly from the gums. It's part pucker, part grin. To everyone except your boss, the pucker-smile is a thousand-watt beacon that says, "I am being a wise-ass now."

Sarcasm is best in person, but it also works well in writing, as the e-mail message below clearly shows. Because it's written, not spoken, the pucker technique is different: Notice how the letter "m" is typed with a slight pucker and the letter "I" has a slight wrinkle over it.*

From: [name withheld]
To: scottadams@aol.com

I thought that you would be interested in another verification of your office viewpoint and how Wally's weekly activity report got into my employment record. After seeing it in one of the daily strips, it seemed perfect for a slot in my annual performance review. So I copied Wally's line, "I streamlined my business processes while honing my participatory style and my proactive attitude, all while valuing diversity," into my description of work in the review. My pointy-haired boss either didn't see the humor in it or didn't read it at all and it is now part of my permanent record as an employee.

*Made you look.

There's a fine line between subtle, professional sarcasm and its cousin, total bull. But both have a valuable place in the business world. Here's an example of someone who crossed the line but still got good results.

From: [name withheld]
To: scottadams@aol.com

Recognizing that there are idiots out there who actually embrace Quality and all it entails, I had to give a Quality briefing the other day.

I know nothing about quality and, frankly, couldn't care less. I made up some slides (Powerpoint, of course) and just wrote what I considered absolute nonsense. I actually pulled suggestions from your book *(The Dilbert Principle)* and inserted buzzwords. The sentences themselves had no meaning that I could discern. I spoke for thirty minutes and said nothing.

I was hailed as having the best presentation that day.

Another good way to avoid punishment for sarcasm is to reword your boss's ridiculous advice into the form that most clearly shows its complete lack of value. Then continue to support the ridiculous advice as though it made perfect sense to you, as in this example.

Sarcasm need not be limited to your boss. Your co-workers are acceptable targets too. The only difference is that your co-workers will realize you're being a wise-ass and seek revenge later. But it's often worth it.

5

Office Pranks

I once worked with a guy who said he wished flies were larger so he could hear them yell when he killed them with a fly swatter. To me, this seemed like a dangerous wish, because you never know when your wish might instantly come true. Imagine how mad you'd be if you spent your one magical wish on fly enlargement. Big flies might be less fun than you think. You'd need a tennis racket to bring one down. If you hit one, there'd be tentacles and fly pieces everywhere. You'd have to burn your clothes and move to a new house every time you swatted one.

And what if you didn't specify how much larger you wished the flies to be? An unspecified wish could get you in trouble. If the flies were too big—say the size of a German shepherd—I'll bet there would be legislation to protect them. They'd be big enough to rip the roof off your house and clean out your pantry while you were at work. Life's hard enough without being attacked by giant doglike flies who have legal immunity.

All things considered, it's probably a good thing that flies are small. And since they are, you'll have to look elsewhere to find satisfying screams of horror. I recommend looking to your co-workers. They're bigger than flies, just as annoying, and always willing to let out a good yelp if the situation calls for it. And there's no legislation against any of the things I'm suggesting, as far as I know. But I must admit I've never read any legislation.

Pranks have a long tradition in the workplace. You can use

them to stimulate creativity, reduce stress, and increase team-work. Or you can use them to humiliate your co-workers in a way that will haunt them for the rest of their mortal existence. Whatever.

Below I have compiled some of the best pranks I have collected from *Dilbert* readers. Use them at your own risk. Most of them will get you fired or beaten.

According to my readers, most *Dilbert* books are enjoyed from the privacy of the "home library" (you know what I mean). You might want to bookmark the following section and save it for that purpose. The prank section is ideally suited for that purpose, because each one is like a little story in its own right.

FAMILY RESEMBLANCE PRANK

Borrow the family photos from your co-worker's desk. Scan them into your computer. Use Photoshop software to replace the faces of family members with your own face. Print your doctored photo on a color printer, put them in the picture frames, and return them to their original place. There are many variations on this prank. For example, if the victim is a married man, replace the face of just one of his children with yours.

RAT DROPPINGS

Start a rumor that a rat has been seen in the office. Get a bag of chocolate sprinkles, the kind used for ice cream. Leave some chocolate sprinkles on your victim's desk, next to some paper that appears to have been gnawed. Tape a toy mouse to your victim's phone receiver, but tucked under so it can't be seen easily. When your victim enters his cubicle and sees the droppings, before he can examine them carefully, call his number.

SOUPED-UP PC

Convince a co-worker that you know a trick for improving PC performance. Explain how you can prop a small book under the back of the PC so the electricity can run downhill on its way to the keyboard. Act like you see a definite difference. Encourage him to share the secret with others.

SECRET MESSAGE

Write a secret message on a blank piece of paper and slip it into the paper tray of the office photocopier, a few sheets down. The next person who makes copies will get your message on his document.

This prank is very flexible. For example, you could write a message in the margin professing love for the recipient of the document and suggesting a rendezvous later. Don't spare the adjectives.

Or your message could look like a margin scrawl that was put there by the vice president of your area—something like, "I never realized how incompetent your co-workers were. Thanks for having the courage to name names.—Jerry."

A variation on this prank is to create a fake organization chart and label it "Proposed Organization." Make sure you give the most heinous morons the best positions. Leave it in the copier's paper tray upside down, so it ends up on the back of someone's document. Another variation is to use a proposed cubicle seating diagram instead of an organization chart.

CAKE IQ TEST

For your next office celebration, frost and decorate a shirt box. Add candles. Do the song. Clap. Give the person of honor a dull knife and ask him to cut the cake. See how long it takes him to figure out he's sawing on a piece of cardboard. Take bets and use a stopwatch to determine the winner.

It's a good idea to have the real cake nearby, since the person you are humiliating will be armed with a dull knife.

PHONE WIRE PRANK

This classic phone prank has been around for years. Call your victim and say you're the phone company and you need his help. Explain that there is too much wire from his line in the central office of the phone company. Ask him to pull the wire on his end to take up the slack. If he does it, encourage him to pull harder because it doesn't seem to be working. You can get some people to yank the wire right out of the wall.

PHONE-CLEANING PRANK

From: [name withheld]
To: scottadams@aol.com

For April Fool's Day I talked our IS department into sending out the following e-mail to the company. It was inspired by the Dilbert Newsletter.

"This weekend the company will be doing a network upgrade and tonight we will be doing some simple maintenance of the company phone system. Shortly after midnight the phone company will be blowing the static from the phone lines to enable better reception. In order to ensure a constant pressure we are asking you to cover your phone receiver and headset in a static bag. You can pick up your static bags from (name) at the IS help desk. The procedure should take about one hour and you may remove the bags in the morning."

About twelve people rushed around looking for the bags and dutifully covered their phones. That night we put shredded paper, lint, and cans in the bags to show them what got "blown" out.

PHONE TONE PRANK

Yet another ageless prank: Call your victim and say you're a line tester for the phone company. Explain that there have been reports of static from other users in your area. Ask the user to whistle the "Star-Spangled Banner" while you run some sound tests on your end. Tell the victim to keep it up until you give the word, otherwise the tests will be useless and you'll have to redo them. Put the phone down and go to lunch.

MICROWAVE PRANK

Put an official Microwave Tracking Form next to the microwave. The form should be both illogical and useless. See how many people put their names on it. Here's an example. Modify it to suit your need.

Microwave Tracking Form

Please help us determine the ideal warm-up times for this microwave oven. Record the length of time you let it warm up before putting your food in. Standard warm-up times are anywhere from 1 to 4 minutes.

Employee	Describe Food	Warm-Up Time
_____	_____	_____
_____	_____	_____
_____	_____	_____
_____	_____	_____

FIRST IMPRESSIONS

Walk up to any two co-workers, let's call them Joe and Bob, and say, "Hey, Joe, do your impression of Bob!" When Joe protests that he doesn't do an impression of Bob, say, "Don't be modest. You had the whole room howling yesterday." Then turn and leave.

MOOCH PRANK

This prank is designed for the office mooch who always wants to eat your goodies. Buy a bag of licorice. Open one end of the hollow licorice and fill it with salt. Wait for the office mooch to ask for a piece. Don't do this in your own cubicle, because there's a good chance there will be some spitting and flailing.

MONITOR UPGRADE

When your computer-illiterate co-worker tries to upgrade from Windows 95 to Windows 98, inform him that it requires a new video monitor. Mumble something about the "video drivers" and shake your head with disgust. When your victim puts in a requisition for a new monitor, and it comes back to him covered with laugh-spittle, say, "I guess they patched that bug."

TELEPHONE SHOUTER

This prank works best with co-conspirators. Have several people call the victim under various pretenses. Ask the victim to talk louder because you can't hear him well. If he offers to call you back, just repeat the process. See how loud you can get him to shout.

This prank has the advantage that it annoys not only your victim but all the people in his vicinity.

ASBESTOS WARNING

From: [name withheld]
To: scottadams@aol.com

Here's a good one. Someone mailed a petri dish and one denture-cleaning tablet to a co-worker, with an official memo that explained it was a test for asbestos in the office environment.

The memo directed "all employees" to conduct a simple test: Fill the petri dish with water and drop the tablet in. If

the water turns blue, there is asbestos in your office and
you must leave immediately.

Dozens of people were standing out on the street, befud-
dled, bemused, and completely had.

CAR KEYS

From: [name withheld]
To: scottadams@aol.com

When one of my office mates went out to lunch and left his
keys on his desk, I went to lunch and made a copy of his
car keys. For the next three months I would do little stuff to
his car—turn it around, move it over a couple spaces or a
couple rows, very subtle things. The one thing not so subtle
I did almost every day was to reset all the preset buttons
on his radio to the local elevator-music channel. For three
months the guy didn't say a word about it to anyone.
Finally, at my going-away party, I walked up to him,
removed his key from my key chain, and handed it to him.
It was very amusing to see the lights come on. I felt really
bad when he told me he took his car into the dealership
four times in futile attempts to get his radio fixed.

E-MAIL TO ALL

From: [name withheld]
To: scottadams@aol.com

In our group, we have group e-mail lists, some that contain
the e-mail addresses of everybody in our group.

A co-worker and myself have been trading rather nasty
jokes by e-mail for several weeks and one day he sent me
the nastiest of all nasty jokes.

So I replied to him with the e-mail he sent me—but I edited
the address headers to look like he had sent it out to the
entire group and not just me. I asked him if he intended to
send it to the whole group!

Well, I think that just about ruined his whole day. I walked
by his cubicle and he was pretty frantic. He told me that
he couldn't believe that he could make such a mistake. He
asked me if there was a way to recall it from the group. I
looked at his panicked condition and just couldn't keep my
face straight.

IF YOU BUILD IT, THEY WILL COME

From: [name withheld]
To: scottadams@aol.com

Shortly after we installed new workstations on every faculty
desk throughout the department, I discovered it was easy
to launch applications remotely on my colleagues'
machines. I created a program to play a sound at random
times, particularly early evenings. I then recorded an
urgent whisper, "Hey, Joe! Over here!" I launched the
application using that sound file on Joe's machine. The
amusement lasted for weeks!

ANAL-RETENTIVE PRANK

From: [name withheld]
To: scottadams@aol.com

I once had a terribly oppressive, controlling boss. He was
an anal-retentive attorney, with every pleat pressed, extra
starch in his collars, his shoes shined just so.

So on days that he gave me a hard time, I would sit at my
desk and toss a single paper clip on the carpet just outside
his door. It never failed—he'd open his door and before he
could go any farther, he had to hitch up his pants legs a little by pinching them exactly on the pleats, bend over, and

pick up the paper clip. Then he'd place it carefully in the paper-clip holder on my desk.

It seemed like he'd get a clue, when I'd do this sometimes 3–4 times a day, but nope.

I used to imagine what would happen if he, say, broke both legs so he couldn't bend over to pick up the paper clip. I bet he'd still be circling around in front of that office door, unable to proceed farther.

BEWARE OF YOUR COMPUTER

If you can get password access to a co-worker's computer, the opportunities for pranks are limitless.

From: [name withheld]
To: scottadams@aol.com

I work in the MIS department of a small firm, which pretty much gives me access to anyone's computer here to do upgrades, fixes, etc. I also had a co-worker who was constantly pulling little pranks on me. It got to the point where it was really annoying.

One day I found a neat little Macintosh extension that allows you to send messages to another Mac user so that it looks just like a system error. I installed it on her computer and one day before lunch set it off with the following message:

"The Radiation Shield of your monitor has failed!! Please move away from the computer as fast as you can."

There was a loud screech and my co-worker came running out of her cubicle, to the laughter of many witnesses.

Revenge . . . oh, how sweet it is.

Note: If someone writes another prank program of that sort, a nice touch would be to make the entire screen distort slightly as if from the radiation leak.

SPEED 3—THE COMPUTER

A variant on the prank above is to send error messages to your victim's computer saying he must press a key every five seconds to avoid a hard disk crash. Show a countdown on screen that resets after any keystroke. See how long you can get your victim to sit there pressing the key. When your victim yells for help, offer to find someone who knows how to fix that exact problem. Then leave for the day.

GOD IS TALKING TO YOU

From: [name withheld]
To: scottadams@aol.com

I was able to gain control of my boss's computer through
the network. I opened up WordPerfect on her computer
and typed, "Come into the light." Upon reflection, this may
have been a little mean, but I still remember not being able
to breathe due to my laughter after she told me that God
had revealed to her that he was coming for her.

SPOOGE BUCKET

From: [name withheld]
To: scottadams@aol.com

The engineering department was on a floor that had no
plumbing. So, instead of walking all the way downstairs to
spill out old coffee, pop, etc., we put a huge white bucket
(commonly referred to as "the spooge bucket") in the furnace room, and disposed of our various unwanted liquids
there.

Normally, the spooge bucket was emptied once a week,
but in this instance, maintenance must have forgotten about
it and the bucket got excessively full. So full, in fact, that

the only things retaining some of the liquid were the law of surface tension and the nice healthy layer of white mold growing over the entire top.

Well, on her first day, our brand-new co-worker needed to spill out her cold coffee and asked where she could do so. One of the enterprising young engineers told her that she could dump it in the "covered bucket" in the furnace room. A minute or so later, a shriek of disgust echoed down the hallway as she plunged her hand into the "lid" to remove it.

I'M WATCHING

From: [name withheld]
To: scottadams@aol.com

Our company does remote video applications. I told someone in our accounting group (who was delaying a number of my expense payments) that I had downloaded a new mouse driver to her PC that allowed me to use her mouse as a camera and microphone. I explained that I did not appreciate what she had recently said and done with my expense paperwork. My expense reports used to take up to two months to get paid, now it happens in days.

Note: A variation of this prank is to tell people that the new computer monitors have built-in video cameras and microphones

so employees can be watched through the local network by anyone who has the right software.

ADD A MEG TO YOUR PC

From: [name withheld]
To: scottadams@aol.com

I came to work early and discovered that one of our VPs
had left his notebook computer on all night with absolutely
no password protection.

I located a sound file, the one where Meg Ryan is doing
that fake orgasm in *When Harry Met Sally*, and installed it
on this VP's PC. I assigned this sound to every single
Windows event so there would be virtually nothing he
could do without exciting Meg.

For good measure, I also cranked the volume on his PC to
maximum, gambling on the probability that he would be so
flustered, he wouldn't be able to find the volume control.

When teaching someone a lesson, it is vitally important
that other people are present so they learn by example.
These are called witnesses, and I had lots.

When the VP triggered the sound for the first time, we
were on the floor with laughter. He didn't know how to
make the sound stop. Shutting the door to his office didn't
help much. The sound still carried halfway through the

building, attracting many more witnesses than I had originally invited.

Forty-five minutes later and after countless attempts (he never found the volume control), the VP finally removed the last of the Meg Ryan sounds.

That night, the VP took his notebook home. Lesson learned.

UPSIDE-DOWN MONITOR

From: [name withheld]
To: scottadams@aol.com

One day while browsing the Web I came upon a font that looks like regular letters except everything is upside down.

I loaded the font onto the computer of a particularly computer-illiterate co-worker and changed the settings so that font would be used by Windows for everything.

I left a note for our tech support guy explaining the prank. When my victim called tech support about his sudden problem, he was told that it would be necessary to order a new part. In the meantime he could try turning his computer monitor upside down.

He was in the process of flipping his monitor over when I stopped by.

POSSESSED ANSWERING MACHINE

From: [name withheld]
To: scottadams@aol.com

There was a particularly annoying employee we wanted to put in her place. We phoned her home during the workday, and when her answering machine answered, we conferenced the call to her work number. Needless to say, she was COMPLETELY FREAKED OUT that her answering machine had CALLED HER AT WORK. Lucky for the three of us involved in the prank, we were able to keep straight faces as she explained what had happened—and even suggested that perhaps her answering machine was possessed. I wonder if she ever figured it out.

LOW BATTERY

From: [name withheld]
To: scottadams@aol.com

If your target carries an alphanumeric pager, send him repetitive pages, with the message, "Low battery."

Be sure your paging terminal does not automatically add a signature or date code to the page.

The victim will constantly change his pager battery or, better, will send the pager to the repair depot only to have it returned with, "No problem found." That's when you start sending the "low battery" pages again.

Many alpha paging systems can now be accessed from the Web, which makes it easy for you to perform this prank while appearing to do your job.

HUBCAPS

From: [name withheld]
To: scottadams@aol.com

One of my co-workers lost two hubcaps off his car; he drove around for months like this. One day we removed the two remaining hubcaps and took them up to his office.

I told him that a friend of mine was scrapping a car just like his, so I grabbed two hubcaps off it before it went to the wreckers. I handed them to my co-worker for his car.

(My accomplices felt I should have won an Oscar for keeping a straight face throughout this.)

He looked at the two hubcaps and noted how they were EXACTLY the same as his; they even had similar dings and scratches!

Later at lunch he took the two "new" hubcaps out to his car. He noticed that the other hubcaps were missing and said, "Oh, man, you should have gotten me four!"

PAINTED FINGERNAILS

From: [name withheld]
To: scottadams@aol.com

We used to do this at a company where I worked a few years ago. When people stand in a co-worker's cubicle, they sometimes rest their hand on the top of the cubicle wall. If you happened to be in the next cubicle, you could easily paint a large dot on each of their fingernails with White-Out.

PHONE FROM HELL

From: [name withheld]
To: scottadams@aol.com

We used to entertain ourselves by going into someone's office and taping down the off-hook button on the phone. Then we would call the person and watch the reaction when the phone doesn't stop ringing after the receiver is picked up.

We used to get one guy this way at least once a week.

FREE MONEY

From: [name withheld]
To: scottadams@aol.com

We have an annual Christmas-tree lighting event hosted by
our CEO. The event is optional and typically only a small
fraction of our workforce shows up. Some of us decided to
play a trick on those who don't go to this heartwarming
event. We all went to our banks and got crisp new $100
bills. After the tree-lighting event we went back to the office
showing off our $100 bills that we "were given" at the
tree-lighting ceremony. I think the attendance will go up this
year.

BLEEP YOU

From: [name withheld]
To: scottadams@aol.com

I wrote a little Visual Basic program that would emit a single beep at random intervals between 17 and 22 minutes.
I installed it on the PC of the guy in the cubicle next to
mine. I put it in his C:\Windows\System directory and set
it to run automatically. The key to keeping a prank file
unnoticed is to give it an official-sounding name, like dev-
sup32.exe. The randomness of the beep makes it all the
more difficult to troubleshoot.

The best part of this prank is that I'm learning all kinds of new words. He usually says something like, "What the heck is that?" But the word "heck" is replaced with something more vulgar.

PHONE YANK

From: [name withheld]
To: scottadams@aol.com

Use a pipe cleaner to tie the receiver cord of a phone to itself, effectively making it very short. When the phone rings, your victim will jerk the entire phone off the desk.

Note: This is especially useful when having meetings with rude co-workers who answer their phone while you're in their office.

PRESUMED DEAD

From: [name withheld]
To: scottadams@aol.com

I used to work with someone who read his (paper) mail only once in a while. He would let it pile up in his in-box until no more would fit, then he'd go through it all at once.

One day, while he was out of the office, a colleague of his took the whole pile from the in-box, wrote "DECEASED" on each piece, and put all the mail in his out-box.

He told me that it took the better part of a year to sort out the resulting mess.

AIR RAID

From: [name withheld]
To: scottadams@aol.com

The burglar alarm in our facility had a test switch, allowing the system to emit a screeching howl. When my co-workers arrived, my manager and I explained that the company required us to have an air-raid drill in case of nuclear attack. Our co-workers, all young, thought that this was stupid, but they believed that the word had come down from on high to stage an air-raid drill.

We explained that when they heard the alarm, the cashiers should all pull out their registers, run to safety zones, and SHIELD THE CASH WITH THEIR BODIES. The drill went off according to training.

A few days later, they were less than amused when we let them in on our little prank.

PEANUTS FROM HEAVEN

From: [name withheld]
To: scottadams@aol.com

On the night before my last day at a job, I spent hours
constructing a delicate setup. When my boss came in the
next morning, while the entire office watched (since I had
told of my prank), he sat down in his chair and read a
note on his desk asking for a certain document. He leaned
over to open his large file drawer. As he opened it, it
pulled a wire that went through a series of pulleys, eventually moving a ceiling tile. Above that tile was 27 cubic feet
of Styrofoam peanuts, corralled and "aimed" using cardboard that was taped together. The peanuts poured down
on my boss for about ten seconds. At the end of this
onslaught was a sign that dangled down from the ceiling:
"Aren't you glad today's my last day?"

POWER STRIPPING

From: [name withheld]
To: scottadams@aol.com

I used to work with a fellow who loved to play pranks on
his supervisor. The supervisor's computer was plugged into
a power strip under his desk. Every morning he would
crawl under his desk to turn on the power strip.

One night our prankster connected a 110 dB emergency horn to the power strip and hid the horn behind the desk. From three doors down, we heard the horn go off, we heard the supervisor's head hit the underside of the desk, and we heard the supervisor yelling the prankster's name.

SNEEZE SLAP

From: [name withheld]
To: scottadams@aol.com

Fill your hands with water, walk behind one of your co-workers, pretend to sneeze, and throw the water on the back of your co-worker's neck. For extra effect, keep walking, staring at your hands, only murmuring under your breath what an amazing sneeze that was, what great distance you got, and how the soakage factor was extra high.

THRONE PHONE

Run fake wires into restroom stalls, originating from someplace hard to trace. Post notices inside the stalls that phones will be installed so employees can avoid downtime. Act like you think it's a good idea and don't know what all the fuss is about.

BAD TECHNICAL ADVICE

Any form of bad technical advice can be entertaining. Try to make your bad advice the kind that will make your victim do something stupid in front of witnesses. Here are some examples of advice to give someone whose computer keeps locking up:

▶ It might be overheating. Try fanning it with a large binder every ten minutes or so.

▶ Hold your phone up to the computer so I can hear it. Then type rhythmically, like a heartbeat.

▶ Your mouseball might be losing flexibility. Try taking it out of the mouse and massaging it.

▶ Your screen might need a sonic degaussment. Try whistling an E flat at the screen. It takes about a minute to work.

▶ Your computer might be picking up interference from CB radio users in the area. Try yelling into the computer, "Please switch to another frequency! Over."

▶ It's a static electricity problem. Remove your shoes and socks when typing. And don't let the keyboard get near any other clothing. Hitch your chair way back and reach forward to the keyboard when using it.

▶ I've been hearing about this problem lately. It's caused by the upcoming solar eclipse. Try putting a pinhole in a shoe box and viewing your screen through it.

▶ To properly ground yourself when the PC case is open, use an antistatic wrist clip. If none is handy, you can use a regular dog leash. Put the collar on yourself and attach the leash to the side of the PC case using a large paper clip.

You can avoid retribution for your bad advice by stating it in the form of a question. That way you don't have to take responsibility when things go terribly wrong. You can say, "Hey, I was only asking." Here are some good questions to ask your PC-illiterate co-workers.

► Have you tried picking it up and shaking it?

► Did you ever think of soaking it in vinegar?

► I wonder what happens if you run a huge magnet over it?

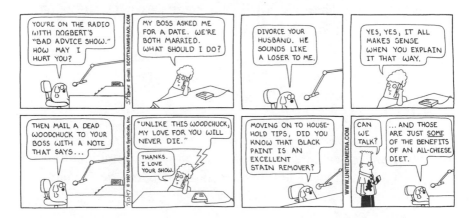

CUBICLE STOOGE

Let's say a co-worker is desperately trying to concentrate on a vital project that is on deadline—the kind where any distraction is a horrible inconvenience. Call a person in the cubicle adjacent to your victim and ask inane questions, like, "In your budget projections, are you assuming a hundred cents to the dollar?" Insist that you have a bad connection and ask the person to speak louder and louder. Not only will the person to whom you're talking get louder, but he will be angry. Plus he will be saying completely nonsensical things like, "TWO PEOPLE WITH SMALL HEADS ARE NOT THE SAME AS ONE HEADCOUNT!!!"

This will make your victim insanely angry, but not at you. You'll be safe and snug in your cubicle yards away.

WHERE'S THAT OPTION?

Make passing references to how you just used the company's new document management system to save yourself a lot of work. Explain how you routed your printer output to the copy machine and had the documents automatically collated and stapled. Then you sent an e-mail message to the In-house Document Delivery Group (IDDG), who distributed all two hundred copies the same day. If your co-worker asks how to do that, give a vague answer involving an icon on his computer that resembles a "cross between a Mobius strip and a picnic." Your co-worker will spend days looking for that icon on his own computer. Anytime he asks for more specifics, change the subject.

FUN WITH SPEAKERPHONES

If one of the people at your meeting is participating from a remote location via speakerphone, this is a good opportunity to find happiness at his expense, without much risk of retaliation. Take one of the life-size moron masks on the following pages—there's one for each gender—and put it over the speakerphone. Or

look between pages 216 and 217 of this book for your very own punch-out speakerphone masks of the Boss and Alice.

SOUNDS THAT DRIVE CO-WORKERS CRAZY

You can produce sounds in the office that will drive your co-workers insane. That can be very entertaining. Every co-worker is different, so you might have to experiment to find the sounds that are the most annoying to your cubicle neighbor. It's worth the effort.

According to my e-mail, the most annoying sound you can project over a cubicle wall is the sound of clipping your fingernails. Dozens of people have written to me to say that the clip . . . clip . . . clip from the adjoining cubicle is enough to drive them to mayhem. Unfortunately, your fingernails don't grow quickly enough to make this sound as often as you might like. But you can compensate for nature's blunder in that area by recording the sound on your computer and replaying it when you're out.

The list of annoying office noises is long. You can probably invent a few on your own. Here's a starter set to get you going. The criterion for selecting good sounds is that they should be rude, but not so rude that a civilized person will want to make a big deal about it. This delicate balance compounds the effectiveness of the annoyance by adding a little voice to the victim's brain that says over and over, "DOESN'T HE REALIZE HOW RUDE THAT IS?????!!!!"

ANNOYING OFFICE NOISES

▶ Coffee slurping

▶ Finger tapping

▶ Whistling

▶ Knuckle cracking

▶ Pen clicking

▶ All things nasal

COUNTERINTELLIGENCE

It can be fun to fill your co-workers with ridiculous "facts," then wait and see if they repeat them later in front of others. Conceptually, it's a lot like raising carrier pigeons. Both hobbies involve attaching information to creatures with tiny brains, then watching in awe as the information returns days later. There's no real purpose to doing this; it's just amazing that it works.

A good category of ridiculous facts is anything involving world events. Tell a co-worker that you're planning a trip to Alaska, assuming you can get a Russian visa. If your co-worker appears puzzled, explain that the United States recently sold Alaska to Russia after it was learned that the much-vaunted Alaskan oil reserves were only diesel oil after all. This sounds vaguely plausible. If you detect any head-nodding, keep riding that bronco as far as it will take you. Talk wistfully about the old days, when Alaska had its own royal family—the Frozington Dynasty. Tragically, the Frozingtons were all rounded up and executed during the Canadian Wars. Many of the native Alaskans "Esks" were forced into servitude as gardeners in Canada. That's where the derogatory phrase "Esk . . . mow" comes from.

Once the evil seeds are planted, wait about a week and make a passing reference to Alaska in a mixed crowd that includes your victim. Your target will be eager to show off his knowledge of Alaska. This can be very amusing, assuming you avoid laughing so hard that you pass a kidney through your urethra.

Here are some other good "facts" to teach co-workers:

► In China, amazingly, no one actually eats Chinese food.

► Light travels faster than sound because of the way your ears are shaped.

► Spanish is basically the same as French, but with fewer words for cheese.

► If a Japanese businessman bows, it means he wants you to rub his head for luck.

► Scientists have determined that smoking is okay if you swallow the smoke instead of letting it in your lungs.

► If you get an unlisted Social Security number, you don't have to pay taxes.

▶ You can request copies of your old mail from the post office.

▶ Every six months, when the earth rotates on its axis, North Korea becomes South Korea and vice versa.

PARANOIA PRANKS

If you know a co-worker who is perpetually paranoid, this trick works well. Take a reusable interoffice envelope—the kind where you cross off the previous address and write in the next on the list—and add two addresses. The victim's name and address should be at the end of the list. The address before the victim's should be Human Resources, or perhaps the legal department, whichever seems scarier in your company. The previous address is the only clue about where the envelope originated from. Tape the envelope closed, mark it "Confidential," then rip it open. Leave the envelope—opened and empty—in the paranoid victim's in-box.

Enlist accomplices to help on the next part. Whenever any of you see the victim, look sincere and say, "Tough break." Or "I don't think you deserved that kind of treatment." Then walk away briskly.

PHONE FUN

If you have at least two co-workers you don't like, that's all you need for phone fun. Sneak into the cubicle of one of them and forward the phone to the other. This is especially effective if they dislike each other as much as you dislike them. Ideally, the two co-workers should be in different buildings or at least on different floors. The person receiving the calls won't be able to call the other victim to sort it out, so they'll have to travel.

A variation on this theme is to call one person, then use the conference-call feature of your phone to call the other. Don't say anything, just connect the two people. Listen to see how long it takes them to figure out neither called the other.

SPEAKERPHONE ABUSERS

The complaint I hear the most about cubicle life is about the idiots who insist on using their speakerphones to conduct business in their cubicles. The resulting noise pollution chokes out productivity in a ten-cubicle radius. You can cure a co-worker of this habit by leaving suggestive messages on the offender's voice-mail system. When the messages are played back, the entire cubicle neighborhood will hear, "Ted, this is Allen from the Sheep Romance Association. Are you thinking of running for treasurer again this year? You've got my vote. In any case, I'll see you at the convention. Wear wool."

Note: Be sure to use an outside line to leave your fake message. Most voice-mail systems transmit the caller's name with the message if you call from a phone on the same system.

FAKE COMPANY POLICIES

Your co-workers have been trained to accept any bizarre company requirement as a matter of course. This gives you great latitude to create your own phony policies to see how many people will believe them.

Employee Organ Donation

Create an Employee Organ Donation form and distribute it to the department. The form should ask for volunteers who wish to have their organs harvested to help defray the expense of providing donuts for company meetings. Include a graph showing the rising cost of pastries. Point out that this is strictly an optional program, although the names of participants will be reported quarterly to the people who make decisions about salaries and promotions.

Employee Dress Code

Create an update to the employee dress code. For realism, make sure it has no basis in common sense. For example, if you already have "casual Friday," you might distribute a memo that introduces "stained Thursday." Stained Thursday would be traditional business clothing, but with slightly relaxed standards for cleanliness, coherence, and odor. It's a transition day to casual Friday. Everyone has at least one great outfit in the closet that has a flaw—a missing button, a permanent stain, a cigarette hole—that sort of thing. Or maybe you're just too lazy to take your outfit to the cleaners, so it smells like a dead giraffe. On stained Thursday those outfits would be considered okay. In your memo, point out that this is the sort of management change that creates winning companies.

Approved Vendor List

Create an "Approved Vendors" list, made up entirely of companies that have gone out of business. Explain in an attached memo that this list has been in development for several years. The new policy requires employees to use the vendors on the list and no others. Find the name of someone who has recently left the company and put that name as the contact person in case there are questions about the policy.

Use What You Sell

Circulate an official-looking e-mail message saying that all employees must use the products your company sells. Suggest that this is a form of punishment for poor performance. If revenues improve next quarter, employees will be allowed to use a competitor's product.

Key Employees

This one is based on a true story: Create a fake policy that says only "key employees" will be allowed to order new business cards. Don't define who the key employees are. This will cause a stampede of people trying to order business cards just to find out if they are "key."

FAXUAL HARASSMENT

Send a fax to a co-worker's regular voice line. Most fax machines will make several attempts to send a fax if it doesn't go through the first time. When your victim answers his phone, he'll get the high-pitched squeal of the fax and realize there is nothing he can do to prevent several more calls just like it. By the fourth call, most victims of this prank will move to a shack in Montana and write a manifesto against technology.

For the more gullible victims, after they complain to you about the repeated calls, tell them to listen carefully to the fax tones because sometimes you can make out the phone number of the calling fax. Explain that fax language is much like human language except more garbled.

MYSTERY MUSIC

Get one of those greeting cards with a music chip that plays an annoying song over and over. Remove the music chip. Sew it into the chair seat of your victim. Or place it above a ceiling tile over the victim's desk. The music should be loud enough to be heard but too faint to be easily located. A similar prank can be performed with a pager instead of a music chip, preferably the victim's pager.

INCREMENTAL INSANITY

This prank has many variations. It involves making slight changes to the placement or dimensions of something in your victim's workspace each day. The changes should be slight enough to avoid immediate detection. For example, lower the height of your victim's chair by one millimeter each day. Eventually the victim will feel he is shrinking. You can compound this feeling by casually mentioning reports you've read lately about how sedentary people get shorter over time. Enlist accomplices to help. Have your accomplices say things like, "Gee, I guess I usually see you wearing higher heels." Or, "That shirt looks a size too big on you."

RESTROOM STALL PRANK

Take an old pair of pants and a pair of shoes and stuff them with newspapers so they appear to be a person's feet as seen from outside the stall. Ideally, match the exact shoe type of your boss. Make a long audio recording of hard-to-identify sounds of ecstasy. The noise should be a random combination of the sounds you make when you . . .

► Scratch an itch in the middle of your back.

► Taste excellent food.

► Have an intense sexual experience.

Feel free to add other unusual sounds—animals screaming, waterfalls, buzzing—depending on how amazingly juvenile and disgusting you are. Put the audiotape in an expensive portable stereo and leave it in the stall with the fake feet. Close the door.

A variation on this prank is to convince a co-worker to pull the prank. Then go in and steal the high-quality stereo. Technically, that's more of a crime than a prank, but it's the kind no one reports.

ANOTHER VERSION OF THE RESTROOM STALL PRANK

From: [name withheld]
To: scottadams@aol.com

One of my co-workers is typically the first in the office each day. One morning, he decided to take a spare pair of men's pants and shoes and place them "appropriately" in one of the stalls of the ladies' rest room.

Many people were quite concerned about this, including one woman who told our HR director, "I think there's a guy in there. But he must be really sick, because he's been in there all morning."

PAVLOVIAN TRAINING FOR CO-WORKERS

You can train your co-workers in the same way Pavlov trained his dogs. It's not immediately obvious why you would want to do this, but it sure is fun, as this report shows.

From: [name withheld]
To: scottadams@aol.com

I work as a security guard. One day, I came back from patrol about five minutes earlier than usual. The guard who watches the doors asked me suspiciously why I had come back early, and accused me of not completing my patrol. She even called our supervisor and complained to him.

I figured that she had a lot of extra time on her hands, so I decided to help her fill some of it.

Her job was to watch the doors and buzz people in with her little access control button. The buzzer is very loud and irritating. There are also access buttons in the security center, where I was stationed. So I pressed the button, just to annoy her. She called me immediately and asked if someone was pressing the button. I innocently told her no. She asked if I knew how she could stop the buzzing. I told her that maybe she should try opening and closing the doors. I watched her on the video monitor as she opened and closed the doors. I stopped the buzzing each time, to convince her that she had discovered the problem. Then I waited and buzzed again. Each time she got up and repeated the successful maneuver.

She never did catch on. She just kept opening the doors and acting all smug that she knew the solution to the problem. But everyone else knew exactly what was going on, and I'm afraid she didn't look like the brightest bulb in the hallway.

INVENTING STRANGE MORALE BOOSTERS

If you've heard of any bizarre and annoying practices at other companies, convince your boss to try it at yours. Better yet, make up a bizarre and annoying practice and tell your boss that it's commonly used in all the *Fortune* 500 companies. I think the poor company below was a victim of just such a prank.

From: [name withheld]
To: scottadams@aol.com

Last week, I received an e-mail message from our highest middle manager in the department. The message explained that, in an attempt to raise morale, the workers would be given an opportunity to play in a "game." To play the game, we all received bright yellow happy faces with our names on them. The purpose of the game was to hold on to the happy face for the duration of one month. Whoever succeeded in doing so would get eight hours extra paid time off.

There's a catch. You lose your happy face if you are ever caught doing something that is construed as a "Non-Positive Attitude." There's no definition of what exactly is a Non-Positive Attitude (NPA). That judgment will be made by what the designers call the "Positivity Police." The Positivity Police are chosen from among the employees by picking names out of a hat. Their job is to report NPA activity to the management.

Once chosen, the e-mail explained, the Positivity Police would reveal their identities only to management.

The funniest part was that no member of the management staff could understand how this could have a negative effect on our attitudes.

MONITORING YOUR CO-WORKERS

If your co-workers are not pulling their weight, and yours too, it might be necessary to measure and report on their performance. This can be a valuable motivator.

From: [name withheld]
To: scottadams@aol.com

A couple of my co-workers would consistently take long breaks and leave early. So another co-worker and I wrote a program that would track the amount of time actually worked compared to time taken for breaks, for each person. The program also allowed us to remotely control their computers. When the person logged on in the morning, a message would appear notifying them of their log-in time. Messages would then appear throughout the day letting them know their work-to-break ratio. If they did not actually work enough hours in a day, when they tried to log off at the end of the day it would not allow them to log off. If they shut off their machines, they would not be allowed to log in the next day (very frustrating).

The Helpdesk could not figure out how the program was working and how to remove it from the computers. A chart report would be generated at the end of each week to show their work and break status. Inevitably, the breaks would add up to almost the same as their actual work.

6

Surviving Meetings

Unless you work alone, one of the biggest assaults on your happiness is something called a meeting. A meeting is essentially a group of people staring at visual aids until the electrochemical activity in their brains ceases, at which point decisions are made. It's like being in suspended animation, except that people in suspended animation aren't in severe physical discomfort and praying for death.

If you attend many meetings, your life will disappear faster than a bag of cash falling off the back of an armored car in front of a homeless shelter for Olympic sprinters. But not everyone feels bored at meetings. The exception to this rule is the people who have such bad personal lives that they use meetings as a substitute for actual social interactions. Avoid these people if you can:

If you absolutely can't avoid meetings, learn how to enjoy them. Your body might have to sit motionless for hours, but you can train your brain to disengage and enjoy itself.

▶ PERSONAL DIGITAL ASSISTANTS

If your co-workers are bringing PalmPilots and other personal digital assistants (PDAs) to meetings, get a Nintendo Gameboy and try to blend in with the crowd. You might want to paint your Gameboy dark gray and file off the logo. Interrupt the meeting to ask people their phone numbers and addresses. Press buttons randomly on your Gameboy to simulate data entry. If someone offers to transfer his business-card information via infrared signal to your PDA, play along. Point your Gameboy in the appropriate direction, then say, "Got it." When the other person complains that he did not receive your information, recommend that he get his PDA repaired. Once your credibility has been established, through the process of being an unscrupulous weasel, you can merrily play with your Gameboy throughout the meeting.

▶ ROBOT VISUALIZATION

My favorite technique for keeping my brain from burrowing out of my head during meetings is what I call the robot visualization. The way this works is that you imagine your body is a gigantic robot and you are a tiny captain inside it, in the control room. Imagine the control room being like the bridge of the Starship Enterprise. The forward screens are the view out of your eyes. Every movement of your huge robotic body becomes fun that way. You hear your little captain issue the command, "Turn neck thirty degrees starboard." When your neck actually turns, it's very cool. You're the captain of this excellent robot. It's just you in the control room, alone with the attractive and ambitious Ensign Raquel. (Adjust the gender to suit your preferences.) There's no end to the robotic possibilities once the two of you start getting frisky and end up on the weapons control panel.

▶ EMBARRASSING THE PRESENTER

If one of your co-workers is making a presentation, amuse yourself by asking questions that are impossible to answer. Don't limit yourself to questions that make any sense or have any relevance. The objective of this game is to make your co-worker get that "please shoot me" expression in front of a roomful of people. For example, if he is doing a presentation on the budget, ask this sort of question:

"Correct me if I'm wrong, but isn't the depreciation rate a good indication of the declining EVA projection from the perspective of a long-term strategy, vis-à-vis the budget gap?"

When your co-worker's eyes start to look like two pie plates with an olive in the middle of each one, make a dissatisfied face and say, "That's okay. I'll ask someone knowledgeable."

It's also fun to raise issues that will create extra work for the presenter. Compete with the other people at your table to see who can make the presenter work the hardest after the meeting. The key is to look earnest and concerned, so your issue seems impossible to ignore. Here are some good issues that fit almost any situation. Any one of these would require more work than could ever be justified, yet they sound almost important.

ANNOYING ISSUES

"What's the impact on all the other departments in our company? Have you checked with them?"

"How would the numbers look if you did 5 percent less of whatever it is that you were talking about? Could you run those numbers for next week?"

"Maybe you should produce a skit to describe your plan and distribute the videotape throughout the company."

The following story is allegedly true, but sounds more like an urban legend. Either way, it suggests a fun joke to pull on a vendor if you can get your co-workers to collude.

From: [name withheld]
To: scottadams@aol.com

This happened at the headquarters of a large mid-Atlantic bank. A vendor came in to talk about some new software. He set up an overhead projector to use with his computer and asked someone to shut off the lights in the conference room. Everyone just sat there. So he looked around for the light switch but couldn't find it.

Finally someone explained that the company replaced the light switches with motion sensors because people were always leaving the conference-room lights on.

When he asked the employees what they did when they had presentations, they replied that they just "sat real still" until the lights went out.

7

Managing Your Co-Workers

If you're unfortunate enough to have co-workers, you must learn how to manage them. Otherwise, like so many wildebeests on the plains of the Serengeti, they will be bumping into you, drinking from your water hole, and generally kicking up a lot of dust. That will cut into your happiness.

You don't have any official power over co-workers, so you must find other forms of persuasion.

▶ CUBICLE FLATULENCE

According to the e-mail reports I'm getting from the field, cubicle flatulence is a mushrooming problem in corporate America. It might replace secondhand smoke as the biggest menace to public health in the workplace. I'm not aware of any scientific studies on the health dangers of secondhand flatulence, but this is exactly the sort of thing that our universities should be studying. For all we know, people are dropping like flies. But I'm not here to talk about the downside of flatulence. This book is about workplace joy.

Dozens of *Dilbert* readers have mentioned one particular coincidence about cubicle flatulence: It seems to attract visitors.

People write to tell me that every time they let one fly, some unsuspecting victim will round the corner and enter their cubicle. This causes a moment of tension, as the visitor, soon aware of the atmospheric disturbance, tries to transact business without the benefit of oxygen. It would be easy to interpret this as a bad situation for all involved. But on more careful observation, it becomes clear that one party in this transaction is getting the benefit of relieved internal pressure and a substantially shorter meeting than would otherwise be the case. It's a classic wind-win situation. The visitor doesn't fare so well. What we can learn from this is that when it comes to flatulence, it's better to give than to receive.

At this writing, I am aware of no companies with written policies forbidding the gassing of co-workers. (You could say it's an open-ended situation.) There might be some international conventions that are applicable, but those are rarely enforced.

▶ BOSSING CO-WORKERS AROUND

Try bossing your co-workers around. Give them assignments; send them to gather information; ask them to work overtime—that sort of thing. Most people will respond with indignation and profanity. But a certain percentage will do exactly as they're told because they're too timid to resist. They might even appreciate the clarity and purpose you have given their lives. Start small, by ordering them to do their own work in ways that will make them look good to their peers. Praise them lavishly for following your orders. Soon they will begin to associate following your orders with pleasant results.

Once you have them conditioned to follow your directions for their own jobs, start to assign some of your work to them. It should be a subtle transition, like asking them to drop things off on the way to other places, or asking them to make copies for you when they are at the copy machine. Slowly expand their assignments to include your core duties. Chastise them for doing their own work before doing yours.

If you have a timid co-worker who vaguely resembles you, give that person a makeover until the two of you are indistinguishable. If you can get someone who looks like you to do your work, you never have to show up at the office again.

▶ BE IN CHARGE OF THE OFFICE MOVE

If your department has to move to new office space, volunteer to be in charge of the move. This will give you absolute power over the future happiness of your co-workers.

During the months leading up to the move, your co-workers will go out of their way to suck up to you. You will live like a cubicle king, meting out punishments and rewards by shuffling the floor layout plan according to who has pleased you lately. Don't worry that taking on this extra duty will keep you from your work. Work is what your serfs are for. They will be glad to pick up your slack in return for a higher priority in the cubicle shuffle.

▶ DEALING WITH IRRATIONAL CO-WORKERS

Nothing can reduce your happiness faster than an argument with an irrational co-worker. You can't win irrational people over to your side by your superior reasoning abilities. And you can't talk them into getting inside abandoned refrigerators and closing the door to see if the light goes out. There simply aren't that many abandoned refrigerators. If you use the refrigerator in the break room, everyone will start whining about how there's no room for yogurt. Until there are more refrigerators, or less yogurt, you will find yourself in frustrating discussions that can have no good endings.

Trying to win an argument with an irrational person is like trying to teach a cat to snorkel by providing written instructions.

No matter how clear your instructions, it won't work. Your best strategy is to reduce the time you spend in that sort of situation.

I have developed a solution to this problem. It is based on the fact that irrational people are easily persuaded by anything that has been published. It doesn't matter who published it, or what the context is, or how inaccurate it is. Once something is published, it's as persuasive as anything else that's ever been published. So I figure that what you need is a publication that supports all of your arguments no matter what they are. This book is that publication.

I have collected the most common arguments made by irrational people into a handy reference guide and titled it "You Are Wrong Because." Circle the irrational arguments that apply to your situation and give a copy to the person who is bugging you. Look smug, as though this were conclusive evidence of your rightness. A rational person might point out that just because something is written down doesn't make it so. But since you're not giving the list to anyone with that much insight, it doesn't really matter. What matters is that you will feel as though you brought closure to a potentially frustrating situation.

You Are Wrong Because

For your convenience, I have circled the brain malfunction(s) that most closely resemble(s) the one(s) you recently made on the topic of (fill in topic): _____.

1. AMAZINGLY BAD ANALOGY

Example: You can train a dog to fetch a stick. Therefore, you can train a potato to dance.

2. FAULTY CAUSE AND EFFECT

Example: On the basis of my observations, wearing huge pants makes you fat.

3. I AM THE WORLD

Example: I don't listen to country music. Therefore, country music is not popular.

4. IGNORING EVERYTHING SCIENCE KNOWS ABOUT THE BRAIN

Example: People choose to be obese/gay/alcoholic because they prefer the lifestyle.

5. THE FEW ARE THE SAME AS THE WHOLE

Example: Some Elbonians are animal rights activists. Some Elbonians wear fur coats. Therefore, Elbonians are hypocrites.

6. GENERALIZING FROM SELF

Example: I'm a liar. Therefore, I don't believe what you're saying.

7. ARGUMENT BY BIZARRE DEFINITION

Example: He's not a criminal. He just does things that are against the law.

8. TOTAL LOGICAL DISCONNECT

Example: I enjoy pasta because my house is made of bricks.

9. JUDGING THINGS WITHOUT COMPARISON TO ALTERNATIVES

Example: I don't invest in U.S. Treasury bills. There's too much risk.

10. ANYTHING YOU DON'T UNDERSTAND IS EASY TO DO

Example: If you have the right tools, how hard could it be to generate nuclear fission at home?

11. IGNORANCE OF STATISTICS

Example: I'm putting ALL of my money on the lottery this week because the jackpot is so big.

12. IGNORING THE DOWNSIDE RISK

Example: I know that bungee jumping could kill me, but it's three seconds of great fun!

13. SUBSTITUTING FAMOUS QUOTES FOR COMMON SENSE

Example: Remember, "All things come to those who wait." So don't bother looking for a job.

14. IRRELEVANT COMPARISONS

Example: A hundred dollars is a good price for a toaster, compared to buying a Ferrari.

15. CIRCULAR REASONING

Example: I'm correct because I'm smarter than you. And I must be smarter than you because I'm correct.

16. INCOMPLETENESS AS PROOF OF DEFECT

Example: Your theory of gravity doesn't address the question of why there are no unicorns, so it must be wrong.

17. IGNORING THE ADVICE OF EXPERTS WITHOUT A GOOD REASON

Example: Sure, the experts think you shouldn't ride a bicycle into the eye of a hurricane, but I have my own theory.

18. FOLLOWING THE ADVICE OF KNOWN IDIOTS

Example: Uncle Billy says pork makes you smarter. That's good enough for me!

19. REACHING BIZARRE CONCLUSIONS WITHOUT ANY INFORMATION

Example: The car won't start. I'm certain the spark plugs have been stolen by rogue clowns.

20. FAULTY PATTERN RECOGNITION

Example: His last six wives were murdered mysteriously. I hope to be wife number seven.

21. FAILURE TO RECOGNIZE WHAT'S IMPORTANT

Example: My house is on fire! Quick, call the post office and tell them to hold my mail!

22. UNCLEAR ON THE CONCEPT OF SUNK COSTS

Example: We've spent millions developing a water-powered pogo stick. We can't stop investing now or it will all be wasted.

23. OVERAPPLICATION OF OCCAM'S RAZOR (WHICH SAYS THE SIMPLEST EXPLANATION IS USUALLY RIGHT)

Example: The simplest explanation for the moon landings is that they were hoaxes.

24. IGNORING ALL ANECDOTAL EVIDENCE

Example: I always get hives immediately after eating strawberries. But without a scientifically controlled experiment, it's not reliable data. So I continue to eat strawberries every day, since I can't tell if they cause hives.

25. INABILITY TO UNDERSTAND THAT SOME THINGS HAVE MULTIPLE CAUSES

Example: The Beatles were popular for one reason only: They were good singers.

26. JUDGING THE WHOLE BY ONE OF ITS CHARACTERISTICS

Example: The sun causes sunburns. Therefore, the planet would be better off without the sun.

27. BLINDING FLASHES OF THE OBVIOUS

Example: If everyone had more money, we could eliminate poverty.

28. BLAMING THE TOOL

Example: I bought an encyclopedia but I'm still stupid. This encyclopedia must be defective.

29. HALLUCINATIONS OF REALITY

Example: I got my facts from a talking tree.

30. TAKING THINGS TO THEIR ILLOGICAL CONCLUSION

Example: If you let your barber cut your hair, the next thing you know he'll be lopping off your limbs!

31. FAILURE TO UNDERSTAND WHY RULES DON'T HAVE EXCEPTIONS

Example: It should be legal to shoplift, as long as you don't take enough to hurt the company's earnings.

32. PROOF BY LACK OF EVIDENCE

Example: I've never seen you drunk, so you must be one of those Amish people.

8

Bringing Humor and Creativity to Your Job

I've heard it said that kindergartners already know how to sing and dance and paint. But as you've probably noticed, that only applies to your own kids. Everyone else's kids are just scribbling, shouting, and jumping around. Their interference is probably the only thing keeping your children's work out of the Louvre.

As far as I can tell, most people don't start life with much in the way of creative skills. And things go downhill from there. In fact, life is one huge process of eliminating any traces of creativity in order to make you more employable. By the time you enter the workforce, you've been scrubbed almost clean. Your employer takes it from there.

There are undeniable economic reasons for eliminating creativity in workers. As a consumer, I know I wouldn't want my doctor to get too creative with me. I want him to give me the same thing that cured the last guy. The last thing you want to hear your doctor say is, "Hey, I wonder if one of these would fit in there!"

When I get on an airplane, I don't want a pilot with any creative urges either.

Air Traffic
Controller: Flight 399, take runway three.

Creative Pilot: I always take runway three. I thought I'd try landing on the roof of the terminal this time.

Air Traffic Controller: Pull up! Pull up!

Same thing with the police. I don't want to get stopped for speeding and be faced with any creativity options there either.

Cop: The rules say I'm supposed to give you a ticket for this sort of thing. But I like to be more creative.

Me: Um . . . what's that mean?

Cop: Greek wrestling.

Too much creativity in the wrong places is clearly bad. The problem with the societywide creativity-squashing system is that is has unintended consequences. Any system that eliminates dangerous creativity will eliminate good creativity too. And where there is no creativity, there is no room for happiness. My goal for the next section of this book is to teach you my special technique for becoming funnier and more creative at work. Most of it will actually be useful.

I treat humor and creativity as one topic because you need creativity to do humor. It comes in handy for other things too, obviously, but I'll focus on humor here.

▶ WHERE CREATIVITY COMES FROM

I can only speak for myself, but I believe my own creativity is 80 percent clever technique, 10 percent genetic abnormality (the good kind), and 10 percent exposure to secondhand smoke.

If you didn't get any secondhand smoke during your childhood development, it's never too late. If you want to make up for lost time, I recommend becoming a barfly or traveling to Europe.

If you're not an adult, and your parents won't let you go to bars or to Europe, you'll need to hang around with the bad kids to get your secondhand smoke. If you don't know any bad kids, I rent myself out as an invisible friend to kids who aren't popular enough to get one without paying. But that's a separate line of business, so send me an e-mail message if you'd like me to be your invisible friend.

For this book, I'll concentrate on the 80 percent of the creative process that is clever technique. That's where I can help the most. In the following section I'll teach you how to make time for creativity. Later, under the topic of humor, I'll get more specific about the techniques for improving creativity.

▶ MANAGE CREATIVITY, NOT TIME

Creativity comes in many forms. You could be creating a better business idea, a better software concept, a better process, or a better anything. Most adults feel they don't have time to develop their creative skills. My theory is that people don't actually have a shortage of time, they're just approaching the question in the wrong way.

Take this quiz to determine whether you understand the implications of good time management:

Time Management Quiz

If you are the first person on your team to finish your
work, you will be rewarded with:

    a. A huge bonus
    b. Recognition as a rising star
    c. More work

The surest way to be permanently unhappy is to manage your
time.

"Managing time" is a concept that made perfect sense for jobs
in the past, such as the job of picking bugs out of another monkey's fur.* The more time you dedicated to the task, the more bugs
you got. It was simple math, even for monkeys. And the creative
alternative—high-pressure steam cleaning—was deemed impractical due to the lack of electricity in the monkey kingdom. For

---

*In the interest of political correctness, since some Creationists will read
this book and be offended by the indirect reference to evolution, you can
substitute the word *apostle* for *monkey* and the point still holds.

monkeys, the time you spent on the job was clearly more important than the level of creativity you demonstrated. But enough about monkeys—I sometimes get carried away because they're so darned cute.

If you have a white-collar job, your best strategy is to manage your creativity, not your time. People who manage their creativity get happy and rich. People who manage their time get tired.

Ask yourself which headline you are more likely to see:

a. CUBICLE WORKER BECOMES BILLIONAIRE THANKS TO CAREFUL SCHEDULING

or . . .

b. POPE DECLARES VIOLENCE IS OKAY WITH HIM, AS LONG AS YOU HAVE A GOOD REASON

An effective way to select a career strategy is to compare it to the odds of the pope endorsing violence. If your strategy has similar odds, consider a new plan.

Scheduling is a blunt instrument when it comes to managing your life. An idea that changes the world can happen in an instant, at any time it pleases. Creativity doesn't need much time. Consider this inspirational little story:

A Little Story About Creativity

Somewhere in a vast wasteland of cubicles, copiers, and conference rooms, an idea is about to be born. It is just the soul of an idea, twinkling in and out of existence, waiting for the right combination of matter and energy to provide form and motion. While it waits, it watches, hidden just beyond the peripheral vision of the human inhabitants, teasing their collective imagination, then backing away, like a name you can't remember or the scent of something familiar. It has no weight or resistance. It is not part of reality. Yet somehow it interacts with reality. It is the mysterious force that appears according to some unpredictable schedule. This is its time. The probability field begins to collapse. Matter and energy are aligning in exactly the right configuration. The idea senses the invitation and begins an instant transformation from nothingness to somethingness. It sparks to life, tiny and weak, hovering just above the carpet. In time, with the right combination of hope and dreams and risk, the idea can become large enough to change the world.

Suddenly, the guy who delivers the copier paper comes around the corner and crushes the idea with his dolly. This is a bigger tragedy than anyone will ever know, because he's delivering the three-hole paper that your inconsiderate co-workers will leave in the copier to ambush you.

As you can see from this inspirational story, creativity doesn't require much time. But creativity always needs your energy. You can't create if you're pooped or your brain is full of junk. A person who manages creativity makes sure his schedule has lots of free spaces, no matter how many priorities are looming. You need a certain amount of free time to recharge your creative energy.

The obvious problem with my advice is that if you manage your life for maximum creativity, you end up looking like a lazy pig. You might as well put an apple in your mouth, spread some hay on the floor of your cubicle, and start napping with your arms and legs out to the side. But you can avoid unkind comparisons to any member of the animal kingdom by using the simple advice that follows. I'll teach you how to cleverly manage your creativity while appearing to be an imbecile who only manages his time.

While it's true that a complete focus on time management will ruin you, you still need *some* discipline in that area. You can't totally separate time management from creativity management. The point is, when you have to pick between managing your creativity and managing your time—and you often have to make that choice—favor creativity. That's where the payoff is.

Here's a true story about how the Human Resources department at one company uses technology to help keep the workload manageable:

From: [name withheld]
To: scottadams@aol.com

I have always thought that HR was staffed by idiots, but now I'm not so sure. After our last semiannual Reorganization Festival, I inadvertently came across the name of my new HR representative (yes, well, it was on the next-to-the-top document in my boss's in-basket, so it was almost in plain sight). I decided to call her just so she'd know that I knew who she was. I called the company operator to get her number.

> Me: I'd like the number for Ima Ghost in HR, please.

> Operator: I'm sorry, that number is unlisted.

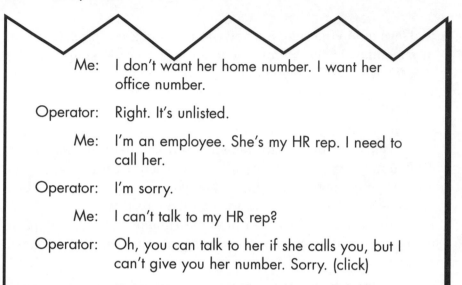

Me: I don't want her home number. I want her
           office number.

Operator: Right. It's unlisted.

Me: I'm an employee. She's my HR rep. I need to
           call her.

Operator: I'm sorry.

Me: I can't talk to my HR rep?

Operator: Oh, you can talk to her if she calls you, but I
           can't give you her number. Sorry. (click)

Undaunted, I walked over to the last rumored location for HR. I found a locked office (at 10:00 A.M.) and a list of 800 numbers taped to the door.

I copied down the "If you need assistance" one and went back to the office. I called the number and tried the first option, which led to four more options, the first of which led to three more. I tried the first one again—it disconnected me. I called back and tried the 1–1–2 option—it disconnected me. Not easily dissuaded, I called every single option. They all disconnected me.

So, at my *Fortune 50* company, we have HR reps with unlisted office phone numbers and an HR "Help" line that disconnects all callers with no human intervention. In fact, it would seem that there are no "humans" in "Human Resources." They're probably in an off-site conference at a local resort, laughing their asses off.

No matter what your job is, there are always more things to do than there are hours in the day. People who manage their time see a hole in their calendar and they fill it faster than a Clydesdale can fill a Dixie cup.

People who manage their creative energy will leave spaces in their day during their most creative hours. For most people, that's either late at night or early in the morning. If you work hard all day, you're probably too tired to use the late-night hours. By process of elimination, that leaves the early morning as the best time to be creative.

Do all your creative thinking in the morning. I recommend that you avoid scheduling any meetings or answering any phone calls before 9:00 A.M.

By the early-afternoon hours, if your brain is normal, it's running strictly on inertia and reflex. All you can do during those hours are the things that are exactly like other things you've done in similar situations. Creativity is out of the question. You might argue that you don't notice any difference in your thinking during the afternoon. That's because you're too dazed to notice anything during those hours. I'm sure that's true for me; I believe you could set my eyebrows on fire during the afternoon and I wouldn't notice until sometime the next morning.

I always schedule my noncreative activities during the afternoon. For example, today I have a meeting with two important business partners. There's no real agenda. The only purpose is to make a personal connection. I guess the reason we're doing it is so that later, if we talk by telephone, we can close our eyes and imagine what each other looks like. It's a poor man's version of videoconferencing.

Creativity Tip

*When you imagine other people, to the extent that they are
clothed, always put them in white culottes. That way you don't
use up any extra memory space for their wardrobe. You can use
the extra memory for storing creative things. Culottes work for
any gender because they're half pants and half skirt. No need to
chew up extra memory space for each gender. The only exception
to the culottes rule is dressing the elderly. You don't want to see
their spindly legs, so put them in blue sweatpants.*

Today's meeting will be at 2:00 P.M., a time when my brain
automatically shuts down all systems not directly related to organ
functions. If you did a Turing* test on me, I would not pass. I suspect that my end of the conversation will not be described by anyone later as "scintillating." It'll probably go like this:

Me:	Hi. Nice to see you.
Guests:	Hi. Nice to see you.
Me:	So, are you two married to each other?
Guests:	Um, no, we work together.
Me:	Too bad. You'd make a nice couple. Would you like a beverage?

It will go downhill from there.

---

*A Turing test is what you use to determine if a computer can display
intelligence that is indistinguishable from human intelligence. No computer has passed the test yet. But that's only because no one has written
a program to make a computer complain about its job all day.

MULTITASKING

You can create more time for yourself by combining mind-numbingly boring tasks (i.e., your job) with fascinating creative tasks (i.e., preparing for your cool new future job). Let's call this process "creative multitasking" so it sounds important.

Creative multitasking works magic because creativity and boredom go together like salt on french fries. No one ever says, "I don't need any french fries, I already have salt." The more you have of one, the easier it is to consume the other. Work can be like that too if you choose your challenges wisely. The more boredom you endure, the more ready your mind will be to take on something interesting. And the more creative stimulation you take on, the more appreciative you'll be of any opportunity to do something boring to give your brain a rest.

Never make the mistake of trying to multitask by combining a boring activity with another boring activity. Your brain will subconsciously associate that level of boredom with old age and send the signal to grow more hair in your ears. And don't multitask with two creative tasks either, such as knitting and ballet. That's just begging for trouble. If you're going to multitask, choose your tasks wisely.

If you work in a cubicle, you already have the boring part of the equation worked out. Look for creative activities that can blend in with the day job without arousing suspicion. For example, if you spend a lot of time on the phone, start a phone-sex business to release your creativity. Your phone-sex customers won't get suspicious if you toss in some corporate phrases such as "Leverage your team member!" and "Enhance the performance of your business unit!" Anyone listening at the office will just think you're bossy and foul-mouthed. That never hurt anyone's career. And if your boss happens to call you on the sex line, that can be a big advantage for your next performance review.

If you don't like talking about sex, try writing a novel in your cubicle. Do it one paragraph at a time, using your e-mail software. Send each installment to your home e-mail account for assembly later. If someone looks over your shoulder, apparently you're composing a brief e-mail message. If your computer hard drive gets audited, not a trace of personal business will be found. I have spoken to several people who are working on their first book in this fashion. (Really.)

Here's a story about someone who almost got away with multitasking two boring jobs, but ultimately it didn't work out. It's a valuable lesson to us all.

From: [name withheld]
To: scottadams@aol.com

This is a true story of a computer programmer who worked as an independent consultant at (company name) in New York City.

The consultant had an interview with a manager on the second floor of the (company) building. He accepted the job. A few days later a second agency he worked with sent him for an interview with another manager of the same company, on the fourth floor of the same building. He accepted that job as well.

He managed to work both of these full-time, 8:00 to 5:00 jobs for over six months without anyone realizing what was going on. He would arrive early for one job, about 7:45, before anyone else got there. Then about 10:00 he would walk down the stairs and show up for the second position, where they believed he was one of those programmers who like to work a later schedule.

He worked little more than eight hours a day but was able to bill for sixteen by convincing each department that he was working full-time just for it.

I know this is true because he was fired just a couple of weeks before I started there. A couple of employees were still shocked and told me the story over lunch. I later asked some other people about it, and they confirmed that it had actually happened.

In the end he was caught when someone from one floor went to the other and saw him working there.

Tip: If you ever get the opportunity to pretend you have two full-time jobs in the same building, cover your tracks by telling everyone how happy you are to be working in the same building as your identical twin.

LOOKING BUSY

The secret to carving out huge chunks of free time from your job is to make your cubicle or office look as though you'll be right back. Meanwhile you can be off creating interesting things, taking challenging classes, or just going on holiday. If you keep up with your e-mail and voice-mail, few people will be the wiser.

To give your cubicle that "back in a flash" look, use a combination of these tricks:

1. Leave a spare jacket on the hanger. No one goes home without his or her jacket.

2. Turn on your computer. (Make sure it's password-protected so you don't get stung by the pranks I explained earlier in the book.)

3. Open a computer software manual to a difficult topic.

4. If you wear glasses, but not all the time, leave your old pair on the technical manual as though you had just set them down. If you don't wear glasses, get some.

You'll need a quiet place to do your creative work while you're avoiding your day job. If you drive to work, you can sit in your car in the parking lot. It's like a home office with a stereo. If you have a cellular phone, you can check your voice mail from a safe distance and be ready to spring into action if an emergency arises.

For those of you who are willing to make a major investment in avoiding work, move to a home that's near your job. After you "stage" your cubicle in the morning, just drive home and enjoy a leisurely brunch. Head back to the office right before lunch. As everyone is leaving for lunch, complain that you will have to work straight through. That will give you all the "face time" you need. When everyone leaves for lunch, use the hour to surf the Web in your cubicle, free from the teamwork and assignments that would normally divert you.

From: [name withheld]
To: scottadams@aol.com

There's a method of "work simulation" that I use almost every day. It's not really funny but it is VERY effective.

I have a laptop as well as a desktop PC on my desk with the backs facing toward the door to my office. I keep my door open so nobody can say I'm trying to hide something, or avoid work. On my laptop, a Web browser is constantly running. On my desktop, my e-mail software is just as vigilant. When I hear someone coming my way, I start rolling my chair back and forth between the computers at a feverish pace, all the while keeping a disturbed look on my face. The intruder will then—without fail—ask if this is a bad time. I will stop between the computers and with my eyes quickly shifting between the two say, "Well . . . no. What's up?"

Usually, the person will assume it's a bad time and leave quickly. But sometimes a visitor is pushy and wants to come in and have a seat. When this happens, I will make eye contact and listen for a while, then slide over and hit a few keys on one of the computers, mumble something, then make eye contact again as if I hadn't moved. Most people become uneasy and leave.

From: [name withheld]
To: scottadams@aol.com

I wrote a program that displays a window on my screen that reads "Compiling! Do Not Touch!" It also has a status bar that moves across the window so it looks like it's actually doing something.

Whenever I sneak out or I'm just sleeping, I run that program. If anyone surprises me at my desk or looks at my screen while I'm away, it looks like I'm a busy guy.

From: [name withheld]
To: scottadams@aol.com

The best way to look busy is to look angry.

From: [name withheld]
To: scottadams@aol.com

This trick always works. Grab a large stack of important-looking papers or an expensive piece of portable equipment and tools. Next, get a VERY contorted look on your face and briskly walk right past your boss muttering gibberish the entire time. Walk to the nearest meeting room, spread out the whole mess on a conference table, and close the door. Your boss will presume this is a very difficult problem. You may now enjoy several hours of peace and quiet.

How long can you keep your job while doing no work whatsoever? I know several people who are apparently conducting long-term trials to determine the answer to that question. The tricky part is explaining what you've been doing all year when it becomes clear that your projects all failed because of your laziness. But if you're lucky enough to be involved with projects that fail for reasons unrelated to your lack of involvement, your trail of sloth can be covered indefinitely.

AVOIDING WORK BY BEING TOO BUSY

If you're too ethical to use cheap tricks to avoid work, you can accomplish the same thing by being so busy that people learn to avoid you. I don't recommend this approach unless you're already in what I call Stage Three of being overworked.

FOUR STAGES OF BEING OVERWORKED

Stage One: Your entire day is filled with one crisis after another.

Stage Two: Your entire day is spent explaining to people that your entire day is filled with one crisis after another.

Stage Three: Your entire day is spent apologizing for the crises you didn't handle because you spent your entire day explaining to other people that your day was filled with crises.

Stage Four: You're so busy that no one even dares call you.

Many people make the mistake of trying to lighten their workload to make time for creative projects. That strategy can never work. If you're an adult, there is no stage below Stage One. If your co-workers, family, friends, and business partners find out that your schedule is not filled with life-threatening crises, they will happily supply them.

It's impossible to free your schedule if other people find out you're doing less work. Your co-workers will try to divert your newly created free time to solving their problems. It's called team-work, and you should avoid it at all costs.

You will never be able to make time for your creative projects by trying to become less busy. Your only path to freedom is to INCREASE your workload until you reach Stage Four. You have to make yourself so busy with important work that no reasonable person would expect you to do anything more. That's when you can stop doing any work whatsoever. Everyone will assume you are so busy helping other people—because that's the kind of person you are—that it would be rude and insensitive to ask you to do more. This is the technique used by CEOs, and it explains why they can take six weeks of vacation every year without hurting the company, but you can't.

BEING UNHELPFUL

In the course of your business day, many people will come to you for assistance. If you make the mistake of being helpful, those people will be back tomorrow. They might even spread the word of your helpfulness. Soon, complete strangers will be trying to get free help from you. The best way to avoid these parasites—a.k.a. co-workers—is to be astonishingly unhelpful, as in these examples.

I'll Meet You There: If one of your co-workers is incessantly bugging you to help on his project, agree to have a meeting with him in a faraway conference room at an agreed time. You buy yourself some free time up front by quickly agreeing to the meeting. And you also get at least thirty minutes while your co-worker sits waiting for you, gently cursing your name for never showing up. Eventually he will hunt you down or call you. Act surprised that it's so late and say you just need to make one more call. Having been on the receiving end of this technique many times, I can assure you that it not only works, but it works repeatedly with the same victims.

Smoking Breaks: If you don't already smoke, consider starting. In the long run you'll die a horrible death, but in the short run you'll get the benefits of being a social pariah who takes too many smoking breaks throughout the day. Nonsmokers have learned the futility of reasoning with smokers, so you'll be able to interrupt any business activity to take your smoking breaks. If you want to end an unproductive meeting with a nonsmoker, invite him to join you on your smoking break so you can talk. Most nonsmokers will discover they have something else they need to do instead.

Harnessing the Power of Your Own Incompetence: If you're naturally incompetent, you already know the freedom and joy that come from being that way. Your co-workers learn to avoid giving you any work that matters, thus freeing your mind to do more of whatever the hell it is that people like you do. If you're not incompetent, you might want to take some tips from this star performer.

From: [name withheld]
To: scottadams@aol.com

A colleague and I wrote a paper for a conference that we
were scheduled to attend the following week. On Monday
we asked the group secretary to copy it onto the department letterhead, telling her we needed it by Thursday. "No
problem," she said. Later that afternoon we realized that a
minor change needed to be made and I asked the secretary for the report back. She squirmed in her chair and
asked if she could get it to me tomorrow. Next morning,
same thing, "Try back after lunch." Early afternoon came
and she said, "Not today, maybe tomorrow."

"What," I asked, "happened to our report?"

"Oh," she said, "I had so many things on my desk to do
yesterday that I put them all in an interdepartmental mail
envelope and mailed them to myself. Then my desk is clear
and I look like I'm getting all my work done. I will work on
the report when it comes back in a day or two."

Wednesday afternoon the envelope returned. I snagged
the report and never asked her to do another thing again.

NEW ETIQUETTE FOR EFFICIENCY

Two hundred years ago, when there weren't many people on
earth, everyone was perfectly happy to listen to stories about any-

thing from tree bark to bunions. This was before electricity was popular, so a good bunion story was better than sitting in the dark doing nothing.

But now we have television to fill the voids in our lives. Still, we often get trapped listening to people who have nothing interesting to say. This can chew up vast blocks of your precious time.

I think we should all agree to revise the standard rules of etiquette to allow a polite way to escape that sort of person. Maybe something like this:

Etiquette Decree:

All people must carry a card that lists their boring stories, including the running time for each. It is the right of any citizen to examine another person's story card in advance and decide whether the story is worth the time.

Bob's Story Card

The Car That Just Wouldn't Start:	Running time 14 minutes
Rake Hit Me in the Groin:	Running time 18 minutes
Damn Dog Ate My Biscuit:	Running time 12 minutes
Why I Hate Art:	Running time 83 minutes

After examining the story card, the potential story victim would have an opportunity to politely decline the abuse, using this suggested form:

> I'd rather not waste ____ minutes of my mortality listening to a story about your toddler's appetite for crayons. But if there's a change my limited time situation, such as the surprising discovery that I am immortal, I will contact you immediately.

This might seem unkind, but it wouldn't be rude if we all agree on the rules. And it makes sense; even a can of peas has a label that shows what's in it. All I ask is that boring people be held to the same safety standard as all the other vegetables.

Here's a story card that you can fill out for a boring co-worker of yours, after you've heard all of his stories several times:

_____'s Boring Story List
      Name

BORING STORY TOPIC   RUNNING TIME

_____   _____

_____   _____

_____   _____

_____   _____

_____   _____

_____   _____

_____   _____

HOW TO SAY NO

In a typical day, the majority of your creative energy will be hijacked by the people around you, primarily your co-workers. For example, just today I was hit up for these unreasonable favors, which I quote:

▶ "May I get a word in edgewise?"

▶ "Please back your car off my foot!"

▶ "Would you mind not staring at my chest for two seconds?"

Imagine how unproductive my day would be if I did what everyone else wanted me to do instead of focusing on my own priorities. Luckily, I have developed a system for saying no to people who try to steer me off the path of creative success. I share these secrets with you, in the hope that I never have to borrow anything from you.

Sounding Pathetic: I have the sort of telephone voice that makes people ask if I'm sick. With me it's natural, but you can fake it if you try. If I get twenty calls in a day, fourteen will ask me if science has a cure for whatever I have. It used to be annoying, but I realized it worked to my advantage. It makes me sound overworked and pathetic. Sympathy is a powerful tool if you want to weasel out of favors. If you play it right, you can convince the person on the other end of the phone that you're too weak to survive any requests for assistance. But always act as though

you're willing to risk it. You don't have to lie. Just let your raspy voice send the misleading signal on its own.

For example, let's say your friend calls and asked this favor:

Friend: Would you help me move some furniture?

You: (raspy and pathetic voice) Is it heavy?

Friend: Well, yeah, that's the point.

You: I could move some knickknacks maybe. Not the big ones. Is that the sort of thing you had in mind?

Friend: Um . . .

You: When I say I could move knickknacks, I don't mean I could lift and carry them. But I could push them to new locations on the shelf.

Friend: Never mind.

You: How about doilies? Do you have any of those in the wrong place? I'm eager to help.

At this point in the conversation, even the densest person will conclude that you must be very sick. He will want to hang up quickly, because you have captured the favor-asking high ground. He knows that at any moment you might ask him to bring you some soup.

Acting Confused: Ideally you want the person you are rejecting to feel foolish for imposing on you. You can do that by asking questions as if you do not understand the request. For example, let's say someone asks you to drive him to the airport during the workday so he can begin his vacation. The wrong approach would be to say exactly what you're thinking:

WRONG

> "You selfish turdling! Since when did I become the source of financing for your vacations? Have you heard of a new invention called the taxi? You make me want to puke."

You can see how the honest response would cause trouble in your relationship later. The correct approach is to act confused and continue to ask for clarification:

CORRECT

Friend: Would you take me to the airport tomorrow?

You: Are you asking me to quit my job and travel the world with you?

Friend: Um, no, I just want a ride to the airport.

You: Did someone steal your car?

Friend: No.

You: Taxi strike?

Friend: No.

You: Well, now I'm really confused.

Friend: Look, I'll owe you a favor.

You: Can I have my favor in advance?

Friend: I guess that's fair. What do you want?

You: I want you to take a cab to the airport.

Saying Yes but Never Doing It: The most time-efficient way to say no to something is to say yes, and then never do it. If your objective is to save yourself time and effort, it's counterproductive to say no to someone, even if you have a bulletproof reason. No matter how good the reason, you will be interrogated further, under the inquisitor's assumption that you are either a lazy, stinkin' liar or you are a lazy, stinkin' idiot who can't think of a way to fit something new into your schedule. This can be both insulting and very accurate. That's why it hurts so much.

To avoid that type of pain, cheerily say yes and then get on with your life as though you had said no. You will build goodwill instead of suffering insult and interrogation. It might seem as though you will pay for your spineless deception later, but observation shows that is rarely the case. My brother discovered this technique as a teen. When Mom would ask him to take out the garbage, he always responded with a cheery "Okay." Then he continued reading his comic books. The pattern would repeat for hours. Mom would get increasingly annoyed with each new request. In response, my brother would become increasingly cheery and agreeable.

"Right away, Mom! I'm on it."

But the garbage never moved. Eventually Mom would recognize the pattern and do the only thing you can do when you have an unresponsive teenager: Reassign the work to the preteen. I've toted a lot of garbage in my day. My brother is a genius.

I've since modified the say-yes technique so it doesn't sound quite so unhelpful. Now I quickly agree to do whatever I'm asked by saying, "Sure! Glad to help. I have about six hundred other favors to do first, but yours is definitely on my list. If there's anything else I can do, don't hesitate to ask."

This serves to lower people's expectations to the point where they will immediately seek alternatives for whatever they needed. With this method you can usually get people to call you before their deadline to tell you it's "already taken care of." They might even thank you for your help. Be gracious and offer to be of assistance in the future. Never say, "How's it feel to suck your own blood, you parasite?" That just causes ill will.

Here's a true report from the field that shows how useful this technique can be.

From: [name withheld]
To: scottadams@aol.com

Last summer I was working on a number of Web pages, and once they were finished, they were placed on the company server so that my co-workers could look at them and give me feedback on them. Fortunately, most of my co-workers are at least semi-Internet-literate, but one was not. This co-worker surfed outside my pages to a new government site and found errors on it. She called me to inform me of these errors. I explained that the government Website was totally out of my control, but she insisted I write the Web master to tell him of the errors. Her rationale was that if we linked to pages that had a few problems, my company would look bad. Knowing that I would just confuse her if I tried to explain the concept of the Internet to her, I just agreed politely and ignored it. Problem solved.

Preemptive Voice-mail Declines: Lately I've been experimenting with using voice-mail to do preemptive turn-downs. My outgoing voice-mail message anticipates most of the typical requests for my time and delivers the bad news without my direct involvement. It changes frequently, but here's a template for your use:

> Hi, this is Scott Adams. At the sound of the beep, please leave your long, rambling message explaining why I should do something that benefits you— something with little or no value to the rest of the solar system. I will send my answer to you via a coded message in your television set. If the answer is no, Larry King will be wearing suspenders tonight. If the answer is yes, *Good Morning America* will announce that their new morning host is Salman Rushdie.

Most people will persist even after hearing the message. But I've found that it softens them up considerably and they don't fight too hard when I say no in person.

Referring People to Your Web Page: If people are always asking you for information, start referring them to your Web page. It's okay if you don't have a Web page, or that your Web page has no useful information. Most people are delighted when you tell them all the information is on your Web page. I guess that sounds like a very cool thing, so they appreciate it at some level. Then they go away.

Saying No in Writing: The best way to say no to something is in writing. That gives you the freedom to completely misinterpret the request, so you can decline using any excuse whatsoever. For example, if someone leaves you a voice mail asking for your help choosing a software vendor, reply by e-mail and say that you can't help because you "already donate to the United Way." Obviously your answer has nothing to do with the question, but it will look like a simple misunderstanding.

SECRETARIES

Never get yourself a secretary. People who have secretaries usually end up with more work than the people who have none.

Every unit of efficiency provided by a secretary will be balanced by a counterefficiency.

Efficiency	Counterefficiency
Takes phone messages.	Writes fours that look like nines, twos that look like sevens, and sevens that look like ones.
Intercepts hundreds of unproductive requests.	Creates thousands of unproductive requests for your time.
Schedules meetings for you.	Schedules meetings with people you'd rather see on milk cartons.
Organizes the diversity workshop for the department.	Accuses you of discrimination.
Keeps time-wasting people out of your office.	Won't stay out of your office.
Buys a gift for your spouse for Valentine's Day.	Expects a gift for birthdays, Secretary's Day, and whatever else Hallmark decides.
Reduces your stress by handling tasks that you would find frustrating.	Increases your stress by sharing personal problems you've never even heard of before.
Files important documents . . .	. . . where you can't find them.

Dogbert Disconnect

I've noticed that about 20 percent of my business calls result in me being put on hold and forgotten or simply disconnected immediately. Being a trusting soul, normally I might assume that multiline telephones are inherently confusing and that busy people make mistakes. But I once worked in a job that involved helping people over the phone, so I know the ugly truth.

In one of my first jobs, at a large bank, I was being trained to work in a customer service department. My trainer excused himself to answer a ringing phone. He put the customer on hold and resumed my training. The lesson for that day was how to make a phone call go away by putting a customer on hold and ignoring him. It worked! I asked my trainer if he ever got in trouble for doing that. He assured me that it's a problem only if you give your real name—always a big mistake in the banking industry. To this day, most of my co-workers think they worked with a short, blond guy named Pat McGroin.

People who work in technical support jobs deal with huge numbers of morons each day. Naturally they have developed the most sophisticated methods for avoiding callers. For example, if you call a tech support number within thirty minutes of the end of their work shift, you will automatically be put on hold for thirty minutes, then disconnected. No tech support person wants to take a chance on getting the call from hell right before closing time. They're professional problem solvers; it's no wonder they figured out how to solve their own problems.

CHANGE YOUR NAME

If you've got a name that's long, or hard to spell, change it to something more efficient. It will save you months over the course of your life. That's time you can use for having fun. My name, for example, is mercifully efficient: Scott Adams. It's easy to spell and it's economical with letters. I can fill out forms like a demon. When someone asks my name, I say it once and I'm off to do other things. The savings add up. I wrote this entire book in the amount of time that Boutros Boutros-Ghali spends trying to rent a car.

Throughout history, the most productive and successful people have been the ones with easy names.

SUCCESSFUL NAMES

Cher

Madonna

Mister T

President John Adams

President John Q. Adams

Only rarely do people with complicated names become successful. They are "the exceptions that prove the rule." Arnold Schwarzenegger is a perfect example. When he was a teenager, the forearm on his writing hand became huge from writing his name on school assignments. The other kids called him "Big Arm." He was forced to lift weights with the other arm so the one oversized arm didn't make him walk in circles. The rest is history.

Consider The Artist Formerly Known As Prince. When he was just called Prince, he had a hit movie and some top-ten albums. When his name was efficient, his career boomed. But then he tried to change his name to that strange symbol thing. He's spent every day since then just trying to make a withdrawal from his bank. I don't know if he still plays an instrument or not.

AVOIDING WORK BY ACTING CREATIVE

An effective way to reduce your workload is to act creative, which is exactly like acting insane but without the involuntary incarceration and ensuing social stigma. It's somewhat similar to being a Technology Prima Donna, but without the burden of pretending to have technical skill.

ACTING CREATIVE

Boss: Does anyone have a status on the project?

You: THE HAIR IN MY NOSE IS PLOTTING TO KILL US!!!

Boss: Remind me not to invite him to the next meeting.

At the next meeting, while the uncreative people are worrying that their fat cells are establishing trading colonies in their buttocks, you'll be off alone, having a good time.

If you want to be known as a creative person, it's important to stay in character all day long. When someone asks you a question, don't be quick to answer. Instead, stare at nothing for an uncomfortably long period and scrunch your eyebrows with a faint suggestion that a Trident-class submarine is navigating through your intestines. Make obscure references to dead people or old movies and act as if everyone should know exactly what you're talking about. This will kill the conversation deader than a shrunken head at a Hacky Sack festival.

Now look at the ground and say something ambiguous that could be construed as either an insult, or a threat, or possibly just a poorly delivered joke. If you're consistent, this type of behavior will buy you some time to be alone so you can create things.

Whatever you do, don't let anyone know that you have math skills, if in fact you have any. Math skill is a sure sign that you're an impostor trying to pass as a creative person. Go out of your way to act math-stupid. For example, after dinner at a restaurant with friends, say, "Okay, there are four of us, we all had the same thing, and the check comes to $40. Did anyone bring a calculator?"

As a creative person, you are not obliged to be logical, since logic is the opposite of creativity. Act confused at every opportunity. If you get into a discussion of world events, take an irrational stand and defend it vigorously. Here are some good positions to take on important issues:

OPINIONS FOR CREATIVE PEOPLE

▶ Animals should be allowed to drive if they can pass the written test.

▶ Maybe we can't reduce global warming by opening our refrigerators at the same time, but shouldn't we at least try?

▶ The smart businesses always lose money, for tax reasons. Why can't we be like that?

FILTERING BAD IDEAS

Are you a good listener? By that I mean when someone talks to you, do you make eye contact and nod your head while thinking about yourself?

You don't have to listen to every single word that people say in order to be a good listener. You can usually get the gist of the topic in the first sentence, then tune out and nod politely until the noise stops. This method is sufficient to get 100 percent of the useful content from most conversations. For example, if someone says, "I'm sad that my goldfish died," and then the person continues talking about the fish, you can safely summarize the entire ensuing conversation—no matter its duration—into "I'm sad that my goldfish died." There's almost nothing that can be added to the goldfish story that will change the basic facts:

1. Fish dead
2. Owner sad

The rest of the story will involve details that are important to the owner of the deceased fish but not to you. You really don't need to know the precise time of day the fish died or the presumed cause of death. Nor do you need to know the ex-fish's name. It's dead. It will not come when called. If you feed it, it will not eat. Soon it will smell bad. It will more likely be flushed down the toilet than buried at Arlington. You can know many things without paying attention.

If you listen to other people at all, you will be forced to hear many incredibly bad suggestions and ideas during the course of your lifetime. You'll need some techniques to filter the 1 percent good ideas from the 99 percent bad ones. This can be a huge time-saver.

No one is smart enough to know in advance what ideas will turn out to be in the 1 percent, but sometimes you can filter out the most worthless ones, thus improving your odds of finding the winners. Over the years I have developed these handy rules for filtering out the worst ideas. These rules actually work:

Rules for Filtering Out Bad Ideas

1. An opinion based on someone's **physical** reaction is better than an opinion based on someone's **thinking**.

2. An **unsolicited** opinion is more useful than one you ask for.

3. It doesn't matter how many people **dislike** an idea. All that matters is how many **like** it.

4. A sensible idea with small **upside potential** is a bad idea.

You'll be amazed at how useful the four rules are for weeding out bad ideas. See for yourself by trying them in this exercise.

Exercise—Find the Bad Ideas

Determine if any of the following ideas are bad. Apply the four filtering rules to each one. If the idea fails any one of the four filters, it is a bad idea.

IDEAS:

A. "Since you asked, yes, your meat loaf is delicious and you should certainly open a chain of stores to sell it."

B. "It's none of my business, and I'm a complete stranger, but I think you should do something about that mole on your forehead. You look like a damn unicorn."

C. "Personally, I don't like the idea of an antigravity invention, so you probably ought to spend your time doing something more useful."

D. "*Dilbert* books arouse me. Someone should write more of them."

E. "You should try rock climbing!"

The filters are deceptively simple, but amazingly effective. If you use them, it will save you vast amounts of time weeding out the bad ideas, without missing any good ideas in the process.

▶ CREATING HUMOR

In this section, I will teach you my *Dilbert*-honed secret formula for turning annoying and frustrating workplace situations into healthy doses of mirth. Once you learn the secret techniques, you'll no longer look upon your co-workers as troublemaking dolts. They will become the raw materials feeding your humor engine. Your boss will seem to transform from an uncaring troll to a gold mine of laugh potential. Once you know the humor secrets, your workplace will suddenly seem like a very amusing place to spend the day.

Some employees use all their energy maneuvering for political advantage. That's called being Machiavellian. After you learn the humor secrets, you can spend your day mocking those employees. I call that Mockiavellian. Given a choice, you will always be happier as a Mockiavellian than a Machiavellian. And since you will seem funnier (and therefore smarter), those Machiavellian employees will eventually work for you. Then you can mock them even more.

ORIGINALITY

For humor to work, it must be original. It's easy to create original humor—or anything else original—if you follow my formula.

Originality Formula

Theft + Lack of talent + Time = Originality

Identify someone who has more creative talent than you do, then try to imitate that person exactly. If you're like me, you can depend on your lack of talent to make your imitation look nothing like the source. Over time, you'll drift even further from the source of your theft, thus becoming "original."

Just a coincidence?

Peanuts © UFS, Inc.   Dilbert © UFS, Inc.

The only way your imitation will be detected is if it looks too similar to the source. If you're cursed with enough talent to be a good imitator, try mixing stolen elements from different sources together until the result is unrecognizable.

In many ways, originality is like car theft. You should have the decency to change the license plates and repaint the car before you drive it past the original owner. That's just common courtesy.

My advice might sound cynical, but as far as I can tell, theft is the only way anyone approaches originality, with the exception of the clinically insane. The difference between what looks original and what looks derivative is the degree to which the theft has been disguised.

PICKING THE COMEDY TOPIC

The hardest part of writing humor is finding a topic that hasn't already been used more times than the only back scratcher at the

Institute of Very Itchy People. Ideally, you want a situation that
makes you smile even before the humor has been added. If you
start with a fresh and inherently funny situation, you're halfway
home. Here are some topics from the corporate world that make
you laugh before the joke is added:

NATURALLY FUNNY WORK TOPICS

▶ Teamwork

▶ Employee of the Week

▶ Cubicles

▶ ISO 9000

If a topic makes you gag, or clench your buns, or laugh, or
sigh, or retch—or react physically in any way—you have a winner.
The best situations are the ones that cause your body to react.
Otherwise, it's just information without any emotional charge.

Emotion is the essence of humor. That's why it's impossible to
do a joke about an object—like a cubicle—unless you add the
human element. What's funny about cubicles is how they make
people feel. Cubicles can inspire a wide range of emotions:

CUBICLE-RELATED EMOTIONS

▶ Despair that you haven't earned an office

▶ Comfort of being in your own little womb

▶ Jealousy at the people who have doors

▶ Anger at all the noise from neighboring cubicles

► Paranoia that passersby notice you're not working

► Claustrophobia

► Pride in your own little patch of real estate

► Feeling trapped by obnoxious co-workers

The most common dead end in trying to write jokes is to focus on objects instead of emotions. For example, one of the most frequently suggested topics for *Dilbert* is "bunk cubicles." The idea is that employees would be stacked in cubicles, like bunk beds. The idea is so visually appealing that it would be easy to construct a gag around the physical appearance of a bunk cubicle. But that would be a dead end. A bunk cubicle, however clever, is still just an object. It wouldn't come alive unless the focus of the joke was on how the employees felt about the idea of being treated like stackable objects. If I were to use the bunk cubicle idea, I would probably avoid drawing a picture of it at all, instead focusing on how the employees react to the concept.

Once you have your topic, you're ready to apply the "Two of Six" rule.

THE "TWO OF SIX" RULE

Some humor experts say the secret to humor is to combine something unexpected with something bad and then make sure it's happening to someone else. But if that's all it took, serial killers would be winning comedy competitions. The evening news is full of unexpected bad things that happen to other people. Most of it isn't funny, unless it involves exploding whales, ear biting, or pies thrown at billionaires.

Plenty of jokes don't have pain. If all jokes had to have pain, some of the most famous jokes in the world would have to be rewritten like this:

Q: Why did the chicken cross the road?
A: Because it was on fire.

Q: Why does a fireman wear red suspenders?
A: Maybe he's on fire too.

While it might be true that most humor has surprise, pain, and distance, that's not very useful information. It won't help you be funny. And there are too many exceptions. Something is clearly missing. That's why I developed a more useful framework for creating humor. I call it the "Two of Six Rule." It's based on my observation that all humor uses at least two of these six dimensions:

SIX DIMENSIONS OF HUMOR

1. Cuteness
2. Meanness
3. Bizarreness
4. Recognizability
5. Naughtiness
6. Cleverness

It doesn't matter which two dimensions you use. It doesn't matter if you use more than two. The only rule is that you have to use at least two of the six.

The way you use this framework is to select a topic that lends itself to one of the dimensions, for example, something that's inherently cute. Then you brainstorm with the other five dimensions to see which one can be layered on to your topic without causing confusion.

The framework alone isn't enough to guarantee laughs. It's

just a starting point. I'll give you some additional tips that can get you 80 percent of the way to Laughville. I'll expand on each of the six dimensions so you can see some examples and get a better idea how to apply them.

CUTENESS

By cuteness, I mean the quality that kids and animals have naturally. Anything with fur is cute, at least until you hit it with your car or make a coat out of it.

Things with big eyes and tiny noses are generally cute, with the possible exception of Michael Jackson. And the jury is still out on the animated cast of *South Park*.

You know cuteness when you see it. There's no strict definition. One thing is for sure: Dogs with hats are always cute.

Do not include in the cute category the adults who believe that although they are not good-looking in the classic sense, they are nonetheless cute.

I used to think I was in that category, but no one supported my claim. So now I tell people I'm inexplicably sexy instead. This position is more defensible because sexiness is more subjective than cute. For example, when you watch a nature program on television and see two love-crazed wolverines going at it like a couple of love-crazed wolverines, you don't say to yourself, "I gotta get me some of that."

No, you don't. But I sure do. Wolverines turn me on. That's my point: Everyone has a different idea of what is sexy.

Now, watch me seamlessly tie this back to the topic.

Unlike sex appeal, where everyone has his own opinion, people generally agree about what is cute. If you have a situation that involves kids or animals, you're halfway home, unless they're ugly kids. All you need to turn a cute situation into a funny situation is another dimension. Meanness is always a good dimension to mix with cuteness. For example, Barney the dinosaur is cute. But Barney the shish kebab is funny. It's cute, it's mean, it's all you need.

Meanness isn't the only thing you can add to cute. It's just the simplest. Here's an example of cuteness and meanness with a dash of cleverness in the form of a play on words.

The following example combines cuteness with meanness and adds a very indirect layer of "I've been there" recognizability.

MEANNESS

When you add meanness to a situation, the humor can easily degenerate into something sophomoric. For example, if you took a Tickle Me Elmo doll, which is cute, and then did something mean with it—like using it to light the charcoal grill at the kindergarten picnic—it would be funny, but somewhat juvenile. I do not condone that sort of humor.

I recommend a more mature approach to cruelty. The meanness should be subtler and more complicated. But it can still involve a Tickle Me Elmo doll. For example, consider this story about a thrifty family.

The parents are too cheap to buy their young daughter the thing she wants more than anything else in the world: a Tickle Me Elmo doll. Instead, the parents decide to rent an Elmo for one month, in the hope their daughter will lose interest before it is time to return it. The daughter, Tina, is delighted with the Elmo and plays with it for thirty straight days, loving it more every day.

At the end of the month, while Tina is at school, the parents return Elmo to the rental store. Wishing to avoid an ugly situation when Tina comes home, they invent a little white lie to explain Elmo's disappearance. They decide to tell Tina that Elmo died because she didn't feed him.

To support their story, the parents decide to bury something in the backyard. The logical choice is the neighbor's Great Dane, because the dog comes when called, thus eliminating the need to lug something heavy. The neighbors hear their dog barking and come outside to see what all the noise is about. Thinking fast, Tina's parents whack the neighbors with shovels and bury them instead of the dog. The neighbors' relatives, all of whom were on the way over for a family reunion, hear the screams and run to the rescue. Tina's parents—by this time quite handy with shovels—slay all of the neighbors' relatives and add them to the pile. Someone calls the police. The sound of shovel whacking fills the air. Eventually the pile in the backyard gets so large that the family opens a luxury ski resort and becomes multimillionaires.

The moral of the story: If life gives you lemons, build a luxury ski resort.

As you can see from that story, there's no law that says your humor can't be mixed with an inspirational message. But watch out when you mix cuteness with meanness. Not everyone is mature enough to realize how funny that sort of thing is.

If you don't feel comfortable taking your meanness all the way to genocide, you can still get plenty of traction by concentrating on rudeness. Rudeness is mean, and almost no one is offended by hearing a story about someone else's rudeness.

BIZARRENESS

Bizarreness refers to any two things that don't belong together. A rhinoceros on a bicycle is bizarre. Managers who care about your personal life are bizarre. Employees who complain of being overpaid are bizarre.

In comics, the most popular way to achieve bizarreness is with animals who act like people. You're halfway home if you have a talking animal, especially if the animal is cute. That's why you see so many cute, talking animals in comics.

Dogbert can say things that only sound funny because he's a little white dog. This cartoon is a perfect example of dialogue that is funny only because it's coming from a dog.

Bizarreness shouldn't be totally random. It works best if there's some pseudo-logic holding everything together. In the case of talking animals, we've all had experience with an animal who seemed practically human at one time or another. It's a small leap to imagine the animal walking on two legs and talking. This approach works with almost anything; you start with the ordinary and then exaggerate it until it becomes bizarre. That way you keep a thread back to the starting point.

By way of contrast, imagine a bowling ball that acts like a refrigerator. It's bizarre, but too illogical to be funny. It's totally random because there is no logical thread between the bowling ball and the refrigerator. It probably won't work for a joke.

But take a human resources director, then exaggerate the uncaring attitude and sadistic streak. What do you have? A cat, of course. That's why Mr. Catbert, the Evil Director of Human Resources, is a bizarreness that works.

Here are two bizarre concepts—sex and household appliances—that can be connected by a thin band of logic. Without the sliver of logic holding these two unrelated things in place, this wouldn't work.

RECOGNIZABILITY

Have you ever been in this situation? You pull up to a red light and there's no one else around for miles. You think about running the light. You look left, then right, then in your rearview mirror. No cops, no witnesses. It would be the perfect crime. You have miles of visibility in all directions. You smile inwardly, feeling evil. It's oddly satisfying. You think to yourself, "I'm bad."

Then the light turns green. You feel like a total weenie for sitting there like a ceramic frog in a coma while telling yourself how rebellious you are. You are not a rebel. You proceed cautiously into the intersection and turn right. Then you remember that in your state it's perfectly legal to turn right on a red light, so you didn't have to wait for the light anyway. You are a slow-witted nonrebel. And you signaled for the turn.

If you ever considered cheating on a red light, the situation I just described gave you the feeling I call "recognizability." You can easily put yourself in the situation and visualize it perfectly.

But visualizing a situation is not enough for humor purposes. You have to *feel* it. Let's say the story was about you stopping at a stoplight and then proceeding—nothing more. You can visualize that perfectly, but there is no emotional charge to the situation. You can't feel it in your gut. That situation wouldn't qualify as "recognizability" for the purpose of humor.

But let's add one element to the stoplight story to give it some juice. Let's say there's another driver behind you. You hesitate for just a moment after the light turns green, and the driver behind you honks his horn in a punitive way. You hate him, because he honked after you'd already started forward. It was an uncalled-for honk. Now the story qualifies as recognizability for humor, more so than in the first example. Start there and add another dimension to get humor.

The main pitfall with the recognizability dimension is that everyone has different experiences. It's hard to come up with a situation that everyone recognizes. Even the stoplight story is meaningless unless you drive a car. But there's a bigger pitfall if you go in the other direction—relying on universal themes like eating, romance, sleeping, and shopping. Those topics have been ridden hard by every funny person on earth. My advice is to write about the things that bug you personally, then hope some other people are feeling the same.

Here's an example that might seem unreal to some people, but it's not. Lots of people wrote to tell me their bosses made the same sort of request I show in this cartoon. For that group of unfortunates, this cartoon has recognizability, cleverness in the form of broken logic (I'll talk about that later), and a thin layer of meanness.

NAUGHTINESS

You might want to skip this section if you're easily offended.

The naughty dimension includes any topic you wouldn't want to mention to your mother. And I do mean specifically *your* mother, not mine. My mom isn't a good standard for naughtiness because she grew up on a dairy farm. Her chores included shoveling gigantic mounds of fecal matter, yanking those dangly things beneath cows, and arranging premarital sex for the chickens. In the same way that Eskimos have developed many words for snow, dairy farmers have also developed an extensive vocabulary for their environment. Farmers like to use everything they produce; that's why much of this colorful vocabulary pulls double duty as obscene expletives. It's important that farmers have a large reserve of expletives, because it's the sort of work that causes you to injure yourself several times per hour. No professional farmer wants to repeat his best material before noon.

The swearing on Mom's farm wasn't all work-related. Some was recreational, bordering on art. Grandfather's hobbies included going out to the barn at night and cursing at the cows until their milk tasted like grapefruit juice. My uncle reportedly knocked a squirrel out of a tree using nothing but carefully chosen words.

The point is, you'll have to use your own mom for the naughtiness test. Mine isn't easily shocked, unless you count her reaction when she reads this section. (Just kidding, Mom!)

Naughtiness is the easiest dimension to work with. You can take almost any ordinary situation, add something naughty to it, and it automatically seems bizarre or recognizable or mean. You get a second dimension of humor without any effort. That's why you see so much of it.

But naughtiness has risks. Many people believe that exposure to naughtiness is harmful to humans. You can test this for yourself by using identical twins who are under the impression that you invited them over for a party. Seal one twin in a soundproof container. Then tell the other twin this classic naughty joke:

> Did you hear about the naked guy who ran through
> a crowded church? They caught him by the organ.

Observe and record the reaction of the twins. The twin in the soundproof container will be beating on the wall yelling, "   !!!" which, roughly translated, is, "Help! Help! There's no air in this soundproof container!!!"

By contrast, the twin who had unprotected exposure to naughtiness will immediately become a crack-selling, ivory-poaching, jaywalking CPA. It won't be pretty. That's why it's wise to steer clear of the naughtiness dimension if you can. However, if you can't resist the siren song of naughtiness, there's a rule you **must** follow for your own protection:

Naughtiness Rule: The funnier the joke, the more
you can get away with.

Never use naughtiness in mixed company, unless your witticism is so funny that your audience will shoot tears of happiness out of their eyes with a velocity sufficient to powerwash a small bus. Any joke that falls short of that standard will make you lose respect in the eyes of everyone except your best friends, who, as you know, lost respect for you long ago. But if your naughtiness makes someone laugh, that person immediately abdicates his right to whine about it later. Humor can insulate you from criticism, at least a bit.

People will also tolerate far more naughtiness if they feel they had a choice about consuming it. For example, hardly anyone complains about romance novels. It's your own choice whether you want to read a naughty book or not. And you can't say you weren't warned. It's no secret what you'll find in a paperback titled *I Was Taken by a One-Eyed Pirate*. But if you put that type of naughtiness in the local newspaper, for example, readers will be caught off guard. They might bump into it inadvertently and feel violated. Imagine how shocking it would be to stumble on to this horoscope:

Scorpio

Oversexed Scorpios find their libidos in hyperdrive all week. If you've considered bestiality as a lifestyle—and what Scorpio hasn't?—this is a good time to grab the bull by the horns.

You don't have to go that far to get in trouble. Some newspapers wouldn't run the following *Dilbert* cartoons. One used the word "hiney" and the other used the colloquialism "sucked." These words wouldn't have raised an eyebrow in book form, but in the context of a newspaper, some editors felt that their communities couldn't handle the shock.

Here are a few jokes that appeared in my book, *Dogbert's Big Book of Etiquette.* No one complained. It's unlikely I could have gotten them published in newspapers.

Now, let's take an ordinary story from my real life—this morning, in fact—and show you how naughtiness can be added to a normal situation to make it funny. This true story already had built-in meanness, so all it needed was one more dimension. As you'll see, it isn't funny until the naughtiness is added. Here's a version of the story *without* naughtiness so you can see for yourself.

Boring Story with No Naughtiness

This morning I accidentally snapped myself with the elastic band of my pajamas. It hurt.

See what I mean? No humor. Now I will tell the same story, adding the naughty element. (This is a completely true story.)

Humorous Story with Naughtiness

I was wearing my red flannel pajamas, as is my custom this time of year. Nature called. For the benefit of the ladies, let me explain something about men's pajamas. There are two possible means of extracting one's manhood from red flannel pajamas, assuming we eliminate the foot holes as possibilities. The civilized way is to use the fly hole that is designed for that very purpose. But that can take more coordination than I have in the morning. The more efficient way is to simply grab the waistband and stretch it down. I chose that method. But being a bit klutzy, my hand slipped, allowing the elastic band to snap back in a vigorous fashion, making brisk contact with the two most sensitive parts of my body, which are not my eyeballs. This is not to say that my eyeballs were completely uninvolved, because they were actually bulging out and touching the wall in front of me at this point.

I jumped around for several minutes doing the *Nutcracker Waltz* while simultaneously singing the lost lyrics, which go something like this: "EEY-OWWW!!! OUCH OUCH OUCH AAAUU-UAAAAHHH!!!"

There, you see how that story didn't come alive until the naughtiness was added?

Naughtiness and meanness both work best when they are subtle or indirect. Here's an example where several mean and naughty elements are mixed together but each of them individually is somewhat subtle. And the reader is forced to reach his or her own conclusion about what the nickname might be.

Naughtiness and vulgarity often work when they happen off-stage, in the imagination of the audience. Here's a good example. Had I shown the suggested gesture explicitly, the comic never would have been published.

You can get away with swearing when it would otherwise be offensive if you allude to the offending word but don't actually use it. In this way you can cause the bad word to register in the reader's head, exactly as you intended, but without committing the sin of writing or speaking it. I have no idea why transmitting a foul word indirectly is less offensive than transmitting it directly, but everyone acts like that's the case, so I don't question it. That's how I was able to get this cartoon published.

CLEVERNESS

As you might guess, the most challenging dimension is cleverness. It doesn't take much brain power to turn an ordinary situation into something mean or recognizable or bizarre or naughty. But cleverness requires some work.

I won't try to define cleverness too strictly. You know it when you see it. It's the thing that makes no sense but still makes sense. It's the thing you wish you'd thought of.

There are several classic paths to cleverness. These are the ones I use the most:

▶ Exaggeration

▶ Play on words

▶ Broken logic

Exaggeration: It's not enough to simply exaggerate something. That wouldn't be clever. There's nothing witty about saying, "This *Dilbert* book must have been written by the sexiest man alive!" That's nothing but a simple exaggeration. (And only barely that.) An exaggeration becomes clever when you take it to the next level. You have to exaggerate so incredibly that your audience is convinced that you could not exaggerate one bit further. Then you do, usually by adding an unexpected layer. That's the clever part.

Consider this cartoon:

It was a simple exaggeration that the boss would leave the building without telling the employees of the bomb threat. That wouldn't be enough to sell that joke. The unexpected layer—the thing that compounds his carelessness—is that he bought a lottery ticket. It's hard to explain why playing the lottery constitutes additional carelessness, but most people would see it that way, so it works.

Exaggeration is one of my favorite devices for writing *Dilbert*. I ask myself, If this is the worst that could happen, what would be even worse? Sometimes I have to suspend the laws of physics or the laws of Congress to make the exaggeration work.

Let's say you work for a company that doesn't care about you.

Normally, the worst thing they could do is fire you. Exaggerate one level more and the worst they could do is kill you. That's almost there. You need yet another level of exaggeration to make it work, as in this strip.

Here's another example, pulled from real life. I got an e-mail message from someone who complained of the photocopier being located in an employee's cubicle. It sounds like a comic exaggeration even though it's real. All I needed was a second level of exaggeration:

Play on Words: Puns are an easy way to be clever, but they don't qualify as funny on their own. A computer could generate puns, but they wouldn't make you laugh. The trick is to insert puns in situations where they would be rude, or mean, or naughty. It's the extra dimension that makes puns work.

There are a few people—very few, actually—who enjoy pure, single-dimensional puns. The people in this group ask only that the puns are sufficiently complex and clever. Technically, this sort of pun worship is a form of appreciation more than it is a form of humor. I include myself in the pun-lover category. I can assure you it is a very lonely category.

Use puns sparingly, as no more than 10 percent of the general population appreciates them, and it's hard to know in advance who those people are. The only correlation I've noticed is that youngsters who have been accepted at Ivy League colleges usually like pure puns. In other words, "Use a pun, go to Yale."

See how lonely I am right now?

Broken Logic: The "Broken Logic" form of cleverness is the most difficult to create—and to me, the best. The trick is to take a normal situation and twist it just enough so that the logic is destroyed, yet not so much that the brain won't try to make sense of it. That's the secret: The brain has to automatically try to "fix" the unfixable, or else it's just random.

Here's an example.

In that example, the book is only **about** glue, not covered with glue. But your brain reflexively tries to make sense of it. At the moment of discomfort when your brain realizes it can't fix what's broken, it triggers a laugh response. I guess your brain doesn't know what else to do.

Here's another example. If you don't get this joke, the explanation follows.

Wally's last line about the missing pillow is a callback to a very old joke that goes like this:

> Last night I dreamed I was eating a giant marshmallow. This morning my pillow was gone.

If you've never heard that joke before, Wally's pillow reference makes no sense. I made a conscious choice to leave some readers on the curb with this one. But if you were familiar with the old marshmallow joke, the *Dilbert* cartoon put your brain in the uncomfortable position of resolving the broken logic between two entirely different jokes.

One of my favorite examples of broken logic was invented by a friend over dinner at a Chinese restaurant years ago. As was our tradition in this little foursome, we were examining the menu for spelling errors and typos before ordering. It became a contest. Each of us searched frantically for the next error, joyfully shouting the discoveries as we found them. Finally, with all spelling errors and typos seemingly identified, one friend pointed to a correctly spelled word and announced triumphantly, "Look! This one is pronounced wrong!"

COMBINING DIMENSIONS

Since many of the dimensions of humor are subjective, you can increase your odds of getting a laugh by using more than two dimensions. Here's one of my favorite multidimensional strips, using cuteness, meanness, bizarreness, cleverness and—for anyone who has ever worked with a consultant—some recognizability too. This cartoon gives almost anyone a reason to like it.

HUMOR EXERCISE

Now that you've read about all six of the dimensions, let's see how good you are at spotting them. Read the story below and see how many of the six elements you can find in this true story.

THE TRUE STORY OF THE SPIDER AND THE CAT

It was time for bed. I drank deeply from my glass of cool water, then placed it on the dresser in its usual spot. I snuggled under the covers and reached for the remote control that operates the bedroom lights. (Yes, I do have a remote control for the room lights. I spent many years around engineers, and some of it rubbed off. Too much, really.)

For some reason, that night the remote control was not on the nightstand where it belonged. No problem. I knew I would find it the next day. I hopped out of bed, turned off the lamps the old-fashioned way, and reclaimed my warm spot beneath the covers.

Things went fine until about 4:00 A.M., when I awoke and noticed the lights were on for some reason. It seemed odd, but I was too groggy to think about it. Realizing I was thirsty, I decided to take a gulp from my ever-ready glass of water. I always drink water when I wake up, because I sleep with my mouth open, so most of the moisture from my guts evaporates during the night. On cool nights, I can actually create a ground fog in the bedroom. Anyway, I've noticed that my guts work better when they're kept moist, so I add water often.

I take great pride in being able to find my water glass in total darkness. I know the number of steps from the bed, the height of the dresser, and the approximate location of the glass on the dresser. Sometimes I make beeping sounds and pretend I'm a bat using my sonar. The beeping doesn't help. I assume this is why bats never drink out of my water glass.

That night, no guesswork was needed, because the light was already on, for some mysterious reason. I picked up the glass, raised it to my lips, and came eye-to-tentacle with the biggest floating spider I have ever seen in my life.

I don't mean to exaggerate here. Imagine a Chihuahua with eight legs. Now imagine the Chihuahua being eaten by this spider. I'm talking about a *big* spider.

THAT MONSTER ALMOST WENT IN MY MOUTH!!!!
The only thing that saved me was the freak coincidence that the lights had somehow been turned on in the middle of the night. I discovered later that my cat Freddie had waddled into the bedroom and used the misplaced remote control for a pillow, accidentally turning on the light. He was still snoozing on it when I discovered his heroism.

Freddie saved me!

As an optimist, I interpreted this as a stroke of incredible luck. The *one* time there is a spider in my water, my cat turns on the lights and saves me. This is very high on the coincidence scale. I believe it proves that either I am the luckiest man on earth, or my cat Freddie has been watching reruns of *Lassie* and picking up a trick or two.

By way of contrast, my girlfriend, Pam, has a different interpretation of this event. She cheerily pointed out that in all likelihood I have consumed thousands of spiders and never noticed it until the one time the lights were on.

THINKING IN OPPOSITES

If you have humor writer's block, a great way to get jump-started is to imagine people and objects as the opposite of what they seem to be.

Take anything that makes sense and turn it inside out and

backwards just to see what it looks like. Sometimes you find gems. It's a good way to get your brain into creative mode.

Two Questions to Ask about Anything

1. What if it's not what it seems?

2. What if it's the opposite of what it seems?

You'll be surprised how easily those two questions can free your thinking.

The method works best with characters. Take a normal character and make him the opposite of what his stereotype would suggest. Lots of times that creates problems for other characters, so you're halfway to Jokeville without even trying. Add a pinch of comedic exaggeration and you've got yourself some instant humor.

For example, you would expect a butler to be helpful and loyal. He would bring hot beverages on request. Now turn it around and exaggerate the opposite. Now you have a butler who despises his employer and tries to injure him as often as possible. He would spill hot beverages on his employer's genitalia, intentionally, several times a day. And then he would complain about being underpaid.

Movies and television shows are full of humorous opposites. In *The Wizard of Oz,* the lion is cowardly. In the movie *Liar Liar,* Jim Carrey plays a lawyer who can't lie. In the movie *Being There,* Peter Sellers is a dolt who becomes president. You can think of a hundred more.

Humorous Opposites

▶ Well-informed boss

▶ Murderous doctor

- ▶ Generous panhandler

- ▶ Small dog who wants to conquer the world

- ▶ Selfish angel

- ▶ Consultant who works for free

- ▶ Teacher who hates children

- ▶ Honest politician

- ▶ Vegetarian wolf

- ▶ Suicidal psychiatrist

Here's one of my favorite strips. It uses a simple opposite: a lazy beaver.

DIALOGUE TIPS

At some point in your career you will be asked to write humorous dialogue for one thing or another. It might be a skit for the department staff meeting, or a radio commercial for your business, or the comic strip you're creating in your cubicle while you steal time from the company. Whatever the reason, you can't avoid writing humor dialogue your whole life. Here are some tips to help you do it well.

Dialogue Tip 1: The average person is ignorant, self-absorbed, and generally evil. Keep that in mind when you're writing humorous dialogue.

If you write dialogue where every character is acting with an exaggerated sense of self-interest, sprinkled with a bit of ignorance, your audience will say to you later, "That was so realistic." The secret to realism is selfishness. The more the better. Slather it on. You can't exaggerate selfishness so much that it appears unrealistic.

Dialogue Tip 2: Real people rarely talk in a question-and-answer format. When someone asks a question, the other person normally responds in one of these ways:

1. *He answers the wrong question intentionally, just to be annoying.*

2. *He ignores the question and talks about something related to himself.*

3. *He makes a joke.*

4. *He wonders aloud how this possibly matters to him.*

5. *He proves by his response that he is too dumb to understand the question.*

6. *He gets offended by the question.*

WRITING STYLE

Humor can't survive complicated sentences. Use the same writing style for humor as you use for good business writing. I don't mean the kind of business writing that you see from your co-workers, filled with incomprehensible nonwords. I mean the kind of business writing that is simple and to the point. It's the kind of business writing you would learn if you took a class called Business Writing. And you should take one, whether you plan to be funny or not. After the course, your written ideas will seem more brilliant and no one will know why. (I discovered that phenomenon after taking a business-writing class. Seriously, it's one of the best things you can do for your career.)

I can't teach you good business writing in this book, but two points are worth mentioning because they are essential to humor.

RULE 1: AVOID INDIRECT SENTENCES

INDIRECT SENTENCE
The log was eaten by a beaver.

DIRECT SENTENCE
A beaver ate the log.

Both sentences say the same thing, but your brain processes the direct sentence faster. It might seem like an insignificant difference, but I've never seen successful humor that used indirect sentences.

RULE 2: KEEP IT SIMPLE. FORGET ABOUT ACCURACY

No one remembers the details of what you say. Get rid of your sentence modifiers. Sometimes you can make an ordinary insight sound funny by simply stripping out the modifiers. Here's an example:

COMPLICATED VERSION (NOT FUNNY)
Often, in the course of normal life, very bad things

can happen to you for no reason at all. It is advisable that you not dwell overlong upon it.

SIMPLE VERSION (FUNNY)
Shit happens.

Here's a good example of a cartoon that would be ruined by adding any clarifying words.

HONESTY IS FUNNY

You can make an ordinary situation funny by substituting honesty where, ordinarily, people would lie or avoid saying anything. Honesty in social situations is so rare that it automatically qualifies as bizarre. And it's usually cruel too. You get two of the six dimensions of humor—bizarre and mean—without much effort. I use this method often, as in this example.

BRAINSTORMING

Brainstorming got its name from a method that was developed during the Dark Ages. The technique involved removing the brains of smart people and leaving them out in a storm. The storm-washed brains would then be beaten against flat stones and hung out to dry. Later they would be ironed to get the crevices out. After the freshly laundered brains were sewn back into their original skulls, the smart people would be expected to come up with good ideas. If they didn't, it was proof they were witches.

This process has lost favor everywhere except in England, where it was credited over the years with creating such good ideas as warm beer, overtaxing the American colonies, Twiggy, and pissing off the Irish.

Everywhere else, the meaning of brainstorming changed over time. Now it refers to a process where you take a group of people who have bad ideas and make them sit in the same room. Consultants have discovered that when you take people with bad ideas and clump them together, you get—and this is the amazing part—a large clump of bad ideas. Some of those ideas are much worse than others. If you sit in a brainstorming session long enough, the least putrid ideas start to sound quite brilliant. But that's not the only benefit of the technique.

When you get a lot of bad ideas in one place, they start to morph into new and exciting bad ideas. Here are some examples of how simple bad ideas can bind to become hybrid, complex bad ideas.

Simple Bad Idea	Hybrid Bad Idea
Give employees monogrammed pencils instead of bonuses . . .	. . . then insist that employees change names so they all have the same initials.

Simple Bad Idea	Hybrid Bad Idea
Invent a beer can with a motorized straw for quicker drinking . . .	. . . equipped with an adapter for the car lighter.

Instead of brainstorming with other people, I recommend brainstorming with yourself. It's faster, and you don't have to keep a straight face when your co-workers exhibit the type of brilliance that gives all mammals a bad name. When you brainstorm alone, all you lose is the knowledge and viewpoints of other people—and that's something you can learn to fake with very little effort.

THINKING CREATIVELY

One of the questions I'm most often asked is "How do you think up a new cartoon idea every day?" Like most things in life, there are some tricks to it. If you know the tricks, it's not as hard as it might seem. I'll tell you how I approach creativity. I doubt that one creative method works for everyone, but it will give you something new to try. Judge for yourself.

The way I look at it, creativity is a matter of pushing bad ideas out of your mind so new ones can flow in. The active part of the process—the part you can develop with practice—is the flushing of bad ideas from your head to make room for new ones.

Getting rid of bad ideas is less scary than trying to create something from nothing. "Creating" is not the sort of mental process anyone can understand or manage in a direct sense. You have to go at it indirectly. That's why it's useful to think of creativity backward—as a process of eliminating bad ideas.

Unless you're a monk with ten years of meditation training, your mind isn't capable of being empty, even for a moment. As soon as one thought leaves, another takes its place. If the new thought isn't good enough for your purposes, don't dwell on it. Just release it. Try to increase the number of ideas you evaluate per minute. The more ideas you evaluate, the better your odds of hitting a winner. Use the odds to your advantage.

The best and quickest way to evaluate your ideas is to use your gut instead of your common sense. I mean that literally. Great ideas have an immediate physical impact on your body. If you're trying to create humor, your body will laugh when the right idea crosses your mind. If you're trying to create an idea with emotional impact, your body will tense up or cry or shake when you think of a winning idea. I've even noticed that my body responds physically to ideas that don't directly involve an emotion, such as a good business idea. (Those make me tingle.)

Technically, your brain is still doing all the evaluating, not your digestive system. But when it comes to creativity, your brain isn't so good at signaling its preferences directly. You have to pick up the messages indirectly, in your muscles and glands and circulatory system.

Listening to your body instead of your brain is against your nature, so it takes practice. It's tempting to give each of your ideas a thorough rational analysis—weighing the pros and the cons—before going to the next. And it's tempting to hold on to an idea that doesn't work, in the hope that further analysis will discover it wasn't such a bad idea after all. Those are normal impulses. You won't learn to trust your gut to make the quick filtering decisions until you've created a good track record for yourself.

Your personality is probably the biggest factor in whether you're able to release ideas quickly. Some people are natural collectors. They hold on to things reflexively. They keep mementos, they take photographs, they dwell on past relationships. My personality is the opposite extreme. I live almost entirely in the next moment. I don't own a camera. I can't watch a movie twice no matter how much I liked it the first time. For me, forgetting an idea is natural and easy most of the time. Yet I still have to remind myself to let go once in a while. If you're the kind of person who never throws anything away, you might have a hard time with this technique.

The surest sign of a bad idea is one that passes the brain test but not the gut test. An idea that "makes sense" is the hardest to release. It's especially hard to release if you've spent some time evaluating it. You become invested. The worst thing you can do with that sort of idea is share it with others. They too will see the sense of it and tell you it's a good idea. Bad ideas that make sense start to get their own weight if you don't banish them right away.

The one big problem I've noticed from listening to my gut is that sometimes an idea will be scary. Then the fear reaction will mask any other physical reaction. This wouldn't be such a big problem except that the ideas that are the scariest (at least in terms of potential embarrassment) are so often the best ones. This true story is a good example.

RAY MEBERT—EXPERT CONSULTANT

I got a call from Tia O'Brien, a freelance writer on assignment for the *San Jose Mercury News*. She had been asked to do a story about me in my role as *Dilbert* cartoonist. The newspaper asked her to approach it from an angle that was fresh and interesting. We discussed some ideas over the phone until we came up with the most frighteningly embarrassing plan of my entire life. Naturally, Tia liked that plan, since it would make a good story no matter how it worked out. The plan was this: I would be disguised by a professional makeup artist and try to pass myself off as a world-class consultant for a major company. Tia would come along as my "assistant." I would see how far I could yank the chains of the executives before they tarred and feathered me.

Tia worked her contacts in the industry and found an accomplice with a sense of fun and adventure: Pierluigi Zappacosta (yes, that's his actual name), co-founder and then vice chairman of Logitech International. (They make computer mice and other input devices.) Pierluigi agreed to call the senior staff together to meet with the famous consultant, code-named "Ray Mebert."* I had two specific goals for the meeting:

1. Lead the executives into creating the longest, most useless, buzzword-heavy mission statement on earth.

2. Get volunteers to agree to put the mission statement to music.

As the makeup artist applied my large puffy brunette wig and my fake mustache that morning, I could feel my various guts arguing with one another about the best way to stop me from doing this. If my intended victims recognized the bad disguise, or if they saw through my act, I would waste a lot of people's time that day. If I yanked their chains too hard, I would find myself in a room full of very angry executives. Tension was high. Tia decided to raise the stakes by bringing a film crew to record the action. Our cover story for the executives was that the video would be made available to the rest of the employees later to get "buy-in."

The executives filed in and took their places around a large conference table. Pierluigi introduced me, then sat down to play his part in the prank. He was to nod approvingly, no matter what I

---

*If a dog is a Dogbert and a cat is a Catbert and a Rat is a Ratbert, I figured I must be a Mebert. But we used the French pronunciation.

said. I started by telling the group a little about my background—my fictitious Harvard MBA, my fictitious experience consulting for several failed endeavors, and most notably my experience on the "Taste Bright" project at Procter & Gamble. I explained that while working at P&G I had discovered through research that people often tasted the detergents and cleansers before using them. My job was to improve the taste of all the soap products. There were murmurs of approval at this "out of box" thinking.

Next, I went to the easel, where I drew a diagram of three rings intersecting and labeled it the "Mission Triad." The circles were labeled: Message, Authority, and Linguistics. The intersection was what I called "The Buy-in Zone." It was all nonsense, but the kind of nonsense that is so pervasive in corporate settings that no one openly questions it. The group waited politely to see if any content would emerge.

Within an hour I managed to lead the executives into creating this mission statement:

Mission Statement

The New Ventures Mission is to scout profitable growth opportunities in relationships, both internally and externally, in emerging, mission-inclusive markets, and explore new paradigms and then filter and communicate and evangelize the findings.

By this time, my credibility and charisma were high enough to ask for their help in putting the mission statement to music. I explained that although this might seem silly on the surface, there is a wealth of evidence that people can remember words more easily if they are put to music. Two executives confessed to having musical talent, and—since they were team players—they agreed to take on the task of the musical mission statement. Mercifully, I ripped off the wig and mustache and revealed my true identity. The shock soon turned to laughter and a good time was had by all. Tia turned the incident into a feature story that got a lot of attention, and no one has tried to kill me yet. That outcome was as good as it could have been. Fortunately for me, Logitech is a confident company with a good sense of humor. (I'm certain I would have gotten the same results at any company on earth, except for maybe the good-sense-of-humor part.)

Had I listened to my gut, I probably wouldn't have undertaken this creative venture. What I've learned over time is that the fear response often comes with the best ideas. If your creative idea doesn't bring with it some risk of embarrassment, it probably isn't too special. When it comes to creativity, fear can be a good signal, as long as it's only fear of embarrassment.

Mild-mannered cartoonist
Scott Adams

Scott Adams disguised as
super consultant Ray Mebert

(Both photos by Richard Hernandez/San Jose Mercury News)

Consultant Ray Mebert works his magic
(Richard Hernandez/*San Jose Mercury News*)

THE MIRACLE OF CREATIVE VOLUME

Most people would be embarrassed to fail 80 percent of the time. Not me. I call that a good week. If I can make someone laugh at one *Dilbert* strip out of five, I know I will be forgiven for the next four. There's a honeymoon effect with humor, as there is with most forms of creativity. Learn to exploit it.

I know people who will make one terrific suggestion to a new boss and then get discouraged when the suggestion is shot down. Or worse, they'll keep hammering at their bosses with the same doomed suggestions, thinking that persistence will pay off. That is a bad strategy.

A better approach is to create *more* ideas that your boss hates. Try twenty more ideas. Ignore the rejections. Eventually, by pure accident, you'll hit an idea that your boss likes. You won't be remembered as the person who had nineteen **bad** ideas. You'll be the employee who had the one **good** idea. Bad ideas that aren't implemented are quickly forgotten.

Try twenty more ideas. If you get lucky a second time, you'll be known as the employee who is full of good ideas, despite your 95 percent failure rate. You might even be able to drag out that first doomed idea and try it again, this time under the halo of your spectacular track record.

Recently I attended an event where a well-known businessman was giving a talk. A member of the audience was acquainted with someone who once served on the board of directors with this businessman. He told me that the businessman was notorious for bringing ten new ideas to every meeting, of which at least nine were incredibly bad. The businessman was Ted Turner, billionaire founder of CNN.

Quiz 1: Name any one of Ted Turner's *bad* ideas.

Quiz 2: What makes you so sure *any* of his ideas
were bad?

If you're going to create, create a lot. Creativity is not like playing the slot machines, where failure to win means you go home broke. With creativity, if you don't win, you're usually no worse off than if you hadn't played. Creativity has very few downsides, except one: critics.

Handling Criticism

9

When I was a kid, I saw a movie where everyone on earth turned into a dangerous zombie except one guy. Every night the zombies would surround his house and try to turn him into a zombie too. Being creative is exactly like being that guy. If you create anything new—even if it's only an idea—the zombies (hereafter referred to as critics) will surround your office or home and try to recruit you into their cult of normalcy. The critics can effectively neutralize any happiness you get from your creativity.

Here's a simple recipe for handling critics:

RECIPE FOR HANDLING A CRITIC

Ingredients: Four cloves of garlic, one small cross, and one bag of fresh parsley

Eat the four cloves of garlic. Hold the small cross directly in front of the critic and say, "Look what I just made. Do you like it?" The critic will be unable to move until he has pointed out the flaws in your design. Breathe normally until you hear the thud of the critic's skull against the floor. Eat the bag of parsley to hide the murder weapon.

Depending on your ethical preferences, that method might not be acceptable to you. For example, some people are morally opposed to eating parsley. If you're one of them, you'll need other strategies. But first you must identify what sort of critic you are dealing with. Critics fall into these four categories:

TYPES OF CRITICS

1. People who reflexively criticize any idea (contrarians)

2. People who enjoy making you suffer (sadists)

3. People who are angry for no good reason (nuts)

4. People with valid criticisms (bastards)

CONTRARIAN CRITICS

Contrarians are the easiest types of critics to deal with. They're motivated by an obsessive need to demonstrate their brilliance at your expense. For the contrarian, there is no such thing as a good idea that comes from someone else. If you say puppies are fun, the contrarian will say they eat your slippers. If you say sunny days make you feel good, he'll say the sun gives you wrinkles.

Fortunately for you, the contrarian's predictability is his downfall. I once worked with a contrarian engineer. I needed his approval for all plans that had an impact on his area. After the tenth consecutive encounter in which he ripped my ideas to bits, I realized he was a compulsive contrarian, and not merely a cantankerous pessimist. Thereafter, I introduced all new plans to him by first proclaiming them to be hideously expensive and physically impossible. This forced him to provide a vigorous defense of my idea followed by enthusiastic approval. When I moved to a new job and no longer needed him alive, I told him it was impossible for him to hold his breath for thirty minutes. The police ruled it a justifiable suicide.*

---

*Not really, but don't you wish it were that easy?

SADISTIC CRITICS

Sadistic critics are the hardest to deal with, especially at work, because you can't escape them. There's no point in reasoning with sadists because they're only in it for the pleasure of making you feel bad. If you show any weakness, it will only encourage them to do it again. That's why I recommend that you respond to the sadistic critic using a strategy that resembles demonic possession. Start by asking yourself, What would Satan do in this situation? Then go with it. If you can spin your head around and spew vomit, that will make a lasting impression on anyone else who was thinking of taking a run at you. The goal is to train all the sadists in your office so that they focus their evil somewhere else.

> **Sadist:** Your idea is ill-conceived and doomed.
>
> **You:** You short-sighted, pompous bag of monkey crap. Your breath smells like the rotting flesh of a thousand corpses!! I'll dance on your grave when my brilliant idea makes billions of dollars! BUWAHHAHAHA!!!

If the sadist complains about your verbal assault, look surprised and say, "Oh . . . I thought that's what we were doing." Obviously the demonic-possession strategy can have no productive business outcome. But it might make you feel better, and that is its own reward.

PEOPLE WHO ARE ANGRY FOR NO GOOD REASON

When you create anything—especially humor—there's a good chance that people will get angry for no good reason. When people get mad for no reason, you will be branded "insensitive."

For example, literally two minutes ago, I got a complaint from someone who was disturbed about this cartoon. I can't figure out why.

I've tried being sensitive to the feelings of other people, but there are six billion other people stomping around the planet, and each one is completely different. My brain is barely big enough to know what my own body is feeling. I mean, sometimes when I get an itch, I scratch three different body parts before I find it. And sometimes I think I'm tired, then I eat a snack, and suddenly I'm not tired anymore. Apparently, I can't even tell the difference between being tired and being hungry. If I'm confused about the feelings in my own body, there's no hope for me to know what anyone else is feeling. Yet society expects me to try. So most of the time I have to fake being sensitive.

Fortunately for me, I've offended so many people in my career that I've learned to recognize patterns that are likely to get me in trouble. That's why I wrote this chapter. It's for people who are hopelessly insensitive but who haven't yet insulted enough people to recognize the patterns.

In this chapter, I'll show you some of the angry responses I've gotten to *Dilbert* comics—ones that might surprise you—so you can see the kinds of things that get people all worked up. Once you recognize the patterns that offend people, you'll be able to steer clear of them, thus giving the false impression that you are sensitive. In time, you'll be able to leverage that false impression into undeserved respect, shallow friendships, and a deep sense of your own moral superiority.

The next section is interactive. See if you can guess who was offended by this cartoon.

The biggest problem was my timing. It turned out to be a particularly bad week to make jokes about nuns. The cartoon was published at the same time Mother Teresa was being buried. (My cartoons are drawn months in advance. I usually don't know which ones are running on any given day.)

The Mother Teresa connection wasn't the only problem. Take a look at the mail I got that week and see how many of the complaints you would have anticipated.

From: [name withheld]
To: scottadams@aol.com

I have enjoyed "Dilbert" since it first appeared in my paper. I must say, however, that I'm very disappointed in, and offended by, the story line currently running in the *Chicago Tribune*. Many people I know must travel by air as part of their job and I fail to see the humor or cause for celebration of the fact that someone may have been lost in an airplane crash. In fact, I think it's about as tasteless as you can get—whether the crash actually happened or not. Let's get on to a new story line!

From: [name withheld]
To: scottadams@aol.com

On the day that the world mourns the passing of Sister Teresa and she is honored in Calcutta, we feel it is in very poor taste that you use nuns as a source of humor. It is the timing rather than the content.

You and your publisher should have adjusted the release to not coincide with the funeral. We often enjoy your brand of humor. This time you have overstepped the bounds.

From: [name withheld]
To: scottadams@aol.com

Your cartoon today was extremely insulting to all people whose loved ones have been involved in aircraft accidents. In addition, it was thoughtless to all religious nuns. At a time when the world is mourning Mother Teresa's death, it seemed heartless and ill-timed. You owe the world an apology.

From: [name withheld]
To: scottadams@aol.com

Let me begin by stating that I usually find your comic strip
quite amusing. (I'll bet you're just waiting for the "however"
well, here it is . . .) HOWEVER, the strip that was in print
on 9-13-97 was quite distasteful. Given the recent death of
Mother Teresa, this was obscene. Whether this strip was
written before Mother Teresa's death is immaterial; you
managed to make fun of the only two groups that are still
politically correct to publicly chastise—Catholics and fat
people.

You were correct that nuns don't do a lot of aerobics; they
spend their time praying, teaching, and ministering to others. One would think that that would exclude them from
being the brunt of such a cruel joke.

Please do not reply with rationalizations or justifications for
your actions—they may help you sleep at night, but I do
not have time to read them.

I pray that you see the inappropriateness of this comic and
regret having written it.

The worst thing you can do when accused of being insensitive
is to defend yourself with clever arguments. For example, I could
argue that nuns would be delighted to go to heaven. And nuns
would be glad to save a person's life. For a nun, my cartoon
described a perfect day. If you look at it logically, my comic was
really an inspirational story with a happy ending. Sure, I *could*
make that argument, but I won't, because I've learned that angry

people are immune to my flawless logic. For some reason, people just get upset when you demonstrate how clever you are.

On occasion, I have responded to charges of insensitivity by pointing out how insensitive it is for anyone to accuse me of insensitivity without fully understanding why I act the way I do. Then I express my hope that one day, insensitive people like me will be loved for what we are, not stereotyped. If you're thinking of trying that approach, I can tell you that it fails every time.

There is only one effective response when accused of insensitivity: Accuse your accuser of a sin called political correctness. Political correctness is a totally meaningless phrase, similar to "insensitivity." Neither has any useful meaning because they both describe every person on earth. Realistically, everyone whines when his or her own demographic group is maligned. We're all politically correct. So it's like accusing a dog of having hair on its body. Yet many people are so bothered by the label "politically correct" that they will withdraw their accusations of insensitivity and apologize for being so testy. This is another case of stupidity triumphing over stupidity. It shouldn't work, but it does. You might as well take advantage of it.

Let's look at another strip that I thought was harmless when I created it. See if you can identify the offensive element.

Several readers wrote to call me a "white racist pig," and other words to that effect, because of the reference to South Korea. I *could* argue that it's insensitive for anyone to call me white, because I have 1/128th Native American blood. That's not enough to open my own gambling casino, but it isn't exactly "white" either. Unfortunately, as you've learned from the prior example, that argument would only make my accusers angrier. And the Native Americans and casino operators wouldn't be too pleased either. That's why I would *not* make that argument.

Here's a comic that caused a minor firestorm. See if you can guess why.

If you guessed that autograph collectors complained because I suggested they are gullible, you'd be wrong. I didn't hear a peep. I was surprised.

But autograph *dealers* complained strenuously. Several wrote to tell me that they did **not** sell forgeries. One dealer said he always provides a signed certificate of authenticity to prove his signed memorabilia are not fake. (Really, he said that.)

The angriest readers were the ones who wrote to say I was "irreverent" and "insulting" to Jesus Christ. Some said I "mocked" religion.

I *could* have made the following argument: If Jesus saw that comic, would he be offended? Or would he laugh, ask for the original, and go off and save souls? I think he'd laugh heartily and give me a couple of backstage passes to his next sermon. Maybe he'd ask for the original. (Unless he was more of a *Ziggy* fan.) My argument, if I were foolish enough to make one, would rhetorically ask, shouldn't the followers of Jesus have the same priorities that he does? Isn't that pretty much the point?

Wisely, I decided *not* to make that argument.

Have you found the pattern of what makes people angry? It doesn't matter what you *say* about a topic, it only matters what context you put it in. I call it the problem of "proximity." It's the most important concept you must understand in order to pretend you are sensitive.

The proximity problem happens when you put two incompatible concepts in the same setting. In the nun comic, the death of Mother Teresa was too recent. Even though the cartoon had nothing to do with Mother Teresa, the proximity exacerbated its offensiveness.

In the comic about South Korea, I mentioned the country in the middle of a cartoon that involved unethical behavior, cruelty, ignorance, and stupidity. It didn't matter that none of those negative traits were ascribed to South Koreans. The proximity problem blended the country and the unrelated negatives all together in people's perception.

In the sports memorabilia cartoon, I made the mistake of including Jesus in a cartoon that addressed unscrupulous behavior and gullibility. I wasn't implicating Jesus in anything negative, but I failed to keep him at a safe distance from it. People were angry but couldn't easily explain why. It was a pure proximity problem.

My biggest proximity mistake was a series of *Dilbert* strips where Wally orders a mail-order bride from the mythical land of Elbonia.

People saw much symbolism in that cartoon. The problem is that it wasn't intended to be a symbolic cartoon. In my mind, the pig was just a pig, albeit a talking pig. It was not a metaphor for anything. I thought it would be funny if, instead of getting a human bride, Wally got ripped off by the mail-order company and got a nonhuman bride. To me, it was a clever indictment of the mail-order industry.

Unfortunately, many people found hidden messages in that cartoon. Women flamed me for suggesting that all women are pigs. People who married mail-order brides flamed me for suggesting their wives were pigs. Mail-order bride companies flamed me for suggesting their clients are pigs. But my favorite letter from the realm of the bizarre was this one:

Dear Mr. Scott Adams,

I have been reading your cartoon *Dilbert* for many years. Could you tell me the meaning of the 1/9/97 cartoon that appeared in the *Dallas Morning News*? Is it talking down to people in general? Or is it talking about the Black slang language Ebonics? I looked up the Internet Directory of Countries in the world and could not find Elbonia. What does the low expectations mean? And is the snout talking about African-American facial features versus European facial features?

As your loyal reader, I anxiously await your reply.
[name omitted]

I never answered that letter, so I would like to take the opportunity to do it here:

Dear [name omitted]

WHAT THE HELL IS WRONG WITH YOU????!!!!

Sincerely,
Scott Adams

The key to faking sensitivity is to abandon any hope that other people will react rationally to what you say and do. No one is rational about anything he cares about. I'm not. You're not. If you want to avoid being called insensitive, avoid the proximity problem and you will eliminate 80 percent of all appearances of insensitivity.

But no matter how careful you are, there are always surprises. In my book *The Dilbert Future* I suggested that people who write down their goals every day get better results than those who don't. Can you see any problem with that? Several people did. Here's a typical one.

From:[name withheld]
To: scottadams@aol.com

I was disappointed about your promotion of the use of the affirmations technique. The "power" you are tapping into is just another element of the New Age panorama, and its workings are manipulated not by you, but by the enemy of our souls. He'd have you believe you are enabling events to occur while all along you are just being given what you want so as to keep you from beholding the Savior of the world, Jesus Christ. The earth and all things in it belong to God, and we are not here to get whatever things we desire. We are here to glorify God in whatever we do. He is reality.

VALID CRITICISM

The worst type of criticism is the kind that is valid. If you are the recipient of valid criticisms you will lose the love and respect that you have worked so hard to earn. Fortunately, you can make up the gap by using trickery to gain additional love and respect that you don't deserve. Let these two cartoons be your guide.

▶ THE TROUBLE WITH NORMAN

Critics can be very annoying when they're right. But they're much worse when they're wrong. Your first reaction might be to hunt them down, strap powerful explosives to their bodies, then videotape the explosion to use later as a screensaver for your computer. But this is illegal in almost every state, except Texas, where you can get away with it if you claim the critic was trying to break into your house. If you don't live in Texas, I recommend that you do what I do: Use your critics for personal gain. This chapter can serve as your model.

Media critic Norman Solomon recently wrote a book called *The Trouble with Dilbert.* It was a scholarly analysis of the danger that the *Dilbert* comic strip poses to civilization. Special attention was given to a discussion of the author's greed, cynicism, and hypocrisy. This hurt me, because in my heart I know I am only greedy and cynical.

When Solomon's book hit the shelves, the media flocked to the story, always eager to find an angle where "man bites Dogbert."

In a widely published AP story, reporter Michael Hill summarized Solomon's complaints in a way that makes it unnecessary for you to read the actual book:

1. *Dilbert* pokes fun at ordinary workers and middle management, as if it's totally their fault workplaces are inefficient.

2. In an era of job cuts and corporate abuses, *Dilbert* lets upper management off the hook.

3. Adams is sympathetic to corporate downsizing tactics.

4. Adams is cynically making scads of money by licensing his creations to anyone.

5. Instead of being a weapon against mind-numbing corporate blather, *Dilbert* is a tool for propagating more of it.

If you're old enough, you might remember the late Gilda Radner's character on *Saturday Night Live*. She played a confused woman—"Emily Litella"—who would hear something incorrectly and launch into a lengthy and emotional monologue against the perceived injustice. When later informed that the real problem is that she misheard something, she ended her act with an embarrassed "Never mind." Norman is in the same situation, as far as I can tell.

It all started when a reporter asked me this question: "Scott, since you constantly attack corporate downsizing in your books and your comic strip, can you think of anything that is *good* about downsizing?"

That's when I made the biggest media blunder of my life: I gave an unbiased opinion. (Mentally insert the sound of Homer Simpson saying, "DOH!") I answered by saying that companies lowered expenses by downsizing. They became more competitive and their stock prices went up. If you're a stockholder, those things are good for you. I rounded out my answer with the observation that at Pacific Bell, my old employer, the bureaucracy decreased as the number of useless managers declined.

I didn't address the obvious bad aspects of downsizing—the disruption of lives, the emotional devastation, the constant fear, and the increased workload of the survivors. The context of the question was that everyone knows that stuff. It's what I talk about all the time in *Dilbert*.

My comments on the "benefits of downsizing" made it into print.

Norman saw my quote in a publication and called me to ask if I had really said that downsizing has benefits. I confirmed my quotes. (DOH! again.) I didn't realize that by now the original context—my continuous writing about the hideous effects of downsizing on employees—had already evaporated. Suddenly I was—to use Norman's words—"in favor of downsizing."

Armed with this valuable piece of misinformation, all the pieces fell into place for Norman: The author of *Dilbert* was evidently a tool of the capitalist pigs who oppress the working class. The most damning evidence was that many large companies pay for *Dilbert*-related activities (licensing, speaking, etc.). I was taking money from the enemy! Apparently this money trail set me apart from all the other published cartoonists who—and this is not widely known—get all of their compensation by breaking into parking meters.

Advice to Norman: Many newspapers, magazines, and book publishers are large corporations. Be sure to avoid taking their money as you pursue your writing career. Otherwise you will lose your credibility.

Norman and his publisher issued a press release and created a media campaign to publicize the anti-*Dilbert* book. Suddenly my phone was ringing and reporters wanted to know my response to the charges. Where there's smoke there must be fire, they reasoned. This controversy must be important because it's in an actual book! For the media, anyone who is opposed to anything is news.

I found myself on the defensive. But I couldn't figure out exactly what I was defending. I've spent so much time around engineers and economics majors that I couldn't see the world the way the journalism majors in the media painted it. For example, it seems to me that the ultimate victory in life is to mock large corporations and have them pay me to do it while everyone watches. To me, that's funny. Maybe even ironic. To the media, that is blatant hypocrisy.

My philosophy is very consistent. For example, if I were attacked by a mugger and somehow I managed to kill him in self-defense, I'd take his wallet before I left the crime scene. Some people would call this hypocritical. I call it good economics. And funny. Maybe even ironic.

Obviously it wouldn't make sense to address Norman's points in my normal rational way, since we have different views of what is rational. Instead, I give you an imaginary interview between Dogbert and Norman Solomon. You could say that all of the quotes attributed to Norman here are total fabrications. But I prefer to think of it as taking his own words out of context. That's what critics do, so it would be hypocritical for him to complain. Besides, there's a good chance that Norman has used all of these words at one time or another, admittedly not in this particular sequence. I'll do my best to "edit" them in a way that captures the intellectual integrity of his argument.

DOGBERT VERSUS SOLOMON

Dogbert: Thank you for agreeing to this interview, Mr. Solomon.

Norman: I didn't agree to it. I'm a fabrication so you won't get sued for libel.

Dogbert: My first question is, what's up with your hair?

Norman: My hair?

Dogbert: Yeah. I mean, your head looks like a mushroom with fur. Do you own a mirror?

Norman: I don't see what that has to do with anything.

Dogbert: Well, I noticed you didn't sell many copies of your book.

Norman: So?

Dogbert: Have you considered renting your head out as a pot scrubber for large hotels?

Norman: Are you going to ask me any questions about my provocative anti-*Dilbert* book?

Dogbert: Fair enough. So, you accuse Mr. Adams of favoring downsizing?

Norman: That's right. Mr. Adams is a cynical man. Downsizing is bad.

Dogbert: What is the alternative to downsizing that you favor?

Norman: Alternative?

Dogbert: Does it start with a "C" and end with the fall of the Iron Curtain?

Norman: Companies should not be able to hire and fire people just to increase profits for greedy owners!

Dogbert: Can you think of any economies that have tried it your way? (Hint: Albania)

Norman: Okay, sometimes it might be necessary to downsize people. But I object to the *way* it's done.

Dogbert: So, then you are in complete agreement with Mr. Adams—one of the most vocal critics of downsizing tactics on the planet earth?

Norman: No, no. That's different. Mr. Adams is only saying bad things about downsizing so he can make money from people. He's obviously cynical about it because he works with big corporations.

Dogbert: Didn't I see you on MSNBC promoting your book?

Norman: So?

Dogbert: Do you know who owns MSNBC?

Norman: I assumed it was the Multiple Sclerosis people. Is that wrong?

Dogbert: You imply that Mr. Adams is anti-worker because he doesn't spend as much time criticizing senior management as he could.

Norman: Yes, that's a logical conclusion based on the facts.

Dogbert: Have you ever published any criticisms of teen pregnancy?

Norman: What's that got to do with anything?

Dogbert: Obviously you're in favor of teen pregnancy. Otherwise you would be speaking out against it right now instead of having this interview.

Norman: Stop it! I refuse to do any more of this fictitious interview!

Norman didn't end his campaign against *Dilbert* with his worst-selling book. He updated his case with an article on the Disgruntled Website in December of 1997, in which he accused me of the following heinous crimes against humanity:

ALLEGED CRIMES OF SCOTT ADAMS

1. Opposing inefficiency

2. Making money

These crimes don't look so bad when they're summarized. But due to the fact that squirrels live in Norman Solomon's skull, the wording of his article made me hate myself when I read it. I could hardly believe what kind of person I had become. Norman knows how to turn a phrase. Here's a quote in which he savages my preference for efficiency:

> During the mid-1990's, *Dilbert* came to function as a stealth weapon against workers. After all, bosses cracking whips are not apt to have much credibility. But a clever satire of inefficiency can go where no whip-cracking is able to penetrate.

If Norman is opposed to people who favor efficiency, it follows logically that he is in favor of inefficiency. That sort of philosophy must make his life very difficult. No wonder he's grumpy. I'm wondering how he gets around town. Efficiency-loving people like me would probably take a car, or perhaps even a bicycle. But Norman is on record in favor of inefficiency. So I'm guessing he glues thousands of hummingbirds to his body and hopes they all fly in the same direction.

I realize that by the time you read this chapter, Norman Solomon may have shed his human "container" to follow a comet. So the debate may have ended on its own. But I couldn't resist the opportunity to use Norman for my own capitalist purposes here. I think it's funny. Maybe even ironic. With any luck, he'll write a sequel.

10

The Downside of Success

If you plan to use the tips in this book to amass wealth and fame, make sure you know what you're getting into. It's not as glamorous as you might think. As a public service, I will describe my own life—a typical day in the life of a semifamous cartoonist. Then you can decide for yourself whether fame and fortune are for you.

First, some background. I share a home with my longtime girlfriend, Pam. Pam is a vice president of a technology company and has never once been the source of humor for a *Dilbert* cartoon, as far as she knows.

One of Pam's quirks is an irrational love of the white carpet that was here when we bought the house. Now, when I say white, I'm talking in terms that are more conceptual than literal. You see, we have two cats, both of whom have holes on each end that constantly spew disgusting things over the allegedly white carpet. It's an old rug, so no stain will clean entirely, no matter what technology is employed. In reality, it's more of a leopard pattern now. Not a healthy leopard either.

This carpet doesn't just allow stains, it *invites* them. If a bumblebee passes gas anywhere in North America, my carpet gets a little browner in sympathy. This is a dangerous carpet to walk on. In fact, my carpet is the only one specifically mentioned in the international land mine treaty. Once a month I have a team from the United Nations stop by to deactivate as much of it as they can. We've lost a few Spaniards and a Canadian.

Since I am the person who works at home all day, it is my job to handle any new carpet disasters. This occupies much of my waking hours. I spray and I rub and I steam, and then I start over on a new area. Much of my day is spent on my hands and knees dealing with cat-related expectorations. For a change of pace, I clean the litter box.

To me, the obvious solution is to replace the stain-loving white carpet with something made in this century—something that resists stains. The technology exists. That way, the carpet would be easy to clean, and when it was done it would be pleasant to look at.

But Pam likes the "white" carpet. I cannot talk her out of it. So I live like a twelfth-century serf, crawling around in the stench and stains of animal debris. Sometimes I fantasize that one of the king's men will gallop by and lop off my head with a broadsword, thus ending my agony.

Meanwhile my cats are shedding hair like an aging dandelion in a hurricane. I believe Freddie can actually aim and shoot a solid stream of hair, like some sort of cat superhero. He's spraying the love seat with hair as I write this.

The other big problem of being famous is that people want to mail you things that you don't want. Most of these people are well-meaning, so I feel bad complaining. But it's a much bigger problem than you'd ever expect. This was an entirely unanticipated downside of being a semifamous cartoonist.

TYPICAL DAILY CONVERSATION

Kind Stranger: So, I hear you have cats.

Me: Yes.

Kind Stranger: What's your mailing address? I'll send over some poems about cats that I wrote when I was drunk. You'll get a kick out of them.

Me: Um . . .

Kind Stranger: I also know a guy who carves potatoes into animals. I'll ask him to make you some cats. When should I drop them off?

Me: Um . . .

So that's my life. It's mostly about cleaning cat stains and avoiding the kindness of strangers. If that sort of thing appeals to you, then by all means follow the advice in this book and leverage your happiness into money, fame, and success. Just don't say you weren't warned.

Final Postscript

Freddie, the aforementioned cat, passed into cat heaven as I was finishing up this book. He was high-maintenance, but he was my biggest source of workplace joy. I would gladly spend a year cleaning carpet stains for another ten minutes with him.

Freddie taught me a lot about finding joy. For him, a nap on top of my warm computer monitor and a baby's sock stuffed full of catnip were all he needed to have a splendid day. Even in his twilight he never missed a chance to find joy or to give it. His frail body would somehow make it down the stairs and to the door to greet me every time I came home, no matter how many times I went in and out during the day. When he ate, it was with a gusto that seemed as if he were tasting food for the first time in his life. When I brushed him, he purred like a lawn mower. He lived in the moment until the moment was gone.

My final advice—and the only one in this book that won't get you fired, sued, or beaten—is to get a pet if you don't have one. That way, at least one thing will go right for you every day. Your job might still suck, but it will suck less. If you already have a pet, give it a hug right now. You're done with this book. There's no excuse. That, my friends, is joy.